Lecture Notes in Bioinformatics 7548

Edited by S. Istrail, P. Pevzner, and M. Waterman

Subseries of Lecture Notes in Computer Science

T0280348

Elia Biganzoli   Alfredo Vellido
Federico Ambrogi   Roberto Tagliaferri (Eds.)

Computational Intelligence Methods for Bioinformatics and Biostatistics

8th International Meeting, CIBB 2011
Gargnano del Garda, Italy, June 30 – July 2, 2011
Revised Selected Papers

 Springer

Series Editors

Sorin Istrail, Brown University, Providence, RI, USA
Pavel Pevzner, University of California, San Diego, CA, USA
Michael Waterman, University of Southern California, Los Angeles, CA, USA

Volume Editors

Elia Biganzoli
Federico Ambrogi
University of Milan
Department of Clinical Sciences and Community
via Vanzetti, 5, 20133 Milan, Italy
E-mail: {elia.biganzoli, federico.ambrogi}@unimi.it

Alfredo Vellido
Universidad Politecnica de la Catalunya
Dpto. de Lenguajes y Sistemas Informáticos (LSI)
C/Jordi Girona 1-3, Ed. Omega, 08034 Barcelona, Spain
E-mail: avellido@lsi.upc.edu

Roberto Tagliaferri
University of Salerno
Department of Mathematics and Information Sciences
Via Ponte don Melillo, 84084 Fisciano (SA), Italy
E-mail: rtagliaferri@unisa.it

ISSN 0302-9743   e-ISSN 1611-3349
ISBN 978-3-642-35685-8   e-ISBN 978-3-642-35686-5
DOI 10.1007/978-3-642-35686-5
Springer Heidelberg Dordrecht London New York

Library of Congress Control Number: 2012954008

CR Subject Classification (1998): F.1, J.3, I.4, I.2, I.5, F.2, G.1.6

LNCS Sublibrary: SL 8 – Bioinformatics

Typesetting: Camera-ready by author, data conversion by Scientific Publishing Services, Chennai, India

Printed on acid-free paper

Springer is part of Springer Science+Business Media (www.springer.com)

Preface

This volume contains selected contributions delivered at the 8th International Meeting on Computational Intelligence Methods for Bioinformatics and Biostatistics (CIBB 2011) held in Gargnano del Garda, Palazzo Feltrinelli, during June 30–July 2, 2011.

The CIBB meeting series is organized by the Special Interest Groups on Bioinformatics of the International Neural Networks Society (INNS) to provide a forum open to researchers from different disciplines to present and discuss problems concerning computational techniques in bioinformatics, system biology, and medical informatics with a particular focus on neural networks, machine learning, fuzzy logic, and evolutionary computational methods. From 2004 to 2007, CIBB meetings were held with an increasing number of participants in the format of a special session of bigger conferences, namely, WIRN 2004 in Perugia, WILF 2005 in Crema, FLINS 2006 in Genoa, and WILF 2007 in Camogli. With the great success of the special session at WILF 2007 that included 26 strongly rated papers, we launched the first autonomous CIBB conference starting with the 2008 conference in Vietri.

CIBB 2011 attracted 24 papers submissions from all over the world. A rigorous peer-reviewed selection process was applied to select the papers included in the conference program. This volume collects the best contributions presented at the conference. Moreover, the volume also includes two presentations from keynote speakers.

The success of CIBB 2011 is to be credited to the contribution of many people. Firstly, we would like to thank the organizers of the special sessions for attracting so many good papers that extended the focus of the main topics of CIBB. Second, special thanks are due to the Program Committee members and reviewers for providing high-quality reviews. Last but not least, we would like to thank the keynote speakers and tutorial presenters Nikola Kasabov (Auckland University of Technology, New Zealand), Clelia Di Serio (Vita-Salute San Raffaele University), Elena Marchiori (Radboud University Nijmegen), Francesco Masulli (University of Genua), and Alexandru G. Floares (SAIA, OncoPredict, IOCN, Romania).

Special thanks are also extended to the people of the local Organizing Committee, to Marco Fornili (University of Milan, Italy) and Giuseppe Marano (University of Milan, Italy). We greatly acknowledge Niccolò Bassani (University of Milan, Italy) for his invaluable work in the editing of the final volume.

October 2012

Elia Biganzoli
Alfredo Vellido
Federico Ambrogi
Roberto Tagliaferri

Special Guest Message for the 150th Anniversary of Italian Unification

Prof. Jon Garibaldi
University of Nottingham, UK

Dear Colleagues,

I am deeply honoured to be invited to say a few words to recognise and celebrate the 150th anniversary of the establishment of a unified Italy. I express my heartfelt gratitude to my dear friend and colleague Elia Biganzoli for extending this invitation. I regret the fact that of duties I cannot be with you at the CIBB 2011 conference, as I am currently in Taiwan attending another conference.

My family bears the name of the great man who helped bring about the unification of Italy, General Giuseppe Garibaldi. While the mists of time and the paucity of documentary records have prevented us from establishing a definitive genealogy, it has been passed down through our family that we are direct descendants, and that Garibaldi is my Great-Great-Great-Great-Great Uncle! Whether or not this is authentic is not too important, because regardless of ancestry, I feel a direct connection to some of Garibaldi's values and beliefs.

Garibaldi believed that a unified Italy would be stronger, collectively, than a divided one. I believe this has been true in the 150 years to today, I believe it is still true and will continue to be so. While acknowledging that there are stronger elements and weaker elements in any such diverse unification, Garibaldi believed, as I do, that it is the duty of the strong to help those not so fortunate. I urge all Italians to believe in the benefits of a unified Italy.

In the same way that I believe in a unified Italy, I also believe in a unified Europe. I feel that Garibaldi would have approved of a strong European Union working together for all its citizens. As scientists, we achieve more by coming together in conferences such as this, sharing our findings, and collaborating, thereby being an example of the potential that lies in unity. So, on the 150th anniversary of Italian Unification, I wish you all well, have a great conference, and work together to achieve great things!

My warmest regards,

Jon Garibaldi

Organization

The 8th CIBB meeting was a joint operation of the Special Interest Groups on Bioinformatics and Biopattern of INNS and of the Task Force on Neural Networks of the IEEE CIS Technical Committee on Bioinformatics and Bioengineering with the collaboration of the Section of Medical Statistics and Biometry of the University of Milan, Italy, and supported by SAS JMP and Quantide Srl.

General Chairs

Elia Biganzoli	University of Milan, Italy
Andrea Tettamanzi	University of Milan, Italy
Alfredo Vellido	Universitat Politecnica de Catalunya, Barcelona, Spain

Biostatistics Technical Chair

Valeria Edefonti	University of Milan, Italy

Bioinformatics Technical Chair

Claudia Angelini	IAC-CNR Naples, Italy

Program Chairs

Luciano Milanesi	CNR-ITB Milan, Italy
Roberto Tagliaferri	University of Salerno, Italy

Program Committee

Sansanee Auephanwiriyakul	Chiang Mai University, Chiang Mai, Thailand
Gilles G. Bernot	University of Nice Sophia Antipolis, France
Chengpeng Bi	Childrens Mercy Hospital, Kansas City, USA
Patrizia Boracchi	University of Milan, Italy
Mario Cannataro	University Magna Graecia Catanzaro, Italy
Adriano Decarli	University of Milan, Italy
Julian Dorado	Universidade da Coruña, Spain
Alfredo Ferro	University of Catania, Italy
Enrico Formenti	University of Nice Sophia Antipolis, France

Christoph Friedrich	Fraunhofer Institute for Algorithms and Scientific Computing, Sankt Augustin, Germany
Salvatore Gaglio	University of Palermo, Italy
Juan Miguel Garcia Gomez	Universidad Politecnica de Valencia, Spain
Antonio Giordano	University of Siena, Italy, and Sbarro Institute for Cancer Research and Molecular Medicine, Center for Biotechnology, Temple University, Philadelphia, USA
Pietro Lio'	University of Cambridge, UK
Paulo J. Lisboa	John Moores University, Liverpool, UK
Giancarlo Mauri	University of Milano Bicocca, Italy
Jos David Martin-Guerrero	Universitat de Valencia, Spain
Ivan Olier	University of Manchester, UK
Nicolas Pasquier	University of Nice Sophia Antipolis, France
David A. Pelta	University of Granada, Spain
Leif E. Peterson	Methodist Hospital Research Institute Houston, USA
Gianluca Pollastri	University College Dublin, Ireland
Mihail Popescu	University of Missouri - Columbia, USA
Riccardo Rizzo	Istituto di Calcolo e Reti ad Alte Prestazioni, (ICAR), sede di Palermo, CNR, Italy
Volker Roth	University of Basel, Switzerland
Giuseppe Russo	Sbarro Institute for Cancer Research and Molecular Medicine, Center for Biotechnology, Temple University, Philadelphia, USA
Federico Mattia Stefanini	University of Florence, Italy
Carmen Paz Suarez-Araujo	University of Las Palmas de Gran Canaria, Spain
Giorgio Valentini	University of Milan, Italy
Yanqing Zhang	Georgia State University, Atlanta, USA

Local Organizing Committee

Federico Ambrogi	University of Milan, Italy
Niccolò Bassani	University of Milan, Italy
Francesco Napolitano	University of Salerno, Italy

CIBB Steering Committee

Pierre Baldi	University of California Irvine CA, USA
Alexandru Floares	Oncological Institute Cluj-Napoca, Romania
Jon Garibaldi	University of Nottingham UK
Francesco Masulli	University of Genoa, Italy, and Temple University Philadelphia, USA
Roberto Tagliaferri	University of Salerno, Italy

Financing Institutions

Department of Mathematics and Informatics, University of Salerno, Italy
Department of Information Technology, University of Milan, Italy
Quantide srl
SAS-JMP
IAC-CNR, Naples, Italy

Endorsing Institutions

Faculty of Medicine and Surgery, University of Milan, Italy

Table of Contents

Invited Lectures

Statistical Learning

Genomics

Computational Intelligence for Health at the Edge

Proteomics

Intelligent Clinical Decision Support Systems (i-CDSS)

Bioinformatics

Data Clustering

Modelling the Effect of Genes on the Dynamics of Probabilistic Spiking Neural Networks for Computational Neurogenetic Modelling

Nikola Kasabov[1,2], Stefan Schliebs[1], and Ammar Mohemmed[1]

[1] KEDRI, Auckland University of Technology, New Zealand
{nkasabov,sschlieb,amohemme}@aut.ac.nz
www.kedri.info
[2] Institute for Neuroinformatics, ETH and University of Zurich, Switzerland

Abstract. Computational neuro-genetic models (CNGM) combine two dynamic models – a gene regulatory network (GRN) model at a lower level, and a spiking neural network (SNN) model at a higher level to model the dynamic interaction between genes and spiking patterns of activity under certain conditions. The paper demonstrates that it is possible to model and trace over time the effect of a gene on the total spiking behavior of the SNN when the gene controls a parameter of a stochastic spiking neuron model used to build the SNN. Such CNGM can be potentially used to study neurodegenerative diseases or develop CNGM for cognitive robotics.

1 Introduction

Computational Neuro Genetic Modelling (CNGM) is a biologically motivated modeling approach that is concerned with the creation of two-level hierarchical computational models, where interaction between large number of dynamic variables (called genes) is modeled over time as a gene-regulatory network model (GRN) that affects the activity of a higher level system – modeled as a spiking neural network (SNN). The behavior of the two systems, in their continuous interaction under certain input-output conditions, have been introduced and studied in [9–11, 13–16]. CNGM constitute the next generation of computational modeling techniques built on the foundations of the traditional neural network techniques.

The goal of this paper is to explore and to develop further the CNGM paradigm through the introduction of stochastic neuronal models (e.g. [5]) used to build stochastic/probabilistic SNN (pSNN). Such pSNN are more biologically plausible, offering some additional advantages [16]. For this purpose genes are used to control parameters and their effect on the behavior of the whole pSNN is modeled and studied.

A specific gene from the genome relates to the activity of a neuronal cell by means of a specific protein. Complex interactions between genes and proteins within the internal gene/protein regulatory network influence the functioning of

E. Biganzoli et al. (Eds.): CIBB 2011, LNBI 7548, pp. 1–9, 2012.

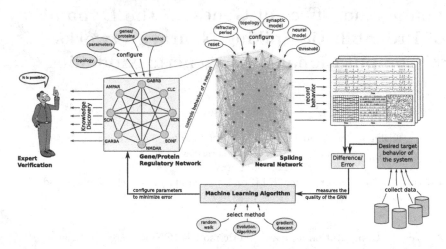

Fig. 1. A schematic illustration of the Computational Neurogenetic Modelling framework

each neuron and a neural network as a whole [19, 7]. With the advancement of molecular research technologies huge amount of data and information is available about the genetic basis of neuronal functions and diseases [19, 7, 22]. This information can be utilized to create models of brain functions and diseases that include models of gene interactions within models of neural networks.

In order to create biologically plausible CNGM we need to integrate knowledge from genomics, proteomics, neuroscience, psychology, and theoretical disciplines such as computer science and physics. To understand the functions of genes, we need to know how they are expressed, when they are expressed, conservation among their products and their response to therapeutic drugs. In addition, we also need to know how they interact and influence the dynamics of neurons in neural networks.

Genetic neuroscience uses principles from cellular and molecular biology to investigate questions about gene actions in the brain. Many techniques are designed to collect data related to the effect of genes and proteins on brain functions, e.g. genetic mutations; gene knockouts; protein purification; gene expression analysis; GAS chromatography; gel electrophoresis; high performance liquid chromatography (HPLC); western blotting, etc. Another multi-gene approach, high throughput genotyping technology, can be used to define single nucleotide polymorphisms that characterize diseases. All these useful techniques however need to be complemented and combined with sophisticated bioinformatics techniques in order to discover complex gene/protein interactions in relation to a given objective function. This is where CNGM can help.

The functioning of a CNGM is illustrated schematically in Figure 1. A Gene/Protein Regulatory Network (GRN) models the interaction of genes/proteins over time. Each of these genes/proteins can affect the behavior of a connected spiking neuron by directly controlling its parameters. For example, some proteins affect the excitability of the neuron (e.g. AMPAR, NMDAR), while others promote neural inhibition (e.g. GARBA, GARBRB) [13–15, 9, 11, 10, 16]. By changing the dynamics of the GRN, a specific behavior can be imposed to the SNN. An optimization algorithm can be used to modify the parameters of the GRN in such a way that a desired SNN output characteristic is obtained. This behavior could, for example, resemble real-world data obtained from clinical experiments. The optimized GRN that causes the desired behavior of the SNN is now expected to contain valuable information about the relationship and dynamics of the involved genes. Studying these dynamics may provide interesting new insights in the area of genetic neuroscience and facilitate new discoveries Several initial studies have investigated the feasibility of the CNGM approach. For example, in [23], a protein regulatory network (PRN) model was obtained from induced epileptic seizure EEG data from mice. With the use of a simple neural model (Integrate-and-Fire [1]), a genetic algorithm [4] was used to optimized the PRN model to match some real data [2].

Using a CNGM approach to build robots was investigated in [20]. The functions of the robot are distributed between a SNN model and a PRN model that enables to implement a principally new concept of functional and structural flexibility in robots. Robotic systems that employed PRN were also introduced as epigenetic robots [21].

The studies in CNGM so far have used simple and deterministic spiking neuron models, such as the Leaky Integrate-and-Fire (LIF) model [1]. However it has already been demonstrated that using probabilistic/stochastic spiking neuron models, that are more biologically plausible, enhances the functionality and the applicability of SNN. The probabilistic approach is motivated by the fact that biological neurons exhibit significant stochastic characteristics. Including non-deterministic elements into the neural model would bring benefits for modelling brain information processes and for modelling stochastic engineering processes too.

One of the problems of using pSNN is to optimize and control the neuronal parameters, even though for many biologically plausible parameters it is already known what genes/protein control them. In a simple experiment this paper demonstrates that it is possible to model the effect of a gene, that controls a particular neuronal parameter, on the spiking activity of the whole pSNN. This will enable a further study and development of pCNGM and their applications.

2   Probabilistic Neural Models

In this section, we describe the probabilistic neural models that we have used to replace the deterministic LIF neurons of a traditional SNN. In this study, we employ some very simple probabilistic extensions of the LIF model.

Models of probabilistic neurons have been proposed in several studies, e.g. in the form of dynamic synapses [18], the stochastic integration of the post-synaptic potential [5] and stochastic firing thresholds [3].

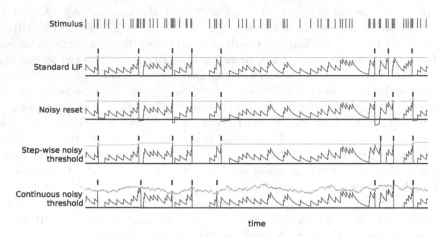

Fig. 2. Evolution of the post-synaptic potential $u(t)$ and the firing threshold $\vartheta(t)$ over time (lower and upper curves respectively) recorded from a single neuron of each neural model. The input stimulus for each neuron is shown at the top of the diagram. The output spikes of each neuron are shown as thick vertical lines above the corresponding threshold curve.

In [12] a probabilistic neuronal model is introduced that has three probabilistic parameters to extend the LIF model: $p_{cj,i}(t)$ is the probability that a spike emitted by neuron n_j will reach neuron n_i at a time moment t trough the connection between n_j and n_i; $p_{sj,i}(t)$ is the probability of the synapse $s_{j,i}$ to contribute to the post synaptic potential $PSP_i(t)$ after the latter has received a spike from neuron n_j; $p_i(t)$ is the probability parameter for the neuron n_i to emit an output spike at time t, once the total post-synaptic potential $PSP_i(t)$ has reached a value above the PSP threshold (a noisy threshold). As a partial case, when all or some of the probability parameters are fixed to "1", the pSNM can be reduced to the LIF.

The LIF neuron is arguably the best known model for simulating spiking networks. It is based on the idea of an electrical circuit containing a capacitor with capacitance C and a resistor with resistance R, where both C and R are assumed to be constant. The model dynamics are then described by the following differential equation:

$$\tau_m \frac{du}{dt} = -u(t) + R\, I(t) \tag{1}$$

The constant τ_m is called the membrane time constant of the neuron. Whenever the membrane potential u crosses a threshold ϑ from below, the neuron fires a spike and its potential is reset to a resting potential u_r. It is noteworthy that the shape of the spike itself is not explicitly described in the traditional LIF model. Only the firing times are considered to be relevant.

We define a *stochastic reset* (SR) model that replaces the deterministic reset of the potential after spike generation with a stochastic one. Let $t^{(f)} : u(t^{(f)}) = \vartheta$ be the firing time of a LIF neuron, then

$$\lim_{t\to t^{(f)}, t>t^{(f)}} u(t) = \mathcal{N}(u_r, \sigma_{SR}) \qquad (2)$$

defines the reset of the post-synaptic potential. $\mathcal{N}(\mu, \sigma)$ is a Gaussian distributed random variable with mean μ and standard deviation σ. Variable σ_{SR} represents a parameter of the model.

We define two stochastic threshold models that replace the constant firing threshold ϑ of the LIF model with a stochastic one.

In the *step-wise stochastic threshold* (ST) model, the dynamics of the threshold update are defined as

$$\lim_{t\to t^{(f)}, t>t^{(f)}} \vartheta(t) = \mathcal{N}(\vartheta_0, \sigma_{ST}) \qquad (3)$$

Variable σ_{ST} represents the standard deviation of the Gaussian distribution $\mathcal{N}$ and is a parameter of the model. According to Eq. 3, the threshold is the outcome of a ϑ_0-centered Gaussian random variable which is sampled whenever the neuron fires. We note that this model does not allow spontaneous spike activity. More specifically, the neuron can only spike at time $t^{(f)}$ when also receiving a pre-synaptic input spike at $t^{(f)}$. Without such a stimulus a spike output is not possible.

The *continuous stochastic threshold* (CT) model updates the threshold $\vartheta(t)$ continuously over time. Consequently, this model allows spontaneous spike activity, i.e. a neuron may spike at time $t^{(f)}$ even in the absence of a pre-synaptic input spike at $t^{(f)}$. The threshold is defined as an Ornstein-Uhlenbeck process [8]:

$$\tau_\vartheta \frac{d\vartheta}{dt} = \vartheta_0 - \vartheta(t) + \sigma_{CT}\sqrt{2\tau_\vartheta}\xi(t) \qquad (4)$$

where the noise term ξ corresponds to Gaussian white noise with zero mean and unit standard deviation. Variable σ_{CT} represents the standard deviation of the fluctuations of $\vartheta(t)$ and is a parameter of the model. We note that $\vartheta(t)$ has an overall drift to a mean value ϑ_0, i.e. $\vartheta(t)$ reverts to ϑ_0 exponentially with rate τ_ϑ, the magnitude being in direct proportion to the distance $\vartheta_0 - \vartheta(t)$.

The dynamics of the four models are presented in Figure 2. For each model a single neuron is shown that is stimulated by a random spike train generated by a Poisson process with mean rate 150Hz. Both the evolution of the post-synaptic potential $u(t)$ and the evolution of the firing threshold $\vartheta(t)$ are recorded and shown in the figure. We note the step-wise and the continuous update of the two threshold models and the stochastic reset of the reset model. Due to the stochastic dynamics each probabilistic model displays a different spike output pattern compared to the deterministic LIF neuron.

3   Modelling the Effect of Gene Dynamics on the Spiking Dynamics of a pSNN for a pCNGM

Here we assume that a pSNN is built with the use of a probabilistic spiking neuron model and that the probability parameters are controlled by genes from the GRN. In order to illustrate the feasibility of modeling the effect of a gene that controls a probabilistic parameter on the functioning of the whole pSNN we have created the following experimental scenario. We constructed a reservoir having a small-world inter-connectivity pattern as described in [17]. A recurrent SNN is generated by aligning 1000 neurons in a three-dimensional grid of size $10 \times 10 \times 10$. In this grid, two neurons A and B are connected with a connection probability

$$P(A, B) = C \times e^{\frac{-d(A,B)}{\lambda^2}} \tag{5}$$

where $d(A, B)$ denotes the Euclidean distance between two neurons and λ corresponds to the density of connections which was set to $\lambda = 3$ in all simulations. Parameter C depends on the type of the neurons. We discriminate into excitatory (ex) and inhibitory (inh) neural types resulting in the following parameters for C: $C_{ex-ex} = 0.3$, $C_{ex-inh} = 0.2$, $C_{inh-ex} = 0.4$ and $C_{inh-inh} = 0.1$. The network contained 80% excitatory and 20% inhibitory neurons. All parameter values are directly adopted from [6].

The SNN is stimulated by a random spike train generated by a Poisson process with a mean rate of 75Hz. This stimulus is injected into 100 spiking neurons that were randomly selected from the reservoir.

The GRN is designed as a single gene that changes periodically its expression. It controls a single parameter of the SNN namely the decay rate τ_m of the LIF

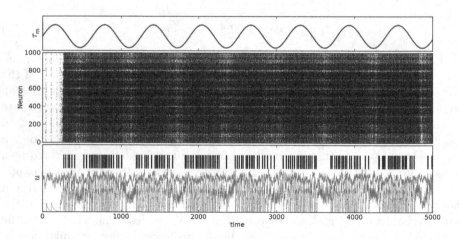

Fig. 3. A Gene Regulatory Network (GRN) interacting with a spiking neural network (SNN) with 1000 neurons. The GRN controls a single parameter, i.e. the decay rate τ, over a period of five seconds. The top diagram shows the evolution of τ. The response of the SNN is shown as a raster plot of spike activity. A point in this diagram indicates a spike of a specific neuron at a specific time in the simulation. The bottom diagram presents the evolution of the membrane potential of a single neuron in the network (lower curve) along with its firing threshold ϑ (upper curve). Spikes of the neuron are indicated as vertical lines in the same diagram.

neuron. The value of τ_m is periodically modified ranging between values of 10 and 30ms. The impact of this temporal change is monitored in a computer simulation over five seconds of real time.

Figure 3 presents the results of the performed computer simulation. The top diagram shows the evolution of τ_m illustrating its periodic changes caused by the GRN output. The neural response of the SNN is depicted in the middle diagram. Here a point indicates the firing time of a particular neuron in the network. Clearly, the network is impacted by the change of its neural parameter τ_m. Lower levels of τ_m result in a decreased activity of the spiking neurons. The same observation is made when looking at the evolution of the membrane potential of a single neuron in the network (lower diagram in Figure 3). We note the stochastic nature of the threshold. The output spikes of the neuron are shown as vertical markers in the lower diagram. Clearly, the spike activity decreases for smaller values of τ_m.

From this simple illustration, we conclude that the dynamics of the pSNN behaviour can be indeed controlled by the dynamics of a GRN as part of a pCNGM. By providing a quality measure for the behaviour of the pSNN, we can employ an optimization method, such as evolutionary algorithms, to match the pSNN output to a desired real-world dataset. After the optimization, a study of the GRN can lead to the discovery of new information.

4   Conclusion and Further Research

The paper demonstrated that using probabilistic models of spiking neurons in CNGM facilitates the study of the interaction between genes in the GRN model and the SNN behaviour. Further development of these models includes evolvability of the pSNN [9, 11, 10]. CNGM is a promising paradigm for future development of intelligent systems and their applications across disciplines. The models will potentially allow to model and trace the progress of neurodegenerative diseases under certain treatments and drugs [16]. Several pilot practical applications are aimed to be developed further across disciplines, including Bioinformatics, Neuroinformatics, Engineering, Economics and Social Sciences.

Acknowledgments. The work on this paper has been supported by the Knowledge Engineering and Discovery Research Institute (KEDRI, www.kedri.info). One of the authors, NK, has been supported by a Marie Curie International Incoming Fellowship within the 7th European Framework Programme. (http://ncs.ethz.ch/projects/evospike/).

References

1. Abbott, L.F.: Lapicque's introduction of the integrate-and-fire model neuron (1907). Brain Research Bulletin 50(5-6) (1999)
2. Benuskova, L., Kasabov, N.: Computational Neurogenetic Modelling. Springer, NY (2007)

3. Clopath, C., Jolivet, R., Rauch, A., Lüscher, H.R., Gerstner, W.: Predicting neuronal activity with simple models of the threshold type: Adaptive exponential integrate-and-fire model with two compartments. Neurocomput. 70(10-12), 1668–1673 (2007)
4. Fogel, D.B.: Evolutionary computation - toward a new philosophy of machine intelligence, 3rd edn. Wiley-VCH (2006)
5. Gerstner, W., Kistler, W.M.: Spiking Neuron Models: Single Neurons, Populations, Plasticity. Cambridge University Press, Cambridge (2002)
6. Grzyb, B.J., Chinellato, E., Wojcik, G.M., Kaminski, W.A.: Which model to use for the liquid state machine? In: IJCNN 2009: Proceedings of the 2009 International Joint Conference on Neural Networks, pp. 1692–1698. IEEE Press, Piscataway (2009)
7. Holter, J.L., Humphries, A., Crunelli, V., Carter, D.A.: Optimisation of methods for selecting candidate genes from cdna array screens: application to rat brain punches and pineal. Journal of Neuroscience Methods 112(2), 173–184 (2001)
8. van Kampen, N.G.: Stochastic Processes in Physics and Chemistry. North-Holland (2007)
9. Kasabov, N.: Evolving Connectionist Systems: The Knowledge Engineering Approach. Springer, London (2007)
10. Kasabov, N.: Evolving intelligence in humans and machines: Integrative connectionist systems approach (feature article). IEEE Computational Intelligence Magazine 3(3), 23–37 (2008)
11. Kasabov, N.: Integrative connectionist learning systems inspired by nature: current models, future trends and challenges. Natural Computing 8, 199–218 (2009), http://dx.doi.org/10.1007/s11047-008-9066-z, doi:10.1007/s11047-008-9066-z
12. Kasabov, N.: To spike or not to spike: A probabilistic spiking neuron model. Neural Networks 23(1), 16–19 (2010)
13. Kasabov, N., Benuskova, L.: Computational neurogenetics. Journal of Computational and Theoretical Nanoscience 1, 47–61 (2004)
14. Kasabov, N., Benuskova, L.: Theoretical and computational models for neuro, genetic, and neurogenetic information processing. In: Rieth, M., Schommers, W. (eds.) Handbook of Computational and Theoretical Nanotechnology, ch. 41. American Scientific Publishers, Los Angeles (2005)
15. Kasabov, N., Benuskova, L., Wysoski, S.G.: Biologically plausible computational neurogenetic models: Modeling the interaction between genes, neurons and neural networks. Journal of Computational and Theoretical Nanoscience 2, 569–573 (2005)
16. Kasabov, N., Schliebs, R., Kojima, H.: Probabilistic computational neurogenetic framework: From modelling cognitive systems to alzheimer's desease. IEEE Trans. on Autonomous Mental Development 3(4), 300–311 (2011)
17. Maass, W., Natschläger, T., Markram, H.: Real-time computing without stable states: A new framework for neural computation based on perturbations. Neural Computation 14(11), 2531–2560 (2002)
18. Maass, W., Zador, A.: Dynamic stochastic synapses as computational units. In: Advances in Neural Information Processing Systems, pp. 903–917. MIT Press (1999)
19. Marcus, G.F.: The Birth Of The Mind: How A Tiny Number of Genes Creates the Complexities of Human Thought. Basic Books (March 2005)
20. Meng, Y., Jin, Y., Yin, J., Conforth, M.: Human activity detection using spiking neural networks regulated by a gene regulatory network. In: The 2010 International Joint Conference on Neural Networks (IJCNN), pp. 1–6 (July 2010)

21. Morse, A., de Greeff, J., Belpeame, T., Cangelosi, A.: Epigenetic robotics architecture (era). IEEE Transactions on Autonomous Mental Development 2(4), 325–339 (2010)
22. NCBI: The nervous system, in genes and disease. National Centre for Biotechnology Information (2003), http://www.ncbi.nlm.nih.gov/books/ bv.fcgi?call=bv.View..ShowSection&rid=gnd.chapter.75
23. Villa, A.E.P., Asai, Y., Tetko, I.V., Pardo, B., Celio, M.R., Schwaller, B.: Cross-channel coupling of neuronal activity in parvalbumin-deficient mice susceptible to epileptic seizures. Epilepsia 46(suppl. 6), 359 (2005)

Biostatistics Meets Bioinformatics in Integrating Information from Highdimensional Heterogeneous Genomic Data: Two Examples from Rare Genetic Diseases and Infectious Diseases

Clelia Di Serio[1], Danilo Pellin[1], Alessandro Ambrosi[1],
Ingrid Glad[2], and Arnoldo Frigessi[3]

[1] University Centre of Statistics in the Biomedical Sciences
Vita-Salute San Raffaele University
[2] Department of Mathematics, University of Oslo, Norway
[3] Department of Biostatistics, University of Oslo, Norway

Abstract. Understanding genetic information to code and interpret disease phenotypes represents one major goal in modern biology. The challenge of integrating separate scientific vocabularies and insight is daunting because of the vastness and rapid evolution of the disciplines. New models and tools are needed to allow scientists to bridge knowledges, integrate concepts and information, and enable complex analysis. In this contribution we show two examples of datasets from Gene Therapy and Tubercolosis to highlight how integration between biostatistics and bioinformatics allows to gain information from the extremely large biogical databases produced with the new biotechnologies, such as Next Generation Sequencing (NGS) data.

Keywords: NGS, gene therapy, sRNA, MTB, hotspots, comparative genomics.

1 Introduction

Biostatistics and Bioinformatics represent two major approaches to integrate knowledge in Biology and Medicine according to their central paradigms (Fig.1). It is not easy and still debatable to distinguish between the two disciplines in genomic contexts since both aspire to contribute to a better understanding of the underlying biological mechanisms in many frameworks in modern biology.

In particular common goals of both perspectives can be summarize as:

- Learn and Generalize: Discover conserved patterns (distributions) of sequences, structures, metabolism & chemistries from well-studied examples.
- Prediction: Infer function or structure of newly sequenced genes, genomes, proteomes or proteins from these generalizations.

E. Biganzoli et al. (Eds.): CIBB 2011, LNBI 7548, pp. 10–20, 2012.

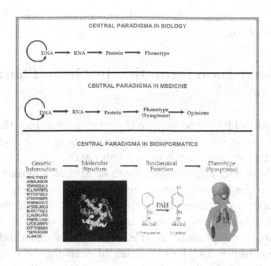

Fig. 1. Central Paradigma in Biology in Medicine and in Bioinformatics

- Organize & Integrate: Develop a systematic and genomic approach to molecular interactions, metabolism, cell signaling, gene expression
- Simulate: Model gene expression, gene regulation, protein folding, protein-protein interaction, protein-ligand binding, catalytic function, metabolism
- Engineer: Construct novel organisms or novel functions or novel regulation of genes and proteins.
- Target: Mutations, RNAi to specifc genes and transcripts or drugs to specific protein targets.

One could summarize some traditional issues of statistics in the following: i) the study of general populations, ii) the study of variation iii) the study of methods of the reduction of data. However dealing with modern biology and genetics many statistical features changed. For instance, with the increasing interest on rare diseases the concept of population changed, and inference needs different tools. Similarly, since humans share about 99,8% of the genetic heritage the definition of variability moved to that of "differential variability". More, one of the main paradigms of statistics was that "what doesn't change is not interesting" [12]. Nowadays, one of the main fundamentals of comparative genomics is that what doesn't vary is extremely informative in terms of evolutionary advantges. Finally, data reduction is not anymore a problem in biostatistics. The use of the complete information is crucial for investigating relationships between organism complexity and genome.

In the next sections we will discuss how biostatistics and bioinformatics represent not just a tool to infer conclusions from highdimensional data but rather a methodology to support biomedical sciences in understanding the underlying biological mechanisms in overall genome characterization and to develop new therapeutic strategies for both rare and high prevalence diseases. In this regard two applicative frameworks are illustrated respectively Gene Therapy and My-cobacterium Tubercolosis.

2   Statistics and Bioinformatics in Gene Therapy Frameworks

Retroviral vectors are widely used in gene therapy to introduce therapeutic genes into patients' cells, since, once delivered to the nucleus, the genes of interest are stably inserted (integrated) into the target cell genome.

Understanding how retroviral vectors (such as Moloney Leukemia Virus based vectors) integrate in the human genome became a major safety issue in the field of gene therapy, since a concrete risk of developing tumors associated with the integration process was assessed in the clinical setting [1,2]. Moloney Leukemia Virus based vectors are apparently characterized by a non-random integration pattern, with a preference for the vicinities of active gene transcription start sites. A main question in this framework concerns how and where gene therapy vectors integrate over the genome.

These two different aspects of integration process are addressed both from a probabilistic and a bioinformatics perspective. First we want to evaluate non randomness of integration process. There is now compelling evidence that integration of retroviral vectors follows non-random patterns in mammalian genome, with a preference for active genes and regulatory regions.

In particular, Moloney Leukemia Virus (MLV), derived vectors show a tendency to integrate in the proximity of the transcription start site (TSS) of genes, occasionally resulting in the deregulation of gene expression and, where proto-oncogenes are targeted, in tumor initiation. This has drawn the attention of the scientific community to the molecular determinants of the retroviral integration process as well as to statistical methods to evaluate the genome-wide distribution of integration sites. In recent approaches, the observed distribution of MLV integration distances (IDs) from the TSS of the nearest gene is assumed to be non-random by empirical comparison with a random distribution generated by computational simulation procedures.

To provide a statistical procedure to test the randomness of the retroviral insertion pattern a probability model (Beta distribution) based on IDs between two consecutive genes has been proposed [3]. The problem of non-random retroviral integration has been approached from a probabilistic point of view. The authors model a normalized integration distance from the transcription start site of the nearest upstream or downstream gene. From this model, a simple and straightforward testing procedure is derived to estimate how the transcription start site of a given gene may or may not attract integration events. This approach overcomes the issues of different gene length, gene orientation, and gene density, which are often critical in analyzing integration distances from transcription start sites. The approach is tested on real experimental data retrieved from human hematopoietic stem/progenitor cells.

A new testing procedure for non-randomness is then built to model the distribution of $Y(*)$ which is the integration distance (ID) from the TSS of the nearest gene (upstream Y_U and downstream Y_D) . Then we normalize the r.v. Y as it follow:

$$Y^* = \frac{Y_U}{Y_U + Y_D} = 1 - \frac{Y_D}{Y_U + Y_D} \tag{1}$$

which describes the ID as a proportion of the total distance between the start sites of two consecutive genes. Notice that Y^* becomes now independent of *gene length*, *gene orietation* and of *gene density*, being always $0 \leq Y^* \leq 1$. In statistical terms we assume as a convenient distribution for Y^* the Beta distribution, which is one of the most widely used in clinical, biological and genetic settings. In fact, Beta distribution models events that are constrained to take value within a finite interval. This includes as a particular case the Uniform distribution on support $[0, 1]$ which coincides with our null hypothesis of "random integration. For these reasons the Beta distribution looks very suitable to describe, within the same parametric family, the integration preferences. This distribution family depends on two free parameters, p and q. The probability density function is given by:

$$B_{Y^*}(p, q) = P_{Y^*}(y^*; p, q) = \frac{(1 - y^*)^{p-1} y^{*q-1}}{B(p, q)} = \frac{\Gamma(p+q)}{\Gamma(p)\Gamma(q)}(1 - y^*)^{p-1} y^{*q-1} \tag{2}$$

with $0 \leq Y^* \leq 1$ and 0 otherwise, $p > 0, q > 0$.

The main aim of the modelling is the estimation of the parameters p and q. The null hypothesis "X is distributed uniformly over the whole genome" corresponds to "Y^* is uniformly distributed in $[0, 1]$", that is equivalent to a Beta distribution with both p and q equal to one.

The parameter estimates have also a practical interpretation: different values of p and q reflect different integration preferences. This can also be easily visualized: a "U shape in the distribution of Y^* indicates that integrations land close to a TSS with higher probability (TSS *attracts* integrations). This occurs when both the beta parameters p and q are less than 1. On the contrary, p and q greater than 1 means that integration around a TSS is *disfavoured*. A straight line for Y^* distribution ($p = q = 1$) indicates that integrations are randomly located with respect to a TSS. Results on a subsample of integrations are shown in Fig. 2.

The second aspect of integration process deals with the identification of genomic areas where integration tend to cluster. These regions are called hotspots. We propose a new approach to compare and highlight different behaviours in different viruses, that is to identify "comparative hotspots". Integration of retroviral vectors in the human genome follows nonrandom patterns that favor insertional deregulation of gene expression and may cause risks of insertional mutagenesis when used in clinical gene therapy. Understanding how viral vectors integrate into the human genome is a key issue in predicting these risks ([4]). We provide a new statistical method to compare retroviral integration patterns. We identify the positions where vectors derived from the Human Immunodeficiency Virus (HIV) and the Moloney Leukemia Virus (MLV) show different integration

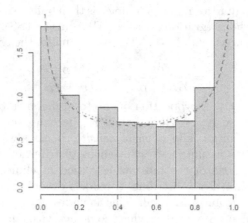

Fig. 2. Observed Y distribution and fitted distributions both with MME (dashed line) and with MLE (dotted line). Kolmogorov Smirnov: MME p-value = 0.909, MLE p-value = 0.8012.

behaviors in CD34+ human hematopoietic progenitor cells. Non-parametric density estimation is used to identify candidates comparative hotspots, which are then tested and ranked. We identified 100 significative comparative hotspots, distributed on all chromosomes. HIV-specific hotspots were wider and contained more genes. For comparative hotspots with HIV preference, GO analysis showed significant enrichment of antigen processing and presentation, and of hormone nuclear receptor activity; both involving exclusively genes located in the MHC locus on chromosome 6. Four methylations were founded to have different mean density in comparative hotspots (H2AZ, H3K4me1, H3K4me3, H3K9me1). Expression did not differ in comparative hotspots from background. Findings suggest the existence of epigenetic or nuclear topology contexts that guide retroviral integration to specific chromosome areas.

We provide a new method to compare retroviral integration patterns. A statistical methodology base on nonparametric kernel density estimation with Gaussian kernels is exploited to detect "comparative hotspots", i.e. areas of the genome where integration intensities of MLV and HIV appear to differ. For details see [5]. Our approach is in two steps: first candidate comparative hotspots are identified by comparing variability bands around estimated integration intensities along the genome, then each candidate comparative hotspot is tested in turn. Our analysis discriminates regions targeted by both viruses, most likely on the basis of their accessibility (high content of active genes), from regions specifically targeted by either MLV or HIV. A representative example is given for Chromosome 20 Fig. 3.

We show that HIV and MLV integrate differently in regions spanning 0.2 to 6 Mb in the human genome, with strikingly specific patterns In particular, HIV-specific hotspots are wider and contain a larger number of genes. The preference of HIV or MLV for these regions cannot be explained by the known viral target

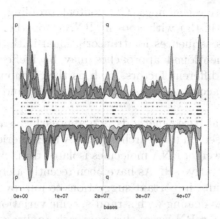

Fig. 3. Integration densities of HIV and MLV in CD34+ cells, for chromosome 20. We analysed each strand separately: the upper half is the + strand and the lower the - strand. In dark grey the estimated variability band at level 0.99 for HIV integrations (n=1629), in light grey for MLV (n=1815). Candidate comparative hotspots are plotted in the two central x-axes.

site selection preferences, or by the expression characteristics of the targeted genes, suggesting the existence of epigenetic or nuclear topology contexts that drive retroviral integration to specific chromosome territories.

We identify the positions where vectors derived from the Human Immunodeficiency Virus (HIV) and the Moloney Leukemia Virus (MLV) show different integration behaviors in human hematopoietic progenitor cells. Non-parametric density estimation is used to identify candidate comparative hotspots, which are then tested and ranked.

We found 100 significative comparative hotspots, distributed throughout the chromosomes. HIV hotspots were wider and contained more genes than MLV ones.

3   Statistics and Bioinformatics in High Incidence Infectious Diseases: An Application to Mycobacterium Tubercolosis

Tuberculosis remains one of the leading causes of morbidity and mortality from infectious disease worldwide, and understanding the patho-physiology of MTB is imperative for developing new drugs and vaccines. Most of the 140 bacterial sRNAs discovered in the past six years were identified by systematic screens using computational methods or experimental-based approaches, including microarray and shotgun cloning [6].

A smaller number of them were discovered by direct labelling or by functional genetic screens. In the recent literature bioinformatic approaches for identification of sRNA molecules in bacteria have been developed, using different combinations of comparative genomics, GC content profiling, sequence alignment of intergenic regions (IGRs) with known sRNAs, together with the search for appropriate consensus sequences for transcriptional initiation and termination sites. However the mentioned approaches may be ineffective when studying mycobacteria due to different factors, such as their genomic composition, the difficulty in defining accurate transcriptional signals, and the lack of verified sRNAs.

Among experimental-based methods two approaches lead to very promising results. The first is based on the search for sRNA in Escherichia coli by the analysis of low-molecular-weight RNA molecules isolated from cultures. According to this approach, nine putative sRNAs have been recently identified in MTB [7]. A second approach provides important suggestions to improve the accuracy of annotation of many genes dealing with strand-specific variation of RNA-seq, called single-strand RNA-seq, ssRNA-seq; this approach applies also to the identification of novel sRNAs. However these methods suffer some limitations. The main one is the strong dependency on both the amount of sRNAs present in the sample as well as experimental conditions. For this reason this methodology identifies only sRNAs highly expressed during the selected experimental conditions.

We propose a new bioinformatic approach for sRNAs identification based on both sRNA-seq data and comparative genomics. We provide a genome-wide identification of sRNAs in MTB.

3.1   Methods

We develop a method which relies mainly on the combination of two genomic features: the first extracts information from RNA-seq data (Reads Map) and the second is based on IGR conservation analysis (Conservation Map).

Reads Maps Construction. The input needed in this step corresponds to the output of standard next generation sequencing mappers such as SOAPv1, Bowtie, ELAND or BWA and two strand-specific databases contains genomic coordinates (start, end position and strand) of regions which are not used as template for transcription, both intergenic and antisense (IGR + AS). A filtering procedure has been implemented in BioPerl to extract from these alignment program output, those reads that uniquely map to any of the genomic interval contained in each of the database files separately. Only reads completely mapping within the IGR or AS region are included.

Two strand-specific reads maps are obtained. From these maps a coverage value is computed at a single base resolution for all screened bases of the IGR + AS portion of the genome. We define a R_i of a specific genomic position i as the count of reads overlapping that position given by $R_i = \sum I_{ij}$ where I_{ij} is the indicator function equal to 1 if the position i is between the start position and the end position of the generic reads r_j and i can assume all values included in the regions contained in IGR + AS genome.

Conservation Map Construction. The following step is based on IGRs conservation analysis. This approach starts from the creation of single-base resolution conservation map. Differently from reads map, conservation map is not calculated in AS regions since these show a very high conservation degree. We first define a conservation set as a set of genome to be used as comparison against our target organism. Using information contained in sequence files .fna and annotation files .gff we create a comparison database of IGR sequences and a target database of IGR sequences. All records contained in the target database was compared using BLASTN 2.0 with the whole contained in the comparison one (E-value threshold: 1e-2). By processing the obtained matches output file, a conservation maps is subsequently created. The *sequence conservation value* of a specific genomic position corresponds to the weighted count of different genome containing that position with at least one alignment satisfying quality criteria $C_i = w_j * I_{ij}$ where C_i corresponds to the conservation value of the *i-th* base on the genome and i takes all values included in genomic regions within target IGR database. I_{ij} is an indicator function that takes value equal to 1 if the j-th genome contains within at least one hit considering the BLAST output fulfilling the quality requirements. w_j is the weight assigned to each genome in the comparison set corresponding to its evolutionary distance to target genome. The distance is calculated accordingly with the method proposed in the recent literature [8]. Thresholds setting leads to definition of ExprT1 and ConsT1 thresholds corresponding to 95th percentile of reads abundance and conservation distributions respectively, while ExprT2 and ConsT2 thresholds correspond to the 90th percentile. This procedure tests the null hypothesis of the presence of a pure background signal with respect to an alternative hypothesis of a mixture of background and sRNA signal, set to a significance level equal to $\alpha=0.05$ and $\alpha=0.10$. Setting the threshold on a combination of background noise and sRNA candidates signal represents a conservative approach since it shifts the discriminating cut-off to a larger value and hence to a higher percentiles producing an effective level α. From the comparative genomics step we consider the percentiles of the conservation distributions as ad hoc cut-offs to identify the more likely promising regions.

3.2   sRNA Candidates Definition

Reads and conservation maps are superimposed to identify putative regions encoding for sRNA candidates. As aforementioned conservation map support is a subset of reads map support. In AS Regions the value of is set equal to 0. In particular we defined a Genomic Region (GR) as sRNA candidate if the following conditions are satisfied:

  - genomic region made up by consecutive nucleotides
  - genomic region length 30 nt and 550 nt

In addition at least one of the further conditions must be tested and satisfied on GR base:

- all GRi has reads abundance Ri value ExprT1 threshold
- all GRi has a conservation Ci value ConsT1 threshold
- all GRi interval has an abundance reads Ri value ExprT2 threshold and a conservation Ci value ConsT2 threshold. Different combinations of three of the previous testing conditions lead to three possible candidates type (type A, type B, type C). The selection of candidates type is crucially affected by the order of testing conditions. In other words finding type A candidates should be the first step which influences step 2 for the search of type B and step 3 for identifying C candidates.

Step 1: identification of regions satisfying conditions 1, 2 and 3 (type A candidates);

Step 2: identification of regions satisfying conditions 1, 2 and 5 (type B candidates);

Step 3: identification of regions satisfying conditions 1, 2 and 4 (type C candidates).

The scheme in Fig.4 helps in visualizing the sRNAs identification process based on superimposing reads map and conservation map.

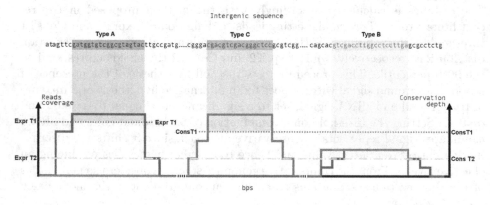

Fig. 4. SRNA identification process. For each IGR, reads (dark grey curve) and conservation (light grey curve) maps are superimposed. First Type A candidates are identified and extracted by testing length constrains (conditions 1 and 2) and reads coverage above ExprT1 (dotted dark grey). On the remaining portions of IGRs, Type B candidates are identified and extracted by testing length constrains (conditions 1 and 2) and contemporaneously both reads coverage above ExprT2 and conservation depth above ConsT2 (dot and dashed light grey lines). Lastly, on remaining part of the IGRs Type C candidate are identified on the base of highly conserved regions (above ConsT1 threshold reported as dotted light grey line).

3.3   Candidates sRNA Encoding Region

Totally 2090 sRNA candidates are identified (1012 strand +; 1078 strand -). sRNA candidates length ranges from 30 to 520 nt with a average length equal to 67 (median value equal to 46). Among these candidates, 236 show a secondary structure Minimum Free Energy (MFE) p-value 5e-2 calculated by means of the Randfold algorithm using simple mono-nucleotide shuffling method.

Comparing sRNA trans-encoded (B11, B55, C8, F6 and G2) and cis-encoded (antisense -AS- to desA1, pks12, Rv 1726 and Rv 1890c reported in Arnvig KB [10] with our result, we highlight the good performance of the algorithm, especially for those with one distinct processed 5 end (B11, B55). A decreasing accuracy in start and end coordinates identification is observed for all the trans- and cis-encoded sRNAs showing multiple 5 ends (C8, F6, G2 and ASdes) as expected. No candidates result in regions around remaining 3 antisense sRNAs (ASpks12, ASRv 1726 and ASRv 1890c). This is probably due to a very low amount or absence of transcript in RNA-seq experiment condition.

We also compare our results with those reported in Livny paper [9], who apply SIPTH algorithm to MTB genome. Using the pure computational approach of SIPTH, a total amount of 102 candidates are identified in MTB. 17 genomic loci are defined as possible coding for sRNAs according to both methods. Since there is no experimental-based (Northern Blot, tiling array) validation on Livny's predictions, performance measures to compare the two algorithms cannot be provided.

In Di Chiara et al. paper [11] (2010) several sRNA are identified in Mycobacterium bovis BCG by means of Northern Blot analysis, on in silico (SIPTH) and experimental (cloning) candidates regions. 20 out of 37 are present also in MTB. In addition, 30 different candidates show a high homology with sRNAs recorded in RFAM db.

4   Final Comments

This contribution shows how integrating bioinformatics and biostatistics with biomedical information may advance the general understanding of biological mechanisms underlying many diseases, both rare, as some immunodeficiencies, as well as infectious such as Tuberculosis where adaptation to the changing environment and control of virulence are still under study.

Bioinformatics allows for a careful organization of data material taking into account experimental constrains and staging multiple data. Data acquisition is a fundamental step in bioinformatic technologies that may be use to reinforce experimental results via a correct design.

Statistics investigates the level of "surprise" in data, the exceptions, the differences, regularities and stochastic variations in data structure, creating models that reproduce, for instance, the so called "in silico" distributions as a sort of probabilistic control distribution for genomic events.

Together, Bioinformatics and Biostatistics create a strong alliance to generate new hypotheses in biology based on High-Throughput Data.

References

1. Baum, C., Dullmann, J., Li, Z., Fehse, B., Meyer, J., et al.: Side effects of retroviral gene transfer into hematopoietic stem cells. Blood 101, 2099–2114 (2003)
2. Montini, E., Cesana, D., Schmidt, M., Sanvito, F., Ponzoni, M., et al.: Hematopoietic stem cell gene transfer in tumor-prone mouse model uncovers low genotoxicity of lentiviral vector integration. Nature Biotechnology 24, 687–696 (2006)
3. Ambrosi, A., Cattoglio, C., Di Serio, C.: Retroviral Integration Process in the Human Genome: Is It Really Non-Random? A New Statistical Approach. PLos Comp. Bio. 4(8) (2008)
4. Cattoglio, C., Pellin, D., Rizzi, E., Maruggi, G., Corti, G., Miselli, F., Sartori, D., Guffanti, A., Di Serio, C., Ambrosi, A., De Bellis, G., Mavilio, F.: High-definition mapping of retroviral integration sites identifies active regulatory elements in human multipotent hematopoietic progenitors. Blood 116(25), 5507–5510 (2010)
5. Ambrosi, A., Glad, I.K., Pellin, D., Cattoglio, C., Mavilio, F., Di Serio, C., Frigessi, A.: Comparative retroviral DNA integration hotspots identify different behaviors of HIV and MLV (2011) (submitted)
6. Waters, L.S., Storz, G.: Regulatory RNAs in bacteria. Cell 136, 615–628 (2009)
7. Levine, E., Hwa, T.: Small RNAs establish gene expression thresholds. Curr. Opin. Microbiol. 11, 574–579 (2008)
8. Qi, J., Wang, B., Hao, B.I.: Whole proteome prokaryote phylogeny without sequence alignment: a K-string composition approach. J. Mol. Evol. 58, 1–11 (2004)
9. Livny, J., Waldor, M.K.: Identification of small RNAs in diverse bacterial species. Curr. Opin. Microbiol. 10, 96–101 (2007)
10. Arnvig, K.B., Young, D.B.: Identification of small RNAs in Mycobacterium tuberculosis. Mol. Microbiol. 73, 397–408 (2009)
11. DiChiara, J.M., Contreras-Martinez, L.M., Livny, J., Smith, D., McDonough, K.A., et al.: Multiple small RNAs identified in Mycobacterium bovis BCG are also expressed in Mycobacterium tuberculosis and Mycobacterium smegmatis. Nucleic Acids Res. 38, 4067–4078 (2010)
12. Fisher, R.A.: Statistical Methods for Research Workers (1925)

Bayesian Models for the Multi-sample Time-Course Microarray Experiments

Claudia Angelini[1,*], Daniela De Canditiis[1],
Marianna Pensky[2], and Naomi Brownstein[3]

[1] Istituto per le Applicazioni del Calcolo CNR, Italy
[2] Department of Mathematics, University of Central Florida, USA
[3] Department of Biostatistics, University of North Carolina at Chapel Hill, USA

Abstract. In this paper we present a functional Bayesian method for detecting genes which are temporally differentially expressed between several conditions. We identify the nature of differential expression (e.g., gene is differentially expressed between the first and the second sample but is not differentially expressed between the second and the third) and subsequently we estimate gene expression temporal profiles. The proposed procedure deals successfully with various technical difficulties which arise in microarray time-course experiments such as a small number of observations, non-uniform sampling intervals and presence of missing data or repeated measurements. The procedure allows to account for various types of errors, thus, offering a good compromise between non-parametric and normality assumption based techniques. In addition, all evaluations are carried out using analytic expressions, hence, the entire procedure requires very small computational effort. The performance of the procedure is studied using simulated data.

Keywords: Bayesian analysis, Classification, Hypothesis testing, Multi-sample problems, Time-course microarray.

1 Introduction

Gene expression levels in a given cell can be influenced by various factors, namely, a pharmacological or a medical treatment, or a specific pathological or environmental state, or a specific experimental set-up. For the sake of brevity, we will simply use the term condition to describe any of such circumstances. One of the goals of modern molecular biology is the high-throughput identification of genes associated with a particular condition of interest. The widely used technology of microarrays allows one to simultaneously monitor the expression levels of thousands of genes. Time-course microarray experiments [2–4, 6, 9, 12, 14, 17] are an increasingly popular approach for understanding the dynamical behavior of a wide range of biological systems.

In this paper we shall consider microarray experiments made over the course of time which involve comparison between several biological conditions. In particular, we consider data consisting of measurements of the expression levels of

---

* Corresponding author.

E. Biganzoli et al. (Eds.): CIBB 2011, LNBI 7548, pp. 21–35, 2012.

N genes collected over time [0,T] under $H \geq 3$ different conditions. The objective is first to identify the genes that are differentially expressed between some of the H conditions and then to estimate the response.

In general, the problem can be formulated as follows. For condition $\aleph$, $\aleph = 1, \cdots, H$, data consists of the records on N genes which are taken at time points $t_{\aleph}^{(j)} \in [0,T]$, $j = 1,..,n_{\aleph}$, and, for gene i at a time point $t_{\aleph}^{(j)}$, there are $k_{\aleph i}^{(j)}$ records available, making the total number of records for gene i in condition $\aleph$ to be $M_{\aleph i} = \sum_{j=1}^{n_{\aleph}} k_{\aleph i}^{(j)}$. Note that the number of time points is relatively small ($n_{\aleph} \approx 10$) and very few replications are available at each time point ($k_{\aleph i}^{(j)} = 0, 1, \ldots K_{\aleph i}$, where $K_{\aleph i} = 1, 2, 3$ or 4) while the number of genes is very large ($N \approx 50,000$). Note that this is a much more general set up than the one which is usually considered since we require neither that the observations for the H conditions are made at the same time points nor that the number of observations for different samples is the same. The only requirement is that the samples are observed over the same period of time.

Each record can be modeled as a noisy measurement of a function $s_{\aleph i}(t)$ evaluated at a time point $t_{\aleph}^{(j)}$, where $s_{\aleph i}(t_{\aleph}^{(j)})$ represents the expression level of gene i measured on condition $\aleph$ at a time point $t_{\aleph}^{(j)}$, $\aleph = 1, 2, \cdots H$. The objective of the analysis is to identify differentially expressed genes (i.e. genes such that $s_{1i}(t) = \ldots = s_{Hi}(t)$ is not verified) and to estimate the expression profiles of the genes. Note that in the case of $H = 2$, this problem translates into selecting the curves $s_{1i}(t)$ and $s_{2i}(t)$, $i = 1, \cdots, N$, such that the difference $s_i(t) = s_{2i}(t) - s_{1i}(t)$ is not identical to zero (see [3]). However, in the case when $H \geq 3$ there are many more possibilities. For example, a particular gene i can be differentially expressed between all H conditions: $s_{1i}(t) \neq s_{2i}(t) \neq \cdots \neq s_{Hi}(t)$, or it can be not differentially expressed for the first $H - 1$ conditions and differentially expressed for the H-th condition: $s_{1 i}(t) = s_{2 i}(t) = s_{H-1 \, i}(t) \neq s_{Hi}(t)$, and so on. In general, in the case of H conditions, one has B_H different possibilities, where B_H is the Bell exponential number, i.e the number of nonempty subsets of the set with H elements. The problem is to identify for each gene which of these B_H situations actually takes place.

The problem of identification of time-course differentially expressed genes under several biological conditions was considered in the recent papers by [3, 13, 17]. The first two papers do not examine every possible situation reducing the problem of finding differentially expressed genes between only two conditions. By contrast, paper [17] studies all possible situations. However, the weakness of the approach is that it tests whether a gene is differentially expressed at a particular time point not overall, thus, ignoring the temporal dependence between the expression levels at different time points. Therefore, the objective of the present paper is to overcome this shortcoming by generalizing the functional approach of [2, 3] to the case of the H-conditions ($H \geq 3$) microarray experiments.

The paper is organized as follows. Section 2 introduces the hierarchical Bayesian model. Sections 2.2 and 2.3, respectively, describe modeling the gene expression profiles and the errors. Section 3 explains how to estimate the gene-dependent parameters. Section 4 describes the inference, while Section 5 outlines the procedures for estimating the gene expression profiles. Section 6 provides the techniques for estimating global parameters. Section 7 summarizes the algorithm. Finally, Section 8 provides an extensive simulation study. The Appendix contains the derivation of the formulae in the previous sections.

2   Statistical Modeling, Estimation and Classification of Gene Expression Profiles

2.1   The Data Structure

The data are assumed to be already pre-processed to remove systematic sources of variation. Normalization procedures depend on the type of platforms used for performing the experiments. For a detailed discussion of the normalization procedures for microarray data we refer the reader to e.g. [7, 10, 15, 16].

The measurements are taken at $n_\aleph$, $\aleph = 1, \cdots, H$, different time points in $[0, T]$ where the sampling grid $t_\aleph^{(1)}, t_\aleph^{(2)}, \ldots, t_\aleph^{(n_\aleph)}$ is not necessarily uniformly spaced and may be different for $\aleph = 1, \cdots, H$. For each array, the data consist of N measurements $z_{\aleph i}^{j,k}$, where $\aleph$ is the sample number, $i = 1, \ldots, N$, is the gene number, index j corresponds to the time point $t_\aleph^{(j)}$ and $k = 1, \ldots, k_{\aleph i}^{(j)}$, $k_{\aleph i}^{(j)} \geq 0$, accommodates for possible technical replicates at time $t_\aleph^{(j)}$. By the structure of the experimental design, $k_{\aleph i}^{(j)}$ are the same for each gene i; however, since some observations may be missing, we let $k_{\aleph i}^{(j)}$ to depend on i.

For each gene i in the sample $\aleph$, we assume that evolution in time of its relative expression is governed by a function $s_{\aleph i}(t)$ and each of the measurements involves some measurement error, i.e.

$$z_{\aleph i}^{j,k} = s_{\aleph i}(t_\aleph^{(j)}) + \zeta_{\aleph i}^{j,k}, \qquad i = 1, \ldots, N, \quad j = 1, \ldots, n_\aleph, \quad k = 1, \ldots, k_{\aleph i}^{(j)}. \quad (1)$$

The measurement errors $\zeta_{\aleph i}^{j,k}$ are assumed to be i.i.d. with zero mean and finite variance. The function $s_{\aleph i}(t)$, $\aleph = 1, \cdots, H$, represents the temporal expression level of gene i in the sample $\aleph$ over the interval $[0, T]$.

2.2   Modeling the Gene Expression Profiles

Each function $s_{\aleph i}(t)$ is globally estimated, since the measurements are available only at a few time points. Specifically, we expand each function over some standard orthonormal basis on the interval $[0, T]$

$$s_{\aleph i}(t) = \sum_{l=0}^{L_i} c_{\aleph i}^{(l)} \phi_l(t) \qquad (2)$$

and characterize each of them by the vector of its coefficients $c_{\aleph i}$. In the present paper we use Legendre polynomials suitably rescaled and normalized in $[0, T]$, but other choices are possible. We emphasize that the degree of the polynomial varies from gene to gene but is common for all H conditions. The values of the coefficients $c_{\aleph i}^{(l)}$ and the degrees of the polynomials L_i are estimated from the observations via a Bayesian approach.

We assume that the genes are conditionally independent, so that combination of (1) and (2) yields

$$\mathbf{z}_{\aleph i} = \mathbf{D}_{\aleph i}\mathbf{c}_{\aleph i} + \boldsymbol{\zeta}_{\aleph i} \tag{3}$$

where $\mathbf{z}_{\aleph i} = (z_{\aleph i}^{1,1} \ldots z_{\aleph i}^{1,k_{\aleph i}^{(1)}}, \cdots, z_{\aleph i}^{n_{\aleph},1}, \ldots z_{\aleph i}^{n_{\aleph},k_{\aleph i}^{(n_{\aleph})}})^T \in R^{M_{\aleph i}}$ is the column vector of all measurements for gene i in condition $\aleph$, $\mathbf{c}_{\aleph i} = (c_{\aleph i}^0, \ldots, c_{\aleph i}^{L_i})^T \in R^{L_i+1}$ is the column vector of the coefficients of $s_{\aleph i}(t)$ in the chosen basis, $\boldsymbol{\zeta}_{\aleph i} = (\zeta_{\aleph i}^{1,1}, \ldots, \zeta_{\aleph i}^{1,k_{\aleph i}^{(1)}}, \cdots, \zeta_{\aleph i}^{n_{\aleph},1}, \ldots, \zeta_{\aleph i}^{n_{\aleph},k_{\aleph i}^{(n_{\aleph})}})^T \in R^{M_{\aleph i}}$ is the column vector of random errors and $\mathbf{D}_{\aleph i}$ is the $M_{\aleph i} \times (L_i+1)$ block design matrix, the j-row of which is the block vector $[\phi_0(t_{\aleph}^{(j)}) \ \phi_1(t_{\aleph}^{(j)}) \ \cdots \ \phi_{L_i}(t_{\aleph}^{(j)})]$ replicated $k_{\aleph i}^{(j)}$ times.

The proposed model is fully Bayesian, since we treat all parameters either as random variables or as nuisance parameters, thus recovered from data. We assume that given σ^2, the vectors of errors $\boldsymbol{\zeta}_{\aleph i}$ are normally distributed $\boldsymbol{\zeta}_{\aleph i} \mid \sigma^2 \sim \mathcal{N}(0, \sigma^2 \mathbf{I}_{M_{\aleph i}})$, hence

$$\mathbf{z}_{\aleph i} \mid L_i, \mathbf{c}_{\aleph i}, \sigma^2 \sim \mathcal{N}(\mathbf{D}_{\aleph i}\mathbf{c}_{\aleph i}, \sigma^2 \mathbf{I}_{M_{\aleph i}}). \tag{4}$$

We also assume that L_i a-priori has the truncated Poisson distribution $Pois^*(\lambda, L_{\max})$ with parameter λ truncated at $L_{\max}$, and we denote its pdf by $g_\lambda(L_i)$:

$$g_\lambda(L_i) = \left[\sum_{l=0}^{L_{\max}} (l!)^{-1}\lambda^l e^{-\lambda} \right]^{-1} (L_i!)^{-1}\lambda^{L_i}e^{-\lambda}, \quad L_i = 0, \ldots, L_{\max}. \tag{5}$$

Parameter λ is proportional to the average degree of the polynomial and $L_{\max}$ refers to the maximal possible degree. The values of both parameters are treated as known constants. In general, λ and $L_{\max}$ should be chosen by considering the number of available time points and the nature of the problem.

Denote

$$\mathbf{C}_i = \{\mathbf{c}_{1i}, \cdots, \mathbf{c}_{Hi}\}, \quad \mathbf{Z}_i = \{\mathbf{z}_{1i}, \cdots, \mathbf{z}_{Hi}\} \tag{6}$$

the set of the vector coefficients and the set of the vector of data. The question of interest now is, for every gene $i = 1, \cdots, N$, to identify whether it is differentially expressed and, if yes, then between which conditions. For this purpose, we introduce B_H classes $\omega_0, \omega_1, \cdots, \omega_{B_H-1}$ that represents all possible combination of the H conditions. We observe that B_H is the Bell exponential number and it can be evaluated recursively as $B_n = \sum_{k=0}^{n-1} \binom{n-1}{k} B_k$, with $B_0 = B_1 = 1$. The formula gives $B_2 = 2$, $B_3 = 5$, $B_4 = 15$, $B_5 = 52$, $B_6 = 203$. Clearly, it will be hard to analyse more than 4 or 5 conditions simultaneously. For example, for $H = 3$ we have five possible classes which can be described as follows:

$$\begin{array}{lll} \omega_0 : c_{1i} = c_{2i} = c_{3i} & \omega_1 : c_{2i} = c_{3i} \neq c_{1i} & \omega_2 : c_{1i} = c_{3i} \neq c_{2i} \\ \omega_3 : c_{1i} = c_{2i} \neq c_{3i} & \omega_4 : c_{1i} \neq c_{2i} \neq c_{3i} \end{array} \tag{7}$$

It is reasonable to assume that a-priori vectors $c_{\aleph i}$, $\aleph = 1, 2, \cdots, H$, are either equal to each other or are group-wise independent with identical distributions. A total of B_H different combinations can occurr. For example, in the case of $H = 3$ we elicit the following priors on the vectors $C_i = \{c_{1i}, c_{2i}, c_{3i}\}$:

$$\begin{aligned} C_i \mid L_i, \sigma^2, \omega_0 &\sim \mathcal{N}(c_{1i} \mid 0, \sigma^2 \tau_{0i}^2 Q_i^{-1}) \delta(c_{1i} = c_{2i} = c_{3i}) \\ C_i \mid L_i, \sigma^2, \omega_1 &\sim \mathcal{N}(c_{1i} \mid 0, \sigma^2 \tau_{1i}^2 Q_i^{-1}) \mathcal{N}(c_{2i} \mid 0, \sigma^2 \tau_{1i}^2 Q_i^{-1}) \delta(c_{2i} = c_{3i} \neq c_{1i}) \\ C_i \mid L_i, \sigma^2, \omega_2 &\sim \mathcal{N}(c_{2i} \mid 0, \sigma^2 \tau_{2i}^2 Q_i^{-1}) \mathcal{N}(c_{1i} \mid 0, \sigma^2 \tau_{2i}^2 Q_i^{-1}) \delta(c_{1i} = c_{3i} \neq c_{2i}) \\ C_i \mid L_i, \sigma^2, \omega_3 &\sim \mathcal{N}(c_{3i} \mid 0, \sigma^2 \tau_{3i}^2 Q_i^{-1}) \mathcal{N}(c_{1i} \mid 0, \sigma^2 \tau_{3i}^2 Q_i^{-1}) \delta(c_{1i} = c_{2i} \neq c_{3i}) \\ C_i \mid L_i, \sigma^2, \omega_4 &\sim \mathcal{N}(c_{1i} \mid 0, \sigma^2 \tau_{4i}^2 Q_i^{-1}) \mathcal{N}(c_{2i} \mid 0, \sigma^2 \tau_{4i}^2 Q_i^{-1}) \\ &\quad \times \mathcal{N}(c_{3i} \mid 0, \sigma^2 \tau_{4i}^2 Q_i^{-1}) \delta(c_{1i} \neq c_{2i} \neq c_{3i}). \end{aligned} \tag{8}$$

where $0 = (0, \cdots, 0)^T$. We assume that a-priori $P(\omega_l) = \pi_l$, $l = 0, \cdots, B_H - 1$, with $\sum_{l=0}^{B_H-1} \pi_l = 1$, so that

$$p(C_i \mid L_i, \sigma^2) = \sum_{l=0}^{B_H-1} \pi_l \, p(C_i \mid L_i, \sigma^2, \omega_l). \tag{9}$$

In formula (8), matrix Q_i is a diagonal matrix that can account for the decay of the coefficients in the chosen basis. Note that if no assumptions are made about smoothness of the gene expression profiles, we can assume $Q_i = I$. Parameters τ_{li}^2, $l = 0, \cdots, B_H - 1$, are gene and class specific and represent the strength of the signal with respect to the noise for a gene i in class l. We treat τ_{li}^2 as unknown nuisance parameters and estimate them from the data by maximizing the marginal likelihood for each gene independently (see Section 3).

2.3 Modeling the Errors

We assume that parameter σ^2 is a random variable

$$\sigma^2 \sim \rho(\sigma^2). \tag{10}$$

The latter choice allows one to account for possibly non-Gaussian errors (quite common in microarray experiments), without sacrificing closed form expressions for estimators and test statistics. In particular, among the possible choices, we consider three types of priors $\rho(\cdot)$:

case 1: $\rho(\sigma^2) = \delta(\sigma^2 - \sigma_0^2)$, the point mass at σ_0^2. The marginal distribution of the error is normal.

case 2: $\rho(\sigma^2) = IG(\gamma, b)$, the Inverse Gamma distribution. The marginal distribution of the error is Student T.

case 3: $\rho(\sigma^2) = c_\mu \sigma^{(M-1)} e^{-\sigma^2 \mu/2}$, where M is the total number of arrays available in the experimental design set-up. If the gene has no missing data, i.e. all replications at each time point are available, then the marginal distribution of the error is double exponential.

The global hyperparameters, $\pi_0, \pi_1, \ldots, \pi_{B_H-1}$, and the $\rho(\sigma^2)$-specific parameters (σ_0^2 for case 1, γ and b for case 2 and μ for case 3), are estimated from the data. Possible strategies for doing this are discussed in Section 6. Once the hyperparameters are estimated, Bayesian analysis is carried out by combining the prior information and the data into the posterior distribution.

3   Estimation of Gene-Dependent Parameters

If the global parameters of the model were known, one could proceed to a gene-by-gene analysis of vectors of coefficients $c_{\aleph i}$, $\aleph = 1, \cdots, H$, $i = 1, \cdots, N$. In this section, we only provide the final formulae, referring the reader to the Appendix for the details of the calculations. To deal with different choices of $\rho(\sigma^2)$, we introduce a function

$$F(A,B) = \int_0^\infty \sigma^{-2A} e^{-B/2\sigma^2} \rho(\sigma^2) d\sigma^2 \tag{11}$$

that can be explicitly calculated in the three cases discussed above as:

$$F(A,B) = \begin{cases} \sigma_0^{-2A} e^{-B/2\sigma_0^2} & \text{in case 1,} \\ \frac{\Gamma(A+\gamma)}{\Gamma(\gamma)} b^{-A}(1 + \frac{B}{2b})^{-(A+\gamma)} & \text{in case 2,} \\ \frac{B^{(M+1-2A)/4} \mu^{(M+1+2A)/4}}{2^{(M-1)/2} \Gamma((M+1)/2)} K_{((M+1-2A)/2)}(\sqrt{B\mu}) & \text{in case 3.} \end{cases} \tag{12}$$

Here M denotes the number of available observations and $K_h(\cdot)$ is the Bessel function of degree h (see [8], Sections 8.4–8.5 for the definition). Note that in the sequel function F will appear with the argument $A = M_i/2$, where $M_i = \sum_{\aleph=1}^H M_{\aleph i}$, denotes the total number of records for gene i.

Then, if the i-th gene has no missing data (i.e. $M_i = M$), expression for case 3 in formula (12) simplifies to

$$F(M/2, B) = \sqrt{\pi} \left[\Gamma((M+1)/2) \right]^{-1} (\mu/2)^{M/2} \exp(-\sqrt{B\mu}).$$

Combining (4), (9) and (10) in a joint pdf and integrating out C_i and σ^2, we obtain

$$p(Z_i|L_i) = (2\pi)^{-M_i/2} |Q_i|^{1/2} \sum_{l=0}^{B_H-1} \pi_l A_{li}(Z_i|L_i, \tau_{li}) \tag{13}$$

where Z_i is defined in (6) and

$$A_{li}(Z_i|L_i, \tau_{li}) = (2\pi)^{M_i/2} |Q_i|^{-1/2} p(Z_i|\omega_l, L_i). \tag{14}$$

In the case of $H = 3$, the expressions for $p(\mathbf{Z}_i|\omega_l, L_i)$ are given by formulae (22) and (23) below. Hence, the joint pdf of $\mathbf{Z}_i$ is

$$p(\mathbf{Z}_i) = \sum_{L_i=0}^{L_{\max}} p(\mathbf{Z}_i|L_i)\, g_\lambda(L_i), \tag{15}$$

and gene-dependent parameters τ_{li}^2, for $l = 0, \ldots, B_H - 1$, can be estimated as

$$(\hat{\tau}_{0i}^2, \ldots, \hat{\tau}_{B_H-1\,i}^2) = \arg\max_{\tau_{0i}^2, \ldots, \tau_{B_H-1\,i}^2} p(\mathbf{Z}_i). \tag{16}$$

However, since the joint pdf of $\mathbf{Z}_i$ is a sum of B_H positive terms (see formula (13)), each depending on a single τ_{li}^2, instead of one B_H-dimensional optimization, one can carry out B_H independent one-dimensional maximization procedures with respect to τ_{li}^2 for $l = 0, \ldots, B_H - 1$:

$$\hat{\tau}_{li}^2 = \arg\max_{\tau_{li}^2} \sum_{L_i=0}^{L_{\max}} A_{li}(\mathbf{Z}_i, L_i|\tau_{li})\, g_\lambda(L_i), \quad l = 0, \cdots, B_H - 1. \tag{17}$$

Maximization (17) represents the most computationally demanding step of the overall algorithm. However, since it is carried out independently for each gene, computations can be accelerated by using parallel computing.

The posterior pdf of the degree L_i given data $\mathbf{Z}$ is calculated as

$$p(L_i|\mathbf{Z}_i) = p(\mathbf{Z}_i|L_i)g_\lambda(L_i)\big/p(\mathbf{Z}_i). \tag{18}$$

For each gene i, we estimate L_i by maximizing the posterior pdf (18) (MAP principle). After τ_{li}^2, $l = 0, \ldots, B_H - 1$, and L_i are estimated, we replace them with $\hat{\tau}_{li}^2$ and $\hat{L}_i$ in all the subsequent calculations.

4 Identification and Classification of Genes

4.1 Evaluation of Class Probabilities

Our main goal now is to carry out classification of genes to classes $\omega_l, l = 0, \cdots, B_H - 1$. We evaluate probability that gene i belongs to class ω_l as

$$p(\omega_l|\mathbf{Z}_i) = \frac{\pi_l\, p(\mathbf{Z}_i|\omega_l)}{p(\mathbf{Z}_i)} = \pi_l \frac{\sum_{L_i=0}^{L_{\max}} g_\lambda(L_i)\, p(\mathbf{Z}_i|\omega_l, L_i)}{p(\mathbf{Z}_i)} \tag{19}$$

with

$$p(\mathbf{Z}_i|\omega_l, L_i) = \int\int p(\mathbf{Z}_i|\mathbf{C}_i, \sigma^2)\, p(\mathbf{C}_i|\omega_l, \sigma^2, L_i)\, d\mathbf{C}_i d\sigma^2 \tag{20}$$

and

$$p(\mathbf{Z}_i) = \sum_{L_i=0}^{L_{\max}} \sum_{l=0}^{B_H-1} \pi_l \, p(\mathbf{Z}_i|\omega_l, L_i) \, g_\lambda(L_i). \tag{21}$$

For example, in the case of $H = 3$, evaluation of $p(\mathbf{Z}_i|\omega_l, L_i)$, $l = 0, \cdots, B_H - 1$, yields

$$p(\mathbf{Z}_i|\omega_0, L_i) = \frac{|\mathbf{Q}_i|^{1/2} \, F(M_i/2, \mathbf{S}_i - \mathbf{v}_i^T \mathbf{V}_i^{-1} \mathbf{v}_i)}{(2\pi)^{M_i/2} \, |\mathbf{V}_i|^{1/2} \, \tau_{0i}^{(L_i+1)}},$$

$$p(\mathbf{Z}_i|\omega_l, L_i) = \frac{|\mathbf{Q}_i|^{1/2} \, F(M_i/2, \mathbf{S}_i - \mathbf{v}_{-li}^T \mathbf{V}_{-li}^{-1} \mathbf{v}_{-li} - \mathbf{v}_{li}^T \mathbf{V}_{li}^{-1} \mathbf{v}_{li})}{(2\pi)^{M_i/2} \, |\mathbf{V}_{-li}|^{1/2} \, |\mathbf{V}_{li}|^{1/2} \, \tau_{li}^{2(L_i+1)}}, \quad l = 1, \cdots, H,$$

$$p(\mathbf{Z}_i|\omega_4, L_i) = \frac{|\mathbf{Q}_i|^{1/2} \, F(M_i/2, \mathbf{S}_i - \sum_{l=1}^{H} \mathbf{v}_{li}^T \mathbf{W}_{li}^{-1} \mathbf{v}_{li})}{(2\pi)^{M_i/2} \, \prod_{l=1}^{H} [|\mathbf{W}_{li}|^{1/2}] \, \tau_{4i}^{H(L_i+1)}}, \tag{22}$$

where

$$
\begin{aligned}
\mathbf{S}_i &= \sum_{k=1}^{H} \mathbf{z}_{ki}^T \mathbf{z}_{ki}, & \mathbf{D}_i &= \sum_{k=1}^{H} \mathbf{D}_{ki}^T \mathbf{D}_{ki}, \\
\mathbf{V}_i &= \mathbf{D}_i + \tau_{0i}^{-2} \mathbf{Q}_i, & \mathbf{v}_i &= \sum_{k=1}^{H} \mathbf{D}_{ki}^T \mathbf{z}_{ki}, \\
\mathbf{V}_{-li} &= \sum_{\substack{k=1 \\ k\neq l}}^{H} \mathbf{D}_{ki}^T \mathbf{D}_{ki} + \tau_{li}^{-2} \mathbf{Q}_i, & \mathbf{v}_{-li} &= \sum_{\substack{k=1 \\ k\neq l}}^{H} \mathbf{D}_{ki}^T \mathbf{z}_{ki}, \\
\mathbf{V}_{li} &= \mathbf{D}_{li}^T \mathbf{D}_{li} + \tau_{li}^{-2} \mathbf{Q}_i, & \mathbf{v}_{li} &= \mathbf{D}_{li}^T \mathbf{z}_{li}, \\
\mathbf{W}_{li} &= \mathbf{D}_{li}^T \mathbf{D}_{li} + \tau_{4i}^{-2} \mathbf{Q}_i, & l &= 1, \cdots, H.
\end{aligned}
\tag{23}
$$

Remark 1. Formulae (22) for the class $l = 1, 2, 3$ are analytically interchangeable, i.e. the H class are equivalent under label permutations.

4.2   Identification and Classification of Differentially Expressed Genes

In a standard Bayesian classification framework (**BC**), each gene is classified according to the highest posterior probability (19). However, this approach does not allow to control the number of false positive among the differentially expressed genes (i.e., those not in class ω_0). For this reason, we also propose a two-stage bayesian approach (**TSB**) as follows. At the first stage, we identify the genes which are differentially expressed among at least two of H conditions. At the second stage, we determine between which of the B_H cases occurs.

In order to proceed, we note that $p(\omega_0|\mathbf{Z}_i)$ can be presented as

$$p(\omega_0|\mathbf{Z}_i) = \pi_0 \left(\pi_0 + \frac{1 - \pi_0}{BF_i(\mathbf{Z}_i)} \right)^{-1}$$

where $BF_i(\mathbf{Z}_i)$ is the Bayes factors, the quotient between the posterior odds ratio and the prior odds ratio, for testing hypotheses $H_{0i} : i \in \omega_0$ versus $H_{1i} : i \notin \omega_0$ (see e.g. [5]):

$$BF_i(\mathbf{Z}_i) = (1 - \pi_0) \frac{\sum_{L_i=0}^{L_{\max}} g_\lambda(L_i) p(\mathbf{Z}_i|\omega_0, L_i)}{\sum_{l=1}^{B_H} \pi_l \sum_{L_i=0}^{L_{\max}} g_\lambda(L_i) p(\mathbf{Z}_i|\omega_l, L_i)}. \tag{24}$$

Note that, although Bayes factors BF_i can be used for independent testing of the null hypotheses H_{0i}, $i = 1, \ldots, N$, the classical Bayesian approach [5] does not account for the multiplicity of comparisons. However, since in microarray experiments N is large, the problem of multiplicity cannot be ignored, therefore we apply the Bayesian multiple testing procedure of [1].

5   Estimation of Gene Expression Profiles

There are at least two approaches for estimating the gene expression profiles: the model-selection based estimator or the model-average based estimator. The model-selection based estimator is constructed under the assumption that gene i belongs to class ω_l, i.e. $\mathbf{c}_{\aleph i}$ is estimated by

$$\hat{\mathbf{c}}_{\aleph i}(\omega_l) = \mathrm{E}\left(\mathbf{c}_{\aleph i} | \omega_l, \mathbf{Z}_i, \hat{L}_i\right).$$

Here, $\hat{L}_i$ is estimated degree of the polynomial for expression profiles for gene i. Hence, $\hat{\mathbf{c}}_{\aleph i}(\omega_l)$ can be evaluated as

$$\hat{\mathbf{c}}_{\aleph i}(\omega_l) = \frac{\int \mathbf{c}_{\aleph i}\, p(\mathbf{C}_i, \mathbf{Z}_i | \omega_l, \sigma^2, \hat{L}_i)\, \rho(\sigma^2)\, d\mathbf{C}_i d\sigma^2}{p(\mathbf{Z}_i | \omega_l, \hat{L}_i)}. \tag{25}$$

In the case of $H = 3$ we derive the following expressions for $\hat{\mathbf{c}}_{\aleph i}(\omega_l)$, $\aleph = 1, 2, 3$, $l = 0, \cdots, 5$:

$$\begin{aligned}
\hat{\mathbf{c}}_{\aleph i}(\omega_0) &= \mathbf{V}_i^{-1} \mathbf{v}_i, & \aleph &= 1, 2, 3, \\
\hat{\mathbf{c}}_{1i}(\omega_1) &= \mathbf{V}_{1i}^{-1} \mathbf{v}_{1i}, & \hat{\mathbf{c}}_{2i}(\omega_1) &= \hat{\mathbf{c}}_{3i}(\omega_1) = \mathbf{V}_{-1i}^{-1} \mathbf{v}_{-1i}, \\
\hat{\mathbf{c}}_{2i}(\omega_2) &= \mathbf{V}_{2i}^{-1} \mathbf{v}_{2i}, & \hat{\mathbf{c}}_{1i}(\omega_1) &= \hat{\mathbf{c}}_{3i}(\omega_1) = \mathbf{V}_{-2i}^{-1} \mathbf{v}_{-2i}, & (26) \\
\hat{\mathbf{c}}_{3i}(\omega_3) &= \mathbf{V}_{3i}^{-1} \mathbf{v}_{3i}, & \hat{\mathbf{c}}_{1i}(\omega_1) &= \hat{\mathbf{c}}_{2i}(\omega_1) = \mathbf{V}_{-3i}^{-1} \mathbf{v}_{-3i}, \\
\hat{\mathbf{c}}_{\aleph i}(\omega_4) &= \mathbf{W}_{\aleph i}^{-1} \mathbf{v}_{\aleph i}, & \aleph &= 1, 2, 3,
\end{aligned}$$

In alternative one can use the model average estimator:

$$\hat{\mathbf{c}}_{\aleph i} = \mathrm{E}\left(\mathbf{c}_{\aleph i} | \mathbf{Z}_i, \hat{L}_i\right)$$

which can be evaluated as

$$\hat{\mathbf{c}}_{\aleph i} = \frac{\sum_{l=0}^{B_H - 1} \pi_l \int \mathbf{c}_{\aleph i}\, p(\mathbf{C}_i, \mathbf{Z}_i | \omega_l, \sigma^2, \hat{L}_i)\, \rho(\sigma^2)\, d\mathbf{C}_i d\sigma^2}{\sum_{l=0}^{B_H - 1} \pi_l p(\mathbf{Z}_i | \omega_l, \hat{L}_i)}. \tag{27}$$

Since it follows from (26) that the integrals in the numerator of formula (27) are equal to $\hat{\mathbf{c}}_{\aleph i}(\omega_l) p(\mathbf{Z}_i | \omega_l, \hat{L}_i)$, one can easily evaluate the estimators $\hat{\mathbf{c}}_{\aleph i}$ as

$$\hat{\mathbf{c}}_{\aleph i} = \frac{\sum_{l=0}^{B_H - 1} \pi_l\, \hat{\mathbf{c}}_{\aleph i}(\omega_l)\, p(\mathbf{Z}_i | \omega_l, \hat{L}_i)}{\sum_{l=0}^{B_H - 1} \pi_l\, p(\mathbf{Z}_i | \omega_l, \hat{L}_i)} \tag{28}$$

where $\hat{\mathbf{c}}_{\aleph i}(\omega_l)$ and $p(\mathbf{Z}_i | \omega_l, \hat{L}_i)$ are defined in (26) and (20), respectively.

6   Estimation of Global Parameters and Prior Hyperparameters

In this section we consider some possible strategies for estimation of the global parameters σ^2, π_l, $l = 0, \cdots, H$, and the $\rho(\sigma^2)$-specific parameters σ_0^2 (case 1), γ and b (case 2), and μ (case 3).

Estimation of σ^2. If replications are available (i.e. , $k_{\aleph i}^{(j)} > 1$ for some $j, \aleph$ and i), one can form statistics

$$\beta_{\aleph i}^{(j)} = \sum_{k=1}^{k_{\aleph i}^{(j)}} (z_{\aleph i}^{j,k} - \bar{z}_{\aleph i}^{j})^2 \quad \text{where} \quad \bar{z}_{\aleph i}^{j} = (k_{\aleph i}^{(j)})^{-1} \sum_{k=1}^{k_{\aleph i}^{(j)}} z_{\aleph i}^{j,k}.$$

It is easy to notice that $\beta_{\aleph i}^{(j)}/\sigma^2$ has chi-squared distribution with $k_{\aleph i}^{(j)} - 1$ degrees of freedom $\chi(k_{\aleph i}^{(j)} - 1)$ if $k_{\aleph i}^{(j)} > 1$ and is identical zero otherwise. Hence,

$$\beta = \sum_{\aleph=1}^{H} \sum_{i=1}^{N} \sum_{j=1}^{n_\aleph} \beta_{\aleph i}^{j} \sim \sigma^2 \chi(\upsilon) \quad \text{with} \quad \upsilon = \sum_{\aleph=1}^{H} \sum_{i=1}^{N} \sum_{j=1}^{n_\aleph} (k_{\aleph i}^{(j)} - 1) I(k_{\aleph i}^{(j)} > 1), \quad (29)$$

so that $\hat{\sigma}^2 = \beta/\upsilon$ is an unbiased estimator of σ^2.

In a general situation, when replications are not available or they are available only at few time points, one can apply the U-statistics version of the Rice estimator derived in [11] with the kernel $K(x) = 3(1 - x^2)_+/4$ gene by gene, After that, the global estimator of the variance σ^2 is obtained by pooling the estimators of the variance for single genes (see [3] for details).

Estimation of $\pi = (\pi_0, \cdots, \pi_{\mathbf{B_H}-1})$. Recall that parameters π_{li}, $l = 0, \cdots$, $B_H - 1$, can be estimated without any knowledge of the values of π_l, $l = 1, \cdots, B_H - 1$. Hence, in principle, π_l, $l = 1, \cdots, B_H - 1$, can be obtained as a solution of a $(B_H - 1)$-dimensional optimization problem

$$\hat{\pi} = \arg\max_{\pi} \ \log p(\mathbf{Z}) = \arg\max_{\pi} \ \sum_{i=1}^{N} \log p(\mathbf{Z}_i) \quad (30)$$

where $p(\mathbf{Z}_i)$ is given by formulae (13) and (15). However, the solution of this optimization problem is highly unstable and computationally demanding. Therefore, we used equally likely prior probability.

Estimation of Case-Specific Parameters. In *case 1*, the natural estimator of σ_0^2 is $\hat{\sigma}^2$. In *case 2*, one can either fix one of the two parameters, γ or b, and then estimate another one by matching the mean of the distribution $IG(\gamma, b)$ with $\hat{\sigma}^2$, or use the MLE estimate of both parameters as proposed in [2]. Similarly, in *case 3*, μ is estimated by $\hat{\mu} = (M - 1)/\hat{\sigma}^2$, so that the mean of the prior distribution $\rho(\sigma^2)$ is centered at $\hat{\sigma}^2$. Other alternative strategies can also be used for estimating parameters without changing the general algorithm.

7   Algorithm

The algorithm can be carried out as follows:

1. Fix prior parameters λ, $L_{\max}$ and ν.
2. Estimate global parameters: σ^2 and case-specific hyper-parameters σ_0^2 (for case 1), γ and b (for case 2) or μ (for case 3), see Section 6.
3. For each gene i, estimate the gene specific parameters, τ_{li}^2, for $l = 0, \ldots, B_H - 1$, using equation (17).
4. Apply **BC** classification procedure by placing gene i into a class with the highest posterior probability (19). Alternatively, apply **TSB** classification procedure, i.e., for each gene i, compute Bayes Factor BF_i using formula (24). See Section 4.2 for details.
5. For each differentially expressed gene i, estimate the most appropriate degree L_i as the mean or the mode of the posterior pdf (18).
6. Estimate the gene expression profiles $s_{\aleph i}(t)$ for differentially expressed genes using formulae (2) and (26) or (27).

Since all evaluations are based on explicit expressions, the algorithm is very computationally efficient.

8   Simulations Results and Discussion

In order to evaluate the performance of the proposed method under different possible scenarios, we carried out a simulation study over various kinds of synthetic data-sets. For simplicity, we dealt only with the case $H = 3$. We considered $N = 10,000$ genes and analyze four different data structures: DATASET1, DATSET2, DATASET3 and DATSET4.

DATASET1 has the same time grid, $t_{\aleph}^{(\cdot)} = [1, 2, 3, 4, 6, 8, 10, 11, 12]$ with 2 replicates at each time point except $k_{\aleph i}^{(3,5,7)} = 1$ for all three conditions $\aleph = 1, 2, 3$, and equal cardinalities of all classes $|\omega_l| = 2000$, for $l = 0, \ldots, 4$. In DATASET2, the time grids are $t_1^{(\cdot)} = [1, 2, 4, 6, 8, 10, 11, 12]$, $t_2^{(\cdot)} = [1, 2, 3, 4, 6, 8, 10, 12]$ and $t_3^{(\cdot)} = [1, 2, 3, 4, 6, 8, 11, 12]$, respectively, with 2 replicates at each time point except $k_{1i}^{(4,6)} = 1$, $k_{2i}^{(5,7)} = 1$ and $k_{3i}^{(3,5)} = 1$, and equal classes' cardinalities. DATASET3 has time grids as in DATSET1, while classes' cardinalities are $|\omega_0| = 5000$, $|\omega_1| = 2500$, $|\omega_2| = 1000$, $|\omega_3| = 500$ and $|\omega_4| = 1000$. DATASET4 has time grids as in DATASET2 while classes' cardinalities as DATASET3.

The data were generated according to model (1) with the noise $\zeta_{\aleph i}^{j,k}$ following the Student distribution with 5 degrees of freedom and scaled so that its standard deviation is $\sigma = 0.2$. The gene expression profiles $s_{\aleph i}(t_{\aleph}^{(j)})$ were generated according to model (2). In particular, for each gene, we first sampled the degree of the polynomial L_i from the discrete uniform distribution $U[0,6]$. Then, we sampled one, two or three different vectors of coefficients $\mathbf{c}_{\aleph i}$ from a normal distribution $\mathcal{N}(0, \sigma^2 \tau_i^2 \mathbf{Q}_i^{-1})$ according to the class participation of the current gene. For example, if the gene belongs to the first class (ω_0), then only one vector of coefficient is generated since all the three samples $\aleph = 1, 2, 3$ are the same. If the gene belongs to class 1,2, or 3, then two different vectors of coefficients were generated with one of the vectors used for the sample which differentiates from the other two. Finally, if the gene belongs to class ω_4, then three different vectors of coefficients were generated, each used for one sample. Matrix $\mathbf{Q}_i$ is set equal to $\text{diag}(1^{2\nu_i}, 2^{2\nu_i}, ..., L^{i^{2\nu_i}})$ with ν_i sampled from the uniform distribution $U([0,1])$. For each gene, the values of τ_i^2 were independently and uniformly sampled in order to produce the signal-to-noise ratio (SNR) in the interval $[2,6]$.

For each data-set the simulations were repeated using 100 randomly generated sets of profiles s_{1i}, s_{2i} and s_{3i} and noise realizations, with the choice $L_{max} = 6$, $\lambda = 9$ and $\nu = 0$. The data were processed using the BC and TBS approaches described in Section 4.2. Results are summarized in Tables 1 and 2, where means and standard deviations (in parenthesis) of, respectively, the sensitivity and the specificity for the 5 classes are reported. Sensitivity measures the proportion of actual members of the class which are correctly identified as such (i.e., for each class, the sensitivity is the percentage of genes correctly classified into the current class). Specificity measures the proportion of samples which do not belong to the class and are correctly identified (i.e., for each class, specificity is the percentage of genes which are correctly classified into a class different from the current). Tables 1 and 2 confirm that the two approaches, BC and TSB, are similar. However TSB is slightly more sensitive in the first class, being proposed for controlling the FDR on ω_0; while is less sensitive on classes ω_l, $l = 1, 2, 3$. On the contrary TSB is slightly less specific on ω_0 and more specific on classes ω_l $l = 1, 2, 3$. The two procedures have the same performance on class ω_4. Moreover, the techniques are invariant under permutation of class labels (if the class labels are permuted, then the results permute accordingly, result not showed here). The unbalanced scenarios, both in terms of time grids and of class cardinality, do not affect the classification precision since the procedures yield very similar results on all four data sets.

In order to be fair in the evaluation of the proposed procedures, we carried out an additional set of simulations which was not model-based. Specifically, in the same four scenarios for time grids and class cardinalities as in data sets DATSET1–4, we generated data according to smooth functions which are not directly represented as linear combinations of Legendre polynomials. For each class, we randomly drew one or more functions from a set of predefined shapes: linear, quadratic, sine, cosine and exponential then we randomly picked its coefficients.

Results of these simulations are presented in Tables 3 and 4.

Table 1. Sensitivities of BC and TSB procedures for model-based data sets

		class ω_0	class ω_1	class ω_2	class ω_3	class ω_4
DATASET1	BC	.9318	.9716	.9720	.9713	.9942
		(00030)	(.0020)	(.0017)	(.0018)	(.0009)
	TSB	.9488	.9684	.9689	.9681	.9942
		(.0024)	(.0021)	(.0018)	(.0019)	(.0009)
DATASET2	BC	.9254	.9685	.9695	.9684	.9935
		(.0027)	(.0018)	(.0019)	(.0020)	(.0010)
	TSB	.9456	.9647	.9657	.9648	.9935
		(.0024)	(.0019)	(.0020)	(.0021)	(.0010)
DATASET3	BC	.9281	.9844	.9857	.9861	.9965
		(.0037)	(.0012)	(.0012)	(.0010)	(.0006)
	TSB	.9463	.9816	.9829	.9832	.9965
		(.0033)	(.0014)	(.0013)	(.0011)	(.0006)
DATASET4	BC	.9219	.9827	.9843	.9843	.9961
		(.0037)	(.0014)	(.0015)	(.0010)	(.0006)
	TSB	.9427	.9797	.9807	.9811	.9961
		(.0032)	(.0016)	(.0017)	(.0011)	(.0006)

Table 2. Specificities of BC and TSB procedures for model-based data sets

		class ω_0	class ω_1	class ω_2	class ω_3	class ω_4
DATASET1	BC	.9935	.8945	.8939	.8940	.6872
		(.0018)	(.0071)	(.0074)	(.0069)	(.0118)
	TSB	.9864	.9066	.9065	.9067	.6873
		(.0026)	(.0066)	(.0069)	(.0066)	(.0118)
DATASET2	BC	.9922	.8841	.8819	.8834	.6593
		(.0018)	(.0066)	(.0074)	(.0074)	(.0107)
	TSB	.9840	.8991	.8970	.8979	.6594
		(.0026)	(.0062)	(.0073)	(.0069)	(.0107)
DATASET3	BC	.9935	.8942	.8930	.8948	.6883
		(.0010)	(.0064)	(.0093)	(.0136)	(.0143)
	TSB	.9864	.9074	.9058	.9082	.6883
		(.0015)	(.0062)	(.0091)	(.0126)	(.0143)
DATASET4	BC	.9923	.8833	.8830	.8849	.6590
		(.0013)	(.0059)	(.0102)	(.0148)	(.0144)
	TSB	.9843	.8981	.8979	.8996	.6590
		(.0017)	(.0057)	(.0096)	(.0142)	(.0144)

Table 3. Sensitivities of BC and TSB procedures for model-free data sets

		class ω_0	class ω_1	class ω_2	class ω_3	class ω_4
DATASET1	BC	.9945	.9599	.9599	.9596	.9937
		(.0009)	(.0022)	(.0020)	(.0019)	(.0008)
	TSB	.9970	.9562	.9562	.9560	.9937
		(.0006)	(.0023)	(.0022)	(.0020)	(.0008)
DATASET2	BC	.9937	.9000	.9565	.9585	.8924
		(.0008)	(.0034)	(.0022)	(.0019)	(.0082)
	TSB	.9967	.8952	.9520	.9548	.8924
		(.0006)	(.0034)	(.0023)	(.0020)	(.0032)
DATASET3	BC	.9942	.9725	.9769	.9782	.9954
		(.0011)	(.0017)	(.0013)	(.0013)	(.0008)
	TSB	.9968	.9636	.9694	.9710	.9954
		(.0007)	(.0019)	(.0017)	(.0015)	(.0008)
DATASET4	BC	.9934	.8187	.9696	.9771	.9476
		(.0013)	(.0039)	(.0017)	(.0014)	(.0023)
	TSB	.9964	.8069	.9604	.9700	.9476
		(.0009)	(.0038)	(.0019)	(.0017)	(.0023)

Table 4. Specificities of BC and TSB procedures for model-free data sets

		class ω_0	class ω_1	class ω_2	class ω_3	class ω_4
DATASET1	BC	.9635	.9822	.9821	.9822	.5604
		(.0047)	(.0029)	(.0029)	(.0028)	(.0114)
	TSB	.9239	.9840	.9838	.9839	.5604
		(.0064)	(.0027)	(.0028)	(.0028)	(.0114)
DATASET2	BC	.7012	.9493	.8092	.7891	.5554
		(.0105)	(.0047)	(.0082)	(.0092)	(.0109)
	TSB	.6549	.9510	.8116	.7912	.5554
		(.0109)	(.0047)	(.0081)	(.0090)	(.0109)
DATASET3	BC	.9638	.9824	.9822	.9828	.5605
		(.0027)	(.0026)	(.0046)	(.0055)	(.0149)
	TSB	.9243	.9841	.9838	.9844	.5605
		(.0039)	(.0025)	(.0044)	(.0053)	(.0149)
DATASET4	BC	.7016	.9499	.8088	.7900	.5581
		(.0058)	(.0041)	(.0120)	(.0189)	(.0150)
	TSB	.6552	.9518	.8109	.7922	.5581
		(.0059)	(.0039)	(.0119)	(.0188)	(.0150)

Acknowledgments. Claudia Angelini and Daniela De Canditiis were partially supported by the FLAGSHIP InterOmics project (PB.P05). Marianna Pensky was partially supported by the National Science Foundation (NSF), grant DMS-1106564. Naomi Brownstein was partially supported by the NSF, grant DMS-0646083.

References

1. Abramovich, F., Angelini, C.: Bayesian maximum a posteriori multiple testing procedure. Sankhya 68, 436–460 (2006)
2. Angelini, C., De Canditiis, D., Mutarelli, M., Pensky, M.: A Bayesian Approach to Estimation and Testing in Time-course Microarray Experiments. Stat. Appl. Gen. Mol. Bio. 6, Art. 24 (2007)
3. Angelini, C., De Canditiis, D., Pensky, M.: Bayesian Models for the Two-Sample Time-course Microarray Experiments. CSDA 53, 1547–1565 (2009)
4. Bar–Joseph, Z.: Analyzing time series gene expression data. Bioinformatics 20, 2493–2503 (2004)
5. Berger, O.J.: Statistical Decision Theory and Bayesian Analysis. Springer Series in Statistics (1985)
6. Conesa, A., Nueda, M.J., Ferrer, A., Talon, M.: MaSigPro: a method to identify significantly differential expression profiles in time-course microarray-experiments. Bioinformatics 22, 1096–1102 (2006)
7. Cui, X., Kerr, M.K., Churchill, G.A.: Transformation for cDNA Microarray Data. Stat. Appl. Gen. Mol. Bio. 2 (2002)
8. Gradshteyn, I.S., Ryzhik, I.M.: Tables of Integrals, Series, and Products. Academic Press, New York (1980)
9. Heard, N.A., Holmes, C.C., Stephens, D.A.: A quantitative study of gene regulation involved in the Immune response of Anopheline Mosquitoes: An application of Bayesian hierarchical clustering of curves. JASA 101, 18–29 (2006)
10. McLachlan, G., Do, K.A., Ambroise, C.: Analyzing microarray gene expression data. Wiley Series in Probability and Statistics (2004)
11. Müller, U., Schick, A., Wefelmeyer, W.: Estimating the error variance in nonparametric regression by a covariate-matched U-statistic. Statistics 37, 179–188 (2003)
12. Storey, J.D., Xiao, W., Leek, J.T., Tompkins, R.G., Davis, R.W.: Significance analysis of time course microarray experiments. PNAS 12, 12837–12842 (2005)
13. Tai, Y.C., Speed, T.P.: On gene ranking using replicated microarray time course data. Biometrics 65, 40–51 (2009)
14. Vinciotti, V., Yu, K.: M-quantile regression analysis of temporal gene expression data. Stat. Stat. Appl. Gen. Mol. Bio. 8, Art. 41 (2009)
15. Wit, E., McClure, J.: Statistics for Microarrays: Design, Analysis and Inference. Wiley (2004)
16. Yang, Y.H., Dudoit, S., Luu, P., Lin, M.D., Peng, V., Ngai, J., Speed, T.P.: Normalization for cDNA microarray data: a robust composite method addressing single and multiple slide systematic variation. Nucleic Acids Research 30 (2002)
17. Yuan, M., Kendziorski, C.: Hidden Markov Models for microarray time course data in multiple biological conditions. JASA 101, 1323–1340 (2006)

Appendix

Without loss of generality, let us consider derivation for $H = 3$, $B_H = 5$, $\mathbf{C}_i = \{\mathbf{c}_{1i}, \mathbf{c}_{2i}, \mathbf{c}_{3i}\}$ and $\mathbf{Z}_i = \{\mathbf{z}_{1i}, \mathbf{z}_{2i}, \mathbf{z}_{3i}\}$. Combine (4), (8) and (10) in a joint pdf

$$p(\mathbf{C}_i, \mathbf{Z}_i, \sigma^2 | L_i) = \frac{\rho(\sigma^2)}{(2\pi\sigma^2)^{M_i/2}} \exp\left\{ -\sum_{\aleph=1}^{3} \frac{(\mathbf{z}_{\aleph i} - \mathbf{D}_{\aleph i}\mathbf{c}_{\aleph i})^T(\mathbf{z}_{\aleph i} - \mathbf{D}_{\aleph i}\mathbf{c}_{\aleph i})}{2\sigma^2} \right\}$$

$$\times \left[\frac{\pi_0 |\mathbf{Q}_i|^{1/2}}{(2\pi\sigma^2\tau_{0i}^2)^{(L_i+1)/2}} \exp\left(-\frac{\mathbf{c}_{1i}^T\mathbf{Q}_i\mathbf{c}_{1i}}{2\sigma^2\tau_{0i}^2} \right) \delta(\mathbf{c}_{1i} = \mathbf{c}_{2i} = \mathbf{c}_{3i}) \right.$$

$$+ \frac{\pi_1 |\mathbf{Q}_i|}{(2\pi\sigma^2\tau_{1i}^2)^{(L_i+1)}} \exp\left(-\frac{\mathbf{c}_{1i}^T\mathbf{Q}_i\mathbf{c}_{1i}}{2\sigma^2\tau_{1i}^2} \right) \exp\left(-\frac{\mathbf{c}_{2i}^T\mathbf{Q}_i\mathbf{c}_{2i}}{2\sigma^2\tau_{1i}^2} \right) \delta(\mathbf{c}_{2i} = \mathbf{c}_{3i} \neq \mathbf{c}_{1i})$$

$$+ \frac{\pi_2 |\mathbf{Q}_i|}{(2\pi\sigma^2\tau_{2i}^2)^{(L_i+1)}} \exp\left(-\frac{\mathbf{c}_{1i}^T\mathbf{Q}_i\mathbf{c}_{1i}}{2\sigma^2\tau_{2i}^2} \right) \exp\left(-\frac{\mathbf{c}_{2i}^T\mathbf{Q}_i\mathbf{c}_{2i}}{2\sigma^2\tau_{2i}^2} \right) \delta(\mathbf{c}_{1i} = \mathbf{c}_{3i} \neq \mathbf{c}_{2i})$$

$$+ \frac{\pi_3 |\mathbf{Q}_i|}{(2\pi\sigma^2\tau_{3i}^2)^{(L_i+1)}} \exp\left(-\frac{\mathbf{c}_{1i}^T\mathbf{Q}_i\mathbf{c}_{1i}}{2\sigma^2\tau_{3i}^2} \right) \exp\left(-\frac{\mathbf{c}_{3i}^T\mathbf{Q}_i\mathbf{c}_{3i}}{2\sigma^2\tau_{3i}^2} \right) \delta(\mathbf{c}_{1i} = \mathbf{c}_{2i} \neq \mathbf{c}_{3i})$$

$$+ \left. \frac{\pi_4 |\mathbf{Q}_i|^{3/2}}{(2\pi\sigma^2\tau_{4i}^2)^{3(L_i+1)/2}} \exp\left(-\sum_{\aleph=1}^{3} \frac{\mathbf{c}_{\aleph i}^T\mathbf{Q}_i\mathbf{c}_{\aleph i}}{2\sigma^2\tau_{4i}^2} \right) \delta(\mathbf{c}_{1i} \neq \mathbf{c}_{2i} \neq \mathbf{c}_{3i}) \right].$$

Completing the squares with respect to $\mathbf{c}_{1i}, \mathbf{c}_{2i}, \mathbf{c}_{3i}$ for each of the terms separately and integrating out $\mathbf{c}_{1i}, \mathbf{c}_{2i}, \mathbf{c}_{3i}$ and then σ^2, we arrive at $p(\mathbf{Z}_i | \omega_l, L_i)$, $l = 0, \cdots, B_H - 1$, given by (22).

A Machine Learning Pipeline for Discriminant Pathways Identification

Annalisa Barla[1], Giuseppe Jurman[2], Roberto Visintainer[2,3],
Margherita Squillario[1], Michele Filosi[2,4],
Samantha Riccadonna[2], and Cesare Furlanello[2]

[1] DISI, University of Genoa, via Dodecaneso 35,
I-16146 Genova, Italy
[2] Fondazione Bruno Kessler, via Sommarive 18,
I-38123 Povo (TN) , Italy
[3] DISI, University of Trento, via Sommarive 14,
I-38123 Povo (TN), Italy
[4] Centre for Integrative Biology (CIBIO) , University of Trento, via delle Regole 101,
I-38123 Mattarello (TN), Italy
{annalisa.barla,margherita.squillario}@unige.it,
{filosi,jurman,riccadonna,furlan,visintainer}@fbk.eu

Abstract. Identifying the molecular pathways more prone to disruption during a pathological process is a key task in network medicine and, more in general, in systems biology. In this work we propose a pipeline that couples a machine learning solution for molecular profiling with a recent network comparison method. The pipeline can identify changes occurring between specific sub-modules of networks built in a case-control biomarker study, discriminating key groups of genes whose interactions are modified by an underlying condition. The proposal is independent from the classification algorithm used. Two applications on genomewide data are presented regarding children susceptibility to air pollution and early and late onset of Parkinson's disease.

Keywords: Pathway identification, network comparison, functional characterization, profiling.

1 Introduction

Nowadays, it is widely accepted that most known diseases are of systemic nature, *i.e.* their phenotypes can be attributed to the breakdown of a set of molecular interactions among cell components rather than imputed to the malfunctioning of a single entity such as a gene. Such sets of interactions are the focus of attention of a new discipline known as network medicine [1] devoted to understand how pathology may alter cellular wiring diagrams at all possible levels of functional organization (from transcriptomics to signaling, the molecular pathways being a typical example). The key tools for this discipline are derived by recent advances in the theory of complex networks [2–6]. Applications can be achieved

E. Biganzoli et al. (Eds.): CIBB 2011, LNBI 7548, pp. 36–48, 2012.

by reconstruction algorithms for inferring networks topology and wiring start-ing from a collection of high-throughput measurements [7]. However, the tackled problem is "a daunting task" [8] and these methods are not flawless [9], due to many factors. Among them, underdeterminacy is a major issue [10], as the ratio between network dimension (number of nodes) and the number of avail-able measurements to infer interactions plays a key role for the stability of the reconstructed structure. Although some initial progress, the stability –and thus the reproducibility– of the process is still an open problem.

Here we propose a machine learning pipeline for identifying disruption of key molecular pathways induced by or inducing a condition, given microarray data in a case/control experimental design. The problem of underdeterminacy in the inference procedure is avoided by focusing only on subnetworks. Moreover, the relevance of the studied pathways for the disease is evaluated from their discriminative relevance for the underlying classification problem. The profiling part of the pipeline is composed by a classifier and a feature selection method embedded within an adequate experimental procedure or Data Analysis Protocol [11]. Its outcome is a ranked list of genes with the highest discriminative power. These genes undergo an enrichment phase [12, 13] to identify whole pathways involved, to recover established functional dependencies that could get lost by limiting the analysis to the selected genes. Finally, a network is inferred for both the case and the control samples on the selected pathways. The two structures are compared to pinpoint the occurring differences and thus to detect the relevant pathway related variations.

A noteworthy point of this workflow is independence from its components: the classifier, the feature ranking algorithm, the enrichment procedure, the in-ference method and the network comparison function can all be exchanged with alternative methods. In particular, this property is desirable for the network comparison section. Despite its common use even in biological contexts [14], the problem of quantitatively comparing networks (e.g. using a metric instead of evaluating network properties) is a widely open issue affecting many scientific disciplines. As discussed in [15], the drawback of many classical distances (such as those of the edit family) is locality, that is focusing only on the portions of the network interested by the differences in the presence/absence of matching links. Alternative metrics can overcome this problem so to consider the global structure of the compared topologies; in particular spectral distances - based on the list of eigenvalues of the Laplacian matrix of the underlying graph - are effective in this task. Within them, the Ipsen-Mikhailov [16] distance has been proven to be the most robust in a wide range of situations.

In what follows we will describe the workflow in details, providing two examples of application in problems of biological interest: the first task concerns the tran-scriptomics consequences of exposure to environmental pollution on two cohorts of children in Czech Republic, while the second one investigates the molecular char-acteristics of Parkinson's disease (PD) at early and late stages. To further validate our proposal, different experimental conditions will be used in the two studies, by varying the algorithm component throughout the various steps of the workflow. In both application studies, biologically meaningful considerations on the occurring subnetwork variations can be drawn, consistently with previous findings.

2   Methods

In this section we will describe the proposed pipeline and its main phases. Each phase can be completed using alternative methods. In the present work we applied: SRDA and $\ell_1\ell_2$ for the feature selection step; WebGestalt toolkit for the pathway enrichment step; WGCN and ARACNE for the subnetwork inference step and the Ipsen-Mikhailov distance to evaluate distances between the reconstructed networks.

2.1   The Pipeline

The proposed machine learning pipeline handles case/control transcription data through four main steps, that connect a profiling task (output: a ranked list of genes) with the identification of discriminant pathways (output: ranked list of GO terms differentiating pathophysiology states), see Figure 1.

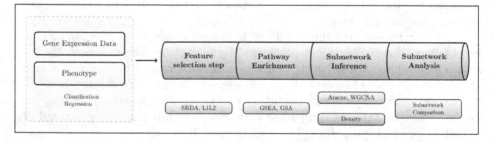

Fig. 1. Schema of the analysis pipeline

In particular, we are given a collection of n samples, each described by a d-dimensional vector x of measurements. Each sample is also associated with a phenotypical label $y = \{1, -1\}$, assigning it to a class (e.g. pollution vs. no-pollution in first experiment hereafter). The dataset is therefore represented by a $n \times d$ gene expression data matrix X ($d \gg n$) and the label vector Y. The pair (X, Y) is used to feed the profiling part of the pipeline, *i.e.* the identification of a predictive classifier and of a set of most discriminant biomarkers. Following [11], biomarker identification is based on Data Analysis Protocol (DAP) to ensure accurate and reproducible results. In our proposal, predictive models are trained on the variables identified either from a sparse regression method (e.g., $\ell_1\ell_2$) or from a classifier (e.g., SRDA) coupled with a feature selection algorithm. For microarray data, the output of the profiling part of the pipeline is a ranked list of genes $g_1, ..., g_d$ from which we extract a gene signature $g_1, ..., g_k$ of the top-k

most discriminant genes. The gene list is chosen as a solution balancing accuracy of the classifier and stability of the signature [11].

In the second part of the pipeline, pathway enrichment techniques (*e.g.*, GSEA or GSA) [12, 13] are applied to retrieve for each gene g_i the corresponding whole pathway $p_i = \{h_1, ..., h_t\}$, where the genes $h_j \neq g_i$ not necessarily belong to the original signature $g_1, ..., g_k$. Extending the analysis to all the h_j genes of the pathway allows us to explore functional interactions that would otherwise be missed.

The subnetwork inference phase requires to reconstruct a network for each pathway p_i by using the steady state expression data of the samples of each class y. The network inference procedure is limited to the sole genes belonging to the pathway p_i in order to avoid the problem of intrinsic underdeterminacy of the task. As an additional caution against this issue, in the following experiments we limit the analysis to pathways having more than 4 nodes and less than 1000 nodes. For each p_i and for each y, we obtain a real-valued adjacency matrix, which is binarized by choosing a threshold on the correlation values. This strategy requires the construction of a binary adjacency matrix N_{p_i, y, t_s} for each p_i, for each y and for a grid of threshold values $t_1, ..., t_T$. For each value t_s of the grid, we compute for each p_i both the distance D (e.g., the Ipsen-Mikhailov distance) between the case and control pathway graphs and the corresponding densities. We choose t_s considering the best balance between the average distance across the pathways p_i and the network density. For a fixed t_s and for each p_i, we obtain a score $D(N_{p_i, y=1, t_s}, N_{p_i, y=-1, t_s})$ used to rank the pathways p_i. A threshold chosen to maximize the scale-freeness of the entire network would not necessarily guarantee the same property for its sub-networks, as shown in [17]. Therefore, as pointed out in [18], it is advisable to maximize the density of the subnetwork of interest in order to have a sufficient amount of information. As an additional scoring indicator for $g_1, ..., g_k$, we also provide the difference between the weighted degree in the patient and in the control network. A final step of biological relevance assessment of the ranked pathways concludes the pipeline. Alternative algorithms can be used at each step of the pipeline: in particular in the profiling part different classifiers, regression or feature selection methods can be adopted. In what follows we describe the elementary steps used in the examples described in Section 4.

2.2 Experimental Setup for the Examples

Spectral Regression Discriminant Analysis (SRDA). SRDA belongs to the Discriminant Analysis algorithms family [19]. Its peculiarity is to exploit the regression framework for improving the computational efficiency. Spectral graph analysis is used for solving only a set of regularized least squares problems avoiding the eigenvector computation. A score is assigned to each feature and can be interpreted as a feature weight, allowing directly feature ranking and selection. The regularization value α is the only parameter needed to be tuned. The method is implemented in Python and it is available within the mlpy library[1].

---

[1] http://mlpy.fbk.eu/

The $\ell_1\ell_2$ Feature Selection Framework ($\ell_1\ell_{2FS}$). $\ell_1\ell_{2FS}$ with double optimization is a feature selection method that can be tuned to give a minimal set of discriminative genes or larger sets including correlated genes [20]. The objective function is a linear model $f(x) = \beta x$, whose sign gives the classification rule that can be used to associate a new sample to one of the two classes. The sparse weight vector β is found by minimizing the $\ell_1\ell_2$ functional: $||Y - X\beta||_2^2 + \tau||\beta||_1 + \mu||\beta||_2^2$ where the least square error is penalized with the ℓ_1 and ℓ_2 norm of the coefficient vector β. The training for selection and classification requires a careful choice of the regularization parameters for both $\ell_1\ell_2$ and RLS. Indeed, model selection and statistical significance assessment is performed within two nested K-cross validation loops as in [21]. The framework is implemented in Python and uses the L1L2Py library[2].

Functional Characterization. WebGestalt is an online gene set analysis toolkit[3]. This web-service takes as input a list of relevant genes/probesets and performs a GSEA analysis [13] in Gene Ontology (GO) [23], identifying the most relevant pathways and ontologies in the signatures. In this set of experiments we selected the WebGestalt human genome as reference set, 0.05 as level of significance, 3 as the minimum number of genes and the default Hypergeometric test as statistical method. Medline[4] was used to retrieve the available domain knowledge on the genes.

Weighted Gene Co-Expression Networks (WGCN). WGCN networks are based on the idea of using (a function of) the absolute correlation between the expressions of a pair of genes across the samples to define a link between them. Soft thresholding techniques are then employed to obtain a binary adjacency matrix, where a suitable biologically motivated criterion (such as the scale-free topology, or some other prior knowledge) can be adopted [18, 24]. Due to the very small sample size, scale-freeness can not be considered as a reliable criterion for threshold selection so we adopted a different heuristics: for both networks in the two classes the selected threshold is the one maximizing the average Ipsen-Mikhailov distance on the selected pathways.

Algorithm for the Reconstruction of Accurate Cellular Networks (ARACNE). ARACNE is a recent method for inferring networks from the transcription level [25] to the metabolic level [26]. Besides being originally designed for handling the complexity of regulatory networks in mammalian cells, it is able to address a wider range of network deconvolution problems. This information-theoretic algorithm removes the vast majority of indirect candidate interactions inferred by co-expression methods by using the data processing inequality property [27]. In this work we use the MiNET (Mutual Information NETworks) Bioconductor package keeping the default value for the data processing inequality tolerance parameter [28]. The adopted threshold criterion is the same as the one applied for WGCN.

---

[2] http://slipguru.disi.unige.it/Research/L1L2Py
[3] http://bioinfo.vanderbilt.edu/webgestalt/ [22]
[4] http://www.ncbi.nlm.nih.gov/pubmed/

Ipsen-Mikhailov Distance. The definition of the ϵ metric follows the dynamical interpretation of a N-nodes network as a N-atoms molecules connected by identical elastic strings, where the pattern of connections is defined by the adjacency matrix of the corresponding network. The vibrational frequencies ω_i of the dynamical system are given by the eigenvalues of the Laplacian matrix of the network: $\lambda_i = -\omega_i^2$, with $\lambda_0 = \omega_0 = 0$. The spectral density for a graph as the sum of Lorentz distributions is defined as $\rho(\omega) = K \sum_{i=1}^{N-1} \dfrac{\gamma}{(\omega - \omega_k)2 + \gamma 2}$, where γ is the common width[5] and K is the normalization constant solution of $\int_0^\infty \rho(\omega)d\omega = 1$. Then the spectral distance ϵ between two graphs G and H with densities $\rho_G(\omega)$ and $\rho_H(\omega)$ can then be defined as $\sqrt{\int_0^\infty \left[\rho_G(\omega) - \rho_H(\omega)\right]^2 d\omega}$. To get a meaningful comparison of the value of ϵ on pairs of networks with different number of nodes, we define the normalized version $\hat{\epsilon}(G, H) = \dfrac{\epsilon(G, H)}{\epsilon(F_n, E_n)}$, where E_n, F_n indicate respectively the empty and the fully connected network on n nodes: they are the two most ϵ-distant networks for each n. The common width γ is set to 0.08 as in the original reference: being a multiplicative factor, it has no impact on comparing different values of the Ipsen-Mikhailov distance. The network analysis phase is implemented in R through the `igraph` package[6].

3   Data Description

In this section we will describe the datasets chosen for the analysis. In the first experiment we used a microarray dataset investigating the effects of air pollution on children. In the second experiment we analyzed gene expression data on PD. Both examples are based on publicly available data on the Gene Expression Omnibus (GEO).

Children Susceptibility to Air Pollution. The first dataset (GSE7543) collects data of children living in two regions of the Czech Republic with different air pollution levels [29]: 23 children recruited in the polluted area of Teplice and 24 children living in the cleaner area of Prachatice. Blood samples were hybridized on Agilent Human 1A 22k oligonucleotide microarrays. After normalization we retained 17564 features.

Clinical Stages of Parkison's Disease. PD data is composed of two publicly available datasets from GEO, *i.e.* GSE6613 [30] and GSE20295 [31]. The former includes 22 controls and 50 whole blood samples coming from patients predominantly at early PD stages while the latter is composed of 53 controls and 40 PD patients with late stage PD. Biological data were hybridized on Affymetrix HG-U133A platform, estimating the expression of 22215 probesets for each sample.

---

[5] γ specifies the half-width at half-maximum (HWHM), equal to half the interquartile range.

[6] http://igraph.sourceforge.net

4 Results

In this section we will report the results obtained from the analysis on air pollution and PD data. In the former case the feature selection and the subnetwork inference tasks were accomplished using SRDA and WGCN while in the latter the same two tasks were carried out using respectively $\ell_1\ell_{2FS}$ and ARACNE.

4.1 Air Pollution Experiment

The SRDA analysis of the effects associated to air pollution provided a molecular profile e.g. a gene signature differentiating between children in Teplice (exposed) and Prachatice (non-exposed) with 76% classification accuracy. Selected by 100× 5-fold cross validation, the signature consists of a ranked list of 50 probesets, corresponding to 43 genes then used for the enrichment analysis.

According to the analysis, 11 enriched ontologies in GO were identified. The most enriched ones concern the developmental processes. This GO class contains ontologies especially related to the development of skeletal and nervous systems, which undergo a rapid and constant growth in children. Other enriched terms are related to the capacity of an organism to defend itself (*i.e. response to wounding* and *inflammatory response*), to the regulation of the cell death (*i.e. negative regulation of apoptosis*, the *multi-organism process*, the *glycerolipid metabolic process*), the response to external stimuli (*i.e. inflammatory response, response to wounding*) and to locomotion.

We then constructed the corresponding WGCN networks for the 11 selected pathways for both cases and controls. In Table 1 (left) we report the pathways together with the number of the included genes, ranked for decreasing Ipsen-Mikhailov distance, *i.e.* difference between cases and controls.

The most disrupted pathway is GO:0043066 (*apoptosis*) followed by GO:0001501 (*skeletal development*). Since the children under study are undergoing natural development, especially physical changes of their skeleton, the high difference between cases and controls of the GO:0001501 and the involvment of pathway GO: 0007275 *i.e. developmental process* is biologically very sound. Another relevant pathway is GO:0006954, representing the response to infection or injury caused by chemical or physical agents. Several genes included in GO:0005516 bind or interact with calmodulin, that is a calcium-binding protein involved in many essential processes, such as inflammation, apoptosis, nerve growth, and immune response. This is a key pathway that is linked with all the above mentioned terms as well as to GO:0007399, which is meaningful, being one of the most stimulated pathways together with the *i.e. skeletal development*. Table 1 (right) also lists the genes that most sensibly change their connection degree, that is, the strength of their interactions within the pathway. Some of them (FKHL18, HOXB8, PROK2, DHX32, MATN3) are directly involved in the development. Furthermore: CLC is a key element in the inflammation and immune system; OLIG1 is a transcription factor that works in the oligodendrocytes within the brain. NRGN binds calcium and is a target for thyroid hormones in the brain. Finally, MYH1 encodes for myosin which is a major contractile protein

Table 1. Air Pollution Experiment: pathways corresponding to mostly discriminant genes ranked by $\hat{\epsilon}$ (left) and differential degree of the top genes belonging to the 11 analyzed pathways (right)

Pathway Code	$\hat{\epsilon}$	# Genes	Agilent ID	Gene	Pathway	Δ Degree
GO:0043066	0.257	21	4701	NRGN	GO:0007399	-2.477
GO:0001501	0.149	89	12235	DUSP15	GO:0016787	-1.586
GO:0009611	0.123	16	8944	CLC	GO:0016787	-1.453
GO:0007399	0.093	252	3697	ITGB5	GO:0007275	-1.390
GO:0016787	0.078	718	4701	NRGN	GO:0005516	-1.357
GO:0005516	0.076	116	12537	PROK2	GO:0006954	1.069
GO:0007275	0.076	453	13835	OLIG1	GO:0007275	0.834
GO:0006954	0.048	180	11673	HOXB8	GO:0007275	-0.750
GO:0005615	0.038	417	16424	FKHL18	GO:0007275	-0.685
GO:0007626	0.000	5	13094	DHX32	GO:0016787	-0.575
GO:0006066	0.000	8	8944	CLC	GO:0007275	0.561
			14787	MATN3	GO:0001501	0.495
			15797	CXCL1	GO:0006954	0.467
			15797	CXCL1	GO:0005615	0.338
			11302	MYH1	GO:0005516	-0.194
			15797	CXCL1	GO:0007399	0.131

component of striated, smooth and non-muscle cells, and whose isoforms show expression that is spatially and temporally regulated during development.

4.2 Parkinson Disease Experiment

The $\ell_1\ell_2{}_{FS}$ analysis of the PD dataset lead to two gene signatures for the early and late stages of PD. The early stage signature consisted of 77 probesets corresponding to 70 genes with a 62% accuracy. The late stage signature consisted of 94 probesets (90 genes, 80% accuracy). The selection was performed within a 9-fold and 8-fold nested cross validation loop.

The enrichment analysis on the two gene lists identified relevant enriched nodes either specific or common between early and late PD. The common pathways have a very general meaning (e.g. *intracellular, cytoplasm, negative regulation of biological process*). Those specific for the early stage concern the immune system, the response to stimulus (i.e. *stress, chemicals or other organism like virus*), the regulation of metabolic processes, the biological quality and cell death. The pathways specific for late stage are related to the nervous system (e.g. *neurotransmitter transport, transmission of nerve impulse, learning or memory*) and to response to stimuli (e.g. *behavior, temperature, organic substances, drugs or endogenous stimuli*).

The relevance networks for late stage PD and for early stage PD were constructed for both cases and controls with ARACNE, for 35 and 42 pathways

Table 2. Parkinson's disease: selected pathways for late (left) and early (right) stage

PD early			PD late		
Pathway Code	$\hat{\epsilon}$	# Genes	Pathway Code	$\hat{\epsilon}$	Genes
GO:0012501	0.49	4	GO:0019226	0.31	20
GO:0005764	0.39	257	GO:0010033	0.20	30
GO:0019901	0.38	116	GO:0007611	0.16	34
GO:0005506	0.38	434	GO:0030234	0.15	20
GO:0008219	0.38	110	GO:0042493	0.15	109
GO:0016323	0.37	111	GO:0032403	0.12	14
GO:0006952	0.37	160	GO:0019717	0.12	79
GO:0046983	0.36	153	GO:0009725	0.11	27
GO:0045087	0.36	112	GO:0030424	0.10	93
GO:0046914	0.35	51	GO:0005096	0.09	252
GO:0016265	0.33	6	GO:0007267	0.09	264
GO:0042802	0.33	473	GO:0050790	0.09	15
GO:0042803	0.32	411	GO:0019001	0.09	34
GO:0050896	0.31	213	GO:0017111	0.09	157
GO:0006955	0.31	778	GO:0007585	0.09	47
GO:0006915	0.31	687	GO:0005516	0.09	215
GO:0042981	0.30	206	GO:0005626	0.09	41
GO:0030218	0.29	33	GO:0045202	0.08	278
GO:0006950	0.28	253	GO:0007610	0.08	40
GO:0020037	0.26	176	GO:0005624	0.08	616
GO:0005938	0.26	50	GO:0043087	0.08	22
GO:0005856	0.24	816	GO:0003779	0.08	423
GO:0016567	0.23	103	GO:0008047	0.07	60
GO:0003779	0.23	431	GO:0042995	0.07	231
GO:0042592	0.22	9	GO:0006928	0.07	166
GO:0051607	0.21	26	GO:0003924	0.07	294
GO:0016564	0.18	229	GO:0007568	0.06	35
GO:0005200	0.16	127	GO:0043234	0.06	233
GO:0030097	0.15	76	GO:0007268	0.06	201
GO:0009615	0.14	111	GO:0030030	0.05	27
GO:0008092	0.12	77	GO:0005525	0.05	450
GO:0030099	0.07	19	GO:0006412	0.05	466
GO:0019900	0.04	32	GO:0043005	0.05	51
GO:0034101	0.00	8	GO:0006836	0.05	42
GO:0051707	0.00	5	GO:0043025	0.04	82
			GO:0042221	0.00	16
			GO:0009266	0.00	6
			GO:0014070	0.00	13
			GO:0046578	0.00	8
			GO:0050804	0.00	11
			GO:0017076	0.00	7

respectively. Pathways and number of included genes are listed in Table 2, ranked for decreasing Ipsen-Mikhailov distance. Again top entries correspond to highest difference due to pathophysiological status.

The functional alteration of pathways characterized for both early and late stage PD allows a comparative analysis from the biological viewpoint. Common pathways between the two stages are considered up to 1000 nodes, hence discarding more general terms in the GO (see 2.1).

Indeed, the only common pathway is GO:0003779, *i.e. actin binding*. Actin participates in many important cellular processes, including muscle contraction, cell motility, cell division and cytokinesis, vescicle and organelle movement, cell signaling. Clearly, this term is strictly associated to the most evident movement-related symptoms in PD, including shaking, rigidity, slowness of movement and difficulty with walking and gait.

In both early and late PD we note some alterations within the biological process class of *response to stimulus*. In the early PD list we identified GO:0006950 *i.e. response to stress*, GO:0009615 *i.e. response to virus* and GO:0051707 *i.e. response to other organism*. In the late PD list we found GO:0042493, *i.e. response to drug*, GO:0009725 *i.e. response to hormone stimulus*, GO:0042221 *i.e. response to chemical stimulus*, GO:0014070 *i.e. response to organic cyclic substance* and GO:0009266 *i.e. response to temperature stimulus*. The pathways specific to early PD identify an involvement of the immune system, which is greatly stimulated by inflammation especially located in particular brain regions (mainly *substantia nigra*). Indeed, we identified: GO:0006952 *i.e. defense response*, GO:0045087 *i.e. innate immuno response* also visualized in Figure 2, GO:0006955 *i.e. immune response* and GO:0030097 *i.e. hemopoiesis*.

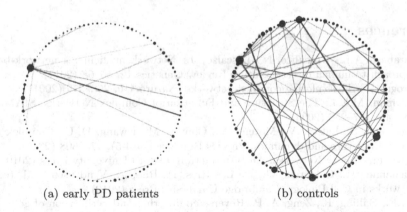

(a) early PD patients   (b) controls

Fig. 2. Networks of the pathway GO:0045087 (*innate immune response*) for Parkinson's early development patients (a) compared with healty subjects (b). Node diameter is proportional to the degree, and edge width is proportional to connection strength (estimated correlation).

In late stage PD, we detected several differentiated terms related to the Central Nervous System (CNS). Among others, we mention: GO:0019226 *i.e. transmission of nerve impulse*, GO:0007611 *i.e. learning or memory*, GO:0007610 *i.e. behavior* and GO:007268 *i.e. synaptic transmission*. These findings are fitting the late stage PD scenario, where cognitive and behavioral problems may arise with dementia.

5 Conclusions

The theory of complex networks has recently proven to be a helpful tool for a systematic and structural knowledge of the cell pathophysiological mechanisms [1]. Here we propose to enhance its value by coupling it with a machine learning preprocessor providing ranked gene lists associated to disease phenotype. This strategy aims at shifting the focus from global to local interaction scales, *i.e.* on pathways which are most likely to change within specific pathological stages. As a side effect, the strategy is also better tailored to deal with situations where small sample size may affect the reliability of the network inference on a global scale. The pipeline has been validated on two disease datasets of environmental pollution (case vs. control) and Parkinson onset (control, early and late PD). In both applications the pipeline has detected differential pathways that are biologically meaningful. All the components of the pipeline are available as open source software.

Acknowledgments. The authors at FBK acknowledge funding by the European Union FP7 Project HiperDART, by the CARITRO Project CancerAtlas and by the PAT funded Project ENVIROCHANGE.

References

1. Barabasi, A.L., Gulbahce, N., Loscalzo, J.: Network medicine: a network-based approach to human disease. Nature Review Genetics 12, 56–68 (2011)
2. Strogatz, S.H.: Exploring complex networks. Nature 410, 268–276 (2001)
3. Newman, M.E.J.: The Structure and Function of Complex Networks. SIAM Review 45, 167–256 (2003)
4. Boccaletti, S., Latora, V., Moreno, Y., Chavez, M., Hwang, D.-U.: Complex networks: Structure and dynamics. Physics Reports 424(4-5), 175–308 (2006)
5. Newman, M.E.J.: Networks: An Introduction. Oxford University Press (2010)
6. Buchanan, M., Caldarelli, G., De Los Rios, P., Rao, F., Vendruscolo, M. (eds.): Networks in Cell Biology. Cambridge University Press (2010)
7. He, F., Balling, R., Zeng, A.-P.: Reverse engineering and verification of gene networks: Principles, assumptions, and limitations of present methods and future perspectives. J. Biotechnol. 144(3), 190–203 (2009)
8. Baralla, A., Mentzen, W.I., de la Fuente, A.: Inferring Gene Networks: Dream or Nightmare? Ann. N.Y. Acad. Sci. 1158, 246–256 (2009)
9. Marbach, D., Prill, R.J., Schaffter, T., Mattiussi, C., Floreano, D., Stolovitzky, G.: Revealing strenghts and weaknesses of methods for gene network inference. PNAS 107(14), 6286–6291 (2010)

10. De Smet, R., Marchal, K.: Advantages and limitations of current network inference methods. Nature Review Microbiology 8, 717–729 (2010)
11. The MicroArray Quality Control (MAQC) Consortium. The MAQC-II Project: A comprehensive study of common practices for the development and validation of microarray-based predictive models. Nature Biotechnology 28(8), 827–838 (2010)
12. Zhang, B., Kirov, S., Snoddy, J.: WebGestalt: an integrated system for exploring gene sets in various biological contexts. Nuc. Acid. Res. 33 (2005)
13. Subramanian, A., Tamayo, P., Mootha, V.K., Mukherjee, S., Ebert, B.L., Gillette, M.A., Paulovich, A., Pomeroy, S.L., Golub, T.R., Lander, E.S., Mesirov, J.P.: Gene set enrichment analysis: A knowledge-based approach for interpreting genome-wide expression profiles. PNAS 102(43), 15545–15550 (2005)
14. Sharan, R., Ideker, T.: Modeling cellular machinery through biological network comparison. Nature Biotechnology 24(4), 427–433 (2006)
15. Jurman, G., Visintainer, R., Furlanello, C.: An introduction to spectral distances in networks. In: Proc. WIRN 2010, pp. 227–234 (2011)
16. Ipsen, M., Mikhailov, A.S.: Evolutionary reconstruction of networks. Phys. Rev. E 66(4), 046109 (2002)
17. Stumpf, M.P.H., Wiuf, C., May, R.M.: Subnets of scale-free networks are not scale-free: Sampling properties of networks. Proceedings of the National Academy of Sciences of the United States of America 102(12), 4221–4224 (2005)
18. Zhang, B., Horvath, S.: A General Framework for Weighted Gene Co-Expression Network Analysis. Statistical Applications in Genetics and Molecular Biology 4(1), Article 17 (2005)
19. Cai, D., He, X., Han, J.: Srda: An efficient algorithm for large-scale discriminant analysis. IEEE Transactions on Knowledge and Data Engineering 20, 1–12 (2008)
20. De Mol, C., Mosci, S., Traskine, M., Verri, A.: A regularized method for selecting nested groups of relevant genes from microarray data. Journal of Computational Biology 16, 1–15 (2009)
21. Fardin, P., Barla, A., Mosci, S., Rosasco, L., Verri, A., Varesio, L.: The l1-l2 regularization framework unmasks the hypoxia signature hidden in the transcriptome of a set of heterogeneous neuroblastoma cell lines. BMC Genomics (January 2009)
22. Zhang, B., Kirov, S., Snoddy, J.: Webgestalt: an integrated system for exploring gene sets in various biological contexts. Nucleic Acids Res. 33 (July 2005)
23. Ashburner, M., Ball, C.A., Blake, J.A., Botstein, D., Butler, H., Cherry, J.M., Davis, A.P., Dolinski, K., Dwight, S.S., Eppig, J.T., Harris, M.A., Hill, D.P., Issel-Tarver, L., Kasarskis, A., Lewis, S., Matese, J.C., Richardson, J.E., Ringwald, M., Rubin, G.M., Sherlock, G.: Gene ontology: tool for the unification of biology. the gene ontology consortium. Nature Genetics 25(1), 25–29 (2000)
24. Zhao, W., Langfelder, P., Fuller, T., Dong, J., Li, A., Horvath, S.: Weighted gene co-expression network analysis: state of the art. Journal of Biopharmaceutical Statistics 20(2), 281–300 (2010)
25. Margolin, A.A., Nemenman, I., Basso, K., Wiggins, C., Stolovitzky, G., Dalla-Favera, R., Califano, A.: Aracne: an algorithm for the reconstruction of gene regulatory networks in a mammalian cellular context. BMC Bioinform. 7(7) (2006)
26. Nemenman, I., Escola, G.S., Hlavacek, W.S., Unkefer, P.J., Unkefer, C.J., Wall, M.E.: Reconstruction of Metabolic Networks from High-Throughput Metabolite Profiling Data. Ann. N.Y. Acad. Sci. 1115, 102–115 (2007)
27. Cover, T.M., Thomas, J.: Elements of Information Theory. Wiley (1991)
28. Meyer, P., Lafitte, F., Bontempi, G.: Minet: A R/Bioconductor Package for Inferring Large Transcriptional Networks Using Mutual Information. BMC Bioinform. 9(1), 461 (2008)

29. van Leeuwen, D.M., Pedersen, M., Hendriksen, P.J.M., Boorsma, A., van Herwij-nen, M.H.M., Gottschalk, R.W.H., Kirsch-Volders, M., Knudsen, L.E., Sram, R.J., Bajak, E., van Delft, J.H.M., Kleinjans, J.C.S.: Genomic analysis suggests higher susceptibility of children to air pollution. Carcinogenesis 29(5) (2008)
30. Scherzer, C.R., Eklund, A.C., Morse, L.J., Liao, Z., Locascio, J.L., Fefer, D., Schwarzschild, M.A., Schlossmacher, M.G., Hauser, M.A., Vance, J.M., Sudarsky, L.R., Standaert, D.G., Growdon, J.H., Jensen, R.V., Gullans, S.R.: Molecular markers of early Parkinson's disease based on gene expression in blood. PNAS (2007)
31. Zhang, Y., James, M., Middleton, F.A., Davis, R.L.: Transcriptional analysis of multiple brain regions in Parkinson's disease supports the involvement of specific protein processing, energy metabolism and signaling pathways and suggests novel disease mechanisms. American Journal of Medical Genetics Part B Neuropsychiatric Genetics 137B, 5–16 (2005)

Discovering Hidden Pathways in Bioinformatics

Paulo J.G. Lisboa[1,*], Ian H. Jarman[1], Terence A. Etchells[1],
Simon J. Chambers[1], Davide Bacciu[2], Joe Whittaker[3], Jon M. Garibaldi[4],
Sandra Ortega-Martorell[5], Alfredo Vellido[6], and Ian O. Ellis[7]

[1] School of Computing & Mathematical Sciences,
Liverpool John Moores University, UK
[2] Dept. of Computer Science, University of Pisa, Italy
[3] Dept. of Mathematics and Statistics, University of Lancaster, UK
[4] School of Computer Science, University of Nottingham, UK
[5] Dept. of Biochemistry and Molecular Biology,
Universitat Autònoma de Barcelona, Spain
[6] Dept. of Computer Languages and Systems,
Universitat Politècnica de Catalunya, Spain
[7] Dept. of Histopathology, School of Molecular Medical Sciences
Nottingham University Hospitals Trust, University of Nottingham

Abstract. The elucidation of biological networks regulating the
metabolic basis of disease is critical for understanding disease progression
and in identifying therapeutic targets. In molecular biology, this process
often starts by clustering expression profiles which are candidates for disease phenotypes. However, each cluster may comprise several overlapping
processes that are active in the cluster. This paper outlines empirical results using methods for blind source separation to map the pathways
of biomarkers driving independent, hidden processes that underpin the
clusters. The method is applied to a protein expression data set measured
in tissue from breast cancer patients (n=1,076).

Keywords: clustering, independent components, hidden sources.

1   Introduction

Disease sub-typing is a priority for interventional medicine. A commonly used
first step to find sub-types in bioinformatics is to cluster expression profiles,
searching for disease phenotypes by grouping observation into naturally recurring patterns. An important aim of disease phenotyping is to gain insights into
the mechanisms that drive metabolic function. These are commonly represented

---

* The authors acknowledge the support of Dr A. Green and other members of the
Breast Cancer Research Team of the University of Nottingham, UK, and Dr. G.
Ball, of Nottingham Trent University, UK, towards the collection of high-throughput
protein expression dataset used in this study, and financial support from the European Network of Excellence Biopattern (FP6-2002-IST-1 No. 508803). A. Vellido is
supported by Spanish R+D project TIN2009-13895-C02-01.

E. Biganzoli et al. (Eds.): CIBB 2011, LNBI 7548, pp. 49–60, 2012.
© Springer-Verlag Berlin Heidelberg 2012

as conditional independence networks that map the multivariate associations between the expression levels of molecular biomarkers.

We hypothesise that individual clusters involve different biological pathways, independently active, which combine in different proportions to form each cluster profile. In mathematical terms, we seek independent components whose mixing coefficients separate when labelled by cluster membership.

Independent Component Analysis (ICA) has been applied to microarray data as a method of unsupervised analysis, reporting a significant improvement in finding biologically relevant transcriptional models [1,2]. Furthermore, expression modes and so-called meta-modes were also derived from microarray data by Lutter and colleagues [3], who remarked that deep exploration by application of ICA is still needed but it is an appropriate tool to uncover underlying biological mechanisms from molecular data. This is mirrored in more recent work by Schwartz and Shackney [4].

However, in these studies each of the identified sources is described by a fixed expression profile, in effect a row of covariates with the same dimensionality as the data. We propose a procedure to identify the conditional independence map for each source. The ultimate aim of this analysis is to elucidate the different biological processes that underpin biological function and explain the contribution of each process to the expression profile of each phenotype.

2   Materials and Methods

2.1   Data

We used a previously studied dataset ($n=1,076$) with 25 protein expression values. The measurements were made from tissue samples collected at initial excision surgery for breast cancer [5]. They are listed in Table 2.1.

2.2   Existing Methods

Clustering methods commonly used in bioinformatics include k-means, Partition Around Medoids and hierarchical algorithms. All of these may be used alone or in combination to form consensus clusters [6]. A fundamental question is whether it is possible to systematically generate cluster solutions that are reproducible in the sense that repeating the analysis will produce approximately the same solutions. A possible approach is to choose a method with a unique outcome, for instance hierarchical clustering. However, with agglomerative methods early stage errors can arise, leading to sub-optimal solutions as compared with partition algorithms [7]. This is especially the case with high dimensional data due to ultrametricity. A robust methodology was applied to the k-means algorithm, by mapping the landscape of solutions obtained for different initializations, using twin directions of within-cluster separation and between-cluster stability [8], to choose a reproducible solution that scores highly in both performance indices.

Low-dimensional visualization of high dimensional data is achieved effectively using the axes defined by the eigenvalues of the separation matrix consisting

Table 1. Protein titles, with short names and dilutions, used in this study

Antibody [clone]	Short Name	Dilution
Luminal phenotype		
16. CK 7/8 [clone CAM 5.2]	CK7/8	1:2
15. CK 18 [clone DC10]	CK18	1:50
17. CK 19 [clone BCK 108]	ck19	1:100
Basal Phenotype		
23. CK 5/6 [cloneD5/16134]	CK5/6	1:100
20. CK 14 [clone LL002]	CK14	1:100
19. SMA [clone 1A4]	ACTIN	1:2000
8. p63 ab-1 [clone 4A4]	p63	1:200
Hormone receptors		-
13. ER [clone 1D5]	ER	1:80
21. PgR [clone PgR 636]	PgR	1:100
12. AR [clone F39.4.1]	AR	1:30
9. EGFR [clone EGFR.113]	EGFR	1:10
24. HER2/c-erbB-2	CERBB2	1:250
4. HER3/c-erbB-3 [clone RTJ1]	CERBB3	1:2
5. HER4/c-erbB-4 [clone HFR1]	CERBB4	6:4
Tumour suppressor genes		
22. p53 [clone DO7]	p53	1:50
6. nBRCA1 Ab-1 [clone MS110]	nBRCA1	1:150
7. Anti-FHIT [clone ZR44]	FHIT	1:600
Cell adhesion molecules		
25. Anti E-cad [clone HECD-1]	E-cad	1:10/20
18. Antl P-cad [clone 56]	P-cad	1:200
Mucins		
3. NCL-Muc-1 [clone Ma695]	MUC1	1:300
2. NCL-Muc-1 core [clone Ma552]	MUC1co	1:250
1. NCL muc2 [clone Ccp58]	MUC2	1:250
Apocrine differentiation		
14. Anti-GCDFP-15	GCDFP	1:30
Neuroendocrine differentiation		
11. Chromogranin A [clone DAK-A3]	Chromo	1:100
10. Synaptophysin [clone SY38]	Synapto	1:30

of the inverse within-cluster scatter matrix multiplied into the between-cluster scatter matrix [9]. The above methods were used to determine the cluster assignment of the protein expression data, into 8 classes, and to visualise the separation. However, the question remains whether the clusters, representing potential sub-types of disease, are separate processes or different mixtures of more basic underpinning processes. To answer this question, we can apply the methodology of blind signal separation in order to identify independent signals buried in the overall data. A suitable approach, in principle, is that of ICA, which finds source signals that are statistically independent and non-Gaussian.

Independent sources may be found by different methods, some of which restrict the mixing matrix coefficients to be positive semi-definite. A family of these methods is Non-negative Matrix Factorisation (NMF) [10,11]. Among these, convex methods (Convex-NMF [12]) consider the factorisation $V \approx WH$, where the data matrix V is of dimension $d \times n$, where n is the number of observations and d is the dimensionality of the data. The mixing matrix H has dimensions $m \times n$, where m is the number of sources extracted from the data (separate from the number of clusters k). The source matrix W has dimensionality $d \times m$.

To achieve interpretability, this method imposes the constraint that the vectors (columns) defining W must lie within the column space of V, i.e. $W = VA$ (where A is an auxiliary adaptive weight matrix that fully determines W), so that $V \approx VAH$. By restricting W to convex combinations of the columns of V we can, in fact, understand each of the basis or sources as weighted sums of data points. Unlike the previous ones, this NMF variant applies to both nonnegative and mixed-sign data matrices. The factors H and A are updated as follows:

$$H^T \leftarrow H^T \sqrt{\frac{(V^TV)^+A + H^TA^T(V^TV)^-A}{(V^TV)^-A + H^TA^T(V^TV)^+A}};$$

$$A \leftarrow A \sqrt{\frac{(V^TV)^+H^T + (V^TV)^-AHH^T}{(V^TV)^-H^T + (V^TV)^+AHH^T}} \tag{1}$$

where $(\cdot)^+$ is the positive part of the matrix, in which all negative values become zeros; and $(\cdot)^-$ is the negative part of the matrix, in which all positive values become zeros.

Once the independent sources are found, it is of interest to map the influence pathways that they represent. This requires a methodology to map the multivariate associations in the data, taking into account all orders of conditioning.

A Directed Acyclic Graph (DAG) represents the joint probability distribution of the data as a graph $G = (V, E)$ with nodes V denoting the random variables $\{X_1, \ldots, X_p\}$ and edges E, whose absence indicates conditional independence relationships among variables. We use a software package termed *CImap*, which uses a constraint-based approach to structure identification by using conditional independence tests to determine whether to sever an edge.

Following the strategy introduced by the PC algorithm [13], *CImap* starts from a fully connected undirected graph and seeks to delete edges that support conditional independence in multiple statistical tests performed at a given level α. *CImap* uses Mutual Information (MI) as a measure of conditional association between variables to test for edge-presence (or independence). In particular, the strength of independence among X_i and X_j conditional on the variable subset induced by $A \subseteq V$ is measured by the conditional mutual information

$$\tilde{I}(i,j,A) = \sum_{x_i,x_j,x_A} p_{ijA}(x_i,x_j,x_A) \log_2 \frac{p_{ij|A}(x_i,x_j|x_A)}{p_{i|A}(x_i|x_A)p_{j|A}(x_j|x_A)} \qquad (2)$$

where p is the joint mass function that is typically approximated with the point estimate n_{ijA}/N. The MI measures the amount of dependency in bits, with the larger the value of $\tilde{I}$ implying the stronger the dependency. A mutual information test retains the edge when the statistic is large. Since MI estimates are known to follow a χ^2 distribution [14], it is possible to determine edge deletion by a chi-squared test on the null hypothesis that the two random variables are independent given X_A. The p-value for the hypothesis is $\tilde{I}(i,j,A) = P(\tilde{I}(i,j,A) > m|H_0)$, where m is the observed MI value: given a significance level α, the edge e_{ij} is deleted if $p_{ijA} > \alpha$ and retained otherwise.

2.3   Proposed Method

The proposed method involves multiple stages, the first of which is standard:

- The first stage is conventional clustering. The results presented in this paper use k-means with the robust selection method to choose the preferred partition from multiple random initialisations of the cluster profiles. The resulting partition is consistent with previously obtained consensus clustering results for the same data [6].
- Separately from the clustering process, methods of blind signal separation are applied to the data to derive profiles of sources whose joint distribution factorises into a product of independent probability distributions. The value of the results is very much dependent on the choice of algorithm. The mutual information of the clusters and mixing matrix of the sources was measured and the highest value used to select the preferred method for source separation. Although the mixing matrix is defined only up to arbitrary scaling, discretising its entries using percentiles for each source removes any dependence on the scaling.
- Conditional Independence tests are now applied to map the multivariate association structure of the sources. To do this requires the derivation of a matrix with the same dimensions as the observed data, where each observation is weighted by its contribution to the value of the source profile. This is explained in more detail in the following.

It follows from the definition of the convex-NMF factorisation that the sources can be recovered from the data matrix, by multiplying from the left with the pseudo-inverse of the mixing matrix

$$\hat{W} = H^+V \qquad (3)$$

Since $H^+H \approx I_m$, to a precision better than 10^{-4}, $\hat{W} \approx W$ and, therefore, the recovery of the source values is accurate.

Recalling that H^+ is $n \times m$, it follows that the values of the first source in $\hat{W}$ are given by the sum of the observations in V, each weighted by the corresponding entry in the first row of H^+, and similarly row-by-row. Therefore, taking each row of the pseudo inverse of the mixing matrix in turn and replicating it d times generates a weighting matrix whose transpose exactly reproduces the unmixing of observations which sums to the profile of each source, i.e. for the first source:

$$V^1_{Weighted} = \begin{bmatrix} H_1^+(1) & \dots & H_1^+(1) \\ \vdots & & \vdots \\ H_1^+(n) & \dots & H_1^+(n) \end{bmatrix} X \qquad (4)$$

where $H_1^+(i)$ denotes element i in row one of H^+, $i = 1, \dots, n$. The weighted matrix has d columns, the summation of which equals the values of the corresponding coordinates in the source.

The conditional independence maps of the sources are generated from the weighted matrices $V^{Source}_{Weighted}$ for each source in turn.

3   Experimental Results

The landscape mapping methodology [8] generates a clear indication of eight clusters shown in fig.1. The hypothesis that the clusters consist of different linear combinations of a basis set of sources is consistent with the separation of the clusters in the space of mixing elements, shown visually in fig.2.

The profiles of each cluster are straightforward to generate and illustrative examples are shown in fig.3 for the two basal/triple negative clusters.

Each cluster generates a conditional independence map (fig.4). Although they show characteristic motifs, the maps are very sparse on account of the relatively small number of observations in each group. Note the highlighted similar. The two basal/triple negative phenotypes that have similar profiles in fig.3 now show distinctive association motifs, highlighted in the bottom row.

The application of blind source separation to the complete data set used $m = 8$ sources, using as a guide the number of principal components that describe 90% of the variance in the data. Source profiles with particular distinguishing features are shown in fig.5.

In fig.5, the *cerbb2* phenotype (cluster 2) and specific independent component (source 6) are linked in the *CImap*. One of the basal/triple negative phenotypes (cluster 3) is highly associated only with the CAD specific component (source 5) whereas the phenotype with elevated *p53* expression (cluster 4) is linked to the corresponding specific component (source 8).

Although one of the sources with basal cytokines is also associated with cluster 5, which is classed as sub-type *luminal N*, this phenotype is largely dominated by source 1.

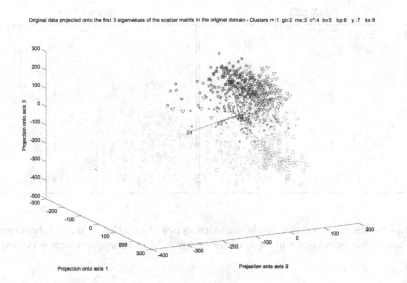

Fig. 1. Visualisation of the original data. The HER-2 positive cluster stands-out to the left while the remaining clusters form two groups, one with 5 luminal subtypes and the other with two basal subtype shown with squares and stars.

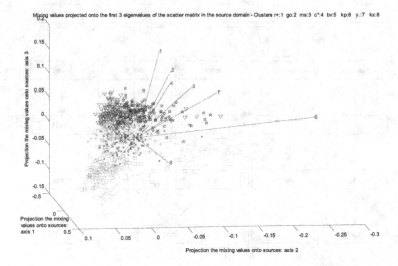

Fig. 2. Visualisation of the mixing matrix coefficients using scatter matrices. The numbered lines show the directions of the sources.

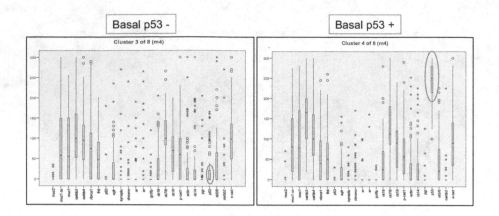

Fig. 3. Profiles of two basal/triple negative types. Note the similarity between the sub-types which is evidence in all markers except p53 expression, which is circled.

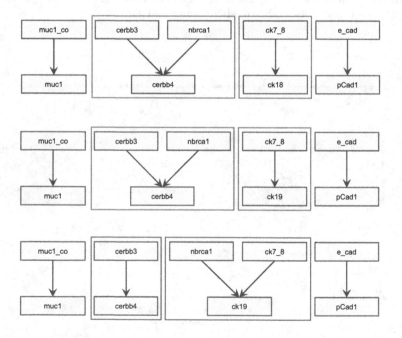

Fig. 4. Conditional independence maps of the Cerbb2 positive group (top) and the Basal/triple negative subtypes with normal (middle) and elevated (bottom) expression levels of p53

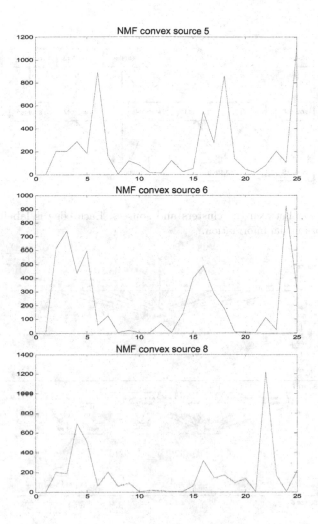

Fig. 5. Profiles for 3 of the 8 independent sources generated by NMFconvex. The order of the markers is listed in Table 1. These particular sources are unique in expressing CADs (top), cerbb2 (middle) and p53 (bottom). In addition sources 5 (top) and 8 (bottom) are the only ones with a profile showing non-zero expression of the basal cytokines ck5/6 and ck14.

The association between the sources and clusters can itself be mapped using conditional independence, as shown in fig.6. The *CImap* can then be applied to the contribution that each observation makes to each source in turn, to discover the multivariate associations for the independent biological process *hidden* in the data. These component maps are shown in fig.7.

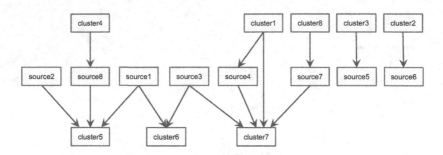

Fig. 6. Association between the clusters and sources. Each edge is labelled with its pairwise value of mutual information.

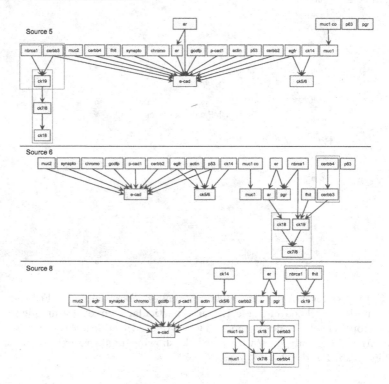

Fig. 7. Component CImaps for three independent processes. Note that the motifs highlighted in fig.4 now show differences in the associations between the expression levels for nbrca1, cerbb3/4 which link with the luminal cytokines. Moreover, the two basal/triple negative phenotypes that have similar profiles in fig. 3 now have clearly distinct graphs.

4 Discussion and Conclusions

The graphs and source profiles are consistent with each other. There are repeated motifs in the conditional independence maps of the sources which match the graph fragments obtained from the clusters, with minor deviations that are consistent with the fact that the sources and clusters are not exactly the same even when a cluster is dominated by a single source, as in the case of the *HER-2* group.

Interestingly, the basal/triple negative clusters, although similar in profile in all respects except for *p53* expression, are associated with considerably different graphs.

While disease subtyping remains the first line of exploratory data analysis in many applications of bioinformatics, with clustering among the most commonly used methodologies, it is relevant to consider the hypothesis that there are independent matrix sources that drive each sub-type and which are expressed in different linear combinations. This hypothesis leads naturally to the identification of independent sources, for which non-negative factorization algorithms provide a principled basis to estimate positive semi-definite mixing matrices.

This paper proposes a methodology to estimate the conditional independence maps for the independent sources. Future work will investigate in more detail the biological plausibility of conditional independence maps interpreted as influence pathways underpinning the independent modes of molecular activity of disease.

References

1. Li, H., Sun, Y., Zhan, M.: The Discovery of Transcriptional Modules by a Two-Stage Matrix Decomposition Approach. Bioinformatics 23(4), 473–479 (2007)
2. Li, H., Zhan, M.: Unraveling Transcriptional Regulatory Programs by Integrative Analysis of Microarray and Transcription Factor Binding Data. Bioinformatics 24(7), 1874–1880 (2008)
3. Lutter, D., Ugocsai, P., Grandl, P., Orso, E., Theis, F., Lang, E.W., Schmitz, G.: Analyzing M-CSF Dependent Monocyte/Macrophage Differentiation: Expression Modes and Meta-Modes Derived from an Independent Component Analysis. BMC Bioinformatics 9, 100 (2008)
4. Schwartz, R., Shackney, S.E.: Applying Unmixing to Gene Expression Data for Tumor Phylogeny Inference. BMC Bioinformatics 11, 42 (2010)
5. Abd El-Rehim, D., Ball, G., Pinder, S., Rakha, E., Paish, C., Robertson, J., Macmillan, D., Blamey, R., Ellis, I.O.: High-Throughput Protein Expression Analysis Using Tissue Microarray Technology of a Large Well-Characterised Series Identifies Biologically Distinct Classes of Breast Cancer Confirming Recent cDNA Expression Aanalyses. Int. J. Cancer 116, 340–350 (2005)
6. Soria, D., Garibaldi, J.M., Ambrogi, F., Green, A.R., Powe, D., Rakha, E., Douglas-Macmillan, R., Blamey, R.W., Ball, G., Lisboa, P.J.G., Etchells, T.A., Boracchi, P., Biganzoli, E., Ellis, I.O.: A Methodology to Identify Consensus Classes from Clustering Algorithms Applied to Immunohistochemical Data from Breast Cancer Patients. Comput. Biol. Med. 40, 318–330 (2010)

7. Zhao, Y., Karypis, G., Fayyad, U.: Hierarchical Clustering Algorithms for Document Datasets. Data Min. Knowl. Disc. 10(2), 141–168 (2005)
8. Jarman, I.H., Etchells, T.A., Bacciu, D., Garibaldi, J.M., Ellis, I.O., Lisboa, P.J.G.: Clustering of Protein Expression Data: A Benchmark of Statistical and Neural Approaches. Soft Computing: A Fusion of Foundations, Methodologies and Applications 15(8), 1459–1469 (2010)
9. Lisboa, P.J.G., Ellis, I.O., Green, A.R., Ambrogi, F., Dias, M.B.: Cluster-Based Visualisation with Scatter Matrices. Pattern Recogn. Lett. 29(13), 1814–1823 (2008)
10. Paatero, P., Tapper, U.: Positive Matrix Factorization: A Non-Negative Factor Model with Optimal Utilization of Error Estimates of Data Values. Environmetrics 5(2), 111–126 (1994)
11. Lee, D.D., Seung, H.S.: Learning the Parts of Objects by Non-Negative Matrix Factorization. Nature 401(6755), 788–791 (1999)
12. Ding, C., Li, T., Jordan, M.I.: Convex and Semi-Nonnegative Matrix Factorizations. IEEE T. Patt. Anal. 32(1), 45–55 (2010)
13. Spirtes, P., Glymour, C., Scheines, R.: Causation, Prediction and Search, 2nd edn. MIT Press, New York (2000)
14. Goebel, B., Dawy, Z., Hagenauer, J., Mueller, J.: An Approximation to the Distribution of Finite Sample Size Mutual Information Estimates. In: IEEE International Conference on Communications, vol. 2, pp. 1102–1106. IEEE Press, New York (2005)

Reliability of miRNA Microarray Platforms: An Approach Based on Random Effects Linear Models

Niccolò Bassani, Federico Ambrogi, Cristina Battaglia, and Elia Biganzoli

University of Milan
{niccolo.bassani,federico.ambrogi,
cristina.battglia,elia.biganzoli}@unimi.it
http://www.unimi.it

Abstract. MiRNAs are short ribonucleic acid (RNA) molecules, acting as post-transcriptional regulators. Intensity levels of thousand of miR-NAs are commonly measured via microarray platforms,with pros and cons similar to those for gene expression arrays.

Data reliability for miRNA microarrays is a crucial point to obtain correct estimates of miRNA intensity, and maximizing biological relative to technical variability is a task that has to be properly addressed.

To such aim, random effects models provide a powerful instrument to characterize different sources of variability. Here we evaluated repeatability of Affymetrix Gene Chip $^{©}$ miRNA Array by fitting random effects models separately for 4 cell lines.

Results indicated good platform performance both in terms of within-sample repeatability and between-lines reproducibility. Validation on publicly available NCI60 dataset showed similar patterns of variability, suggesting good reproducibility between experiments.

Future research will explore the possibility to use this method to compare normalization methods as well as genomic platforms.

Keywords: miRNA, reliability, random effects, variance components, technical variation.

1 Introduction

MicroRNAs (miRNAs) are small single-strand non-protein-coding RNA molecules, of 17-25 nucleotides in length. miRNAs function as negative post-transcriptional gene regulators, regulating mRNA translation and degradation in animals, plants and viruses [1,2], and are believed to account for more than 3% of all human genes [3]. Recent evidences demonstrated that miRNAs play a critical role in many biological processes, also including haematopoietic cell differentiation, apoptosis, cell proliferation, organ development and stress response. They also have been implicated in tumorigenesis: in fact, recent evidences showed that the expression profiles of relatively few miRNAs (about 200 genes) were required to accurately classify human cancers, allowing their diagnosis and prognosis [4,5].

E. Biganzoli et al. (Eds.): CIBB 2011, LNBI 7548, pp. 61–72, 2012.

Microarray analysis of miRNAs dates back to 2004, when Miska *et al.* [6] first proposed to exploit microarray technology for measuring intensity level for a large set of mammalian microRNAs. Hence, a relevant increase in the use of this strategy has led to a large amount of studies that aimed at exploring miRNA expression profiles in a various range of conditions. In parallel, several study have investigated analytical performance of this platform, mainly focusing on an overall degree of correlation between miRNA expression measurements, both within and between platforms.

In particular, Sato *et al.* [7] compared five different miRNA microarray platforms in terms of reproducibility and repeatability, evaluating coefficients of varation and the Spearman rank-based correlation index. Moreover, within each platform pairs of samples were investigated or differential miRNA expression and percentages of miRNAs commonly differentially expressed was reported. Similarly, Ach *et al.* [8] compared Agilent miRNA platform and quantitative PCR by means of miRNA-wise linear regressions and Pearson correlation coefficient. Other works [9,10,11] dealt with such an issue, mainly by evaluating correlation between and within platforms, often reaching similar conclusions.

Evaluating repeatability of a microarray platform is however a hard task that can not be addressed simply via correlation coefficients, mainly because this measure is not able to separate the amount of variability due to biological aspects of the experiments (different samples or treatment groups) and that due to technical variation because of laboratory and experimental effects that can not be fully controlled (sample preparation, temperature, etc.). Tipycally, one is interested in maximizing the first component (i.e. the biological one) which carries relevant information for the researcher, and, in the meanwhile, minimizing all the remaining components that can simply be considered as noise.

In this work a linear mixed effects model [12,13] was proposed to evaluate repeatability of miRNA microarray platform, using variance components estimate to assess contribution of each source of variability to the overall assay variation. The proposed method was applied to a repeatability experiment performed using the Affymetrix GeneChip© miRNA Array on 4 cell lines (3 renal tumors and one universal reference) in order to assess performance of this platform in a well controlled and balanced experiment. These cell lines were replicated 3 times, resulting in a total of 12 arrays. Analysis were performed only on the 847 human miRNAs available on the platform, for each of which there were 4 replicate measurements randomly spotted on the array. These probe-level data were log10 transformed and non-normalized. The method has also been applied on another set of data coming from the NCI60 set of tumor cell lines, using a slightly different version of the Affymetrix array.

The paper is organized as follows: in section 2 general principles of random effects models are presented, Affymetrix GeneChip© miRNA Array is shortly described and the model considered is presented and discussed; in section 3 we report main results for both experimental and validation dataset, in terms of variance components and ANOVA table for the model; in section 4 advantages and limitation of the proposed approach are discussed and finally, in section 5, possible extension of the approach are presented.

2   Materials and Methods

The Affymetrix GeneChip© miRNA Array contains information on 7815 different probe sets of miRNA, of which only 847 are human. For each of this 847 miRNAs there are 4 replicate measurements randomly spotted on the array: our analysis regarded only human miRNAs so the study was perfectly balanced.

To estimate between-array variability, each sample was replicated 3 times, and no experiment-wise normalization (e.g. quantile, loess, etc.) was performed. This is because our goal is to evaluate raw data repeatability, and normalization is expected to remove noise and variability due to technical reason in order to highlight biological variation which is of relevance when planning genomic experiments. Technical variability was also assessed by evaluating miRNAs' spot replicates, to understand whether these measures are consistent within miRNAs.

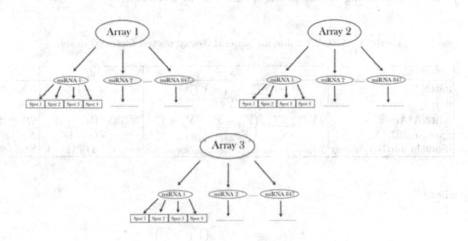

Fig. 1. Experimental design, within cell line

All factors considered (miRNA for biological variation, array replicate and different miRNA spots for technical variation) have been considered as random effects. The effect of miRNA and Array are considered to be *crossed*, that is that the Array named as 1 for miRNA A is the Array named 1 for miRNA B, and miRNA A is the same on Array 1 and Array2; on the contrary, miRNAs' spots is considered to be a random effect *nested* within miRNA, since the spot numbered as 1 for miRNA A as no direct relationship with the spot numbered as 1 for miRNA B. In this sense, the experiment is a *nested-factorial* one [14], that is an experiment which include both *nested* and *crossed* factors. Note that the 4 lines have been analyzed separately, since there is no interest in evaluating variation between different biological conditions. Experimental design is graphically represented in figure 1.

The model can thus be specified as follows

$$y_{ijkl} = \beta + a_i + b_j + (ab)_{ij} + c_{k(i)} + (bc)_{jk(i)} + e_{ijkl} \tag{1}$$

where greek letters represent fixed effect and latin letters represent random effects. In particular, β is the fixed intercept, or grand-mean, of the model, a_i is the effect of the i-th miRNA, b_j is the effect of the j-th replicate array, $(ab)_{ij}$ is the interaction between miRNA and array, $c_{k(i)}$ is effect of the k-th replicate miRNA spot nested within the i-th miRNA, , $bc_{jk(i)}$ is the interaction between array and spot nested in miRNA and e_{ijkl} is the error component of the model. The model specified in this way leaves no degrees of freedom ($l = 1$) for the estimation of this last error component since no replicates for the highest-order interaction are available. Such a specification is however useful to have an explicit reference to all source of technical variation, a matter of fundamental importance in this study. It is thus possible, starting from the model in (1), to compute a classical ANOVA table as a starting point for estimating variance components for the model effects.

Table 1. ANOVA table for general 3-way nested factorial design

Effect	SS	df	MS
miRNA	$rs \sum_{i=1}^{m} \left(\overline{Y}_i - \overline{Y} \right)^2$	$m - 1$	SS_a/df
Array	$ms \sum_{j=1}^{r} \left(\overline{Y}_j - \overline{Y} \right)^2$	$r - 1$	SS_b/df
miRNA*Array	$s \sum_{i=1}^{m} \sum_{j=1}^{r} \left(\overline{Y}_{ij} - \overline{Y}_i - \overline{Y}_j + \overline{Y} \right)^2$	$(m-1)(r-1)$	SS_{ab}/df
Spot in miRNA	$SS_{Spot} + SS_{Spot*miRNA}$	$m * (s - 1)$	SS_c/df
(Spot in miRNA)*Array	$SS_{Array*Spot} + SS_{Array*miRNA*Spot}$	$m * (r - 1) * (s - 1)$	SS_{bc}/df

where

$$SS_{Spot} = mr \sum_{k=1}^{s} (\overline{Y}_k - \overline{Y})^2 \tag{2}$$

$$SS_{miRNA*Spot} = r \sum_{i=1}^{m} \sum_{k=1}^{s} (\overline{Y}_{ik} - \overline{Y}_i - \overline{Y}_k + \overline{Y})^2 \tag{3}$$

$$SS_{Array*Spot} = m \sum_{j=1}^{r} \sum_{k=1}^{s} (\overline{Y}_{jk} - \overline{Y}_j - \overline{Y}_k + \overline{Y})^2 \tag{4}$$

$$SS_{Array*miRNA*Spot} = \sum_{i=1}^{m} \sum_{j=1}^{r} \sum_{k=1}^{s} (\overline{Y}_{ijk} - \overline{Y}_{ij} - \overline{Y}_{ik} - \overline{Y}_{jk} + \overline{Y}_i + \overline{Y}_j + \overline{Y}_k + \overline{Y})^2 \tag{5}$$

Note that $\overline{Y}$ is the grand mean of log10 intensity values, and that indexed mean are the group-specific means of miRNA intensity. Starting from table 1, it is possible to estimate the variance components as described in table 2.

Table 2. Expected Mean Squares and variance components estimates for the effects in model (1)

Effect	Expected MS	σ^2
miRNA	$rs\sigma_a^2 + r\sigma_c^2 + s\sigma_{ab}^2 + \sigma_{bc}^2$	$(MS_a - MS_c - MS_{ab} + MS_{bc})/rs$
Array	$ms\sigma_b^2 + s\sigma_{ab}^2 + \sigma_{bc}^2$	$(MS_b - MS_{ab})/ms$
miRNA*Array	$s\sigma_{ab}^2 + \sigma_{bc}^2$	$(MS_{ab} - MS_{bc})s$
Spot in miRNA	$r\sigma_c^2 + \sigma_{bc}^2$	$(MS_c - MS_{bc})/r$
(Spot in miRNA)*Array	σ_{bc}^2	MS_{bc}

Estimation of confidence intervals for these variance components is based on Satterthwaite's approximation [15]. Confidence interval at level α for σ_a^2 (i.e. miRNA component) can be obtained as

$$\left(\frac{r\hat{\sigma}_a^2}{\chi_{\alpha/2,r}^2} \quad , \quad \frac{r\hat{\sigma}_a^2}{\chi_{1-\alpha/2,r}^2} \right) \tag{6}$$

where r is defined as

$$r = \frac{(MS_a - MS_c - MS_{ab} + MS_{bc})^2}{\frac{MS_a^2}{(m-1)} + \frac{MS_c^2}{m(s-1)} + \frac{MS_{ab}^2}{(m-1)(r-1)} + \frac{MS_{bc}^2}{mr(s-1)}} \tag{7}$$

Starting from tables 1-2 it is thus possible to obtain confidence intervals estimates for all variance components of the effects included in the model. The model (1) and the estimates (both pointwise and intervals) will be computed separately for each of the 4 samples available since we are not interested in evaluating variation between different biological conditions. All analysis have been performed in the R environment, using package lme4 and *ad hoc* functions.

3 Results

3.1 Experimental Data Description

Experimental data refer to 4 different cell lines, named A498, CAKI-2, HK-2 and hREF. A498 [16], CAKI-2 [17] and HK-2 [18] represent 3 renal tumor lines whereas hREF is a pool of 20 normal human tissues, thus it is expected to show a higher biological variability.

Distribution of log10-transformed intensity of probe-level data for 847 human miRNAs is reported in figure 2. Technical replicates for sample A498 show some differences in terms of densities, since the first replicate (solid line) seems to account for generally lower values than the other two arrays. Several other

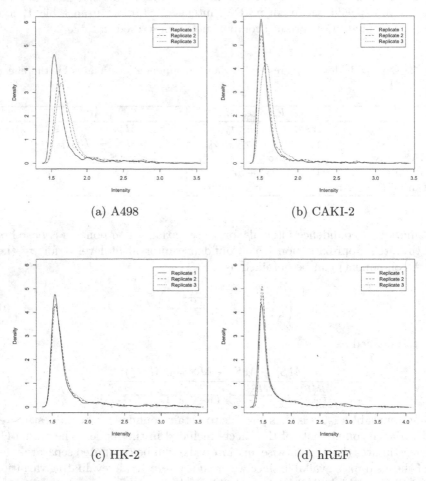

Fig. 2. Kernel density estimates of miRNA intensities within samples

transformation have been considered for reducing skewness (cubic root, square root, Rocke-Durbin, Box-Cox), but no general improvement has been found. Log10 has been chosen for convenience, and analysis has been performed on these transformed data.

3.2   Model Estimation

As already stated, we have fitted the model in (1) separately for each experimental sample. Diagnostic plots for the residuals of the model are presented in figure. Both the quantile-quantile plots and the residuals vs predicted plots show that assumptions of the model are questionable. However, it has to be noted that main problems occur for low values of intensity, that is for miRNAs that are likely to be poorly detected by the microarray technology.

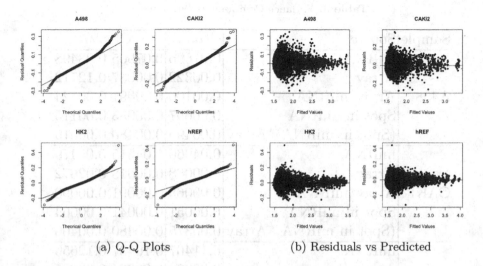

(a) Q-Q Plots   (b) Residuals vs Predicted

Fig. 3. Diagnostic plots for model (1). In the left panel quantile-quantile plots are shown, with the line of perfect concordance; in the right panel predicted values of the model are plotted against residuals.

In table 3 variance component estimates for the models fitted are reported. Sum of squares and mean squares are not reported for ease of reading. It is interesting to note that Array variability within cell line A498 is somewhat larger than for the other cell lines, whereas other sources of technical variability appear to be much more similar for all lines. Notably, biological variation is the largest source of variability for all samples, especially for hREF (but this is expected since it is a pool of 20 human samples). Generally, there seem to be a good level of platform repeatability: miRNA-array interaction appears to be quite low, suggesting good concordance of miRNA intensity levels across arrays; different spots mapping to the same miRNA show very low variability, indicating that it is possible to average over multiple measurements of the same miRNA to obtain a single intensity/expression value to be used for biologically relevant analysis.

From this analysis some interesting conclusions can be drawn: the Affymetrix platform shows good performance in terms of repeatability, since technical variation components are quite low and account for a small portion of total variability within each line, and of reproducibility, since technical variance components across samples show quite similar patterns, with the exception of Array component for A498 line, which is to be better explored to understand why the Array component is so *large* when compared to other samples.

In such a perspective we have evaluated separately the four lines in terms of ranks of replicate spots. That is, for each sample first we have averaged over spots mapping to the same miRNA within each array, than we have ranked the averaged measurements of each miRNA between the three replicates, evaluating for each replicate how many miRNAs were ranked as 1st, 2nd and 3rd. In fact,

Table 3. Variance Components estimates

Sample	Source	σ^2	CI95%
A498	miRNA	0.07696	0.07005 0.08498
	Array	0.00322	0.00087 0.12712
	Array*miRNA	0.00106	0.00091 0.00124
	Spot in miRNA	0.00097	0.00083 0.00115
	(Spot in miRNA)*Array	0.00499	0.00480 0.00519
CAKI2	miRNA	0.04960	0.04515 0.05479
	Array	0.00068	0.00018 0.02672
	Array*miRNA	0.00065	0.00091 0.00090
	Spot in miRNA	0.00051	0.00041 0.00064
	(Spot in miRNA)*Array	0.00375	0.00480 0.00406
HK2	miRNA	0.11467	0.10437 0.12650
	Array	0.00020	0.00005 0.00785
	Array*miRNA	0.00117	0.00091 0.00149
	Spot in miRNA	0.00087	0.00075 0.00101
	(Spot in miRNA)*Array	0.00387	0.00373 0.00403
hREF	miRNA	0.19199	0.17484 0.21172
	Array	0.00007	0.00002 0.00276
	Array*miRNA	0.00084	0.00075 0.00096
	Spot in miRNA	0.00081	0.00071 0.00091
	(Spot in miRNA)*Array	0.00266	0.00256 0.00277

it is possible that one array may over- (under-) express intensity of miRNAs by means of a systematic factor , thus leading to falsely high (low) detected values on one of the replicates. Such a situation, characterized by *systematic bias* could possibly be an explanation for such a high inter-array variation in the A498 line, and could provide useful information on results discussed previously.

In the plots of figure 4 our hypothesis is confirmed: on the first array of line A498 90.9% of miRNA's intensity values are the lowest value between the 3 replicates, and on the third intensity of 72.5% of miRNAs is the highest. Similarly, also line CAKI2 show similar patterns, but this results in an array variance component substantially in line with HK-2 and hREF.

The approach considered thus suggests that the Affymetrix GeneChip© miRNA Array is a repeatable and reproducible platform in terms of variance components associated to different experimental factors. To furtherly validate this platform we applied the proposed method to an external dataset which included quadruplicates of three cell lines coming from the NCI60 samples.

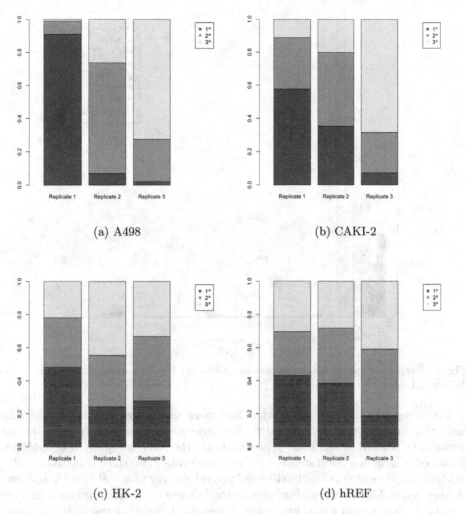

(a) A498 (b) CAKI-2

(c) HK-2 (d) hREF

Fig. 4. Distribution of ranked, spot-averaged miRNA intensities for each replicate array, within sample

3.3 Validation

Validation data consists of quadruplicate arrays of three tumor lines from the NCI60 experiment [19]: KM-12 (Colon), PC-3 (Prostate) and OVCAR-8 (Ovarian). To compare estimates of variance components between different experiments a barplot has been drawn in figure 5. Whereas biological variation is characterized by different levels of intensity, it is possibile to see that sources of technical variation seem to be quite similar between lines, with the exception of the miRNA*Array interaction, which shows slightly higher values for the NCI60 lines (mainly PC-3 and OVCAR-8) than for our experimental samples.

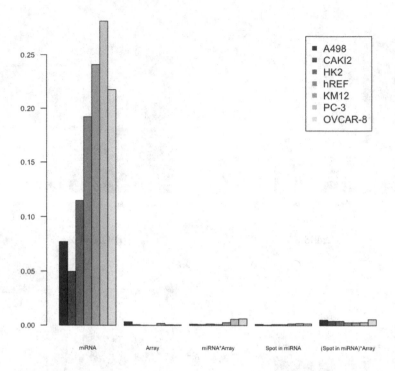

Fig. 5. Barplot of variance components in model (1) for both experimental and validation cell lines

These results tend to confirm what had been seen previously in section 3.2, and are a further proof of the good performance of the platform, in terms of repeatability (within sample) and reproducibility (between samples). The method proposed is kind of a novel strategy for such an evaluation, since it helps in highlighting specific sources of variability and provides a way to reveal possible sources of bias/noise. Moreover, random effects models are commonly implemented in standard software and a wide literature is available to help the researcher in specifying the correct model depending on the specific experimental design.

4   Discussion

Technical evaluation of microarray reproducibility and repeatability is an issue that researchers have been dealing with since the dawn of genomics era, and miRNA microarray are not different in this sense. However, many published works make use of (ranked or not) correlation coefficients or compare list of differentially expressed miRNAs to evaluate these technical aspects.

The method proposed is very useful because it provides specific information on different sources of variability that characterize each experiment: being able to distinguish between variation due to biological matters and technical ones is relevant because it allows us to understand if the platform carries biological or noisy information. In this experiment the platform was shown to have high repeatability within both sets of cell lines, and highly reproducible, with very similar variance components. It is of interest to note that the model presented in (1) is extremely flexible, and can be modified to account for different experimental designs or specification of factors types (e.g. mixed effects).

The choice of considering raw (e.g. not normalized) data is mainly due to the fact that normalization is a task which addresses removal of artifacts induced by the platform that were the goal of our investigation. Thus, had we considered filtered and normalized data we would have probably lost relevant information for our purposes. Considering only human miRNAs has been a practical choice, since functional (or differential, etc) analysis mainly involve analysis of this set of microRNAs.

5 Conclusions

miRNA are short RNA molecules that have been shown to play a key-role in several pathways and in the regulation of expression of several disease-markers. For such a reason, the use of miRNA microarrays is fundamental to measure intensity level of thousands of miRNA simultaneously, in order to have a deeper understanding of the mechanisms which regulate the organism.

These platforms however suffer from the same drawbacks associated with gene expression microarrays, thus need to be properly evaluated in terms of sources of variability, in order to maximize biological information and reduce technical noise. Most studies investigate reproducibility and repeatability of these platform by means of standard correlation coefficients or evaluating miRNAs that are commonly differentially expressed between replicates experiments. In this paper we suggest to use random effects model to study variance components associated to different factors involved in the study (replicate array, replicate spot, specific miRNA), and to compare these components between different samples to understand how much does technical variation in this platform amount to. Application of this strategy on experimental and validation data suggest the idea of good performance, and provides useful information on how to properly design future experiments.

Since this method aims at quantifying noise from a microarray platform, it could be extremely useful to evaluate the process of chip normalization, i.e. the removal of non-biological information. Future work will consider the possibility to stud this feature, as well as extension and application of the method to other platforms (Illumina, Agilent, etc.)

References

1. Ambros, V.: MicroRNA Pathways in Flies and Worms: Growth, Death, Fat, Stress, and Timing. Cell 113, 673–676 (2003)
2. Lai, E.C.: microRNAs: Runts of the Genome Assert Themselves. Curr. Biol. 13, R925–R936 (2003)

3. Bentwich, I., Avniel, A., Karov, Y., Aharonov, R., Gilad, S., Barad, O., Barzilai, A., Einat, P., Einav, U., Meiri, E., Sharon, E., Spector, Y., Bentwich, Z.: Identification of Hundreds of Conserved and Nonconserved Human microRNAs. Nat. Genet. 37(7), 766–770 (2005)

4. Esquela-Kerscher, A., Slack, F.J.: Oncomirs - microRNAs with a Role in Cancer. Nat. Rev. Cancer 6, 259–269 (2006)

5. Lu, J., Getz, G., Miska, E.A., Alvarez-Saavedra, E., Lamb, J., Peck, D., Sweet-Cordero, A., Ebert, B.L., Mak, R.H., Ferrando, A.A., Downing, J.R., Jacks, T., Horvitz, H.R., Golub, T.R.: MicroRNA Expression Profiles Classify Human Cancers. Nature 435(7043), 834–838 (2005)

6. Miska, E.A., Alvarez-Saavedra, E., Townsend, M., Yoshii, A., Sestan, N., Rakic, P., Constantine-Paton, M., Horvitz, H.R.: Microarray analysis of microRNA expression in the developing mammalian brain. Genome Biol. 5(9), R68.1–R68.13 (2004)

7. Sato, F., Tsuchiya, S., Terasawa, K., Tsujimoto, G.: Intra-Platform Repeatability and Inter-Platform Comparability of MicroRNA Microarray Technology. PLoSONE 4(5), e5540 (2009)

8. Ach, R.A., Wang, H., Curry, B.: Measuring microRNAs: Comparisons of Microarray and Quantitative PCR Measurements, and of Different Total RNA Prep Methods. BMC Biotechnology 8 (2008)

9. Chen, Y., Gelfond, J.A.L., McManus, L.M., Shireman, P.K.: Reproducibility of Quantitative RT-PCR Array in miRNA Expression Profiling and Comparison with Microarray Analysis. BMC Genomics 10 (2009)

10. Pradervand, S., Weber, J., Lemoine, F., Consales, F., Paillusson, A., Dupasquier, M., Thomas, J., Richter, H., Kaessmann, H., Beaudoing, E., Hagenbuchle, O., Harshmann, K.: Concordance among digital gene expression, microarrays, and qPCR when measuring differential expression of microRNAs. BioTechniques 48(3), 219–222 (2010)

11. Yauk, C.L., Rowan-Carroll, A., Stead, J.D.H., Williams, A.: Cross-platform analysis of global microRNA expression technologies. BMC Genomics 11 (2010)

12. Laird, N.M., Ware, J.H.: Random-Effects Models for Longitudinal Data. Biometrics 38, 963–974 (1982)

13. Pinheiro, J.C., Bates, D.M.: Mixed-effects Models in S and S-PLUS. Springer, New York (2000)

14. Montgomery, D.C.: Design and Analysis of Experiments. Wiley, New York (2009)

15. Satterthwaite, F.E.: An Approximate Distribution of Estimates of Variance Components. Biometr. Bull. 2(6), 110–114 (1946)

16. Giard, D.J., Aaronson, S.A., Todaro, G.J., Arnstein, P., Kersey, J.H., Dosik, H., Parks, W.P.: In vitro cultivation of human tumors: establishment of cell lines derived from a series of solid tumors. J. Natl. Cancer Inst. 51(5), 1417–1423 (1973)

17. Fogh, J., Trempe, G.: Human tumor cells in vitro. In: Fogh, J. (ed.). Academic Press, New York (1975)

18. Ryan, M.J., Johnson, G., Kirk, J., Furstenberg, S.M., Zager, R.A., Torok-Storb, B.: HK-2: an immortalized proximal tubule epithelial cell line from normal adult human kidney. Kidney Int. 45(1), 48–57 (1994)

19. Ross, D.T., Scherf, U., Eisen, M.B., Perou, C.M., Rees, C., Spellman, P., Iyer, V., Jeffrey, S.S., Van de Rijn, M., Waltham, M., Pergamenschikov, A., Lee, J.C.F., Lashkari, D., Shalon, D., Myers, T.G., Weinstein, J.N., Botstein, D., Brown, P.O.: Systematic variation in gene expression patterns in human cancer cell lines. Nat. Genet. 24, 227–235 (2000)

A Bioinformatics Procedure to Identify and Annotate Somatic Mutations in Whole-Exome Sequencing Data

Roberta Spinelli, Rocco Piazza, Alessandra Pirola, Simona Valletta,
Roberta Rostagno, Angela Mogavero, Manuela Marega, Hima Raman,
and Carlo Gambacorti-Passerini

Dept. of Clinical Medicine, University of Milano-Bicocca, Milan, Italy
via Cadore, 48 - 20900, Monza (MB) Italy
roberta.spinelli@unimib.it

Abstract. The application of next-generation sequencing instruments
generates a tremendous amount of sequencing data. This leads to a challenging bioinformatics problem to store, manage and analyze terabytes of
sequencing data often generated from extremely different data-sources.
Our project is mainly focused on the sequence analysis of human cancer
genomes, in order to identify the genetic lesions underlying the development of tumors. However, the automated detection procedure of somatic
mutations and a statistical based testing procedure to identify genetic
lesions are still an open problem. Therefore, we propose a computational
procedure to manage large scale sequencing data in order to detect exonic
somatic mutations in a tumor sample. The proposed pipeline includes
several steps based on open-source softwares and R language: alignment,
detection of mutations, annotation, functional classification and visualization of results. We analyzed whole exome sequencing data from 3
leukemic patients and 3 paired controls plus 1 colon cancer sample and
paired control. The results were validated by Sanger sequencing.

Keywords: next-generation sequencing, computational procedure, somatic mutations, leukemia, colon cancer.

1 Introduction

The development of high-throughput sequencing technology provides a great op-
portunity to identify molecular mechanisms, genetic alterations and structural
changes involved in tumor genesis [1] allowing the identification of new therapeutic targets in diseases. Whole exome-sequencing had been widely applied to
identify exonic lesions underlying the tumor growth and to provide a molecular
framework for the development of rational, biology-driven therapies in cancer [2].
In order to identify somatic mutations occurring in cancer genomes, we implemented a bioinformatic procedure using open-source softwares and R language
(http://www.r-project.org/). We applied our strategy to Illumina whole exome sequencing data from Atypical Chronic Myeloid Leukemia (aCML) patients
plus a Colon Cancer patient.

E. Biganzoli et al. (Eds.): CIBB 2011, LNBI 7548, pp. 73–82, 2012.

Our pipeline allowed the identification of somatic mutations occurring in the cancer genomes but not in autologous normal lymphocytes. These mutations were confirmed by Sanger sequencing, indicating that our pipeline is able to effectively process high-throughput sequencing data and extract genes, or genomic region, important to discover new genes associated with diseases suitable for further investigations.

2   Materials and Methods

Genomic DNA from leukemic cells (minimum content 80%) and normal lymphocytes was extracted from 3 aCML patients; furthermore tumor and paired peripheral blood DNA was extracted from a patient affected by colon cancer. The samples were sequenced by Illumina Genome Analyzer IIX with 76 bp paired-end reads. Genomic DNA was prepared for whole-exome sequencing according to the manufacturer's protocols [3,4]. After cluster amplification and sequencing, the images were acquired by Illumina Genome Analyzer Sequencing Control Software (SCS 2.6) and analyzed by Real Time Analyzer (RTA 1.6) to obtain base calls, quality metrics and read calls. RTA 1.6 outputs the results in *Solexa/Illumina-FastQ* format (http://www.illumina.com/).

To compare sequencing data from cancer cells with similar data from healthy non neoplastic cells and to identify somatic mutations, we developed a computational strategy including several steps: alignment of sequences versus Human Genome Reference; detection of single nucleotide variations (SNVs) and small insertions or deletions (INDEL, less than 15bp); identification of candidate somatic mutations, extracting the variations subset occurring only in cancer genomes; annotation and functional prediction of somatic mutations (Fig. 1). At each step, different bioinformatic tools were used: BioPython (http://biopython.org/wiki/Main_Page), SAMtools [5], R language, SIFT (http://sift.jcvi.org/www/SIFT_chr_coords_submit.html) and the genomic visualization of results was carried out using the Integrative Genomics Viewer (IGV) (http://www.broadinstitute.org/igv/).

In our procedure we set a number of parameters in order to assure a high quality control of the data generated. The parameters concern the minimum read coverage, the minimum frequency/percentage of substitution and the minimum average Phred [6] quality score calculated at each genomic position [7].

Data Processing Pipeline
The Data Processing pipeline includes 3 main steps.

STEP 1: Sequences Data Analysis

In the first step we describe the base-pair reads and the information at each chromosomal position of sample to facilitate SNP/indel calling (Fig. 2).

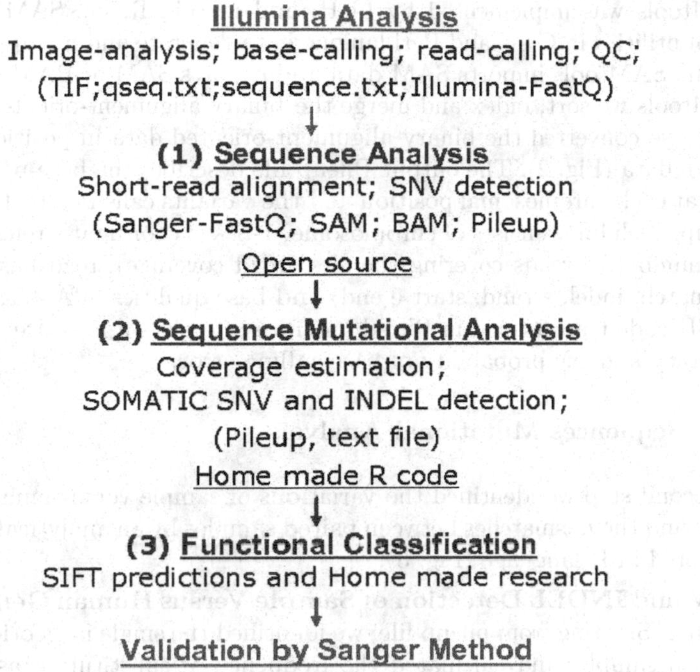

Illumina Analysis
Image-analysis; base-calling; read-calling; QC;
(TIF;qseq.txt;sequence.txt;Illumina-FastQ)
↓

(1) Sequence Analysis
Short-read alignment; SNV detection
(Sanger-FastQ; SAM; BAM; Pileup)
Open source
↓

(2) Sequence Mutational Analysis
Coverage estimation;
SOMATIC SNV and INDEL detection;
(Pileup, text file)
Home made R code
↓

(3) Functional Classification
SIFT predictions and Home made research
↓

Validation by Sanger Method

Fig. 1. The basic workflow of Computational Procedure: from input Illumina sequences data; preprocessing analysis; somatic variations detection and functional annotation of coding variants, to candidate somatic mutations to validate by Sanger method

1. **Preprocessing of Illumina Sequences Dataset.** We converted tumor and normal sequence data from *Solexa/Illumina-FastQ* format in *Sanger-FastQ* using *SeqIO.convert* function in BioPython.
2. **Alignment of Sequences.** We aligned 76bp paired-end reads versus Human Genome Reference hg18 by Burrows-Wheeler Alignment (BWA) algorithm (http://bio-bwa.sourceforge.net/bwa.shtml). BWA is implemented in BWA Tool and published by Li H. and Durbin R. [8]. BWA tool aligns relatively short sequences (queries) to a sequence database (target), such as the human genome reference; implements an algorithm based on Burrows-Wheeler Transform (BWT) and does gapped global alignment queries. BWA is one of the fastest short read alignment algorithms and supports paired-end reads. Using BWA we aligned the paired-end reads in Sequence Alignment Map (SAM) file and filtered the reads mapped in proper pair to further process only the reads that were correctly aligned. Moreover, we restricted the analysis only to the uniquely mapped reads. SAM is a text and standard format for storing large nucleotide sequence alignments.
3. **Conversion from Alignment-Oriented Data to Position-Oriented Data.** We converted the SAM files in Binary Alignments format, BAM (SAM binary) file by SAMtools (http://samtools.sourceforge.net/).

SAMtools was implemented by Li H. and Durbin R. [5]. SAM Tools is a set of utilities in C++ and Perl language, to generate and manipulate alignments. SAMtools imports SAM data and exports SAM or BAM format. By SAMtools we sort, index and merge the binary alignment-oriented data. Finally, we converted the binary alignment-oriented data in position-oriented *pileup* data (Fig. 2). The output Pileup file describes the base-pair information at each chromosomal position and the variants calls in a text format. In pileup, each line consists of chromosome, 1-based coordinate, reference base, the number of reads covering the site (read coverage), read bases (match, mismatch, indel, strand, start e end) and base qualities in ASCII code. The ASCII code transformed in Phred quality score gives a measure of base call accuracy and the probability of base-calling error.

STEP2: Sequences Mutational Analysis

In the second step we identified the variations of sample versus human genome reference and the mismatches between paired samples by an analytical procedure implemented in R language (Fig. 3).

1. **SNV and INDEL Detection of Sample Versus Human Genome Reference.** Starting from pileup file, we identified the single nucleotide variants of each sample, and calculated the frequency of substitution as the absolute frequency of variant allele, the percentage of substitution as the relative frequency of variant allele and the average Phred score of substitution as a measure of average base-call accuracy. At each single nucleotide variants the ASCII code was transformed in Phred quality score and the average was calculated. The R code outputs two lists of variations detected between the sample and the reference, SNVs and INDEL files. Each variation was described in table by chromosome, 1-based coordinate, reference base, read coverage, read bases and base qualities in ASCII code, frequency of substitution, percentage of substitution, average Phred score of substitutions.

2. **Somatic SNV and INDEL Detection by Paired Analysis.** At this step we identified the hypotetical somatic mutations by paired mutational analysis. We discriminated between variants occurring in the cancer genome but not in paired healthy sample and variants occurring in both (SNPs). To obtain robustness of mutation detection we filtered out variations in cancer sample with the following criteria: read coverage less than 20, frequency of substitution less than 6, percentage of substitution less than 25%, average Phred quality less than 30, corresponding to a probability of incorrect base call greater than 0.001. Finally, variations present in matched healthy sample with a frequency lower than or equal to 10% are tolered. Two text files are generated as output; the first one list the somatic variations and the second can be imported directly in SIFT to do functional classification. Each somatic mutation is described in a table by chromosome, 1-physical position, reference base, read coverage, absolute frequency of mutation, percent of mutation and average Phred score of mutation in cancer and in healty sample.

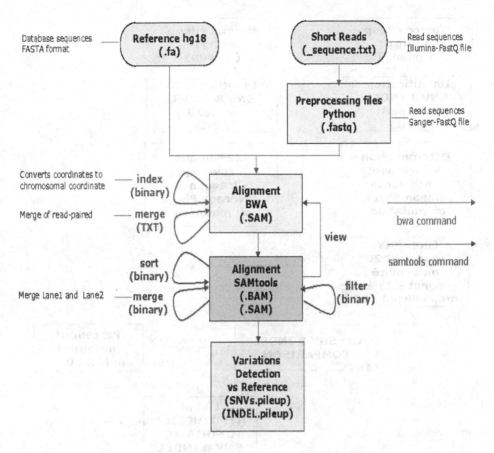

Fig. 2. Workflow to detect SNVs/indel calling

STEP3: Functional classification of Coding Variant

In the third step we annotated and evaluated the functional effect of exonic hypothetical mutations filtering out know polymorphism (Fig. 4).

We used SIFT Genome [9] to predict whether an amino acid substitution affects protein function based on sequence homology. By SIFT we extract coding variants from a large list of hypothetical somatic mutations providing the annotation and the functional prediction. Therefore, using SIFT annotation we filtered out the mutations predicted synonymous and polymorphic and we confirmed the SIFT functional prediction by querying ANNOVAR (http://www.openbioinformatics.org/annovar/, 2011May06 version). ANNOVAR [10] is a freely functional annotation tool of genetic variant for next-generation sequencing data that can identify whether SNPs cause protein coding changes and the amino acids that are affected. Moreover, by ANNOVAR we were able to flexibly use RefSeq genes to annotate the mutations at gene level; identify variants that are reported in dbSNP, or common SNPs (MAF > 1%) in the 1000 Genome Project and discover vari-

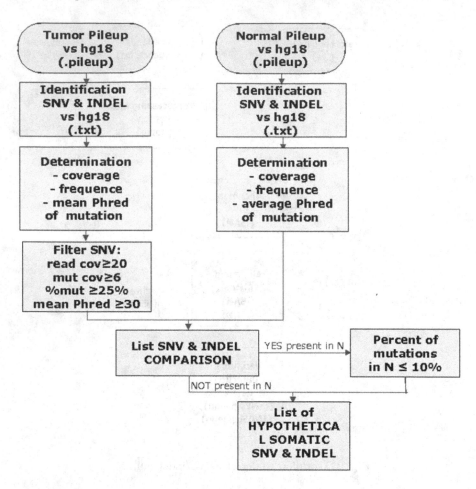

Fig. 3. Workflow to detect SOMATIC SNVs/indel in tumor sample

ants in conserved regions among 44 species or in segmental duplication regions. Moreover we selected the annotated candidate genes for Sanger validation according to the following criteria: genes previously linked and associated with leukemia (data extracted by search in PUBMED); genes know to participate in metabolic and biological process relevant to cancer (gene functional categories evidenced by Ingenuity Pathway Analysis (IPA), http://www.ingenuity.com/). Then all the critical data generated by our algorithm and SIFT were merged using dedicated R scripts. SIFT predictions (nucleotides position reference base and substitution, region belonging, dbSNP ID, SNP Type, Gene Name, Gene Description, Transcript ID, Protein Family ID) were merged with the sequence data (coverage, absolute frequency of mutation, and percent of mutation, average Phred score of mutation in cancer and the same fields for healty sample). Finally, all selected somatic mutations were checked for quality control in pileup and BAM files and visualized by IGV, then sequenced by Sanger method.

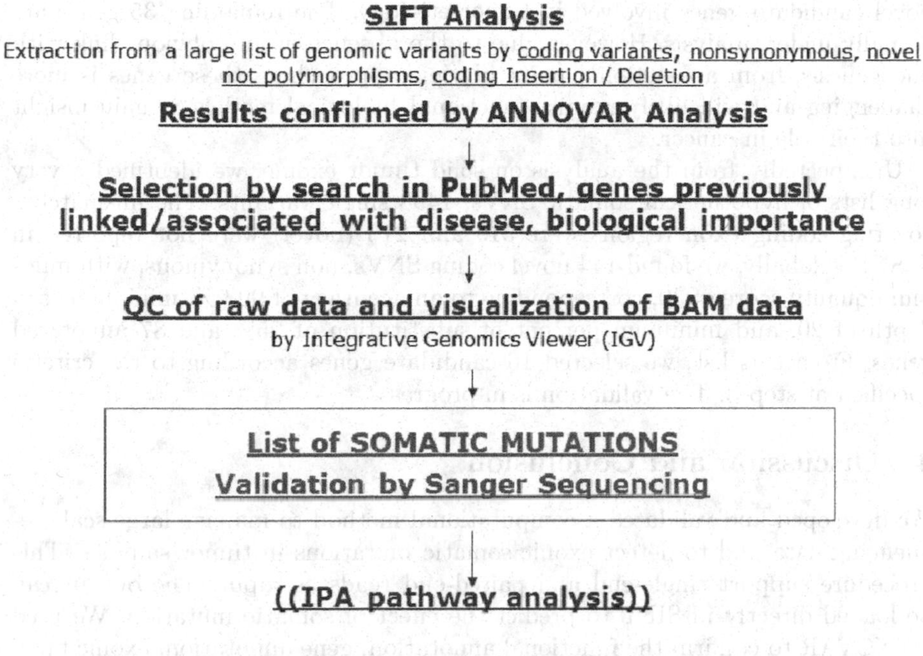

SIFT Analysis

Extraction from a large list of genomic variants by coding variants, nonsynonymous, novel not polymorphisms, coding Insertion / Deletion

Results confirmed by ANNOVAR Analysis

↓

Selection by search in PubMed, genes previously linked/associated with disease, biological importance

↓

QC of raw data and visualization of BAM data

by Integrative Genomics Viewer (IGV)

↓

List of SOMATIC MUTATIONS
Validation by Sanger Sequencing

↓

((IPA pathway analysis))

Fig. 4. Functional classification and selection of candidate genes

3 Results

The entire procedure was applied to whole exome sequencig of 3 leukemia (L) patients and 3 paired controls plus 1 solid tumor sample and paired control.

On average, 42 million of paired-end reads and 5.4 gigabases (Gb) of sequences were generated per individual. The percentage of reads matching the reference human genome (hg18, NCBI36.1) was over 90%, with a mean exon coverage of over 70-fold. For both the leukemic sample and the control, more than 90% of exons had a mean coverage of over 20-fold.

In the leukemia dataset we found several patterns of hypothetical somatic mutations. In particular we identified lists of hypothetical somatic mutations of 113, 146, 517 single variants for each leukemic patient. The mutations in coding regions were 31/113, 42/146, 55/517 respectively. Of them, 27/31, 24/42 and 43/55 weren't reported in dbSNP (novel). Then, we detected in leukemia dataset a total of 69 mutations in exon regions, novel, non synonymous, with minimum average Phred quality score of 30 corresponding to an accuracy of 99.9%, minimum read depth of 20, confirmed by at least 6 individual sequences and minimum percent of mutation equal to 25% in 56 annotated genes. Additionally, the candidates genes were selected for Sanger sequencing analysis according to the criteria specified at step 3. This analysis allowed us to focus on 21 genes validated by Sanger sequencing method (data not shown). Pathway analysis of these genes performed by IPA confirms that they belong to Cell Cycle network function and cancer disease. The remaining 35 genes may represent putative novel candidate genes involved in tumor etiology. The remaining 35 genes are actually under analysis. However, due to the absence of any obvious link with oncogenesis, from a functional point of view approaching these genes is more challenging and will likely require functional biological models to gain insight into their role in cancer.

Unexpectedly from the analysis on solid tumor exome, we identified a very long lists of hypothetical somatic SNVs, 1498 single variants. The mismatches covering coding exon regions were 319 and 213 (novel) were not reported in dbSNP. Globally, we found 144 novel coding SNVs, non synonymous, with minimum quality score of 30, corresponding to an accuracy of 99.9%, minimum read depth of 20, and minimum percent of substitution of 25% and 87 annotated genes. From this list, we selected 16 candidate genes according to the criteria specified at step 3. The validation is in progress.

4   Discussion and Conclusion

We developed and validated a computational method to manage large scale sequencing data and to detect exonic somatic mutations in tumor samples. This procedure support single-end and paired-end reads as input. The output can be loaded directly in SIFT to predict the effect of somatic mutation. We used ANNOVAR to confirm the functional annotation, gene annotation, exonic function, amino acid change, SNP annotation, conservation analysis obtained by SIFT. Moreover, whole-exome pre-computed PolyPhen v2, PhyloP (commonly used euristic methods), MutationTaster, LRT scores from dbNSFP database [11] are available as ANNOVAR annotation database to give more detailed annotation of non-synonymous mutations in humans, in addition to SIFT. dbNSFP is a lightweight database of human nonsynonymous SNPs and their functional predictions to distinguish deleterious mutations from the massive number of nonfunctional variants. However, the overlap between predictions made by LRT, SIFT and PolyPhen is very low, only 5% of predictions are shared across all three methods [12].

We found genomic regions containing interesting genes potentially implicated in our diseases and suitable for further investigations. Recently a new algorithm Bambino [13] was published. Bambino is a tool to detect variations, somatic or germinal and LOH from single or pooled samples. It is useful to visualize the genomic results. It is a java tool, flexible and fast but trivial to annotate and do functional annotation. However, neither our procedure or Bambino provides a statistical based testing to identify SNVs. Moreover, the list of somatic variants can be influenced by the settings used for variant detection and filtering of putative sites. Recently GAMES [14], a new tool useful to identify and annotate mutations in next-generation sequencing was published but it is not implemented for somatic analysis. Further improvements are in progress in our procedure to identify common aberrations in multiple data sets, to introduce functional annotations of SNVs located in intronic and intergenic regions and to combine DNA data analysis with gene expression profiles. The combination of DNA analysis and gene expression profiling provides powerful approach to understand the functional effect. Moreover, we plan to improve the genomic view of results by CIRCOS (http://mkweb.bcgsc.ca/circos/intro/genomic_data/). By using this software we will display in a circular representation the genome and explore the relationships between the DNA events (SV, SNV) and the genomic positions involved and describe in synthesis the structural abnormalities of an individual. In addition we will apply a new machine learning theory to discriminate molecular pathways involved in leukemic pathological process by using a novel and promising method described in Barla et al. [15]. The new pipeline can be applied to perform biomarker study in a leukemic and control data set; moreover, we plan to apply a 'modified' pipeline to a single group of leukemic patients to establish a correlation between the deregulated molecular pathways and the prognosis of patients samples known the somatic mutations.

Acknowledgments. We are grateful to the patients. This work was supported by AIRC 2010; PRIN 2008 program; Fondazione Cariplo (2009-2667); Lombardy Region (ID-16871; ID14546A); Ministry of Health, Programma Integrato di Oncologia (RFPS-2006-333974).

References

1. Campbell, P.J., Stephens, P.J., Pleasance, E.D., O'Meara, S., Li, H., Santarius, T., Stebbings, L.A., Leroy, C., Edkins, S., Hardy, C., Teague, J.W., Menzies, A., Goodhead, I., Turner, D.J., Clee, C.M., Quail, M.A., Cox, A., Brown, C., Durbin, R., Hurles, M.E., Edwards, P.A., Bignell, G.R., Stratton, M.R., Futreal, P.A.: Identification of somatically acquired rearrangements in cancer using genome-wide massively parallel paired-end sequencing. Nat Genet. 40(6), 722–729 (2008)
2. Jiao, Y., Shi, C., Edil, B.H., de Wilde, R.F., Klimstra, D.S., Maitra, A., Schulick, R.D., Tang, L.H., Wolfgang, C.L., Choti, M.A., Velculescu, V.E., Diaz Jr., L.A., Vogelstein, B., Kinzler, K.W., Hruban, R.H., Papadopoulos, N.: DAXX/ATRX, MEN1, and mTOR pathway genes are frequently altered in pancreatic neuroendocrine tumors. Science 331(6021), 1199–1203 (2011)
3. SureSelect Human All Exon Kit Illumina Paired-End Sequencing Library Prep Protocol Version 1.0.1, Agilent Technologies (October 2009)
4. Paired-End Sequencing Sample Preparation Guide.pdf, http://www.illumina.com
5. Li, H., Handsaker, B., Wysoker, A., Fennell, T., Ruan, J., Homer, N., Marth, G., Abecasis, G., Durbin, R.: 1000 Genome Project Data Processing Subgroup. The Sequence Alignment/Map format and SAMtools. Bioinformatics. 25(16), 2078–2079 (2009)
6. Ewing, B., Green, P.: Base-calling of automated sequencer traces using phred. II. Error probabilities. Genome Res. 8(3), 186–194 (1998)
7. Ng, S.B., Turner, E.H., Robertson, P.D., Flygare, S.D., Bigham, A.W., Lee, C., Shaffer, T., Wong, M., Bhattacharjee, A., Eichler, E.E., Bamshad, M., Nickerson, D.A., Shendure, J.: Targeted capture and massively parallel sequencing of 12 human exomes. Nature 461(7261), 272–276 (2009)
8. Li, H., Durbin, R.: Fast and accurate long-read alignment with Burrows-Wheeler transform. Bioinformatics 26(5), 589–595 (2010)

9. Kumar, P., Henikoff, S., Ng, P.C.: Predicting the effects of coding non-synonymous variants on protein function using the SIFT algorithm. Nat. Protoc. 4(7), 1073–1081 (2009)
10. Wang, K., Li, M., Hakonarson, H.: ANNOVAR: functional annotation of genetic variants from high-throughput sequencing data. Nucleic Acids Res. 38(16), e164 (2010)
11. Liu, X., Jian, X., Boerwinkle, E.: dbNSFP: a lightweight database of human non-synonymous SNPs and their functional predictions. Hum. Mutat. 32(8), 894–899 (2011)
12. Chun, S., Fay, J.C.: Identification of deleterious mutations within three human genomes. Genome Res. 19(9), 1553–1561 (2009)
13. Edmonson, M.N., Zhang, J., Yan, C., Finney, R.P., Meerzaman, D.M., Buetow, K.H.: Bambino: a variant detector and alignment viewer for next-generation sequencing data in the SAM/BAM format. Bioinformatics 27(6), 865–866 (2011)
14. Sana, M.E., Iascone, M., Marchetti, D., Palatini, J., Galasso, M., Volinia, S.: GAMES identifies and annotates mutations in next-generation sequencing projects. Bioinformatics 27(1), 9–13 (2011)
15. Barla, A., Jurman, G., Visintainer, R., Squillario, M., Filosi, M., Riccadonna, S., Furlanello, C.: A machine learning pipeline for discriminant pathways identification. In: Proceedings CIBB 2011, 8th International Meeting on Computational Intelligence Methods for Bioinformatics and Biostatistics, Gargnano, Italy (2011)

Feature Selection for the Prediction
and Visualization of Brain Tumor Types Using
Proton Magnetic Resonance Spectroscopy Data

Félix Fernando González-Navarro* and Lluís A. Belanche-Muñoz

[1] Instituto de Ingeniería,
Universidad Autónoma de Baja California Bulevard Benito Juárez,
21280 Mexicali, Mexico
fernando.gonzalez@uabc.edu.mx
[2] Dept. de Llenguatges i Sistemes Informàtics,
Universitat Politècnica de Catalunya Jordi Girona,
1-3, 08034 Barcelona, Spain
belanche@lsi.upc.edu

Abstract. In cancer diagnosis, classification of the different tumor types is of great importance. An accurate prediction of basic tumor types provides better treatment and may minimize the negative impact of incorrectly targeted toxic or aggressive treatments. Moreover, the correct prediction of cancer types in the brain using non-invasive information –e.g. ^{1}H-MRS data– could avoid patients to suffer collateral problems derived from exploration techniques that require surgery. We present a feature selection algorithm that is specially designed to be used in ^{1}H-MRS (Proton Magnetic Resonance Spectroscopy) data of brain tumors. This algorithm takes advantage of the fact that some metabolic levels may consistently present notorious differences between specific tumor types. We present detailed experimental results using an international dataset in which highly attractive models are obtained. The models are evaluated according to their accuracy, simplicity and medical interpretability. We also explore the influence of redundancy in the modelling process. Our results suggest that a moderate amount of redundant metabolites can actually enhance class-separability and therefore accuracy.

Keywords: Cancer, Brain tumours, Feature selection, Classification.

1 Introduction

Proton (or Hydrogen) Magnetic Resonance Spectroscopy (^{1}H-MRS) has been used extensively in biochemistry for *in vitro* chemical analysis of small samples for several years. As a technique for *in vivo* sampling of biological tissue, it provides a quantified biochemical fingerprint of metabolite concentrations [1]. ^{1}H-MRS data has the appearance of a plot of peaks along the x-axis, with the

---

* Corresponding author.

E. Biganzoli et al. (Eds.): CIBB 2011, LNBI 7548, pp. 83–97, 2012.

peak position depending on the resonant frequency of the associated metabolite [2]. An example of a ^{1}H-MRS dataset is shown in Fig. 1.

Nowadays, ^{1}H-MRS has been proven its value as a powerful tool in the clinical assessment of several pathologic conditions -e.g. epilepsy, multiple sclerosis, cancer– and specially in neurological affections [3], [4]. It is the only spectroscopic method for which a complete interpretation of the entire spectrum can be normally expected. Framed as a minimal invasive technique, its application in brain tumor oncological diagnosis carries tremendous benefits to patients, relieving them from complicated surgical procedures and minimizing trauma to normal tissue surrounding the particular lesion or other vital elements. With modern instruments good data may be obtained from samples weighing less than a milligram.

The use of systematic approaches based on ^{1}H-MRS data for the diagnosis and grading of adult brain tumors is subject of an extensive scientific research. One of these growing approaches takes as backbone well-established machine learning techniques to develop predictive models able to discern between several classes of brain tumors [5], [6], [7]. This particular task is quite challenging, mainly because of the high dimensionality and relatively low number of observations. Therefore, the use of *dimensionality reduction* (and, in particular, feature selection) methods becomes an option in order to present low complexity and interpretable models to oncologists.

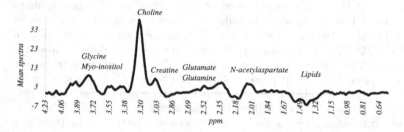

Fig. 1. An example of a long time of echo ^{1}H-MRS dataset. Some of the metabolites visible in this kind of spectrum are the Choline, which is a combination of multiple metabolites and is elevated in all brain tumors; the Creatine, a marker of oxidative metabolism of cells; the N-acetylaspartate, a neuronal density marker; and the Lipids, seen in necrosis conditions.

In this study, an *ad hoc* feature selection (FS) algorithm is used to generate relevant subsets of spectral frequencies (considered as features). The developed algorithm takes advantage of a distinctive aspect shown in typical ^{1}H-MRS readings: some metabolite levels are quite different between types of tumors. Bootstrap resampling is used to reduce sampling variability and obtain more stable readings. We report experimental work in which small subsets of frequencies are able to offer highly accurate and yet simple predictive models (linear classifiers, in this case). The proposed solution is also discussed in terms of visual appearance and interpretation of the involved metabolites.

2   Literature Review

First attempts using ^{1}H-MRS data in assessing human brain tumors *in vivo* are back to [3]. It was found that spectra differ significantly from normal brain spectra and between tumors by detecting the presence/absence of different metabolites. Even though no machine learning (ML) analysis of spectra was done in establishing these differences, it was concluded that ^{1}H-MRS spectroscopy may help to differentiate tumors for diagnostic and therapeutic purposes, limiting the need for invasive and risky diagnostic procedures such as biopsies.

At this point, ML techniques arise in order to *automate* the classification tasks. Artificial neural networks (e.g. [8], [9]) and linear discriminant analysis (LDC) (e.g. [5], [10]) are commonly used methods. Later studies perform dimensionality reduction, either considering the *peak* signals, ratios between peak signals or *feature extraction* based in principal component analysis or independent component analysis [11], [12], [13]. First studies in performing an explicit feature selection process have used simple well-known search algorithms to select subset of spectral points, such as *forward selection* [14], the Fisher criterion or the Relief feature weighing algorithm [15]. More recent works in FS properly speaking are found in [7], [16], [17], [18], which address a multi-class problem on the same dataset analyzed in this work. The dominant techniques are single-layer neural networks or classical feature selection search algorithms wrapping several classifiers, among which LDC usually yields the best predictive models.

3   Class-Separability Feature Selection

It is known that metabolites (spectral points) in ^{1}H-MRS data present notorious differences among tumors. For example, theoretically, meningiomas do not contain N-acetyl aspartate (NAA) and present the choline (CHO) elevated (up to 300 times the normal reading). Metastases present a moderate reduction in NAA and a decreased creatine (CR) signal. Lipid levels located at 1.3 ppm are mainly arisen in high-grade brain malignancies. These *fingerprints* that distinguish each tumor could lead us to try to establish a measure of physical distance between kinds of tumors that expresses the separability between classes. A very simple choice is taken in this study for this measure: the distance (absolute difference) between the *median* profiles across the different *pairs* of classes (tumour types).

Taking as primary data a bootstrap distribution, averaged estimations of such distances from the ^{1}H-MRS data can be computed very fast. The bootstrap distribution of these values offers other quantities of interest (such as the variance), but these are not used here. The median is used (instead of the mean) with the goal of reducing the influence of possible abnormally high (or low) profiles. If used, these profiles could signal a fake high separability.

3.1   A Criterion for Class-Separability

The separability degree of metabolites with respect to each tumor is assessed by the cumulative differences between pairs of elements –i.e. between tumors– thereby obtaining a new feature vector based on distances. It is hypothesized that the direction that best separates tumors taking as basis the metabolites that present abnormal values is partly expressed in this vector.

Algorithm 1. CSFS Class Separability Feature Selection

input : set of bootstrap resamples $S_1, \ldots, S_B$; $\mathcal{L}$ classifier
output: BSS: Best Spectral Subset

1 **foreach** *sample* $b \in \{1, \ldots, B\}$ **do**
2   **foreach** *spectral point* s **do**
3   **foreach** *class* c **do**
4           $m[b, s, c] \leftarrow$ median of spectral point s for class c in S_b

5 $\bar{m}[s, c] = \frac{1}{B} \sum_{b=1}^{B} m[b, s, c]$

6 **foreach** *spectral point* s **do**
7   **foreach** *pair of different classes* (c_i, c_j) **do**
8        $DS[s] \leftarrow DS[s] + |\bar{m}[s, i] - \bar{m}[s, j]|$

9 Sort DS in decreasing order
10 $BSS \leftarrow \varnothing$
11 $Jbest \leftarrow 0$
12 **repeat**
13   ***Forward Stage***
14   **for** $i \in \{1, \ldots, |DS|\}$ **do**
15   **foreach** *sample* $b \in \{1, \ldots, B\}$ **do**
16           $J[b] \leftarrow \mathcal{L}(S_b, S \setminus S_b, BSS \cup \{DS[i]\})$
17       $\bar{J} \leftarrow \frac{1}{B} \sum_{b=1}^{B} J[b]$
18   **if** $\bar{J} > Jbest$ **then**
19          $Jbest \leftarrow \bar{J}$
20          $BSS \leftarrow BSS \cup DS[i]$

21   ***Backward Stage***
22   **repeat**
23   **for** $j \in \{1, \ldots, |BSS|\}$ **do**
24   **foreach** *sample* $b \in B$ **do**
25              $J[b] \leftarrow \mathcal{L}(S_b, S \setminus S_b, BSS \setminus \{BSS[j]\})$
26          $\bar{J} \leftarrow \frac{1}{B} \sum_{b=1}^{B} J[b]$
27   **if** $\bar{J} \geq Jbest$ **then**
28             $Jbest \leftarrow \bar{J}$
29             $BSS \leftarrow BSS \setminus \{BSS[j]\}$

30   **until** *no more Backward improvement*
31 **until** *no more Forward or Backward improvement*

To capture the aforementioned behavior, the **CSFS** algorithm (which briefs for *Class-Separability Feature Selection*) is designed and outlined in Algorithm 1. Taking as primary data a bootstrap distribution from the ^{1}H-MRS data, stable distance estimations are computed, and a centroid $\bar{m}$ for every spectral point within each tumor is computed (lines 1-5) and a vector of centroids is generated by averaging them over the B bootstrap samples. In order to asses the separability degree of metabolites with respect to each tumor, the cumulative difference between pairs of elements –i.e. between tumors– is computed (lines 7-9), obtaining a new feature vector based on distances named DS (sorted in decreasing order in line 9). Hence, the algorithm takes advantage of abnormal presence of certain metabolites that allows to identify specific tumors. As a consequence, its operation is guided by the metabolites presenting a higher averaged degree of separability, as expressed in the ordered vector.

Once the class-separability evaluation is complete, a combined Forward-Backward search strategy for feature selection is implemented, fed by the ordered DS vector, as follows: a Forward step is carried out taking the first element in DS (lines 13-20) and its average performance is evaluated against the bootstrap resamples via a classifier $\mathcal{L}$. In order to avoid the inclusion of redundant features, a Backward stage takes place right after every single Forward stage, with the difference that this latter process is executed as much as necessary, and until no improvement is achieved (lines 21-30).

4   Experimental Work

In this section, the experimental conditions are outlined. The ^{1}H-MRS dataset employed is described jointly with the brain pathologies involved. Several off-the-shelf classifiers are used to measure the subsets performance as long as statistical tests to asses uncertainty about comparisons between models.

4.1   Datasets

An essential variable in the acquisition of ^{1}H-MRS spectra is the choice of echo time. With short times of echo (around 20 ms), larger numbers of metabolites are detected (myoinositol, glutamate, glutamine), but it is more likely that peak superimposition will occur, causing difficulty in spectroscopic curve interpretation. By using long times of echo (more than 135 ms), most metabolites in the brain are lost (except that of choline, creatine, NAA and lactate), but with better definition of peaks, thereby facilitating graphic analysis[19]. There are a few studies comparing the classification potential of the two types of spectra (see e.g. [10], [6]). These works seem to give a slight advantage to using short time of echo information or else suggest a combination of both types of spectra.

The targeted ^{1}H-MRS data is drawn from a database belonging to the *International Network for Pattern Recognition of tumors Using Magnetic Resonance* (INTERPRET). An European research project aimed to develop systematic tools to enable radiologists and other clinicians without special knowledge or expertise to diagnose and grade brain tumors routinely using magnetic resonance spectroscopy [20]. The dataset is constructed by single voxel ^{1}H-MR spectra acquired *in vivo* from brain tumor patients in two configurations: Long Time of Echo (PRESS 135-144 ms), named LTE, and Short Time of Echo (PRESS 30-32 ms), named STE. Brain pathologies that conform both configurations are distributed as following:

- LTE: 195 observations, including 55 meningiomas, 78 glioblastomas, 31 metastases, 20 astrocytomas grade II, 6 oligoastrocytomas grade II and 5 oligodendrogliomas grade II.
- STE: 217 observations, including 58 meningiomas, 86 glioblastomas, 38 metastases, 22 astrocytomas grade II, 6 oligoastrocytomas grade II, and 7 oligodendrogliomas grade II.

A third configuration was prepared in order to explore the discriminative power
of the *fusion* of LTE and STE data, namely the 195 common observations of
these two datasets and the concatenation of their metabolites, which is labeled
as LSTE. In all three sets, the spectra were grouped into three super-classes:
high-grade malignant tumors (metastases and glioblastomas), low-grade gliomas
(astrocytomas, oligodendrogliomas and oligoastrocytomas) and meningiomas.

Table 1. Summary of the results obtained with CSFS. The number in square brackets
is the size of the final Best Spectral Subset (BSS). The right number is the averaged
10x10 CV accuracy in the three ^{1}H-MRS datasets.

	NN	LDC	QDC	LR	lSVM	rSVM
LTE	[11] 89.70	[15] 93.51	[9] 89.09	[7] 91.48	[9] 91.82	[10] **93.88**
STE	[8] 92.21	[16] 93.34	[6] 87.40	[8] 90.48	[12] 93.14	[8] **94.48**
LSTE	[17] 96.14	[26] **98.27**	[8] 92.83	[7] 92.07	[14] 94.83	[12] 94.77

Table 2. Spectral points as selected by the best solutions –see bold faced models in
Table 1. The prefix L (Long), S (Short) in LSTE signals the original time of echo of
the metabolite; all values are expressed in ppm.

Best model ppm
LTE-rSVM 3.74, 2.94, 2.54, 2.35, 1.72, 1.61, 1.25, 1.10, 0.72, 0.66
STE-rSVM 3.81, 3.64, 3.51, 3.07, 2.44, 2.43, 2.37, 2.27
LSTE-LDC L3.81, L3.66, L3.11, L3.07, L2.98, L2.90, L2.75
L2.69, L2.29, L2.18, L1.86, L1.55, L0.83, L0.62
S4.19, S3.81, S3.66, S3.53, S3.49, S2.29, S2.25
S1.32, S1.13, S1.04, S0.70, S0.66

4.2 Experimental Settings

The three ^{1}H-MRS datasets $S = \{LTE, STE, LSTE\}$ were used to generate
three independent sets of $B = 1,000$ bootstrap samples $S_1, \ldots, S_B$ that play the
role of *training sets* in the feature selection process: each classifier $\mathcal{L}$ is developed
on each S_b resample and its performance is assessed on the test sample $S \setminus S_b$,
and *averaged* across the B bootstrap samples. The chosen classifiers for this
study are the *nearest-neighbor* technique (NN), the *Logistic Regression* (LR),
a *Linear* and *Quadratic Discriminant Classifier* (LDC, QDC), *Support Vector
Machine* with *linear* kernel (lSVM) and parameter C (regularization constant)
and *Support Vector Machine with* radial *kernel* (rSVM) and parameters C and
σ^2 (amount of smoothing in the kernel)[1].

---
[1] C and σ^2 are optimized via a grid search.

This process yields a different Best Spectral Subset (or BSS) for each of the three datasets (Algorithm 1). Once these BSSs are obtained, their performance is assessed using 10 times 10-fold Cross Validation (10x10 CV). Then Wilcoxon's signed rank test is applied in order to evaluate a possible statistical significance in the performance of the different models.

5   Discussion of the Results

The outcome of the CSFS process is displayed in Table 1. For LTE data, the rSVM yields the best performance, giving a 93.88% of accuracy with only 10 spectral points; quite close comes LDC at second position with a very similar figure at 93.51% accuracy and 15 spectral points. Precisely, the Wilcoxon signed rank test at 95% level (p-value < 0.05) show significant results comparing the rSVM results against all the others, except with LDC (p-value is 0.160). The STE data experiments show exactly the same behavior, but offering higher readings. The rSVM reaches 94.48% with only 8 spectral points; its first place in this data configuration is supported against all the rest (all p-values are lower than 0.002).

The LSTE experiments render the best results in all cases. The best final performance corresponds to LDC with 98.27% of accuracy using 26 spectral points. Wilcoxon's test p-values give statistical confirmation to this competitive model against all the others. The LSTE-LDC model yields one of the best reported values using this data set *with this particular configuration of super-classes* [16],[6],[11],[12],[21]. Recent work reports a very similar final performance, claiming a 98.46% accuracy using 5x5 CV resampling (instead of 10x10 CV as in this study) using 18 spectral points by means of a single-layer neural network [18]. This is a very attractive solution since it uses a lesser number of spectral points. However, the LSTE-LDC solution uses a classifier that requires no parameter tuning in training phase, which is then computationally cheaper. It is also interesting to note that both methods (LDC and the neural network) offer *linear* decision boundaries. The spectral points selected in the best solutions are displayed in Table 2. The final *selected* feature subset of the best LSTE-LDC model, as positioned in the whole spectrum, is displayed in Fig. 2. In order to better appreciate the solution in its spectral environment, the mean spectra for the three super-classes are added to the plot.

5.1   Data Visualization

Data visualization in a low-dimensional space may become extremely important to radiologists, helping them to gain insights into what undoubtedly is a complex domain. We use in this work a method based on the decomposition of the scatter matrix with the property of maximizing the separation between the projections of data (tumor classes, in this work). This is a linear method, thus easier to use in a real decision-making process that requires an intuitive representation of results. It has been recently improved by a process that involves the sphering of the data, followed by a projection onto the space defined by the class means.

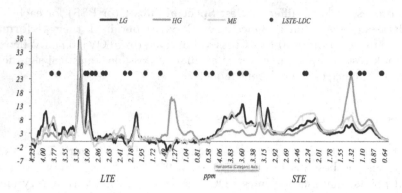

Fig. 2. Best Spectral Subset from LSTE-LDC model as positioned in the whole spectrum

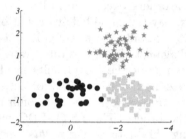

Fig. 3. Projection of the dataset (using the selected feature subset of the best LSTE-LDC model) onto the first two eigenvectors of the scatter matrices as coordinate system. Filled squares represent the HG class: high-grade malignant tumors (metastases and glioblastomas), circles the LG class: low-grade gliomas (astrocytomas, oligodendrogliomas and oligoastrocytomas); stars represent the ME class: meningiomas.

It leads to the definition of low-dimensional projective spaces that preserve the discrimination between classes obtained by the classifiers, even when the data covariance matrix is singular [24].

The result of such visualization is illustrated in Fig. 3. These scatter plots are the two-dimensional projections of the three classes using the first two eigenvectors of the scatter matrices. It is seen that the three supper-classes are notoriously well separated, although a few points cannot be clearly distinguished.

5.2   Metabolic Interpretation

The metabolites detected and their known biological function are listed in Table 3. It is necessary to clarify that some metabolites posses resonances at different positions in the spectrum –e.g. Threonine or Valine. For a complete description refer to the source at [22]. The *Glycerol-phosphocholine-choline* and the

Ethanolamine both deserve a particular comment, given that they show an interesting behavior in appearing in the two parts of the LSTE dataset, the Long and the Short times of echo. Looking for common metabolites with [18] (previously discussed in literature review) the following were found: Alanine, Myo-Inositol, Taurine, Choline, Glutamate and Glutamine.

Table 3. Metabolic interpretation in the best model. The prefix L (Long), S (Short) signals the original time of echo of the metabolite; all values are expressed in ppm.

Metabolite	Biological interpretation
Glycerol-phosphocholine-choline	An end product of membrane phospholipid degradation and increased concentrations have been associated with cerebral ischemia, seizures and traumatic brain injury. {L3.66 S3.66}
Ethanolamine	Increased levels of this metabolite has been observed in ischemic brain tissue of rats and gerbils. {L3.81 S3.81}
Glutathione-glutamate	An anti-oxidant, essential for maintaining normal red-cell structure. Altered levels have been reported in Parkinsons's disease and other neurodegenerative diseases. {L2.18}
Alanine	A nonessential amino acid that has been observed in increased levels in meningiomas. {L1.55}
Threonine	A large neutral amino acid essential to the diet. {S4.19 S1.32}
Valine	An essential amino acid necessary for protein synthesis observed in brain abscesses. {S2.25 S1.04}
Phenylalanine	An aromatic amino acid that presents elevated readings in phenylketonuria, an abnormal phenylalanine metabolization. {L3.11 L3.07}
Glutathione-cysteine	See Glutathione-glutamate. {L2.98 L2.90}
Aspartate	An excitatory amino acid that performs as a neurotoxin in elevated concentrations [23]. {L2.75}
NAA-Aspartate	A free amino acid whose function is poorly understood, but is is commonly believed to provide a marker of neuronal density. {L2.69}
GABA	A primary inhibitory neurotransmitter whose altered concentrations are associated with neurological disorders. {L2.29 L1.86 S2.29}
Myo-inositol	Its function is not enough understood, although it is believed to be a requirement in cell growth. Altered levels have been linked with Alzheimer's disease, hepatic encephalopathy and brain injury. {S3.53}
Choline	A combination of multiple metabolites and is elevated in all brain tumors. It is required for the synthesis of neurotransmitters constituents of membranes. {S3.49}
Not identified	{L0.83 L0.62 S1.13 S0.70 S0.66}.

5.3   The Effect of Redundancy in Class Separability

In spite of the stabilizing effect of bootstrap resampling, the inevitable variability due to randomly sub-sampling an already finite sample warns agaimts taking the feature order found in the vector DS to the letter. It is also clear from the spectra that the metabolites show very different separability degrees. Therefore a safe departing hypothesis is that distant positions in the vector represent big differences in separability; on the contrary, nearby positions should not be taken as a strict order. Assuming then that the ordered vector has captured the basic ability to separate the classes by ranking the features (metabolites) in decreasing order (the *relevance*), a very important issue is then found in their *redundancy*.

In this vein, the ^{1}H-MRS data can be considered as a spatial series, in the sense that spectral points are ordered in the metabolic spectrum. It is then quite

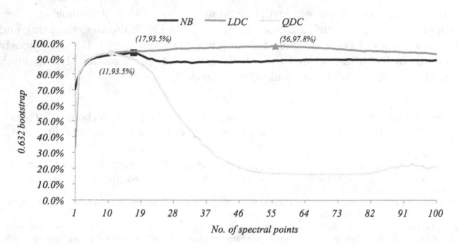

Fig. 4. Performance curves for the LTE ^{1}H-MRS data set. The horizontal axis is the size of the subset being evaluated, following the order given by the vector DS, as described in the text. The vertical axis is the 0.632-Bootstrap classification performance. The numbers in brackets are the size of the subset with best performance and its estimated performance. For conciseness, only the first 100 spectral features are shown.

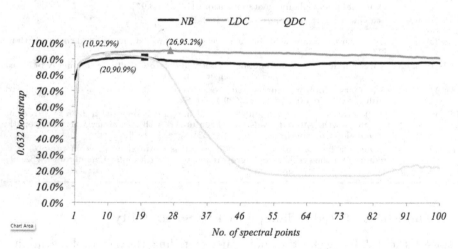

Fig. 5. Performance curves for the STE ^{1}H-MRS data set. See caption of Fig. 4.

likely that contiguous spectral points offer similar separability values and hence will be found indexed in nearby or even consecutive positions in DS (note the reciprocal is not necessarily true[2]). For instance, the Creatine peak, located at 3.03 ppm in the spectrum will have a separability value similar to that of the 3.01 ppm spectral point, which *almost* defines the same metabolite. So far in

---

[2] Consecutive metabolites in DS will have similar separability values but need not be necessarily contiguous in the spectrum.

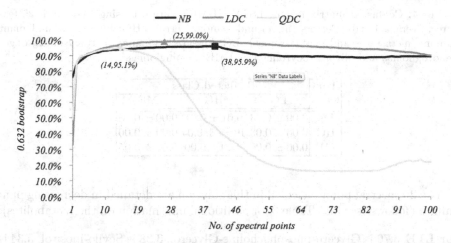

Fig. 6. Performance curves for the LSTE ^{1}H-MRS data set. See caption of Fig. 4.

this work, this redundancy has been dealt with by performing a rather elaborate Forward-Backward search strategy (lines 12-30 in in Algorithm 1).

Should we include *some* redundant metabolites in the model? We conjecture that the answer could be 'yes', for one precise reason. If a metabolite is important for prediction purposes, and there is another metabolite that plays a similar role, then the presence of both in a model can reduce the uncertainty (stochastic variability) on the (unique) information they carry. We also reckon that this redundancy among metabolites must be limited, otherwise the model would be overly complex and the model fitting process may end up overfitting the data.

To test this conjecture a new set of experiments is performed in the same conditions. This time, however, the Forward-Backward search strategy (lines 12-30 in Algorithm 1) is replaced by a simpler and computationally cheaper Forward search strategy: the chosen classifier is fed using the vector *DS* one feature at a time in an incremental way, with no removals. To make the process even faster, only the fastest classifiers are used: again the *Linear* and *Quadratic Discriminant Classifier* (LDC, QDC) and the *Naive Bayes* (NB) classifier.

We show performance curves for the three ^{1}H-MRS data types using these three classifiers in Figs. 4 to 6. Given that these classifiers have no parameters to tune and the incremental nature of the feature selection process, *model selection* reduces to finding the peaks in the graphics.

The best result found across this simple incremental sequence uses 25 spectral frequencies (namely, the first 25 frequencies according to the *DS* vector) and is again obtained using the LSTE ^{1}H-MRS data with LDC. The 0.632-bootstrap estimated classification accuracy is 99.0% (an average error of 1%). The estimated averaged 10x10 CV accuracy is 99.64% (an average error of 0.36%). This prediction is detailed as an average confusion matrix in Table 4.

Table 4. Confusion matrix for the LSTE ^{1}H-MRS data set using LDC with 25 features: average 10x10cv errors (in %) and standard errors. HG: high-grade malignant tumors (metastases and glioblastomas), LG: low-grade gliomas (astrocytomas, oligo-dendrogliomas and oligoastrocytomas) and ME: meningiomas.

True	Predicted Class		
Class	LG	HG	ME
LG	3.09 ± 0.03	0.01 ± 0.01	0.00 ± 0.00
HG	0.06 ± 0.02	10.84 ± 0.04	0.00 ± 0.00
ME	0.00 ± 0.00	0.00 ± 0.00	5.50 ± 0.05

The 25 spectral points selected in this solution are detailed in decreasing ppm value as follows (see also Table 3 for additional information on the metabolites):

for LTE 3.70 is Glycero-phosphocholine-Glycerol, 3.38 is Scyllo-inositol, 3.34 is Scyllo-inositol, 3.07 is Tyrosine, 2.98 is Histamine, 2.96 is Homocarnosine-GABA, 2.90 is Glutathione-Cysteine, 2.56 is Glutathione-Glutamate, 2.29 is GABA, 2.18 is Glutathione-Glutamate, 2.12 is Glutamate, 1.86 is GABA, 1.78 is unknown, 1.61 is unknown, 0.92 is Valine, 0.75 is unknown.

for STE 4.25 is Threonine, 3.47 is Tryptophan, 3.34 is Scyllo-inositol, 2.62 is Aspartate, 2.31 is GABA, 1.30 is Lactate, 1.27 is Lactate, 0.83 is unknown, 0.79 is unknown.

These points are positioned in the joint LSTE spectrum as displayed in Fig. 7. They show *some* redundancy, as exemplified by Scyllo-inositol in LTE or by Lactate in STE. For clarity, again mean spectra for the three super-classes are added to the plot. This remarkably accurate solution is attractive for a number of reasons that go beyond accuracy. First, it uses a moderate number of spectral points (25); second, the used classifier (LDC) requires no parameter tuning in training phase and is computationally cheap. And third it offers a *linear* decision boundary between tumour types. This is illustrated in Fig. 8 which, as before,

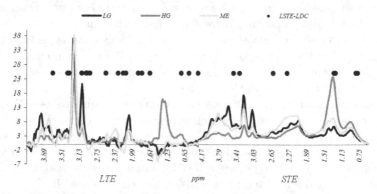

Fig. 7. Best Spectral Subset from the redundant LSTE-LDC model as positioned in the whole spectrum

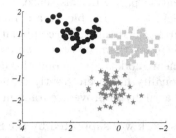

Fig. 8. Projection of the dataset (using the redundant feature subset of the best LSTE-LDC model) onto the first two eigenvectors of the scatter matrices as coordinate system. Filled squares represent the HG class: high-grade malignant tumors (metastases and glioblastomas), circles the LG class: low-grade gliomas (astrocytomas, oligodendrogliomas and oligoastrocytomas); stars represent the ME class: meningiomas.

shows the two-dimensional projection of the three classes using the first two eigenvectors of the scatter matrices. It is seen that the three supper-classes are now perfectly separated.

6 Conclusions

A feature selection algorithm has been introduced as a strategy to select subsets of spectral points from ^{1}H-MRS spectral data of brain tumors. The proposed algorithm takes advantage of the differential presence of certain metabolites that could allow to identify a specific tumor. It also accounts for possible redundancies introduced in the selected subsets of spectral points that could be derived from this approach. The particular task that has been addressed poses many challenges. Interpretability of the solution (e.g., as given by linear models), low number of spectral points, accuracy and stability are not easy to satisfy simultaneously. However, any solution lacking one or more of this characteristics will certainly fall short of what medical standards can expect.

In this vein, the final model obtained is considerably competitive in terms of accuracy, complexity (of both the model and the algorithmic process needed to obtain it), and clinical interpretability, with respect to other solutions in the literature. Most of the identified metabolites present in the final model have been positively defined by the medical literature; some concordances can also be found with other successful recent machine learning works.

Some words of warning may be in order with respect to the feature selection process. Although a "best" subset of spectral points could certainly exist to solve the task at hand, it is extremely unlikely that it is found by a search process, for two reasons. The first reason is an algorithmic one, given the exponential size of the set of all possible solutions. The second reason has to do with statistical significance (all computations with finite samples are uncertain and, to some extent, unreliable) and to model assessment (the classifiers are prone to overfit small datasets). This is the reason why we complement the solution with the interpretation and visualization parts. In this sense, the expertise provided by radiologists and other clinicians is invaluable for a complete evaluation.

This study has also confirmed that the LSTE combination offers better subsets in terms of classification accuracy than the other two datasets alone. Moreover, the results suggest that linear models are among the best suited for the task, provided that the dimensionality has been greatly reduced, and that a limited degree of redundancy may actually improve accuracy in this case.

Acknowledgments. This work was supported by the Spanish MICINN under grant TIN2009-13895-C02-01. Authors acknowledge the former INTERPRET European project partners. Data providers: Dr. C. Majós (IDI), Dr. À. Moreno-Torres (CDP), Dr. F.A. Howe and Prof. J. Griffiths (SGUL), Prof. A. Heerschap (RU), Prof. L Stefanczyk and Dr. J. Fortuniak (MUL), and Dr. J. Calvar (FLENI); data curators: Drs. Julià-Sapé, Candiota and Olier, Ms. Delgado, Ms. Martín and Mr. Pérez (GABRMN-UAB). Prof. C. Arús (GABRMN coordinator).

References

1. Zamani, A.: Proton MR Spectroscopy. In: Minimal invasive Neurosurgery, pp. 75–86. Humana Press (2005)
2. Sibtain, N.: The clinical value of proton magnetic resonance spectroscopy in adult brain tumours. Clinical Radiology 62, 109–119 (2007)
3. Bruhn, H., et al.: Noninvasive differentiation of tumors with use of localized h-1 mr spectroscopy in vivo: initial experience in patients with cerebral tumors. Radiology 172, 541–548 (1989)
4. Hansen, J., et al.: [1]h-mr spectroscopy of the brain: Absolute quantification of metabolites. Radiology 246(2), 318–332 (2006)
5. Tate, A., et al.: Development of a decision support system for diagnosis and grading of brain tumours using in vivo magnetic resonance single voxel spectra. NMR in Biomedicine 19, 411–434 (2006)
6. Garcia, J., et al.: On the use of long te and short te sv mr. spectroscopy to improve the automatic brain. tumor diagnosis. Tech. rep. (2007), ftp://ftp.esat.kuleuven.ac.be/pub/SISTA/ida/reports/07-55.pdf
7. Vellido, A., et al.: Outlier exploration and diagnostic classification of a multi-centre [1]h-mrs brain tumour database. Neurocomputing 72, 3085–3097 (2009)
8. Usenius, J., et al.: Automated classification of human brain tumors by neural network analysis using in vivo 1h magnetic resonance spectroscopic metabolite phenotypes. Neuroreport 7(10), 1597–1600 (1996)
9. Ala-Korpela, M., et al.: Artificial neural network analysis of 1h nuclear magnetic resonance spectroscopic data from human plasma. Neurocumputing 13-15, 3085–3097 (2009)
10. Majos, C., et al.: Brain tumor classification by proton mr spectroscopy: Comparison of diagnostic accuracy at short and long te. American Journal of Neuroradiology 25, 1696–1704 (2004)
11. Devos, A.: Quantification and classification of mrs data and applications to brain tumour recognition. Ph.D. thesis, Katholieke Univ. Leuven (2005)
12. Lukas, L., et al.: Brain tumor classification based on long echo proton mrs signals. Artificial Intelligence in Medicine 31, 73–89 (2004)

13. Huang, Y., Lisboa, P., El-Deredy, W.: Tumour grading from magnetic resonance spectroscopy: a comparison fo feature extraction with variable selection. Statistics in Medicine 22, 147–164 (2003)
14. Nikulin, A., et al.: Near-optimal region selection for feature space reduction: novel preprocessing methods for classifying mr spectra. NMR in Biomedicine 11, 209–216 (1998)
15. Luts, J., et al.: A combined mri and mrsi based multiclass system from brain tumour recognition using ls-svms with class probabilities and feature selection. Artificial Ingelligence in Medicine 40, 87–102 (2007)
16. González, F., et al.: Feature and model selection with discriminatory visualization for diagnostic classification of brain tumors. Neurocomputing 73, 622–632 (2010)
17. Romero, E., Vellido, A., Sopena, J.M.: Feature Selection with Single-Layer Perceptrons for a Multicentre ^{1}h-mrs Brain Tumour Database. In: Cabestany, J., Sandoval, F., Prieto, A., Corchado, J.M. (eds.) IWANN 2009, Part I. LNCS, vol. 5517, pp. 1013–1020. Springer, Heidelberg (2009)
18. Lisboa, P., et al.: Classification, dimensionality reduction, and maximally discriminatory visualization of a multicentre ^{1}h-mrs database of brain tumors. In: ICMLA 2008: Proceedings of the 2008 Seventh International Conference on Machine Learning and Applications, pp. 613–618. IEEE Computer Society (2008)
19. Castillo, M., Kwock, L., Mukherji, S.: Clinical applications of proton mr spectroscopy. AJNR 17, 1–15 (1996)
20. INTERPRET, International network for pattern recognition of tumours using magnetic resonance project (2002), http://azizu.uab.es/INTERPRET
21. Ladroue, C.: Pattern recognition techniques for the study of magnetic resonance spectra of brain tumours. Ph.D. thesis, St. George's Hospital Medical School (2003)
22. Govindaraju, V., Young, K., Maudsley, A.: Proton nmr chemical shifts and coupling constants for brain metabolites. NMR in Biomedicine 13(3), 129–153 (2000)
23. Farooqui, A., Ong, W., Horrocks, L.: Glutamate and Aspartate in Brain. Springer, New York (2008)
24. Lisboa, P., et al.: Cluster based visualisation with scatter matrices. Pattern Recognition Letters 29(13), 1814–1823 (2008)

On the Use of Graphical Models to Study ICU Outcome Prediction in Septic Patients Treated with Statins

Vicent J. Ribas[1], Jesús Caballero López[2], Anna Sáez de Tejada[3],
Juan Carlos Ruiz-Rodríguez[2], Adolfo Ruiz-Sanmartín[2], Jordi Rello[4],
and Alfredo Vellido[1]

[1] Dept. Llenguatges i Sistemes Informàtics,
Universitat Politècnica de Catalunya 08034, Barcelona - Spain
{vribas,avellido}@lsi.upc.edu
[2] Servei de Medicina Intensiva, SODIR Research Group
Hospital Universitari Vall d'Hebrón, Vall d'Hebrón Institut de Recerca Autonomous
University of Barcelona, Barcelona - Spain
{jecaballero, jcruiz}@vhebron.net
[3] Llenguatges i Sistemes Informàtics,
Sabirmedical S.L. Barcelona - Spain
[4] Servei de Medicina Invensiva, CRIPS Research Group,
Centro de Investigación Biomédica en Red de Enfermedades Respiratorias
(CIBERES) Hospital Universitari Vall d'Hebrón,
Autonomous University of Barcelona, Barcelona - Spain
jrello@vhebron.net

Abstract. Sepsis is a common pathology in Intensive Care Units (ICU).
At its most acute phase, namely septic shock, mortality rates can be as
high as 60%. Early administration of antibiotics is known to be crucial for
ICU outcomes. In particular, statins, a class of drug usually associated
to the regulation of the biosynthesis of cholesterol, have been shown
to present good anti-inflammatory properties. In this brief study, we
hypothesized that the pre-admission use of statins should improve ICU
outcomes, reducing the mortality rate. We tested this hypothesis in a
prospective study with patients admitted with severe sepsis and multi-
organ failure at the ICU of Vall d'Hebrón University Hospital (Barcelona,
Spain). Outcome was predicted using statistic algebraic models and the
Bayesian Networks that can naturally be derived from these models.

Keywords: Sepsis, intensive care unit, outcome prediction, statistic algebraic models, Bayesian Networks.

1 Introduction

Sepsis and its associated complications, Septic Shock and Multiorganic Dysfunction Syndrome (MODS), are considered to be the most frequent causes of
morbidity and mortality for patients admitted to the ICU [1].

E. Biganzoli et al. (Eds.): CIBB 2011, LNBI 7548, pp. 98–111, 2012.

Sepsis is characterized by the systemic response to infection and, from a clinical point of view, it is recognized by a set of clinical signs and symptoms corresponding to the response of the organism to the presence of microorganisms or their toxic products.

The evolution and prognosis of septic patients is variable and unpredictable. Some patients with Sepsis have a fulminant evolution leading, within hours, to death due to refractory Septic Shock. However, other patients survive the hyperacute phase and develop MODS, which also leads to death. Fortunately, other patients present a favorable evolution and successfully recover from Sepsis.

The diagnosis of a Septic Shock is not trivial and it is usually carried out in challenging clinical emergency situations. Early recognition of signs of decreased perfusion before the onset of hypotension, appropriate therapeutic response, and removal of the center of the infection, are the keys to the survival of patients with Septic Shock. Given the criticality of this pathology, it is of capital importance to have available an early indication of this condition in order to allow doctors to act rapidly at the onset of Sepsis.

Needless to say, the ICU environment can be unforgiving in terms of decision making tasks. Clinicians in general might benefit from at least partially automated computer-based decision support. Those clinicians making real-time executive decisions at ICUs will require computer-based methods that are not only reliable, but also, and this is a key issue, readily interpretable. This study aims to address these needs through the design and development of computer-based decision making tools to assist clinicians at the ICU. These developments will focus on the problem of Sepsis in general and, more specifically, on the problem of survival prediction for patients with Severe Sepsis that have been treated with Statins prior to their admission to the ICU.

Statin drugs inhibit 3-hidroxi-methylglutaril reductase. Beyond its hypolipemic properties, statins also exercise anti-inflammatory, immunomodulator and antioxidant actions and are capable of modulating vasoreactivity in the coagulation system through its actions at endothelial cell level [7] [8]. Recent studies suggest that chronic treatment with statins would have beneficial effects on infection prevention and treatment as well as on ICU outcomes [9], [10],[11], [12], [13]. Despite this evidence, several studies have found an inconclusive neutral effect [14], or even a greater mortality in patients treated with statins [15]. None of these studies addresses the effect of statins in patients with severe sepsis or MODS.

In this paper, we examine the association between the administration of statins in pre-admission at the ICU and the mortality rates in the ICU over a population of 750 patients with severe sepsis and MODS through algebraic statistical techniques for conditional independence analysis and the associated Bayesian Networks. The use of Bayesian Networks in this context complies with the aforementioned requirements of reliability and interpretability. It must be noted that the patients' database used for the current study, as described in the following section, is larger than any other used for the same research purposes. Its origin is one of the biggest hospital ICUs in the Spanish public health care system.

2   Materials

This work is based on a prospective study approved by the Clinical Investigation Ethical Committee of the *Vall d'Hebron* University Hospital in Barcelona, Spain, which resulted in a prospective database collected by the Research Group on Shock, Organic Dysfunction and Resuscitation (SODIR) of Vall d'Hebron's Intensive Care Unit (VH-ICU). The database consisted of information collected from all patients admitted in the ICU with severe sepsis and MODS between July 2004 and December 2009.

During this period, 750 patients with severe sepsis and MODS were admitted to the ICU (including medical and surgical patients). The mean age of the patients in the analyzed database was 57.07 (with standard deviation ±16.65) years; 47.91% of patients were female; and the diagnosis on admission was 67.83% *medical* and 32.17% *surgical*. The origin of primary infection for the cases on the database was 40.28% pulmonary, 23.20% abdominal, 10.76% urinary, 7.21% skin/muscle, 4.88% central nervous system (CNS), 1.55% catheter related, 1.00% endovascular, 4.99% biliar, 1.55% mediastinum, and 4.58% unknown. Also, 14.13% of patients ($n = 106$) received pre-admission statins.

Organ dysfunction was evaluated with the SOFA Score [18], which quantifies the dysfunction and failure of six organs/systems (Cardiovascular, Respiratory, CNS, Hepatic, Renal and Hematologic), as shown in Table 1. SOFA is a score going from 0 (normal function) to 4 (maximum failure). Severity was evaluated referring to the APACHE II score [19], which is a composite indicator taking into consideration: temperature, blood pressure, pH, white blood cell count, heart rate, oxygenation, age, and so on. The resulting mean APACHE II in our study was 23.03(±9.62 standard deviation). The APACHE II score ranges from 0 to 71; higher scores correspond to more severe disease and a higher risk of death.

Table 1. List of SOFA scores, with their corresponding mean and standard deviation values for the analyzed dataset

Cardiovascular (CV)	2.86 (1.61)
Respiratory (RESP)	2.31 (1.15)
Central Nerv. Sys. (CNS)	0.48 (0.99)
Hepatic (HEPA)	0.49 (0.92)
Renal (REN)	1.06 (1.20)
Haematologic (HAEMATO)	0.78 (1.14)
Global SOFA score	7.94 (3.83)

3   Methods

3.1   Statistic Algebraic Models

Algebraic statistics have been successfully applied to problems in the areas of genomics and proteomics, to obtain Maximum Likelihood amino acid sequences in phylogenetics [21], [22]. More generally, algebraic statistics are used in phylogenetics to show the necessary marginal independence conditions in the analysis of biological sequences. The idea behind this approach is that marginal independence conditions induce a Markov field (undirected graph), which under some factorization conditions (see definition below) can define a Bayesian Network. Both graphs can be used for inference [23], [24].

A statistical model is defined as a family of distributions over a sample space Ω. In our case, Ω is finite with cardinal N. If the distributions are given by polynomials over the parameters, this model is defined as an Algebraic Statistical Model.

Definition 1. An Algebraic Statistical Model (ASM) is a polynomial application [21]

$$\psi : \mathbb{R}^d \to \mathbb{R}^N$$
$$\Theta = (\theta_1, \ldots, \theta_d) \to (\psi_1(\Theta), \ldots, \psi_N(\Theta)). \tag{1}$$

Here X is a random variable $X = (x_1, \ldots, x_d)$ where each x_k is mapped to the integer state space $\{1, .., N\}$, the model parameters are given by $\Theta = (\theta_1, \ldots, \theta_d)$; $\psi_i(\Theta)$ is defined as $\psi_i(\Theta) = P(x_k = i|\Theta)$ for some $k \in \{1, \ldots, d\}$ and ψ is restricted to the probability simplex (Δ^{N-1}). More particularly, ψ is defined over a set $U \subseteq \mathbb{R}^d$ and $\psi(u) \cap \Delta^{N-1} \subseteq \mathbb{R}^N$.

3.2   Models of Conditional Independence

Let a set of discrete random variables $X_1, \ldots, X_n$ where X_i takes values over the probability space Σ_i. Then a distribution over the sample space $\Sigma_1 \times \ldots \times \Sigma_n$ is equivalent to a matrix $(p_{i_1, \ldots, i_n}) \in \Sigma_1 \times \ldots \times \Sigma_n$ where $p_{i_1, \ldots, i_n} = Prob(X_1 = i_1, \ldots, X_n = i_n)$.

Definition 2. Given three disjoint subsets $A, B, C \neq \varnothing$ of $\{X_1, \ldots, X_n\}$, A is independent of B given C, $A \perp\!\!\!\perp B|C$ iff $Prob(A = a, B = b|C) = Prob(A = a|C = c)Prob(B = b|C = c)$ $\forall a, b, c$ such that $Prob(C = c) > 0$. The following theorem (Hammersley-Clifford) [25] shows the connection between the parametrization ψ and the collection of conditional independence statements presented below.

Theorem 1 (Hammersley-Clifford). A probability distribution P with positive and continuous density f satisfies the pairwise Markov property with respect to an undirected graph $\mathcal{G}$ if and only if it factorizes according to $\mathcal{G}$.

It is important to note that Definition 2 translates into a set of quadratic equations in the unknowns $(p_{i_1, \ldots, i_n})$.

Proposition 1. A probability distribution $P = (p_{i_1, \ldots, i_n})$ satisfies $A \perp\!\!\!\perp B|C$ if and only if

$$P_{a,b,c}P_{a',b',c} = P_{a,b',c}P_{a',b,c}.$$
$$\forall a, a' \in \prod_{x_i \in A} \Sigma_i,$$
$$\forall b, b' \in \prod_{x_j \in B} \Sigma_j, \tag{2}$$
$$\forall c \in \prod_{x_k \in C} \Sigma_k,$$

where

$$P_{a,b,c} = Prob(A = a, B = b, C = c)$$
$$P_{a',b',c} = Prob(A = a', B = b', C = c)$$
$$P_{a,b',c} = Prob(A = a, B = b', C = c)$$
$$P_{a',b,c} = Prob(A = a', B = b, C = c).$$

(3)

Equivalently, this proposition implies that the rank of M_c is ≤ 1 where:

$$M_c = \begin{pmatrix} P_{a,b,c} & P_{a,b',c} \\ P_{a',b,c} & P_{a',b',c} \end{pmatrix}_{\forall c \in \prod_{x_k \in C} \Sigma_k}$$

(4)

Here, each of the probabilities are translated into a linear form in the unknowns $(p_{i_1,...,i_n})$. This means that $Prob(A = a, B = b, C = c)$ is replaced by a marginalization which is the sum of all $p_{i_1,...,i_n}$ that satisfy:

 - for all $X_\alpha \in A$ the X_α-coordinate of a equals i_α,
 - for all $X_\beta \in B$ the X_β-coordinate of b equals i_β,
 - for all $X_\gamma \in C$ the X_γ-coordinate of c equals i_γ.

The set of quadratic forms in the unknowns $p_{i_1,...,i_n}$ resulting from this substitution is defined as $Q_{A \perp\!\!\!\perp B|C}$, for a given indexing [21].

3.3 Bayesian Networks

Definition 3. $\mathcal{K}$ is a Bayesian Network with respect to the undirected graph $\mathcal{G}$ if its joint probability density function factorizes as a product of the individual density functions, conditional on their parent variables:

$$p(x) = \prod_{v \in V} p(x_v | x_{pa(v)}).$$

(5)

Here $pa(v)$ is the set of parents of v and V is the set of marginally dependent variables.

From this definition and theorem 1 we know that if $\mathcal{K}$ is a Bayesian Network from the more general graph $\mathcal{G}$, then the pairwise Markov condition (i.e. each node is independent of its non descendants) will hold. In other words, our support $\{X_1, ..., X_n\}$ will define a Markov field [23], [21].

4   Results

4.1   Marginal Dependence between the Pre-admission Use of Statins and the ICU Outcome

We aim to find the relation between the administration of statin drugs prior to ICU admission and the mortality rate in severe sepsis patients. For that, we tested the null hypothesis that the ICU outcome is independent of the pre-admission use of statins for given APACHE II and SOFA scores. More specifically, we tested the following null hypothesis H_o:

$$H_o : \{X_1\} \perp\!\!\!\perp \{X_4\}|\{X_2\}, \{X_3\} \qquad (6)$$

where $\{X_1\}$ is the ICU outcome, $\{X_4\}$ the pre-admission use of statins, $\{X_3\}$ the SOFA score, and $\{X_2\}$ the APACHE II score. In our case, $\{X_1\}$ is 1 for ICU survival and 0 corresponds to exitus. Also, $\{X_4\}$ is 1 if the patient followed pre-admission statin treatment, and 0 if the patient did not follow it. The APACHE II and SOFA scores were stratified according to the minimum value that results in a significant increase in the mortality rates (see Figs. 1 and 2). This means that APACHE II scores lower than, or equal to 21 were set to 0, while scores higher than 21 were set to 1. In clinical practice [19], the 0 coding corresponds to moderate/low mortality rates (i.e. between 30% 40%), whereas the 1 coding corresponds to high mortality rates. With a similar criterion, SOFA scores lower than or equal to 7 were set to 0, while they were set to 1 if the SOFA score was above the selected threshold. Again, in clinical practice [20], this 0 coding corresponds to moderate/low mortality rates (i.e. between 20% 37%), whereas the 1 coding corresponds to high mortality rates.

From section 3.1, we now have a $4 \times 2 \times 2$ matrix M of relative frequencies and from definition 2 we know that all the minors of M should have a rank lower than 1 for H_0 to hold. In our case the four minors of M are:

$$M_{0,0} = \begin{pmatrix} 0.0217 & 0.0014 \\ 0.1655 & 0.0176 \end{pmatrix}$$

$$M_{0,1} = \begin{pmatrix} 0.0163 & 0.0014 \\ 0.0380 & 0.0054 \end{pmatrix}$$

$$M_{1,0} = \begin{pmatrix} 0.0258 & 0.0027 \\ 0.1723 & 0.0285 \end{pmatrix}$$

$$M_{1,1} = \begin{pmatrix} 0.1981 & 0.0285 \\ 0.2266 & 0.0502 \end{pmatrix}$$

The rank of all the minors above was calculated using the singular value decomposition (SVD) algorithm [28]. Table 2 shows that all minors of matrix M are full rank, and, therefore, the null hypothesis can be rejected. This means that the ICU outcome is in fact marginally dependent on the pre-admission use of statins for given APACHE II and SOFA scores (severity and organ dysfunction). These results are also consistent with a χ^2 test, which rejected the null hypothesis with a $p < 0.05$. However, it must be stressed that the performance of this χ^2 would not have yielded the graphical model outlined here.

In order to construct the graph $\mathcal{G}$, we also need to study the marginal dependences between the remaining variables, as shown in Appendix 1.

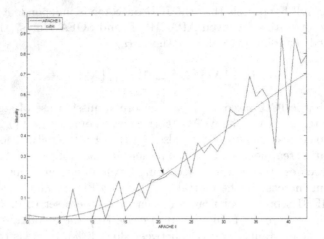

Fig. 1. APACHE II threshold selection: The jagged curve represents the true APACHE II mortality rate, while the smooth curve is the APACHE II mortality rate interpolated with a cubic polynomial. The arrow points to the first inflection point of the polynomial, which, in this study, corresponds to the selected APACHE II threshold for stratification (i.e. APACHE II = 21). This means that APACHE II scores lower than this threshold are set to 2 in our Bayesian Network. Conversely, the APACHE II values higher than 21 are set to 1 in our Bayesian Network.

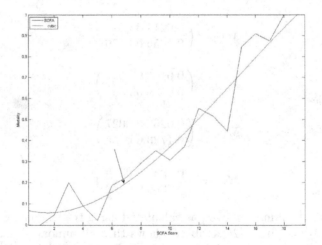

Fig. 2. SOFA score threshold selection: The jagged curve represents the true SOFA score mortality rate, whilst the smooth curve is the SOFA score mortality rate interpolated with a cubic polynomial. As in the previous figure, the arrow points to the first inflection point of the polynomial, which is selected as SOFA score threshold for stratification (i.e. SOFA = 7). This means that SOFA scores lower than this threshold are set to 2 in our Bayesian Network. Conversely, the SOFA values higher than 7 are set to 1 in our Bayesian Network.

Table 2. Ranks of Minors Obtained with SVD

Minor	Rank	Tolerance
$M_{0,0}$	2	$5.55 \cdot 10^{-17}$
$M_{0,1}$	2	$1.39 \cdot 10^{-17}$
$M_{1,0}$	2	$5.55 \cdot 10^{-17}$
$M_{1,1}$	2	$1.11 \cdot 10^{-16}$

4.2 Study of the Protective Effect of Pre-admission Use of Statins with Bayesian Networks

The graphical model $\mathcal{G}$ resulting from section 4.1 and Appendix 1 is the fully connected graph:

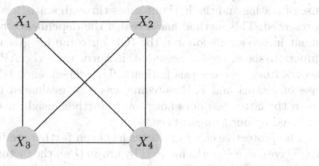

Also the marginal probabilities for the ICU result node X_1 is summarized in Table 3. In this Table, the pre-admission use of statins, Moderate/Low SOFA scores and Moderate/Low APACHE II scores are coded as 1.

Table 3. Marginal probabilities of survival (CPT Table) for ICU results

Statins	SOFA	APACHE II	Result=1	Result=0
1	2	2	0.64	0.36
2	2	2	0.53	0.47
1	1	2	0.80	0.20
2	1	2	0.70	0.30
1	2	1	0.91	0.09
2	2	1	0.87	0.13
1	1	1	0.93	0.07
2	1	1	0.88	0.12

The results in Table 3 confirm our initial hypothesis that the pre-admission use of statins plays an important role for ICU outcome, consistently increasing the probability of survival. This effect becomes more apparent for high severity and moderate organ dysfunction as measured by the SOFA score and APACHE II (0.80 vs 0.70). However, this effect is even more important for both high organ dysfunctions and severities (0.64 vs 0.53).

5   Conclusions

Anecdotal but sound clinical evidence suggests that the use of statins may play an important role in the prognosis of severe sepsis. Despite this, the studies that have addressed this problem so far have been inconclusive.

In this study, we have provided sound evidence that the administration of statin drugs plays an important role in the prognosis of severe sepsis in the ICU context. A simple method to evaluate the dependence between the pre-admission use of statins and the ICU outcomes through statistic algebraic models has been presented. This method has revealed the dependence between the statins treatment in pre-admission and the ICU outcome for given severity and organ dysfunction/shock levels, measured, in turn, with the APACHE II and the SOFA scores from severe sepsis patients. The dependence between the pre-admission use of statins and ICU outcome was also evaluated through a χ^2 test. However, the latter test does not provide further insight about the graphical models induced by our sample space.

The protective effect of statins has been further studied using the corresponding Bayesian Networks induced by graph $\mathcal{G}$ on the factorized sample space distribution (c.f. Table 3). The main conclusion of this study is that these protective effects become more important for severe multi-organic failures accompanied by high APACHE II scores (showing a decrease in the mortality rate of about 10%). This same effect is also observed in moderate organ dysfunction syndromes and high severities.

These are encouraging results that are also consistent with clinical practice. Importantly, Bayesian Networks provide transparent rules that could straightforwardly be used in ICU practice.

Acknowledgment. This research was partially funded by Spanish MICINN R+D Plan TIN2009-13895-C02-01 project.

Appendix 1: Marginal Independence for all Variables

For $H_0 : \{X_1\} \perp\!\!\!\perp \{X_2\}|\{X_3\}, \{X_4\}$:

$$M_{0,0} = \begin{pmatrix} 0.0217 & 0.0258 \\ 0.1655 & 0.1723 \end{pmatrix}$$

$$M_{0,1} = \begin{pmatrix} 0.00140 & 0.00270 \\ 0.01760 & 0.02850 \end{pmatrix}$$

$$M_{1,0} = \begin{pmatrix} 0.0163 & 0.1981 \\ 0.0380 & 0.2266 \end{pmatrix}$$

$$M_{1,1} = \begin{pmatrix} 0.00140 & 0.02850 \\ 0.00540 & 0.05020 \end{pmatrix}$$

Table 4. Ranks, $H_0 : \{X_1\} \perp\!\!\!\perp \{X_2\}|\{X_3\}, \{X_4\}$

Minor	Rank	Tolerance
$M_{0,0}$	2	$1.07 \cdot 10^{-16}$
$M_{0,1}$	2	$1.49 \cdot 10^{-17}$
$M_{1,0}$	2	$1.35 \cdot 10^{-16}$
$M_{1,1}$	2	$2.57 \cdot 10^{-17}$

For $H_0 : \{X_1\} \perp\!\!\!\perp \{X_3\}|\{X_2\}, \{X_4\}$:

$$M_{0,0} = \begin{pmatrix} 0.0217 & 0.0163 \\ 0.1655 & 0.0380 \end{pmatrix}$$

$$M_{0,1} = \begin{pmatrix} 0.00140 & 0.00140 \\ 0.01760 & 0.00540 \end{pmatrix}$$

$$M_{1,0} = \begin{pmatrix} 0.0258 & 0.1981 \\ 0.1723 & 0.2266 \end{pmatrix}$$

$$M_{1,1} = \begin{pmatrix} 0.00270 & 0.02850 \\ 0.02850 & 0.05020 \end{pmatrix}$$

Table 5. Ranks, $H_0 : \{X_1\} \perp\!\!\!\perp \{X_3\}|\{X_2\}, \{X_4\}$

Minor	Rank	Tolerance
$M_{0,0}$	2	$7.62 \cdot 10^{-17}$
$M_{0,1}$	2	$8.21 \cdot 10^{-18}$
$M_{1,0}$	2	$1.50 \cdot 10^{-16}$
$M_{1,1}$	2	$2.82 \cdot 10^{-17}$

For $H_0 : \{X_2\} \perp\!\!\!\perp \{X_3\}\|\{X_1\}, \{X_4\}$:

$$M_{0,0} = \begin{pmatrix} 0.0217 & 0.0163 \\ 0.0258 & 0.1981 \end{pmatrix}$$

$$M_{0,1} = \begin{pmatrix} 0.0014 & 0.0014 \\ 0.0027 & 0.0285 \end{pmatrix}$$

$$M_{1,0} = \begin{pmatrix} 0.1655 & 0.0380 \\ 0.1723 & 0.2266 \end{pmatrix}$$

$$M_{1,1} = \begin{pmatrix} 0.0176 & 0.0054 \\ 0.0285 & 0.0502 \end{pmatrix}$$

Table 6. Ranks, $H_0 : \{X_2\} \perp\!\!\!\perp \{X_3\}|\{X_1\}, \{X_4\}$

Minor	Rank	Tolerance
$M_{0,0}$	2	$8.91 \cdot 10^{-17}$
$M_{0,1}$	2	$1.27 \cdot 10^{-17}$
$M_{1,0}$	2	$1.41 \cdot 10^{-16}$
$M_{1,1}$	2	$2.63 \cdot 10^{-17}$

For $H_0 : \{X_2\} \perp\!\!\!\perp \{X_4\}\|\{X_1\}, \{X_3\}$:

$$M_{0,0} = \begin{pmatrix} 0.0217 & 0.0014 \\ 0.0258 & 0.0027 \end{pmatrix}$$

$$M_{0,1} = \begin{pmatrix} 0.0163 & 0.0014 \\ 0.1981 & 0.0285 \end{pmatrix}$$

$$M_{1,0} = \begin{pmatrix} 0.1655 & 0.0176 \\ 0.1723 & 0.0285 \end{pmatrix}$$

$$M_{1,1} = \begin{pmatrix} 0.0380 & 0.0054 \\ 0.2266 & 0.0502 \end{pmatrix}$$

Table 7. Ranks, $H_0 : \{X_2\} \perp\!\!\!\perp \{X_4\} | \{X_1\}, \{X_3\}$

Minor	Rank	Tolerance
$M_{0,0}$	2	$1.50 \cdot 10^{-17}$
$M_{0,1}$	2	$8.92 \cdot 10^{-17}$
$M_{1,0}$	2	$1.07 \cdot 10^{-16}$
$M_{1,1}$	2	$1.04 \cdot 10^{-16}$

For $H_0 : \{X_3\} \perp\!\!\!\perp \{X_4\} \| \{X_1\}, \{X_2\}$:

$$M_{0,0} = \begin{pmatrix} 0.0217 & 0.0014 \\ 0.0163 & 0.0014 \end{pmatrix}$$

$$M_{0,1} = \begin{pmatrix} 0.0258 & 0.0027 \\ 0.1981 & 0.0285 \end{pmatrix}$$

$$M_{1,0} = \begin{pmatrix} 0.1655 & 0.0176 \\ 0.0380 & 0.0054 \end{pmatrix}$$

$$M_{1,1} = \begin{pmatrix} 0.1723 & 0.0285 \\ 0.2266 & 0.0502 \end{pmatrix}$$

Table 8. Ranks, $H_0 : \{X_3\} \perp\!\!\!\perp \{X_4\} | \{X_1\}, \{X_2\}$

Minor	Rank	Tolerance
$M_{0,0}$	2	$1.21 \cdot 10^{-17}$
$M_{0,1}$	2	$8.96 \cdot 10^{-17}$
$M_{1,0}$	2	$7.58 \cdot 10^{-17}$
$M_{1,1}$	2	$1.29 \cdot 10^{-16}$

References

1. Livingston, D.H., Mosenthal, A.C., Deith, E.A.: Sepsis and multiple organ dysfunction syndrome: A clinical-mechanistic overview. New Horizons 3, 257–266 (1995)
2. American College of Chest Physicians/Society of Critical Care Medicine Consensus Conference, Definitions for sepsis and organ failure and guidelines for the use of innovative therapies in sepsis. Crit. Care Med. 20, 864–874 (1992)
3. Levy, M.M., Fink, M.P., Marshall, J.C., Edward Angus, A., Cook, D., Cohen, J., Opal, S.M., Vincent, J.L., Ramsay, G.: 2001 SCCM/ESICM/ACCP/ATS/SIS International Sepsis Definitions Conference. Intensive Care Med. 29, 530–538 (2003)

4. Esteban, A., Frutos-Vivar, F., Ferguson, N., Penuelas, O., Lorente, J., Al, G.F., Honrubia, T., Algora, A., Bustos, A., Garcia, G., Rodriguez, I., Ruiz, R.: Sepsis incidence and outcome: contrasting the intensive care unit with the hospital ward. Crit. Care Med. 35(5), 1284–1289 (2007)
5. Angus, D.C., Linde-Zwirble, W.T., Lidicker, J., Clermont, G.L., Carcillo, J., Pinski, M.R.: Epidemiology of severe sepsis in the United States: analysis of incidence, outcome, and associated costs of care. Crit. Care Med. 29(7), 1303–1310 (2001)
6. Martin, G.S., Mannino, D.M., Eaton, S., Ross, M.: The epidemiology of sepsis in the United States from 1979 through 2000. N. Eng. J. Med. 348(16), 1546–1554 (2003)
7. Almog, Y., Novack, V., Eisinger, M., Porath, A., Novack, L., Gilutz, H.: The effect of statin therapy on infection-related mortality in patients with atherosclerotic diseases. Crit. Care Med. 35, 372–378 (2007)
8. Chopra, V., Flanders, S.A.: Does Statin Use Improve Pneumonia Outcomes? Chest 136, 1381–1388 (2009)
9. Gao, F., Linhartova, L., Johnston, M., Thickett, D.R.: Statins and sepsis. Br J. Anaesth 100, 288–298 (2008)
10. Thomsen, R.W., Hundborg, H.H., Johnsen, S.P.J., Pedersen, L., Sorensen, H.T., Schonheyder, H.C., Lervang, H.H.: Statin use and mortality within 180 days after bacteremia: A population-based cohort study. Crit. Care Med. 34, 1080–1086 (2006)
11. Tleyjeh, I.M., Kashour, T., Hakim, F.A., Zimmerman, V.A., Erwin, P.J., Sutton, A.J., Ibrahim, T.: Statins for the prevention and treatment of infections. A systematic review and meta-analysis. Arch. Intern. Med. 169, 1658–1667 (2009)
12. Christensen, S., Thomsen, R.W., Johansen, M.B., Pedersen, L., Jensen, R., Larsen, K.M., Larsson, A., Tonnesen, E., Sorensen, H.T.: Preadmission statin use and one-year mortality among patients in intensive care. A cohort study. Crit. Care 14, 29 (2010)
13. Schmidt, H., Hennen, R., Keller, A., Russ, M., Muller-Werdan, U., Werdan, K., Buerke, M.: Association of statin therapy and increased survival in patients with multiple organ dysfunction syndrome. Intensive Care Med. 32, 1248–1251 (2006)
14. Majumdar, S.R., McAlister, F.A., Eurich, D.T., Padwal, R.S., Marrie, T.J.: Statins and outcomes in patients admitted to hospital with community acquired pneumonia: population based prospective cohort study. BMJ 333(7576), 999–1001 (2006)
15. Kapoor, A.S., Kanji, H., Buckingham, J., Devereaux, P.J., McAlister, F.A.: Strength of evidence for perioperative use of statins to reduce cardiovascular risk: systematic review of controlled studies. BMJ 333, 1149 (2006)
16. Fernandez, R., De Pedro, V.J., Artigas, A.: Statin therapy prior to ICU admission: protection against infection or a severity marker? Intensive Care Med. 32, 160–164 (2006)
17. Bellazzi, R., Zupan, B.: Predictive data mining in clinical medicine: Current issues and guidelines. International Journal of Medical Informatics 77, 81–97 (2008)
18. Vincent, J.L., Moreno, R., Takala, J., Willats, S., De Mendoça, A., Bruining, H., Reinhart, C.K., Suter, P.M., Thijs, L.G.: The SOFA (Sepsis Related Organ Failure Assessment) Score to describe organ dysfunction/failure. Intensive Care Med. 22, 707–710 (1996)
19. Knaus, W.A., Draper, E.A., Wagner, D.P., Zimmerman, J.E.: APACHE II: A severity of disease classification system. Crit. Care Med. 13, 818–829 (1985)
20. Lopes Ferreira, F., Peres Bota, D., Bross, A., Melot, C., Vincent, J.L.: Serial Evaluation of the SOFA Score to Predict Outcome in Critically Ill Patients. JAMA 286, 1754–1758 (2001)

21. Pachter, M., Sturmfels, B.: Algebraic Statistics for Computational Biology. Cambridge University Press (2005)
22. Pistone, G., Riccomagno, E., Wynn, H.P.: Algebraic Statistics: Computational Commutative Algebra in Statistics. Chapman and Hall, CRC Press (2001)
23. Lauritzen, S.: Graphical Models. Oxford University Press (1996)
24. Geiger, D., Meek, C., Sturmfels, B.: On the Toric Algebra of Graphical Models. Ann. Statist. 34(3), 1463–1492 (2006)
25. Hammersley, J.M., Clifford P.: Markov Fields on Finite Graphs and Lattices (1971) (unpublished manuscript),
   http://www.statslab.cam.ac.uk/~grg/books/hammfest/hamm-cliff.pdf
26. Hastie, T., Tibshirani, R., Friedman, J.: The Elements of Statistical Learning: Data Mining, Inference, and Prediction, 2nd edn. Springer Series in Statistics. Springer (2009)
27. Breiman, L., Friedman, J., Stone, C.J.: Classification and Regression Trees. Chapman and Hall/CRC (1984)
28. Golub, G.H., Reinsch, C.: Singular value decomposition and least squares solutions. Numer. Math. 14(5), 403–420 (1970)

Integration of Biomolecular Interaction Data in a Genomic and Proteomic Data Warehouse to Support Biomedical Knowledge Discovery

Arif Canakoglu, Giorgio Ghisalberti, and Marco Masseroli

Dipartimento di Elettronica e Informazione, Politecnico di Milano,
Piazza Leonardo Da Vinci 32, 20133 Milano, Italy
{canakoglu,ghisalberti,masseroli}@elet.polimi.it

Abstract. The growing available genomic and proteomic information gives new opportunities for novel research approaches and biomedical discoveries through effective data management and analysis support. Integration and comprehensive evaluation of available controlled data can highlight information patterns leading to unveil new biomedical knowledge. For this purpose, the University Politecnico di Milano, is developing a software framework to create and maintain a Genomic and Proteomic Data Warehouse (GPDW) that integrates information from many data sources on the basis of a conceptual data model that relates molecular entities and biomedical features.

Here we illustrate and discuss the extension of framework for integrating biomolecular interaction data in the GPDW. The comprehensive and mining of the reliable interaction data together with the other biomolecular information in the GPDW constitutes a powerful computational support for novel biomedical knowledge discoveries.

Keywords: Proteomic and genomic interaction data, Automatic data parsing and integration, Data warehousing.

1 Introduction

Biomolecular interaction information is used very frequently by biologists and bioinformaticians to interpret experimental results in the context of a global protein interaction network and to test new hypotheses. Protein interaction databases are very important to capture interaction information from the literature and experimental results and present it in a well-structured format. Nonetheless there is no single database which covers the entire interaction information and, in order to achieve the possible widespread coverage, it is a necessity to combine data from different databases often provided in different formats[1,2,3].

Difficulties in comprehensively using available biomolecular data can be summarized as follow.

- Databases are geographically distributed and they could contains duplicate data. In recent years, it has been working on the integration of distributed

E. Biganzoli et al. (Eds.): CIBB 2011, LNBI 7548, pp. 112–126, 2012.

data into single databases. For this purpose, data warehousing and other data integration approaches can be used to manage and maintain the content. This involves the problem of managing the large amount of heterogeneous data, integrates and offers them to the users within a system as homogeneous as possible.

- Lack of widely adopted standards for data format and exchange data.
- Controlled vocabulary issue. Despite vocabularies used for controlled annotations of molecular entities claims to be orthogonal to each other, often there are relationships between a controlled vocabulary and another, especially when the vocabularies are managed by different organizations.
- Quality of biomolecular annotations in databases. This is not only related to curators' validation of new annotations but also the management and the maintenance of these annotations.

To facilitate the exchange and integration of molecular interaction by data providers, databases and data users, the Molecular Interaction group of the Human Proteome Organization Protein Standard Initiative, proposed a data representation standard (current version PSI-MI 2.5) [4]. This standard has been adopted by the major molecular interaction (e.g protein-to-protein interaction (PPI)) databases and formed the basis for the emergence of the International Molecular Exchange (IMEx) consortium (http://imex.sourceforge.net/) [5]. IMEx follows the model of similar initiatives in different domains of biological data, such as the nucleotide sequence exchange between EMBL [6], GenBank [7] and DDBJ [8], and aims at distributing the curation workload between participating databases thus avoiding work duplication and increasing literature coverage.

Although the experimental data are imported into databanks with the guidance of curators, biomolecular interaction data may contain some false negative and false positive interaction data. With the quality control mechanisms, the number of erroneous data may be decreased.

Comprehensive evaluation of data with other available information in data warehouse can lead to select most reliable information and to provide a paramount support data analysis and mining aimed at biomolecular knowledge discoveries. Towards this aim, we extended previously developed software framework to integrate genomic and proteomic information with biomolecular integration data.

After this introduction, paper is organized as follows. Sect. 2 shows the similar works to this project, Sect. 3 introduces data warehouse and the framework for integration of data warehouse, Sect. 4 gives information about the quality controls on the integrated data, Sect. 5 explains the biomolecular interaction databanks, Sect. 6 is about the integration results and analysis on the results, Sect. 7 concluded the paper.

2   Related Work

There are many approaches to integrated the data sources for resolving the accessing multiple heteroeneous data source problem. One of the main approach for biomedical data is data warehousing. EnsMart [9] is a data warehouse organizing data from individual databases into one query-optimized system. It is based on the principle of creating a generic system from specific data sources. Another system similar to described in this paper is BioWarehouse[10]. It is an evolving open source toolkit for constructing data warehouses that combines different collections of bioinformatic DBs within a single physical DB management system (DBMS), in order to ease queries that span multiple DBs. BioWarehouse aims to be a toolkit capable of supporting multiple alternative warehouses by combining different collections of DBs. The main differences between our proposal and BioWarehouse are in methodological choices concerning the global data schema adopted and data loading procedures. Our data schema is more flexible and easy to be expanded with needs stemming from the integration or modification of data sources, and supports full data provenance tracking. Our loading and updating procedure are more regular, so as to ease the integration of new data types and sources, as well as the adaptation to structural modifications of previously integrated data.

3   Genomic and Proteomic Data Warehouse (GPDW)

To effectively take advantage of the numerous genomic and proteomic information sparsely available in many heterogeneous and distributed biomolecular databases accessible via the Internet, we previously developed the Genome Function INtegrated Discoverer (GFINDer) project [11,12].

GFINDer is based on a multi-organism genomic and proteomic data warehouse (GPDW). In the GPDW several controlled terminologies and ontologies, which describe gene and gene product related biomolecular processes, functions and phenotypes, are imported and stored together with their associations (annotations) with genes and proteins of several organisms. In the GPDW all such data from several different databases are integrated by interconnecting the imported annotations to the genes and proteins they refer to by means of their provided IDs and cross-references.

GPDW framework handles the import and integration process, starting from the creation of a database that contains the metadata necessary for the operation of the application. The method for integration of heterogeneous data collected from the web is divided in two macro-phases:

- *import data from different sources*
- *integration of imported data*

Both steps are controlled by well-defined XML which is controlled by XSD schema. This configurable XML controls all the processes. The configurable parameters are as follows: the files which will be downloaded for each source and its extraction path for the zip files; the definition of the importing java classes, responsible for the process; selection of the sources and the files to import. With this XML, metadata schema is created and then it is used as a reference for the complex queries. We defined another configurable XML file in order to configure the logical schema of the database tables. This second XML defines the creation of the database table column definition, constraints and the indexes the tables.

3.1   Data Import Procedures of GPDW

The main tasks performed by the implemented automatic procedure in the data import step of the integration factory are illustrated in the sequence diagram in Fig. 1.

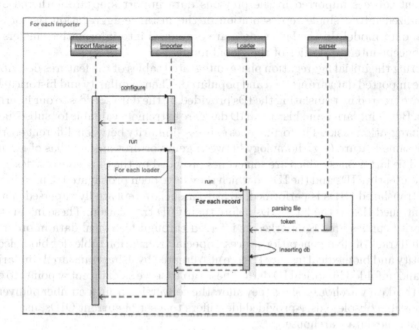

Fig. 1. Sequence diagram of the main tasks of the implemented automatic procedures for data import

The procedure is guided by an Import manager that configures an Importer for each considered data source and starts the procedure. Since each Importer is designed to be self contained, data from many different sources can be imported in parallel to speed up the process. Each source specific Importer coordinates a set of Loaders (a loader for each data file, or group of homogeneous data files, taken from the source) and a set of Parsers (a parser for each data file format). Each parser extracts the data from its associated input files and produces data tokens usable by the loader. Loader and parser use a producer consumer pattern. Each loader is responsible for associating a semantic meaning to the tokens produced by the associated parser(s) and inserting them into the data warehouse. Each tuple inserted from different files or data source contains the the source and data file field as binary values. If a tuple, in other words a feature or relation between features, is repeated in different source or different file, then it is detected by the automatic procedures and the duplicated data is removed and at the end the distinct tuple contains the ID of the both source.

3.2   Data Integration Procedures of GPDW

The main tasks automatically performed in the data integration step of our factory are described in the sequence diagram in Fig. 2. They can be grouped into an aggregation and an integration phase. In the former, data from the different sources imported in the previous data import step are gathered and normalized into a single representation in the instance-aggregation tier of our global data model. In the latter, data are organized into informative clusters in the concept-integration tier of the global model.

During the initial aggregation phase, integrated tables of the features described by the imported data are created and populated. Then, similarity and historical ID data are created by translating the IDs provided by the data sources to our internal OIDs. Both similarity and historical ID data are extremely valuable for subsequent data integration tasks. The former ones express similarity between different entries of the same feature (e.g., homology between genes or proteins, or alias of feature IDs). The latter ones, which are sometimes provided by the data sources, describe obsolete feature IDs and the IDs to which they have been propagated. Unfolding of their translated OIDs is performed, so as to associate repeatedly superseded and discontinued IDs to the latest IDs before their OID translation. These integrated similarity entries are also marked as inferred through historical data in order to keep full track of their generation process. Special translation tables for biomolecular entity and biomedical feature IDs are also created by using translated similarity data and unfolded historical ID data. These tables serve as main entry points to explore the data warehouse, since they allow the conversion from a number of diverse and possible obsolete user-provided identifiers to a set of current OIDs, usable to navigate the data warehouse.

Finally, relationships (annotations) between pairs of feature entries are created by performing OID translation of the imported relationship data expressed through the native IDs. In doing so, relationship data are coupled with the related feature entries. Due on the imported data sources and on their mutual synchronization, relationship data may refer to feature entries, or even features, that have not been imported in the data warehouse. In this case, missing integrated feature entries are synthesized and marked as such (i.e., inferred through synthesis from relationship data). However, if a missing entry has an obsolete ID and through unfolded translated historical data it is possible to extract a more current ID for it, the relationship is first transferred to the latest ID and then marked as inferred through historical data. This relationship translation policy preserves, between the integrated data, all the relationships expressed by the imported relationship data and allows their subsequent use for biomedical knowledge discovery (e.g., by transitive closure inference, involving also the synthesized entries).

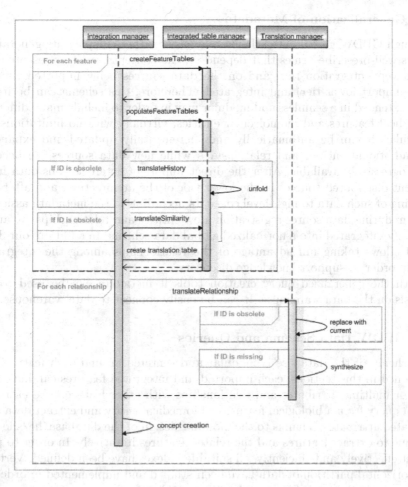

Fig. 2. Sequence diagram of the main tasks of the implemented automatic procedures for data integration

During the final integration phase, by doing a similarity analysis, it has been tested whether single feature instances from different sources represent the same feature concept. In this case, they are associated with a new created single concept OID. Different biomolecular entity concept instances are also further integrated under a single gene concept when they represent biomolecular entities related to the same gene. Then new entries can be inferred from the integrated data (e.g., annotations can be inferred from other annotations by transitive closure inference). The Inferred field is used in all integrated tables to keep track of the method of inference used to derive an entry.

At the end of the integration process, on all integrated tables the defined index, unique, primary and foreign key integrity constraints are enforced in order to detect (and resolve) possible data duplications and inconsistencies, thus improving the time of access to the integrated data, as well as their overall quality.

3.3   Generalization of Metadata

Although GPDW global data schema may seem rather complex, its generation follows well-prescribed rules that depend on the concepts to be represented (in the concept-integration tier) and on the data sources being imported (in the source-import lower tier) and integrated. Therefore, this schema can be iteratively extended in a seamless and modular way in order to include many different biomedical features and biomolecular entities, virtually with no limitations. In particular, it can be automatically and incrementally updated and expanded with additional entities and relationships while new data sources are becoming progressively available. After the direct import of heterogeneous data from different distributed sources in the lower tier of the architecture, and after the mapping of such data to high-level concepts according to the metadata assigned to them during data source registration, new entities and relationships are automatically integrated into a normalized global data schema. In addition, our data model allows taking full advantage of the relationships among the integrated data in order to support knowledge discovery.

With the generalized query creation tools it metadata can be used to do analysis on the data warehouse. It can be easily connect to data warehouse.

3.4   GPDW Data Schema and Queries

The schema of the database is modular and centered around each feature. As mentioned in this sections, each imported and integrated features can have singular or multiple attributes and relationships with other feature. The user can start a query from a biological feature or biomedical entity and extract data and its related attributes. Thanks to the modular design of the database, he/she can continue to extract features and the related features iteratively. In order to perform it effectively and efficiently, all suitable indexes have been defined. Vertical and horizontal partition of data have been studied and implemented in order to obtain good running performance for all general queries.

4   Quality Controls of Integrated Data

There are many techniques to improve data quality such as source trustworthiness, error localization and correction and many other [13,14,15]. GPDW framework is focused on the improvement of two data quality dimensions of integrated biomolecular data accuracy and consistency[16].

Possible errors and inconsistencies are detected by using a set of automatic procedures for data quality checking on the public biomolecular databases. These procedures checks data structure and completeness, ontological data consistency, ID format and evolution, unexpected data values and consistency in single and between multiple sources. They also check presence of obligatory attributes of the data according to the conceptual and logical analysis of the data source provided data. When data source provide data do not pass all the above quality checking steps, they are not imported in the data warehouse.

Most of biological databases provides the whole of their data, or part of them, within text files in different formats, including flat, tabular, XML and RDF formats. This allows reimplementing locally the entire database, or part of it, and integrating its data with those from other databases by automatically parsing the data file contents and importing them in a local data warehouse, such as our GPDW. In subsequent versions of such files, data vary according to the data updated in the database. Also changes in data file structure are not infrequent and can produce erroneous data import and integration. To check consistency of both data and their data file structure, we created automatic procedures in which strict checking of data parsed from source data files is enforced and assured by the created data parsers. This enables us to automatically verify absence of inappropriate missed data and inconsistent data structures, and monitor data structure modifications (e.g. variation of expected tags in XML data files, or data columns in tabular data files) in new versions of source data files.

Furthermore, whenever syntactic or semantic information (e.g. tags in XML file format, or an explanatory header in tabular file format) are available for a source data file, we use them for semantic identification and control of imported data. When data structure modifications or incompatible data are found, such data are not imported in the local data warehouse and warnings are shown for their supervised management.

Several different types of IDs or accession numbers are used to identify data in biological databases. Usually, each database adopts its own IDs and provides their mapping or association with the IDs of other most recognized databases (e.g.Ensembl IDs[17], RefSeq IDs[18] or UniProt IDs [19] for proteins). The different types of IDs have several different formats, but most of them have a well

Table 1. Regular expressions of biomolecular databank's IDs are described in GPDW

ID source	ID type	Regular expression
chebi	small molecule	CHEBI:[0-9]+
embl	protein, trancript, dna sequence	[A-Z]{3}[0-9]{5}(.[0-9]+)?
ensembl	protein	ENS[A-Z]{3}P[0-9]{11} ENSP[0-9]{11}
ensembl	transcript	ENST[0-9]{11} , ENS[A-Z]{3}T[0-9]{11}
entrez	transcript, dna sequence, protein	[0-9]+
intact	protein, transcript, dna sequence, small molecule	EBI-[0-9]+
ipi	protein	IPI[0-9]{6,8}
refseq	dna sequence	N[CGSTW]_[0-9]{6,9}.[0-9]+ NZ_[A-Z]{4}[0-9]{8}.[0-9]+ AC_[0-9]{6}.[0-9]+
refseq	protein	[ANXYZ]P_[0-9]{6,9}
refseq	dna sequence	AC_[0-9]{6}.[0-9]+
uniprot	protein	[A-NR-Z][0-9][A-Z][A-Z0-9][A-Z0-9][0-9] [OPQ][0-9][A-Z0-9][A-Z0-9][A-Z0-9][0-9]

defined numerical or alphanumerical format, with a fixed or variable number of digits or characters. These formats can be described with regular expressions; some databases like RefSeq and UniProt provide regular expressions describing their ID formats (Table 1).

5   Integrated Biomolecular Interaction Data

We considered the molecular interactions(MI) data provided by two of well known MI databank MINT [1] and IntAct [2]. The considered databanks have information about molecular interaction (MI) by extracting experimental details from work published in peer-reviewed journals. In other words, the data available in the databases originates entirely from published literature and is manually annotated by expert biologists to a high level of detail, including experimental methods, conditions and interacting domains.

5.1   Conceptual and Logical Analysis

The IntAct and MINT projects support PSI-MI 2.5 standard. The PSI-MI format is a data exchange format for molecular interactions. This paper is focused on mainly MITAB2.6 and PSI-MI XML v2.5. MITAB is data interchange format, a common tab delimited format XML standard is described below:

The Proteomics Standards Initiative Molecular Interaction XML format (PSI-MI)[20] was developed by the Proteomics Standards Initiative, one initiative of the Human Proteome Organisation (HUPO). The aim of the initiative is to develop standards for data representation in proteomics to facilitate data comparison, exchange and verification. One of those is the PSI-MI standard for protein to protein interaction and also other data type interactions. The format is intended for exchange of data on molecular interactions. All data in PSI-MI are structured around an entry. An entry describes one or more interactions that are grouped together for some reason. The "experimentlist" describes experiments and links to publications where the interactions are verified. The pathway itself is described via the "interactorlist", which is a list of proteins participating in the interaction, and the "interactionlist", a list of the actual interactions. For each interactor information about, for instance, substructure can be defined. For each interaction it is possible to set the type of interaction and also a database reference to more information about the interaction. The type of the interaction, e.g. aggregation, is chosen from an externally defined controlled vocabulary, that can be chosen by the user. The participating proteins are described by their names or references to the "interactorlist". It is also possible to set a confidence level for detecting this protein in the experiment, the role of the protein and whether the protein was tagged or over-expressed in the experiment. In addition each interaction has a description of availability and experiments which normally are references to the lists above.

With the well documented definition and with some more analysis on the data, as a first step, the conceptual analysis is done. In the conceptual analysis,

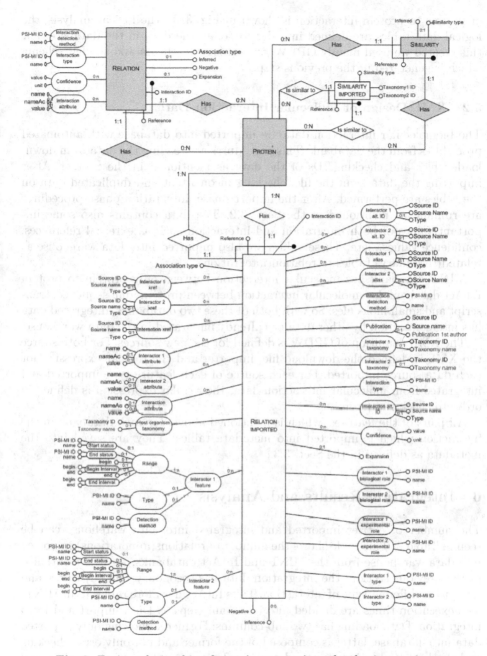

Fig. 3. Entity relationship of protein to protein molecular interaction

we identify the columns and draw and entity-relationship schema show the interaction data columns as conceptually and they are defined with a schema which
is well-matched to the GPDW general schemas. The entity relationship schema

of protein to protein interaction is shown in Fig. 3. In the logical analysis, the logical data tables are defined in order to create the data in the database. For this created we used mainly GPDW general logical schema and the ER schema which is generated in the previous step.

5.2   XML Design of Molecular Interaction Data

The biomolecular interaction data are imported into database with automated procedures from the databank. This procedures are reading the data from downloaded files and checking IDs of the data as mentioned in the Sect. 4. After importing the data from the file, checking inconsistent and duplicated data on the tables are performed. After the import phase, integration phase procedures are running as mentioned in the Sect. 3.2. The data contains also some important values of both integration and interaction such as external references, confidence values,...etc. These values are also imported into data warehouse as related(secondary) tables to relation(integration).

MINT databank has molecular interaction between only protein to protein IntAct databank has molecular interaction between protein, dna sequence, transcript and small molecules. So with both of these two databanks, integrated data has interconnection by other data has already integrated in the data warehouse.

The XML definition of GPDW is defined for the new sources. For both source the XML is defined the download file, importer and the regular expression for each data source imported. For each source of each feature type imported and integrated from molecular interaction data, the regular expression is defined in order to check the errors.

All pairs of the features, which is mentioned above, for each databank in the interaction which is imported into metadata tables. They are saved into the metadata as defined in the Sect. 3.3.

6   Integration Results and Analysis

The number of entries imported and integrated into data warehouse can be seen in Table 2. This table shows the number of relations(annotations) imported into data warehouse from the MINT and IntAct databanks. As it is mentioned in the previous section, the integration data has secondary(related) tables and IntAct has different type of interaction. Thus IntAct has more tables than MINT. The execution times are divided into two main steps as Data import and Data integration. Data loading has two sub-columns: Former is showing only imported data into database, latter is composed of the former and not only error checking and duplicates cleaning on the data but also the creation of constraints and index on the tables. The integration column contains the execution times of second(integration) phase. The system is executed on Intel XEON CPU E5320 1.86 GHz with 16 GB of RAM, running a Windows 2008 Server Edition:SP2 using PostgreSQL database management system. All the processes is running on Java 1.6 64 bit Server Edition. With our current system, the total execution

Table 2. Number of entries integrated and processes' execution time

Databank	Content Type	Number of tables	Number of relation entries	Number of all entries	Execution time (sec)		
					Data loading		Data integration
MINT	binary	11	116,880	1,630,941	280	444	108
	complex	11	8,126	137,184	23		
IntAct	both	98	248,817	12,353,159	1,789	8,506	959

Table 3. Number relation of entries integrated

(a) *Between same type of relation*

Relation type	Number of relation entries	Number of distinct feature entries
protein - protein	125,006*	30,815*
	239,271	52,480
dna sequence - dna sequence	10	15
transcript - transcript	11	14
small molecule - small molecule	23	19

(b) *Between different type of relation*

Relation type	Number of relation entries	Number of distinct first feature entries	Number of distinct second feature entries
dna sequence - protein	987	349	420
transcript - protein	558	81	420
protein - small molecule	1,936	717	129
dna sequence - small molecule	20	10	4
transcript - small molecule	1	1	1

* data.from MINT; all the others from IntAct

time is 02:46:57 and total number of entries is 14,121,284. Although it is not short, the total processing time is acceptable because of handling and processing of the highly amount of data.

In the Tables 3, the number tuples can be easily seen on different relation types. These tables contain the number of relations and the number of distinct features(interactors). It is easy to see that the number of protein to protein interactions are much more than the others. There is quite high amount of distinct proteins, that are imported into database. These proteins are interconnected to other biomolecular feature types that are already imported into database.

In the Table 4, the integrated protein to protein interaction data is interconnected to biomolecular features in the database. The relationship between feature and theirs sources are as follows: Enzyme from ExPASy Proteomics Server[21], Pathway from KEGG [22], and Genetic Disorder from OMIM [23]. And also the

Table 4. Number of entries of the features that are interconnected to proteins, defined in protein to protein interaction

Feature	Number of annotations	Number of distinct protein	Number of feature items
Enzyme	8,121	7,549	1,512
Biological Process	112,789	34,817	1,252
Molecular Function	173,804	44,250	3,623
Cellular Component	161,739	38,829	6,790
Pathway	27,997	9,808	305
Genetic Disorder	5,102	1,532	1,795

table contains the data of Gene Ontology(GO) [24] and Reactome [25]. The total number of protein interactions is 364,277 and the total number of distinct proteins of the interactions is 58,225. More than 60% of proteins integrated to data warehouse are connected to Biological Process, Molecular Function and Cellular Component. The around 13% of proteins has interconnection with enzyme and around 17% of proteins has interconnection with pathway. The proteins from molecular interaction has relation to 33% of enzymes and 20% of genetic disorder in the database.

7   Conclusions

In this paper, we described the integration and quality checking of biomolecular interaction data to Genomic and Proteomic Data Warehouse(GPDW) and the integrated biomolecular interaction data have a connection to the other biomolecular features currently available in the data warehouse. The analysis of interaction data with the other biomolecular feature is highly enough, in other words the interconnection of the newly integrated data is highly. With integration of biomolecular interaction data, GPDW provides better support many algorithms and helps researchers to prediction of new algorithms.

Acknowledgments. This research is part of the Search Computing project (2008-2013) funded by the European Research Council (ERC), IDEAS Advanced Grant.

References

1. Ceol, A., Chatr Aryamontri, A., Licata, L., Peluso, D., Briganti, L., Perfetto, L., Castagnoli, L., Cesareni, G.: MINT, the molecular interaction database: 2009 update. Nucleic Acids Res. 38(Database issue), D532–D539 (2009)
2. Aranda, B., Achuthan, P., Alam-Faruque, Y., Armean, I., Bridge, A., Derow, C., Feuermann, M., Ghanbarian, A.T., Kerrien, S., Khadake, J., et al.: The IntAct molecular interaction database in 2010. Nucleic Acids Res. 38, D525–D531 (2010)

3. Jayapandian, M., Chapman, A., Tarcea, V.G., Yu, C., Elkiss, A., Ianni, A., Liu, B., Nandi, A., Santos, C., Andrews, P., et al.: Michigan Molecular Interactions (MiMI): putting the jigsaw puzzle together. Nucleic Acids Res. 35, 566–571 (2007)
4. Kerrien, S., Orchard, S., Montecchi-Palazzi, L., Aranda, B., Quinn, A.F., Vinod, N., Bader, G.D., Xenarios, I., Wojcik, J., Sherman, D., et al.: Broadening the horizonlevel 2.5 of the HUPO-PSI format for molecular interactions. BMC Biol. 5, 44 (2007)
5. Orchard, S., Kerrien, S., Jones, P., Ceol, A., Chatr-Aryamontri, A., Salwinski, L., Nerothin, J., Hermjakob, H.: Submit your interaction data the IMEx way: a step by step guide to trouble-free deposition. Proteomics 7(suppl. 1), 28–34 (2007)
6. Kulikova, T., Akhtar, R., Aldebert, P., Althorpe, N., Andersson, M., Baldwin, A., Bates, K., Bhattacharyya, S., Bower, L., Browne, P., et al.: EMBL Nucleotide Sequence Database in 2006. Nucleic Acids Res. 35, D16–D20 (2007)
7. Benson, D.A., Karsch-Mizrachi, I., Lipman, D.J., Ostell, J., Wheeler, D.L.: GenBank. Nucleic Acids Res. 36, 25–30 (2008)
8. Sugawara, H., Ogasawara, O., Okubo, K., Gojobori, T., Tateno, Y.: DDBJ with new system and face. Nucleic Acids Res. 36, D22–D24 (2008)
9. Kasprzyk, A., Keefe, D., Smedley, D., London, D., Spooner, W., Melsopp, C., et al.: EnsMart: A Generic System for Fast and Flexible Access to Biological Data. Genome Res. 14(1), 160–169 (2004)
10. Lee, T.J., Pouliot, Y., Wagner, V., Gupta, P., Stringer-Calvert, D.W., Tenenbaum, J.D., Karp, P.D.: BioWarehouse: A Bioinformatics Database Warehouse Toolkit. BMC Bioinformatics 7(170), 1–14 (2006)
11. Masseroli, M., Martucci, D., Pinciroli, F.: GFINDer: Genome Function INtegrated Discoverer through dynamic annotation, statistical analysis, and mining. Nucleic Acids Res. 32(suppl. 2), W293–W300 (2004)
12. Masseroli, M., Galati, O., Pinciroli, F.: GFINDer: genetic disease and phenotype location statistical analysis and mining of dynamically annotated gene lists. Nucleic Acids Res. 33(suppl. 2), W717–W723 (2005)
13. Batini, C., Scannapieco, M.: Data Quality: Concepts, Methodologies and Techniques. Springer (2006)
14. Batini, C., Cappiello, C., Francalanci, C., Maurino, A.: Methodologies for Data Quality Assessment and Improvement. ACM Comput. Surv. 41(3), 16, 1–52 (2009)
15. Madnick, S.E., Wang, R.Y., Lee, Y.W., Zhu, H.: Overview and Framework for Data and Information Quality Research. ACM J. Data Inform. Quality 1(1), 2, 1–22 (2009)
16. Ghisalberti, G., Masseroli, M., Tettamanti, L.: Quality Controls in Integrative Approaches to Detect Errors and Inconsistencies in Biological Databases. J. Integr. Bioinform. 7(3), 2010–2119 (2010)
17. Hubbard, T.J., Aken, B.L., Ayling, S., Ballester, B., Beal, K., Bragin, E., Brent, S., Chen, Y., Clapham, P., Clarke, L., et al.: Ensembl 2009. Nucleic Acids Res. 37(Database issue), 690–697 (2009)
18. Pruitt, K.D., Tatusova, T., Maglott, D.R.: NCBI reference sequences (RefSeq): a Curated Non-Redundant Sequence Database of Genomes, Transcripts and Proteins. Nucleic Acids Res. 35(Database issue), D61–D65 (2007)
19. UniProt Consortium. The Universal Protein Resource (UniProt) 2009. Nucleic Acids Res. 37(Database issue), D169–D174 (2009)
20. Hermjakob, H., Montecchi-Palazzi, L., Bader, G., Wojcik, J., Salwinski, L., Ceol, A., Moore, S., Orchard, S., Sarkans, U., et al.: The HUPO PSI's molecular interaction format–a community standard for the representation of protein interaction data. Nature Biotechnology 22(2), 177–183 (2004)

21. Gasteiger, E., Gattiker, A., Hoogland, C., Ivanyi, I., Appel, R.D., Bairoch, A.: Ex-PASy: the proteomics server for in-depth protein knowledge and analysis. Nucleic Acids Res. 1, 31(13), 3784–3788 (2003)
22. Kanehisa, M., Goto, S.: KEGG: Kyoto Encyclopedia of Genes and Genomes. Nucleic Acids Res. 28(1), 27–30 (2000)
23. Amberger, J., Bocchini, C.A., Scott, A.F., Hamosh, A.: McKusick's Online Mendelian Inheritance in Man (OMIM). Nucleic Acids Res. 37(Database issue), 793–796 (2009)
24. Ashburner, M., Ball, C.A., Blake, J.A., Botstein, D., Butler, H., Cherry, J.M., et al.: Gene Ontology: Tool for the Unification of Biology. Nat. Genet. 25(1), 25–29 (2000)
25. Matthews, L., Gopinath, G., Gillespie, M., Caudy, M., Croft, D., de Bono, B., et al.: Reactome Knowledgebase of Human Biological Pathways and Processes. Nucleic Acids Res. 37(Database issue), D619–D622 (2009)

Machine-Learning Methods to Predict Protein Interaction Sites in Folded Proteins

Castrense Savojardo[1,2], Piero Fariselli[1,2], Damiano Piovesan[1],
Pier Luigi Martelli[1], and Rita Casadio[1]

[1] Biocomputing Group University of Bologna
via Irnerio 42, 40126 Bologna, Italy
[2] Department of Computer Science, University of Bologna
via Mura Anteo Zamboni 7, 40127 Bologna, Italy
{savojard,piero,piovesan,gigi,casadio}@biocomp.unibo.it
http://www.biocomp.unibo.it

Abstract. A reliable predictor of protein-protein interaction sites is necessary to investigate and model protein functional interaction networks. Hidden Markov Support Vector Machines (HM-SVM) have been shown to be among the best performing methods on this task. Furthermore, it has been noted that the performance of a predictor improves when its input takes advantage of the difference between observed and predicted residue solvent accessibility. In this paper, for first time, we combine these elements and we present ISPRED2, a new HM-SVM-based method that overpasses the state of the art performance (Q2=0.71 and correlation=0.43). ISPRED2 consists of a sets of Python scripts aimed at integrating the different third-party software to obtain the final prediction.

Keywords: Hidden Markov Support Vector Machines, Prediction of Interaction sites, Protein-Protein Interaction, Machine Learning, Evolutionary Information, Solvent Accessibility.

1 Introduction

Identifying protein-protein interaction sites on a protein surface is a fundamental step for investigating protein functions and interactions. In the last years, several computational tools have been introduced to address this problem and described in several reviews [33,9,11]. The different methods are based on Neural Networks [32,12,13,22,6,23,24], Support Vector Machines [17,4,3,26,7,31,10,29,19,21], Random Forest [5,27], Conditional Random Fields [17], Hidden Markov Support Vector Machines [20] and meta predictors or ensemble methods [25,8]. A direct comparison of the different methods is difficult since the various authors adopted different data sets, different measures of performances and different definitions of interaction sites. Nonetheless, from the previous efforts, we are able to identify some relevant features that a predictor of protein interaction sites, starting from the protein 3D structure, should include [33,11]. First of all, input has to

E. Biganzoli et al. (Eds.): CIBB 2011, LNBI 7548, pp. 127–135, 2012.

incorporate evolutionary information, better if in the form of Position Specific Scoring Matrix (computed with PSI-BLAST). Moreover solvent accessibility (or its variants, such as protrusion index or residue depth) plays a relevant role [11]. A further improvement was achieved by exploiting the information derived from the difference between the observed and predicted residue accessibility [24]. It was also noted that the relation between labels of neighboring residues is useful for prediction of protein binding sites [20]. For this reason HM-SVMs are the best performing method when input consists of spatial neighbors (encoded as sequence profile vectors) and computed residue accessibility [20]. Finally, the prediction performance is increased by averaging over the predictions of spatial neighbors [13]. Here we implement ISPRED2 a new method that for the first time incorporates all the above-mentioned predictive strategies in order to achieve the state of the art performance.

2   Dataset

For training and testing our method we adopted the data set selected by Liu and co-workers [20] with a low level of sequence identity. Starting from the protein structures included in the PDB, multi-chains, non-NMR structures and structures with resolution < 4 Å were retained. Protein chains of <40 residues were discarded. The PQS web-server [14] was also checked to retain only biologically functional complexes and avoid the presence of crystal packing ones. In order to reduce redundancy, the NCBI BLASTClust program [1] was adopted to cluster sequences with identity above 25% over at least 90% of the pairwise alignment length. This means that two protein chains falling into different clusters have pairwise sequence identity below 25%. 1,124 chains are collected by selecting one representative for each cluster. A 5-fold cross-validation of the dataset is adopted to score the performance of the new prediction method.

3   Definition of Protein Surface, Interaction Contacts and Patches

In order to locate patches of interaction over the surface, we adopted a simplified representation of the protein structure. The entire residue information is condensed in its carbon alpha (CA) so that the overall protein structure is the collection of the three CA coordinates of each of its residues. This representation is the simplest one, since one residue corresponds to only one atom and also because it is rather independent of the conformational changes that eventually can occur to a given side chain upon complex formation. Nevertheless it contains all the sufficient information to investigate surface interactions [12]. Following this definition of protein structure, two residues from two chains are defined to be in contact when the Euclidean distance between their CA atoms is below a fixed threshold. After a comparison with the interaction sites obtained using a complete representation of the protein structure (namely, each residue with all its atoms), the threshold has been fixed to 1.2nm [12]. Accordingly, the protein surface is then the collection of the CA coordinates belonging to the exposed residues. Each protein complex has been split into different files containing only the coordinates of a single chain and solvent exposure has separately been computed for each chain, using the DSSP program [16]. For the definition of an exposed or buried residue, we selected a cut-off of 16% of the relative solvent accessibility [12].

4   ISPRED2 Implementation

Evolutionary information is presently encoded in a Position Specific Scoring Matrix (PSSM), a type of scoring matrix used in protein alignment search that stores amino acid propensities for each position in a protein multiple sequence alignment. We compute PSSM matrices using three rounds of PSI-BLAST for each sequence with the E-value cut-off set to 0.001.

Our method is based on a Hidden Markov Support Vector Machine (HM-SVM). As previously described [28], HM-SVM is a machine learning discriminative technique that combines two learning algorithms, Support Vector Machine (SVM) and Hidden Markov Model (HMM). While exploiting the basic discriminative features of SVMs, it also preserves the Markov chain dependency at the basis of HMMs. In this way higher order relations between surface residues can be taken into account. The SVM^{hmm} software (http://www.cs.cornell.edu/ People/ tj/ svm_light/ svm_hmm.html) has been trained/tested to predict whether each surface residue (represented by a CA atom) is in contact or not with another protein. Briefly, the method is fed using a 17 residue-long window, centered on the surface residue to be predicted that is surrounded by the 16 spatially nearest neighbors (whose CA Euclidean distance with respect to the CA of the central residue is below 1.2 nm). Each residue within the protein structure is encoded with the information contained in the corresponding structural window. It is important to note that residues included in the input window are close in space but not necessarily adjacent in the linear sequence. For this reason, they represent an approximation of the local surface. A recent method highlighted the fundamental role of Relative Solvent Accessibility (RSA) as a fingerprint for interacting sites [24]. On the basis of this observation the central residue is also encoded with the average of the differences between the predicted and the observed relative solvent accessibility of the 17 residues $(i = 1, W)$ within the window as:

$$dRSA_{av} = \frac{1}{W} \sum_{i=1}^{W} RSA_{pred}(i) - RSA_{obs}(i) \tag{1}$$

The predictions are obtained with the SABLE program [30] that provides reliable predictions consistent with the observed RSA and that, among RSA predictors [24], provides the best discrimination between interacting and non interacting sites. Thus, each residue within the window is coded as a vector of 21 elements, whose values are the propensities in the corresponding positions as extracted from the computed PSSM and the computed dRSAav. The system has a binary output: 1 for predicted interacting surface residues, 0 for predicted non-interacting surface residues.

To assess the effective relevance of the Markov model in the prediction we compare the results with the best performing Neural Network system trained with the same input encoding provided to the HM-SVM.

5   Measures of Accuracy

The performance of the method is evaluated using the following measures. The overall accuracy ($Q2$) is defined as

$$Q2 = \frac{p}{N} \tag{2}$$

where p is the number of correct predictions and N is the total number of predictions.

The Matthews correlation coefficient (MCC) for a given class s (in our case, interacting residue and non interacting residue) is defined as:

$$MCC = \frac{p(s)n(s) - u(s)o(s)}{\sqrt{(p(s) + u(s))(p(s) + o(s))(n(s) + u(s))(n(s) + o(s))}} \tag{3}$$

where $p(s)$ and $n(s)$ are respectively the true positive and true negative predictions for class s, while $o(s)$ and $u(s)$ are the numbers of false positives and false negatives. The sensitivity for each class s is defined as

$$Sn(s) = \frac{p(s)}{p(s) + u(s)} \tag{4}$$

The specificity is the probability of correct predictions and it is expressed as follows:

$$Sp(s) = \frac{p(s)}{p(s) + o(s)} \tag{5}$$

Finally $F1$ index is computed using Sn and Sp as follows:

$$F1 = \frac{Sp(s) * Sn(s)}{(Sp(s) + Sn(s))} \tag{6}$$

6   ISPRED2 at Work

Training and testing our method is performed using the dataset recently introduced by Liu and co-workers [20]. In order to generate a reliable testing procedure based on 5-fold cross-validation we split the set into five subsets constraining that sequence similarities between each pair of sequences from two different subsets is less than 25%. Here we consider as interaction sites the surface residues in contact with at least one residue of the other chain (distance between CA <1.2nm) [12]. Different definitions of interaction sites do not affect the overall performance (Table 3). We evaluated different input encoding schemes: i) Profile+RSA = sequence profile of the neighboring residues + relative solvent accessibility (RSA) as computed by the DSSP program [16]; ii) PSSM+RSA=Position Specific Scoring Matrix as computed by PSI-BLAST (-Q option)+RSA; iii) PSSM+dSA=PSSM+the difference between the observed and predicted (with SABLE) residue solvent accessibility [24]. ISPRED2 is based on a Hidden Markov Support Vector Machine (HM-SVM). HM-SVM exploits the basic discriminative features of SVMs and preserves the Markov chain dependency at the basis of HMMs. In this way higher order relations between surface residues can be taken into account. HM-SVM software (SVM^{hmm}) has been trained/tested to predict whether each surface residue is in contact or not. The performance of the HM-SVM is tested in comparison with a Neural Network based method (NN) (described in [12] and here retrained by adopting the same cross-validation procedure).

Optimal NN architectures are compared to optimal HM-SVM models (Table 1). As an example, in Table 2 we report the ISPRED2 cross-validation accuracy as a function of the dimension of the input window. From Table 2, it is evident that there is a weak dependence of the method accuracy on the dimension of the input window, with a slight higher performance around an input window of 17 spatial neighbors. The same picture holds also for the other machine learning models.

In Table 1, HM-SVMs perform better than NNs, indicating they can detect relationships between consecutive neighboring residues. Furthermore encoding based on PSSM has a stronger predictive power if compared to the simple sequence profile (Profile). The difference between the predicted and observed residue accessibility (dSA) significantly improves the method performance. Averaging over the predictions of surface nearest neighbours (< (PSSM+dSA)>) further increases the performance of both methods achieving a correlation coefficient >40%.

7   The Effect of the Definition of Interaction Patches

In this paper we used a definition of interaction site based on the CA-CA distance (see section 3). However, other authors adopted a different definition of interacting residues based on the difference between the accessible surface areas (ASA) of exposed residue. In particular, Jones and Thornton (1997) [15] defined as interacting those residues with side-chains possessing an ASA that decreased by >1 Å^2 on complexation. The accessible surface areas (ASA) were calculated using the program ACCESS[34]. Similarly, Liu et al., 2009 [20], considered the same measure to define interface residues but they computed the ASA using the DSSP program [16]. In order to study the effect of the different definitions of interacting residues, we tested ISPRED2 in cross-validation using the three different definitions described above (Table 3). From Table 3, it is clear that, at least for the data set at hand, there are no significant differences in the adoption

Table 1. Cross-validation performance of the different methods

Method	Q2(%)	Sp(%)	Sn(%)	MCC(%)	Encoding
NN	64	55	77	31	(Profile+RSA)
NN	66	62	84	35	(PSSM+RSA)
NN	69	65	82	39	(PSSM+dSA)
NN	69	65	85	40	<(PSSM+dSA)>*
HM-SVM	68	70	65	36	(Profile+RSA)
HM-SVM	70	72	66	40	(PSSM+RSA)
HM-SVM	71	73	67	42	(PSSM+dSA)
ISPRED2	71	73	68	43	<(PSSM+dSA)>*

*=prediction averaged over a window of 11 neighbors. NN= neural network as described in [12]. HM-SVM=Hidden Markov Support Vector Machine. Q2=overall accuracy. Sp= interaction site specificity. Sn=interaction site sensitivity. MCC=Matthews' correlation coefficient. Profile=sequence profile. PSSM=position specific scoring matrix as computed by BLAST.

Table 2. ISPRED2 performance as a function of the number of spatial neighbors in the input window

Window	Q2(%)	Sp(%)	Sn(%)	MCC(%)
5	69.0	71.5	63.8	38.2
7	69.8	72.1	65.0	39.7
11	70.9	73.0	67.0	42.0
13	70.7	72.7	66.9	41.5
15	71.3	73.2	67.8	42.7
17	71.4	73.2	68.1	43.0
19	71.2	73.3	67.9	43.0

Table 3. Comparison of PredPPI (HM-SVM) performance as function of different definitions of interaction sites

Interaction site definition	Q2(%)	Sp(%)	Sn(%)	MCC(%)
Liu et al. 2009 [20]	71	73	67	43
Jones and Thornton 1997 [15]	71	73	67	42
Fariselli et al. 2002(This paper)	71	73	68	43

of one of the three definitions. This means that the three different interaction site definitions describe almost the same kind of physical features, even though there are small variations in the number and type of involved residues.

8 Comparison with Other Method

Although performance comparison between our method and previously developed methods is rather difficult owing to the different data sets (with the exception of Liu et al., 2009[20]), in Table 4 we report the accuracy of ISPRED2 with respect to other recently developed machine-learning approaches. Table 4 shows that. ISPRED2 improves over the recently introduced predictors of interaction sites (Table 4). This achievement is due to the fact that ISPRED2 exploits relevant input features (difference between predicted and observed solvent accessibility and evolutionary information), includes temporal chain dependency among consecutive accessible residues (by means of the HM-SVMs) and takes advantage of a smoothing approach (by averaging the different predictions that are in their spatial proximity).

Table 4. Comparison with other recent methods

Method	Q2(%)	Sp(%)	Sn(%)	MCC(%)	F1(%)
Wang et al. (2006) [31]	NA	65	69	28	67
Nguyen-Rajapakse (2006) [21]	NA	93	36	33	52
Deng et al. (2009) [8]	NA	63	77	35	69
Liu et al. (2009) [20]*	69	54	59	33	56
ISPRED2 *	71	73	68	43	71

*= On the same data set. The reported performances are taken from the corresponding papers (with the exception of ISPRED2). NA=not available.

9 Conclusions

In this paper, we implement ISPRED2 a new HM-SVM-based method that takes advantage of the difference between observed and predicted residue solvent accessibility. In cross-validation, ISPRED2 overpasses the state of the art performance achieving an overall accuracy of 0.71 with a correlation coefficient of 0.43. ISPRED2 is therefore advisable for determining over the protein structure putative interaction sites and it can be applied in structural Systems Biology studies aiming at validating at a molecular level protein-protein interaction networks [2].

Acknowledgments. CS is the recipient of a MIUR (Ministero Istruzione Universit Ricerca) fellowship supporting his PhD program. The project is partially funded by a MIUR-FIRB grant for the LIBI project delivered to RC.

References

1. Altschul, S.F., Gish, W., Miller, W., Myers, E.W., Lipman, D.J.: Basic local alignment search tool. Journal of Molecular Biology 213(3), 403–410 (1990)
2. Bartoli, L., Martelli, P.L., Rossi, I., Fariselli, P., Casadio, R.: The prediction of protein-protein interacting sites in genome-wide protein interaction networks: The Test Case of the Human Cell Cycle. Curr. Protein Pept. Sci. 11, 601–608 (2010)
3. Bordner, A.J., Abagyan, R.: Statistical analysis and prediction of protein-protein interfaces. Proteins 60(3), 353–366 (2005)

4. Bradford, J.R., Westhead, D.R.: Improved prediction of protein-protein binding sites using a support vector machines approach. Bioinformatics 21(8), 1487–1494 (2005)
5. Chen, X.W., Jeong, J.C.: Sequence-based prediction of protein interaction sites with an integrative method. Bioinformatics 25(5), 585–591 (2009)
6. Chen, H., Zhou, H.X.: Prediction of interface residues in protein-protein complexes by a consensus neural network method: test against NMR data. Proteins 61(1), 21–35 (2005)
7. Chung, J.L., Wang, W., Bourne, P.E.: Exploiting sequence and structure homologs to identify protein-protein binding sites. Proteins 62(3), 630–640 (2006)
8. Deng, L., Guan, J., Dong, Q., Zhou, S.: Prediction of protein-protein interaction sites using an ensemble method. BMC Bioinformatics 10, 426 (2009)
9. DeVries, S.J., Bonvin, A.M.J.J.: How Proteins Get in Touch: Interface Prediction in the Study of Biomolecular Complexes. Current Protein and Peptide Science, 394–406 (2008)
10. Dong, Q., Wang, X., Lin, L., Guan, Y.: Exploiting residue-level and profile-level interface propensities for usage in binding sites prediction of proteins. BMC Bioinformatics 8, 147 (2007)
11. Ezkurdia, I., Bartoli, L., Fariselli, P., Casadio, R., Valencia, A., Tress, M.L.: Progress and challenges in predicting protein-protein interaction sites. Brief Bioinform. 10(3), 233–246 (2009)
12. Fariselli, P., Pazos, F., Valencia, A., Casadio, R.: Prediction of protein–protein interaction sites in heterocomplexes with neural networks. Eur. J. Biochem. 269(5), 1356–1361 (2002)
13. Fariselli, P., Zauli, A., Rossi, I., Finelli, M., Martelli, P.L., Casadio, R.: A neural network method to improve prediction of protein-protein interaction sites in heterocomplexes. In: IEEE Int. Workshop on Neural Network on Signal Processing 2003, Toulouse (FRANCE), pp. 33–41. IEEE Press (2003)
14. Henrick, K., Thornton, J.M.P.Q.S.: A protein quaternary structure file server. Trends Biochem. Sci. 23(9), 302–305 (1998)
15. Jones, S., Thornton, J.M.: Analysis of protein-protein interaction sites using surface patches. J. Mol. Biol. 272, 121–132 (1997)
16. Kabsch, W., Sander, C.: Dictionary of protein secondary structure: pattern recognition of hydrogen-bonded and geometrical features. Biopolymers 22(12), 2577–2637 (1983)
17. Koike, A., Takagi, T.: Prediction of protein-protein interaction sites using support vector machines. Protein Eng. Des. Sel. 17(2), 165–173 (2004)
18. Li, M.H., Lin, L., Wang, X.L., Liu, T.: Protein-protein interaction site prediction based on conditional random fields. Bioinformatics 23(5), 597–604 (2007)
19. Li, N., Sun, Z., Jiang, F.: Prediction of protein-protein binding site by using core interface residue and support vector machine. BMC Bioinformatics 9, 553 (2008)
20. Liu, B., Wang, X., Lin, L., Tang, B., Dong, Q., Wang, X.: Prediction of protein binding sites in protein structures using hidden Markov support vector machine. BMC Bioinformatics 10, 381 (2003)
21. Nguyen, M.N., Rajapakse, J.C.: Protein-Protein Interface Residue Prediction with SVM Using Evolutionary Profiles and Accessible Surface Areas. In: CIBCB 2006, pp. 1–5 (2006)
22. Ofran, Y., Rost, B.: Predicted protein-protein interaction sites from local sequence information. FEBS Lett. 544(1-3), 236–239 (2003)
23. Ofran, Y., Rost, B.: ISIS: interaction sites identified from sequence. Bioinformatics 23(ECCB 2006), e13–e16 (2006)

24. Porollo, A., Meller, J.: Prediction-based fingerprints of protein-protein interactions. Proteins 66(3), 630–645 (2007)
25. Qin, S., Zhou, H.X.: meta-PPISP: a meta web server for protein-protein interaction site prediction. Bioinformatics 23(24), 3386–3387 (2007)
26. Res, I., Mihalek, I., Lichtarge, O.: An evolution based classifier for prediction of protein interfaces without using protein structures. Bioinformatics 21(10), 2496–2501 (2005)
27. Šikić, M., Tomić, S., Vlahoviček, K.: Prediction of Protein-Protein Interaction Sites in Sequences and 3D Structures by Random Forests. PLoS Comput. Biol. 5(1), e1000278 (2009)
28. Tsochantaridis, I., Joachims, T., Hofmann, T., Altun, Y.: Large Margin Methods for Structured and Interdependent Output Variables. Journal of Machine Learning Research 6, 1453–1484 (2005)
29. Yan, C., Dobbs, D., Honavar, V.: A two-stage classifier for identification of protein-protein interface residues. Bioinformatics 20(suppl. 1), I371–I378 (2004)
30. Wagner, M., Adamczak, R., Porollo, A., Meller, J.: Linear regression models for solvent accessibility prediction in proteins. Journal of Computational Biology 12, 355–369 (2005)
31. Wang, B., Chen, P., Huang, D.S., Li, J.J., Lok, T.M., Lyu, M.R.: Predicting protein interaction sites from residue spatial sequence profile and evolution rate. FEBS Lett. 580(2), 380–384 (2006)
32. Zhou, H.X., Shan, Y.: Prediction of protein interaction sites from sequence profile and residue neighbor list. Proteins 44(3), 336–343 (2001)
33. Zhou, H.X., Qin, S.: Interaction-site prediction for protein complexes: a critical assessment. Bioinformatics 23(17), 2203–2220 (2007)
34. Hubbard, S.J.: ACCESS: A Computer Program Written in C. University College, London (1989)

Complementing Kernel-Based Visualization of Protein Sequences with Their Phylogenetic Tree

Martha Ivón Cárdenas[1], Alfredo Vellido[1], Iván Olier[2], Xavier Rovira[3], and Jesús Giraldo[4]

[1] Departament de Llenguatges i Sistemes Informàtics,
Universitat Politècnica de Catalunya 08034, Barcelona - Spain
avellido@lsi.upc.edu

[2] School of Psychological Sciences, The University of Manchester M13 9PL,
Manchester - United Kingdomand
Ivan.Olier@manchester.ac.uk

[3] Department of Molecular Pharmacology Institute of Functional Genomics (IGF)
CNRS UMR5203, INSERM U661, University of Montpellier 141 rue de la Cardonille
F34094 Montpellier cedex 5, France
xavier.rovira@igf.cnrs.fr

[4] Institut de Neurociències, Unitat de Bioestadística,
Universitat Autònoma de Barcelona, 08193, Bellaterra (Barcelona) - Spain
Jesus.Giraldo@uab.es

Abstract. The world of pharmacology is becoming increasingly dependent on the advances in the fields of genomics and proteomics. This dependency brings about the challenge of finding robust methods to analyze the complex data they generate. In this brief paper, we focus on the analysis of a specific type of proteins, the G protein-couple receptors, which are the target for over 15% of current drugs. We describe a kernel method of the manifold learning family for the analysis and intuitive visualization of their protein amino acid symbolic sequences. This method is shown to reveal the grouping structure of the sequences in a way that closely resembles the corresponding phylogenetic trees.

Keywords: Kernel GTM, Phylogenetic Tree, Data Visualization, GPCR, Protein Sequence.

1 Introduction

Just over 10 years have elapsed since the publication of the first draft of the human genome decoding. The detailed description of the human genome is a milestone for science in general and for medicine in particular. It has opened the doors to new approaches to the investigation of pathologies and, with it, to the advent of personalized medicine.

It also means that medicine is quickly becoming a data-intensive area of research. One in which new data-acquisition technologies and a wider variety of

E. Biganzoli et al. (Eds.): CIBB 2011, LNBI 7548, pp. 136–149, 2012.

investigative goals coalesce to make it one of the most important challenges for intelligent data analysis [1]. Genomics and proteomics have contributed the most to this data deluge. As explicitly stated in [2]: "[...] the need to process terabytes of information has become the rigueur for many labs engaged in genomic research".

Arguably, drug research has contributed more to the progress of medicine during the past century than any other scientific factor. One of the main areas of drug research is related to the analysis of proteins. The function of the proteins depends directly on their 3D structure, which is embodied in their amino acid sequence. Such 3D structure is difficult to unravel, but protein sequences, which are easy to acquire, can be an alternative target for our analyses.

The gene-family distribution of targets by drug substance reveals that more than 50% of drugs target only four key gene families, from which almost the 30% correspond to G protein-couple receptors (GPCRs). This family regulates the function of most cells in living organisms and is the target of our study.

The challenge of analyzing GPCR protein sequences invites us to go beyond traditional statistics and resort to computational intelligence approaches. In particular, statistical pattern recognition and machine learning methods bear the potential to deal robustly with this non-trivial type of data. Sound statistical principles are essential to trust the evidence base built with any computational analysis of medical data [4]. Statistical machine learning methods are already establishing themselves in the more general field of bioinformatics [5].

The grouping of GPCRs into types and subtypes based on sequence analysis may significantly contribute to helping drug design and to a better understanding of the molecular processes involved in receptor signaling, both in normal and pathological conditions. The current study is specifically motivated by the need of a robust probabilistic method for grouping and visualizing symbolic protein sequences. As stated in [6], there is no biologically-relevant manner of representing the symbolic sequences describing proteins using real-valued vectors. This does not preclude the possibility of assessing the similarity between such sequences. Kernel methods can be used to this purpose if understood as similarity measures.

In this work, we show that an unsupervised kernel-based method of the manifold learning family, oriented to data visualization, is able to reveal the structure of GPCR types and subtypes in surprising detail. Here, we report evidence that this fine structure closely resembles the organization of these types and subtypes in their corresponding phylogenetic trees. The reported results support the importance of the simultaneous visualization and grouping of the protein sequences in the quest for interpretability.

2   Proteins and Pharmacology

As stated in [7], there is a paradox in the fact that an industry such as pharma that spends billions of US dollars yearly on R+D has not been able to generate substantial knowledge about the set of molecular targets that are the object of its products. For this reason, drug target discovery has of late received much attention in different areas of biochemistry-related drug research.

In biochemistry, a receptor is a protein located in the membrane or inside the cell, to which signalling molecules may attach. Certain types of receptors are the targets with the most number of drugs approved. The idea of a receptor as a selective binding site for chemotherapeutic agents and its pharmacological characterization in almost all organs, including the brain, has provided the basis for a large number of very diverse drugs. Cell membrane receptors, largely GPCRs, constitute the largest subgroup with 45% of all targets. They represent very attractive drug targets in the case of allergies, cancer, autoimmune diseases, or asthma.

GPCRs consist of a single protein chain that crosses the membrane seven times [8]. They constitute the most abundant family of membrane receptors and one of the largest in the whole human genome [9]. The great importance of the GPCR family comes from its ubiquity in terms of location and function. Nearly a thousand GPCRs exist, mediating a host of molecular physiological functions by serving as receptors for hormones, neurotransmitters, cytokines, lipids, small molecules, and various sensory signals (such as light and odors), to name a few.

All GPCRs share a common general protein structure. The seven transmembrane helices are connected between them by three intracellular and three extracellular loops with varying lengths for each receptor subtype.

The GPCRDB[1] [8], a database system for GPCRs, divides the GPCR superfamily into five major families (A to E) based on the ligand types, functions, and sequence similarities (summarized in table 1). Within the families, proteins are further divided into groups (types and subtypes) which bind common agents on the extracellular side of the membrane. The evolutionary relationship between groups is not known; they may have diverged from a common ancestor or be the result of convergent evolution, in which functional constraints lead to unrelated proteins from different organisms with the same design.

Table 1. G-protein coupled receptor families

Superfamily	Description
Family A	Receptors related to Rhodopsin and the beta2-adrenergic Receptors
Family B	Receptors related to the Calcitonin and PTH/PTHrP Receptors
Family C	Receptors related to the Metabotropic Receptors
Family D	Receptors related to the pheromone Receptors
Family E	Receptors related to the cAMP Receptors

While the identification of the function of GPCR sequences has a great importance in biomedical and pharmaceutical research, identifying and classifying this membrane protein superfamily is a difficult task due to the high levels of divergence observed among the GPCR family members. Therefore, it becomes

---

[1] http://www.gpcr.org/7tm/

important that there be a way to accurately and efficiently identify any new GPCRs from genomic data. As a consequence, this would benefit the pharmaceutical research and give us a better understanding of GPCR functions. GPCRs are used in this study due to their scientific importance, and also as an example of highly diverged protein families.

In this study, we will pay special attention to metabotropic glutamate receptors (mGluRs, GPCRs Class C), which offer new possibilities for drug discovery. They play important roles in regulating cell excitability and synaptic transmission. The mGlu receptors are widely distributed throughout the central nervous system, and a whole range of neurological and psychiatric disorders might be treated using drugs that act directly on these receptors. There are eight types of mGlu receptors (8 genes encoding for mGlu1 to mGlu8 in human) divided into three groups based on structure, pharmacology and mechanism of signal transduction [10].

3 Materials and Methods

The grouping of GPCRs into types and subtypes based on sequence analysis may significantly contribute to helping drug design and to a better understanding of the molecular processes involved in receptor signalling both in normal and pathological conditions [11].

In order to group GPCR sequences, we need a measure of similarity between them. Pattern recognition and machine learning techniques can help us in this task. Unsupervised data analysis using clustering algorithms provides a useful tool to explore data structures. Broadly speaking, the aim of clustering methods is to group patterns on the basis of a similarity (or dissimilarity) criteria where groups or clusters are set of similar patterns. Unsupervised methods that were capable of providing simultaneous grouping and visualization of sequence data would be especially adequate for the problem at hand, as visualization can help us to intuitively interpreting the grouping and classification results. The visualization of the high-dimensional GPCR sequences would indeed considerably help understanding their global grouping structure. In what follows, we provide details about one such method.

3.1 Kernel Generative Topographic Mapping

The GTM is an unsupervised statistical machine learning model of the manifold learning family. It performs simultaneous clustering (as a constrained mixture of distributions model) and low-dimensional visualization of multivariate data. It is defined as a nonlinear mapping from a latent space in $\Re^\ell$ (with ℓ being usually 1 or 2 for visualization purposes) onto a manifold embedded in the data $\Re^D$ space. This is expressed as a generalized regression function: $\mathbf{y} = \mathbf{W}\phi(\mathbf{u})$, where $\mathbf{y} \in \Re^D$, $\mathbf{u} \in \Re^\ell$, $\mathbf{W}$ is an adaptive matrix of weights, and ϕ is a vector with the images of S basis functions ϕ_s. The prior distribution of $\mathbf{u}$ in latent space is constrained to form a uniform discrete grid of M centres. Each component m

in the mixture defines the probability of an observable data point $\mathbf{x}$ given a latent point $\mathbf{u}_m$ and the model parameters:

$$p(\mathbf{x}|\mathbf{u}_m, \boldsymbol{\Theta}) = \left(\frac{\beta}{2\pi}\right)^{D/2} \exp\left\{-\frac{\beta}{2}\|\mathbf{x} - \mathbf{y}_m\|^2\right\} \qquad (1)$$

where $\mathbf{y}_m = \mathbf{W}\boldsymbol{\phi}(\mathbf{u}_m)$ and the adaptive parameters $\boldsymbol{\Theta}$ are $\mathbf{W}$ and the common inverse variance β. With these probabilities, a density model in data space can be generated for each component m of the mixture, leading to the definition of a complete model likelihood. The adaptive parameters of the model can be optimized by Maximum Likelihood (ML) using the Expectation-Maximization (EM) algorithm. Details can be found in [12].

Kernelization is a method originally defined for Support Vector Machines (SVM). In recent years it has been extended to other models, including Sel-Organizing Maps, which are functionally similar to GTM [13]. The idea is that a method formulated in terms of kernels can use the one that best suits the problem and data type to be analyzed. GTM was originally defined for quantitative data in the real domain. The type of data analyzed in this study though, which could be considered as a *text-like* sequence of symbols, should benefit from a kernel formulation of the model.

Observed data $\mathbf{X}$ can be implicitly mapped into a high-dimensional feature space H via a nonlinear function: $\mathbf{x} \to \psi(\mathbf{x})$. A similarity measure can then be defined from the dot product in space H as follows:

$$K(\mathbf{x}, \mathbf{x}') = \langle \psi(\mathbf{x}), \psi(\mathbf{x}') \rangle \qquad (2)$$

K is a kernel function that should satisfy Mercer's condition. Data are expressed in the high-dimensional dot product space H, usually known as feature space. This use of the feature space reduces the computational cost by employing the kernel function K instead of directly computing the dot product in H.

The kernelization of GTM entails the redefinition of Eq.1 in feature space as:

$$p(\psi(\mathbf{x})|\mathbf{u}_m, \boldsymbol{\Theta}) = \left(\frac{\beta}{2\pi}\right)^{D/2} \exp\left\{-\frac{\beta}{2}\|\psi(\mathbf{x}) - \mathbf{y}_m\|^2\right\} \qquad (3)$$

Note that the prototypes $\mathbf{y}_m$ are now defined in the feature space and not in data space, as originally. The expression $\|\psi(\mathbf{x}) - \mathbf{y}_m\|^2$ can be reformulated in terms of kernel functions by expanding the prototypes on the data in feature space. That is $\|\psi(\mathbf{x}) - \mathbf{y}_m\|^2 = K_{nn} + (\boldsymbol{\Lambda}\boldsymbol{\phi}_m)^T \mathbf{K}\boldsymbol{\Lambda}\boldsymbol{\phi}_m - 2\mathbf{k}_n\boldsymbol{\Lambda}\boldsymbol{\phi}_m$, where $\mathbf{K}$ is a kernel matrix with elements $K_{nn'} = \langle \psi(\mathbf{x}_n), \psi(\mathbf{x}_{n'}) \rangle$, and row vectors $\mathbf{k}_n$. The adaptive parameters of the model are now $\boldsymbol{\Lambda}$ (an adaptative weight matrix) and β, which can again be optimized by ML using EM (see details in [14]).

We are specially interested in one of the results of the expectation step of EM, namely the estimation of the posterior $R_{mn} = p(\mathbf{u}_m|\psi(\mathbf{x}_n), \boldsymbol{\Lambda}, \beta)$.

This R_{mn} measures the degree of responsibility (probability) of a point $\mathbf{u}_m$ in the latent space for the generation of a $\psi(\mathbf{x}_n)$ GPCR data subsequence, and it allows us to visually represent each sequence on the 2-dimensional latent space of KGTM through its *mode projection*, defined as:

$$m_{mode} = arg\max_m R_{mn} \tag{4}$$

Note that using equation 4 entails selecting that latent point for which the responsibility for a given sequence is maximum. This could be understood as a summary measure (*winner takes all*) according to which we can assign a given sequence to a specific latent point (or *cluster representative*). Even if only this summary measure is used to simplify the visualization procedure, we should not forget that there is still a non-zero probability of a given sequence belonging to any other cluster (latent point in the KGTM grid in Figure 1).

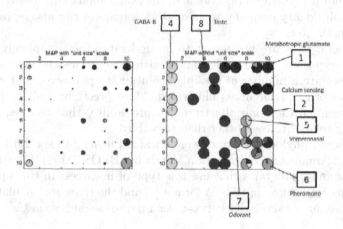

Fig. 1. Data visualization on a 10x10 representation map using the mode projection as described in the text. Left) Pie charts represent latent points and their size is proportional to the ratio of sequences assigned to them. Each portion of a chart corresponds to the percentage of sequences belonging to each sequence type. Right) The same map without sequence ratio size scaling, for better visualization. Type labels: 1: Metabotropic glutamate, 2: Calcium sensing, 4: GABA-B, 5: Vomeronasal, 6: Pheromone, 7: Odorant, 8: Taste.

3.2 The GPCR Data

The dataset analyzed with the KGTM algorithm consists of 232 protein sequences obtained from GPCRDB [8], corresponding to 7 types, namely types 1,2,4,5,6,7 and 8. Type 3 was excluded from analysis of family C as it was not available in GPCRDB for the extracted dataset. Each position in a sequence is called a residue, which in turn may be one of 20 possible amino acids. Each amino acid has a standard one-letter code, and a sequence is therefore represented by a combination of these letters. The number of residues by sequence in the dataset is 253 (data dimensionality). In our experiments, we built the kernel function as a quantitative measure of similarity between two GPCR sequences.

3.3 Phylogenetic Trees

Generally speaking, a phylogenetic tree is a dendogram-like graphical representation of the evolutionary relationship between taxonomic groups. In biology, the term phylogeny refers to the evolution or historical development of a plant or animal species. Taxonomy is the system of classifying species by grouping them into categories according to their similarities. A phylogenetic tree can be seen as a specific type of cladogram where the branch lengths are proportional to the predicted or hypothetical evolutionary time between groups. Cladograms are branched diagrams that illustrate patterns of relatedness, where the branch lengths are not necessarily proportional to the evolutionary time between groups. [15]. The evolutionary path of protein or DNA sequences can also be represented by phylogenetic trees.

Phylogenetic trees are not meant to be understood as completely true and accurate descriptions of the evolutionary paths they represent, because in any of them there are a number of possible evolutionary pathways that could produce the pattern of relatedness illustrated. More precisely, and in the case of protein sequences, they only illustrate the probability that two sequences are more closely related to each other than to a third one.

In this paper, phylogenetic trees were obtained using Jalview 2.6.1 [16], with the Blocks of Amino Acid Substitution Matrix 62 (BLOSUM62) [17], which is the standard for most programs that use this type of matrices. In this application, sequences are introduced in FASTA format [3] and the trees are calculated on the basis of a measure of similarity between each pair of sequences in the alignment.

4   Results and Discussion

When two sequences are compared, the basic mutational processes under consideration are *substitutions*, which change residues in a sequence, and *insertions* and *deletions*, which add or remove amino acids in the sequence. Insertions and deletions are together referred to as *gaps*. The kernel function designed to analyze the GPCR sequences with KGTM is a variation on that in [14] and was used in [19]. It is based on the mutations and gaps between sequences:

$$K\left(x,x'\right) = \exp\left\{\nu\frac{\pi\left(x,x'\right)}{\sqrt{\pi\left(x,x\right)\pi\left(x',x'\right)}}\right\} \tag{5}$$

where x and x' are two sequences and ν is a prefixed parameter; $\pi\left(\cdot\right)$ is a score function commonly used in bioinformatics and expressed as: $\pi\left(x,x'\right) = \sum_r s\left(x_r,x'_r\right) - \gamma$, where x_r and x'_r are the rth residue in the sequences. The value of $s\left(x_r,x'_r\right)$ can be found in a mutation matrix and γ is a gap penalty (usually the number of gaps in sequences). A normalization factor, defined as

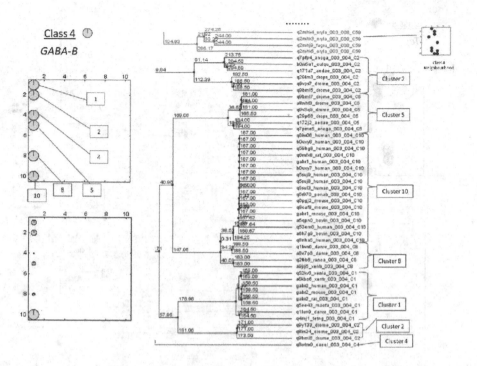

Fig. 2. Data visualization of type 4 (GABA-B), using the mode projection of equation 4 (left; top: Pie charts with size proportional to the ratio of sequences assigned to them; bottom: without that proportionality); right: its corresponding phylogenetic tree

the geometric mean of the maximum scores for each of the sequences, is used in 5 instead of their sum, as used in [14]. The modified kernel function now has a proper delimitation of its range.

The basic visualization of the sequence groupings obtained with KGTM is shown in Fig.1 [19]. Sequences were mapped onto the visualization space of KGTM according to their mode projection, as described in 4. That is, each sequence was assigned to a KGTM cluster and a cumulative view of the sequences, according to pie charts (to also include the sequence type information), is provided.

There is quite clear separation between many of the GPCR class C types, which are visualized in the latent space using the *mode projection*. Many types occupy a rather differentiated area on the map, showing little overlapping. A few of them, though, have overlapping representations. Both cases could be the source of insight on the peculiarities of subtype structure. *Metabotropic glutamate* (class 1), *GABA-B* (4), and *Taste* (8) are clearly differentiated from the rest of types, which show significant overlapping between them.

Before applying the method to construct the phylogenetic tree, a previous data processing was done in order to verify the correct location of the clusters once the tree had been created. With that purpose, sequences were labelled as

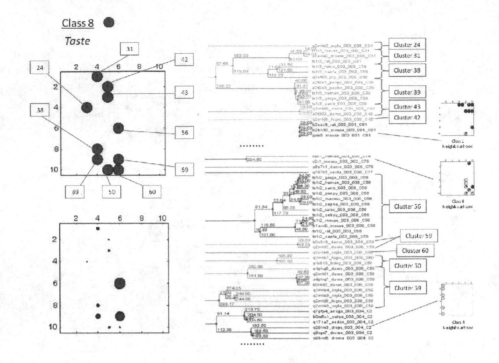

Fig. 3. Data visualization of type 8 (Taste), as in previous figure

well as the final cluster disposition in KGTM, adding the number of the cluster at the end of the sequence ID (See figure 2 for more details).

The distance method applied to the referred distance matrix BLOSUM62 was the Unweighted Pair-Group Method with Arithmetic Mean (UPGMA) [18], which examines the structure present in a pairwise distance matrix (or a similarity matrix) and then, build the phylogenetic tree. UPGMA works by progressively clustering the most similar sequences until all the sequences form a rooted tree.

Ultimately, UPGMA yields a distance-based sequence clustering solution in the same sense that KGTM provides one. There are radical differences between them, though. UPGMA is strictly hierarchical in nature and proceeds agglomeratively. It means that once agglomerated, clusters cannot be partitioned any longer throughout the procedure. This introduces a directional bias in the solution. Also importantly, cluster assignments at each level of the tree hierarchy are completely symmetrical; that is, the relative position of a sequence within each cluster is arbitrary, which makes the direct interpretation of proximity not too straightforward, specially for big trees.

On the other hand, KGTM is not hierarchical or agglomerative in nature, which avoids any directional bias. Also, its visualization map makes the assessment of proximity far more intuitive and devoid of any symmetry-related artifacts.

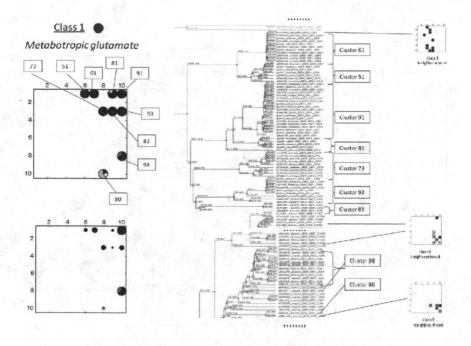

Fig. 4. Data visualization of type 1 (Metabotropic glutamate), as in previous figure

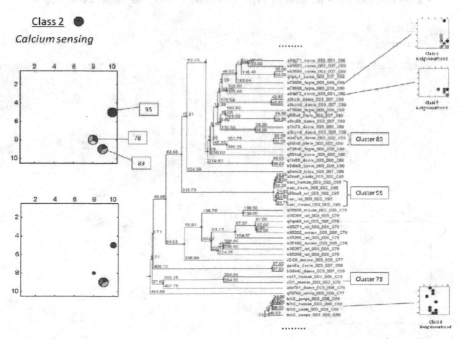

Fig. 5. Data visualization of type 2 (Calcium sensing), as in previous figure

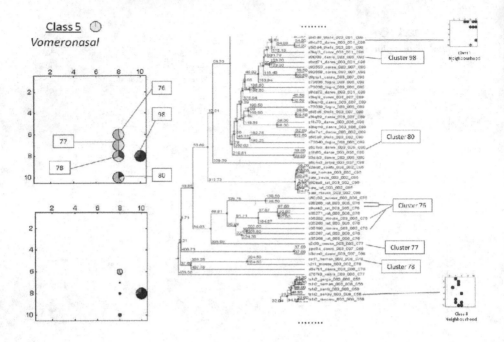

Fig. 6. Data visualization of type 5 (Vomeronasal), as in previous figure

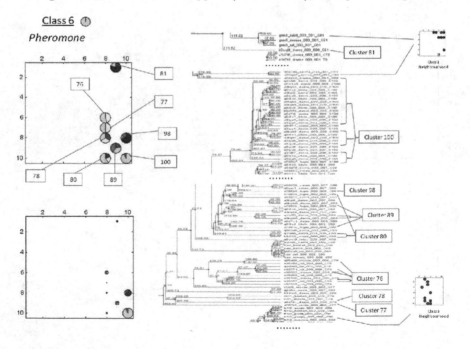

Fig. 7. Data visualization of type 6 (Pheromone), as in previous figure

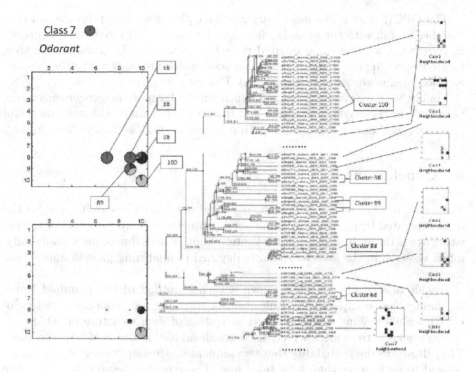

Fig. 8. Data visualization of type 7 (Odorant), as in previous figure

In the following figures, we display the KGTM visualization of each of the GPCR types together with the portion of the phylogenetic tree they correspond to. A visual comparison of both reveals striking similarities.

GPCR type 4 (GABA-B) is neatly separated from the rest of types in the KGTM representation (See figure 2). The phylogenetic tree reproduces this isolation not only globally (all type 4 sequences occupy contiguous tree branch locations) but even to the detail of individual KGTM clusters (each of the 6 clusters allocated by KGTM correspond, quite accurately, to contiguous subregions of the tree).

Type 8 is also clearly isolated from the rest in the KGTM map, with no mixing in its composition. However, the phylogenetic tree separates it in two clearly differentiated branches. This separation corresponds to two clear cluster locations: one group of clusters located at the top of the KGTM map and the other at the bottom (See Fig. 3).

A clear neighbourhood relationship between GPCR type 8 and types 4, 1 and 6, is also revealed in both KGTM and the phylogenetic tree. A single sequence belonging to type 8 provides us with a very illustrative example: the phylogenetic tree locates it in a very differentiated tree branch, at the top of the tree in Fig. 3. By itself, it forms KGTM cluster 24, which is clearly isolated from the rest of type 8.

The GPCR type 1 also has a very compact phylogenetic representation that matches overall with the grouping provided by the KGTM model (See figure 4). In particular, we find some isolated type 1 sequences in the phylogenetic tree, located between type 6 and type 7 sequences, which are assigned to the isolated location of clusters 80 and 98 in the KGTM map.

Finally, we have types 2,5,6 and 7 which show a far more heterogeneous structure both in the phylogenetic tree and in the KGTM map, although they still preserve neighbouring relations in both representations (See figures 5,6,7 and 8).

5 Conclusions

The world of pharmacology is pointedly veering towards research based on the data generated by pharmacogenomics and proteomics. More than half of the existing drugs target just a handful of protein families and, due to data availability, much research in the area is currently devoted to analyzing protein amino acid sequences.

In this brief study, we have shown a kernel method of the manifold learning family that is capable of simultaneously revealing the grouping structure of GPCRs while making the intuitive visualization of such structure possible.

Phylogenetic trees are a widely used graphical tool in the field of proteomics. They illustrate the probability that two sequences, are more closely evolutionary related to each other than to a third one. The reported results show that the unsupervised mapping of GPCR sequences yielded by KGTM closely resembles the corresponding phylogenetic trees to a great deal of detail. This corroborates that KTGM could be used as a complement to the phylogenetic tools, as it provides users with a very detailed while easy to interpret visual grouping of the sequences that is fully consistent with the more complex phylogenetic tree representation.

References

1. Lisboa, P.J.G., Vellido, A., Tagliaferri, R., Napolitano, F., Ceccarelli, M., Martin-Guerrero, J.D., Biganzoli, E.: Data mining in cancer research. IEEE Computational Intelligence Magazine 5(1), 14–18 (2010)
2. Kahn, S.D.: On the future of genomic data. Science 331(6018), 728–729 (2011)
3. Lipman, D.J., Pearson, W.R.: Rapid and sensitive protein similarity searches. Science 227(4693), 1435–1441 (1985)
4. Lisboa, P.J.G.: A review of evidence of health benefit from Artificial Neural Networks in medical intervention. Neural Networks 15, 9–37 (2002)
5. Baldi, P., Brunak, S.: Bioinformatics: The Machine Learning Approach. The MIT Press, Cambridge (2001)
6. Schölkopf, B., Tsuda, K., Vert, J.-P.: Kernel Methods in Computational Biology. The MIT Press, Cambridge (2004)
7. Overington, J.P., Al-Lazikani, B., Hopkins, A.L.: How many drug targets are there? Nature Reviews Drug Discovery 5, 993–996 (2006)

8. Horn, F., Weare, J., Beukers, M.W., Horsch, S., Bairoch, A., Chen, W., Edvardsen, O., Campagne, F., Vriend, G.: GPCRDB: an information system for G protein-coupled receptors. Nucleic Acids Research 26, 275–279 (1998)

9. Pierce, K.L., Premont, R.T., Lefkowitz, R.J.: Seven-transmembrane receptors. Nature Reviews: Molecular Cell Biology 3, 639–650 (2002)

10. Rondard, P., Goudet, C., Kniazeff, J., Pin, J.-P., Prézeau, L.: The complexity of their activation mechanism opens new possibilities for the modulation of mGlu and GABAB class C G protein-coupled receptors. Neuropharmacology 60, 82–92 (2011)

11. Cobanoglu, M.C., Saygin, Y., Sezerman, U.: Classification of GPCRs using family specific motifs. IEEE/ACM Transactions on Computational Biology and Bioinformatics (in press), doi:10.1109/TCBB.2010.101

12. Bishop, C.M., Svensén, M., Williams, C.K.I.: The Generative Topographic Mapping. Neural Computation 10(1), 215–234 (1998)

13. Villa, N., Rossi, F.: A comparison between dissimilarity SOM and kernel SOM for clustering the vertices of a graph. In: Proceedings of the 6th Workshop on Self-Organizing Maps (WSOM 2007), Bielefield, Germany (2007)

14. Olier, I., Vellido, A., Giraldo, J.: Kernel Generative Topographic Mapping. In: Verleysen, M. (ed.) Proceedings of the 18th European Symposium on Artificial Neural Networks (ESANN 2010), pp. 481–486 (2010)

15. Felsenstein, J.: Inferring phylogenies from protein sequences by parsimony, distance, and likelihood methods. Methods Enzymol 266, 418–427 (1996)

16. Waterhouse, A.M., Procter, J.B., Martin, D.M.A., Clamp, M., Barton, G.J.: Jalview Version 2-a multiple sequence alignment editor and analysis workbench. Bioinformatics 25(9), 1189–1191 (2009)

17. Henikoff, S.: Amino acid substitution matrices from protein blocks. PNAS 89, 10915–10919 (1992)

18. Sokal, R., Michene, C.: A statistical method for evaluating systematic relationships. Science Bulletin 38, 1409–1438 (1958)

19. Vellido, A., Cárdenas, M.I., Olier, I., Rovira, X., Giraldo, J.: A probabilistic approach to the visual exploration of G Protein-Coupled Receptor sequences. In: Verleysen, M. (ed.) Proceedings of the 19th European Symposium on Artificial Neural Networks (ESANN 2011), pp. 233–238 (2011)

DEEN: A Simple and Fast Algorithm
for Network Community Detection

Pavol Jancura, Dimitrios Mavroeidis, and Elena Marchiori*

Radboud University Nijmegen,
Intelligent Systems , Institute for Computing and Information Sciences,
Postbus 9010 6500GL Nijmegen, The Netherlands
{jancura,D.Mavroeidis,elenam}@cs.ru.nl
http://www.cs.ru.nl/~jancura,
http://sites.google.com/site/mavroeid/,
http://www.cs.ru.nl/~elenam

Abstract. This paper introduces an algorithm for network community detection called DEEN (Delete Edges and Expand Nodes) consisting of two simple steps. First edges of the graph estimated to connect different clusters are detected and removed, next the resulting graph is used for generating communities by expanding seed nodes.

DEEN uses as parameters the minimum and maximum allowed size of a cluster, and a resolution parameter whose value influences the number of removed edges. Application of DEEN to the budding yeast protein network for detecting functional protein complexes indicates its capability to identify clusters containing proteins with the same functional category, improving on MCL, a popular state-of-the-art method for functional protein complex detection. Moreover, application of DEEN to two popular benchmark networks results in the detection of accurate communities, substantiating the effectiveness of the proposed method in diverse domains.

Keywords: Community detection, protein interaction networks, graph sparsification, heuristic search.

1   Introduction

Many real world phenomena can be modeled as complex interaction networks. Community detection in these networks amounts to detecting groups of nodes such that the nodes belonging to the same group are more connected to each other than to nodes in the rest of the network. Community detection is of high practical relevance in domains as diverse as protein complex detection, community discovery in social networks and many others.

There is a large amount of methods for finding communities in a network (see for instance [9], a recent survey on this subject). Recently, an alternative view on this problem has been proposed in [25], based on the observation that a

---

* Corresponding author.

E. Biganzoli et al. (Eds.): CIBB 2011, LNBI 7548, pp. 150–163, 2012.

network consists of communities which are embedded in a background, that is, a set of nodes that do not belong to any community. The authors proposed a sequential method for detecting communities (and background nodes). Specifically, they formalized the task of finding one community by means of an optimization problem, which was tackled using an heuristic local search algorithm based on tabu-search, and use a parameter specifying the maximum size of a cluster as termination criterion when the desired number of communities is not specified a priori. A drawback of this algorithm is that it requires a number of random starting values and random orders of nodes for finding one community.

In this paper we present an alternative method for community (and background) detection, called DEEN (Delete Edges and Expand Nodes), consisting of the following two steps. First, edges considered to link different clusters are detected and deleted from the network. Next, the resulting network is used for generating clusters in a sequential way, each time starting from one seed node having highest degree.

The main advantages of DEEN with respect to other methods for community detection, like the one above mentioned, are its simplicity and efficiency. Indeed, DEEN uses a simple probabilistic local criterion for scoring edges. Edges with score bigger than a given threshold value are deleted. Communities with minimum and maximum size specified by the user are sequentially generated from seeds using a simple node expansion procedure.

In order to test the effectiveness of DEEN we applied it to two benchmark networks for which a "true" community structure is known. Moreover we applied DEEN to the protein-protein interaction (PPI) network in budding yeast, previously analyzed in [6].

Results of these experiments show that DEEN is capable of detecting communities with high accuracy, substantiating its competitiveness with state-of-the-art methods.

A preliminary version of this paper appeared in [13].

2   The Algorithm

Before introducing the proposed algorithm, we describe the notation and terminology used throughout the paper. A network is represented by an undirected graph $G = (V, E)$, where V is the set of nodes denoted by $s, t, u, v, \ldots$ and E the set of edges connecting pairs of nodes, denoted by $e, g \ldots$. An edge $e = uv \in E$ represents the relation between nodes u and v (for instance, in a PPI network, an interaction between two proteins).

Given a graph $G = (V, E)$, nodes joined by an edge are called *adjacent*. A *neighbor* of a node $u \in V$ is a node adjacent to u. We denote by $N(u)$ the the set of neighbors of u. The degree of u, denoted by k_u, is the number of elements in E containing the vertex u. In the sequel we assume that G has n nodes and m edges.

The size of a set S is denoted by $|S|$ and the set-theoretical difference between two sets S, T is denoted by $S \smallsetminus T$.

2.1   DEEN: Delete Edges and Expand Nodes

The proposed algorithm consists of two steps, called "Delete Edges" and "Expand Nodes", respectively. These steps are explained in detail in the sequel.

Delete Edges. The procedure for deleting edges is based on a local scoring function w that assigns a weight to each edge in E. Edges with weight bigger than a given threshold are deleted.

The scoring function $w : E \to \Re$ maps edges to real numbers, such that for $e = st$

$$w(e) = \begin{cases} \frac{(|N(s) \smallsetminus N(t)|-1)(|N(t) \smallsetminus N(s)|-1)}{(m-2|N(t) \cap N(s)|-1)} \frac{(m-1)}{(|N(s)|-1)(|N(t)|-1)} & \text{if } |N(s)| \cdot |N(t)| > 0 \\ 1 & \text{otherwise} \end{cases}$$

The weight $w(e)$ quantifies the strength of the signal induced by e in a local neighborhood of that edge. Specifically, we define the *local signal induced by e* to be the set of other edges occurring in triangles passing through e, that is,

$$signal(st) = \{sr, tr \mid r \in N(s) \cap N(t)\}.$$

Then we can show that $w(e)$ is the quotient of the expected number of edges between s and t under the *configuration null model* (see, e.g., [18]) between the two following graphs: G where both e and the signal induced by e have been removed, and G where only e has been removed.

Indeed, in the configuration null model, a vertex can be attached to any other vertex of the graph and the probability that vertices s and t, with degrees k_s and k_t, are connected, can be calculated directly as follows. In order to form an edge between s and t one needs to join two stubs (i. e., half-edges), incident with s and t. The probability p_s to pick at random a stub incident with s is $\frac{k_s}{2m}$, as there are k_s stubs incident with s out of a total of $2m$. The probability of a connection between s and t is then given by the product $p_s p_t$, since edges are placed independently of each other. The result is $p_s p_t = \frac{k_s k_t}{4m^2}$, which yields an expected number $P_{st} = 2m p_s p_t = \frac{k_s k_t}{2m}$ of edges between s and t.

One can verify that

$$w(e) = \frac{P_{st}^{G_1}}{P_{st}^{G_2}},$$

where G_1 is the subgraph of G with the same set of nodes and with set of edges equal to $E \setminus (\{e\} \cup signal(e))$ and G_2 is obtained from G by removing only the edge e.

If s and t have no common neighbors, that is, $N(s) \cap N(t) = \emptyset$, then $w(e) = 1$. If either s or t have degree 1 then $w(e) = 0$ reaches its minimum value.

The scoring function w is used to perform edge deletion: edges with score greater than a threshold γ are removed from G. The parameter γ influences the resolution of the communities to be found. In general, using a low value of γ will result in the removal of more edges, hence a larger amount of nodes will become background.

Expand Nodes. After deleting all edges of G with $w(e) > \gamma$ we obtain a new graph, say G'. We build clusters by applying to G' the following local clustering procedure that iteratively selects and expands a seed node.

Specifically, a clustering is generated as follows: a node u with highest degree is selected (ties are broken at random) and used as first element of a cluster. This cluster is expanded by adding the set $N(u)$ of all neighbors of u in G'. Such expansion step is applied to all the elements added to the cluster. The procedure is iterated until either no neighbor can be added, or a given upper bound (max_size) on the maximum size of a cluster is reached, or when there are more edges with both nodes in the cluster than edges with only one node in the cluster (this latter condition corresponds to the notion of weak community as defined in [19]). At that point the nodes of the constructed cluster are removed from G' and a new seed (node with highest degree) is selected and expanded. The process continues until all nodes have been assigned to a cluster. The set of nodes occurring in clusters with size smaller than a given lower bound (min_size) form the background.

Time Complexity. The time complexity of DEEN is dominated by the computation of the score of each edge. Assuming the adjacency lists for each node to be pre-sorted, intersecting the adjacency lists for two nodes takes number of operations proportional to the sum of their degrees. Since a node s of degree k_s requires k_s intersections, the total number of operations is proportional to $\sum_s k_s^2$. Nevertheless, using fast approximation techniques (see [4,20]) one can compute an estimate of the score of all edges in linear time on the number $|E|$ of edges.

3   Related Work

Our approach is related to other methods for community detection and clustering in networks based on seed expansion, like those used for clustering PPI networks, SPICi [14], DPClus [2], and SCAN [17], our previous work on modular network comparative analysis [12], and other methods not specifically developed for analyzing biological networks (e.g., [1]). Their appropriateness essentially depends on the input graph properties. For instance, for graphs with small diameter a breadth-first search (BFS) style expansion strategy may be more heavily influenced by the graph's small world properties (i.e., small shortest paths between all the graph nodes) rather than the node community structure; while in the cases of graphs with large diameter a BFS approach may present a simple and easy way to implement a strategy for detecting the desired clusters. While these methods employ a more involved criterion for seed selection and expansion, DEEN acts on a sparsified graph which allows one to use a very simple cluster expansion criterion based on node degree.

DEEN is also related to approaches that transform the graph prior to clustering. An example of this approach is the algorithm proposed in [21]: hub proteins (with degree greater than a given threshold) are first selected and their neighborhood graphs are subsequently constructed. A hub-duplication strategy is then applied to detect dense subgraphs in these neighborhood graphs with multi-functional hub proteins assigned to multiple clusters. While the goal of this method is to better identify overlapping complexes with multi-functional proteins, DEEN aims at identifying boundaries between clusters, characterized in terms of edges.

Another example of a related approach is the popular Girvan-Newman algorithm for community detection [11], applied to detect functional complexes in PPI network, e.g., in [7]. This clustering algorithm is based on a measure that tells us which edges are more likely to be "between" communities. The communities are detected by progressively removing edges from the original graph, in a greedy fashion, until a criterion measuring the modularity of the resulting network partition is satisfied. The measure employed in the algorithm is the so-called edge betweeness, defined as the number of shortest paths between pairs of nodes that pass through that edge. If there is more than one shortest path between a pair of nodes, each path is assigned equal weight such that the total weight of all of the paths is equal to one. Edges connecting communities will have high edge betweenness (at least one of them). By removing these edges, the groups are separated from one another and so the underlying community structure of the network is revealed.

DEEN differs from the Girvan-Newman algorithm in three main aspects: (a) it uses a different *local* measure for quantifying the likeliness of an edge to be between clusters, which employs information on the nodes adjacent to the two nodes of that edge; (b) it removes edges in one step, instead of iteratively; (c) it detects communities by performing seed expansion on the network resulting from the application of the edge deletion step. Thus DEEN is a fast local heuristic method, which uses graph transformation as a pre-processing instead of as a core step of a clustering algorithm.

Many variants of the Girvan-Newman algorithm have been proposed, including algorithms based on local measures for edges or nodes (for an overview see [9]). In particular, the measure used in DEEN for edge removal is related to the notion of edge-clustering coefficient used in the local method for community detection presented in [19]. Edge-clustering coefficient, is defined as the number of triangles (or other higher order cycles) to which a given edge belongs plus one, divided by the number of triangles that might potentially include it, that is, the minimum of the degrees of the edge nodes minus one.

Conceptually, the edge deletion component of our framework is also related to graph sparsification techniques that remove graph-edges with the general goal of approximating certain graph properties of interest. Most relevant to our work are the graph sparsification approaches that aim in preserving cuts (up to a multiplicative error) in the reduced, "sparsified" graph (i.e. [10] and references therein). As opposed to these approaches our work defines a probabilistic local model for removing the edges and does not directly aim in approximating cluster-structure properties of the full graph. Other related work is local graph sparsification for scalable clustering [20], which tries to remove edges in order to enable faster graph clustering.

4 Experimental Evaluation

4.1 Benchmark Networks

To illustrate the proposed method and test its performance, we apply it to
two popular benchmark networks: the karate club network and the US College
football network. We measure the quality of discovered communities in terms of
cluster purity, that is, the fraction of all pairs of nodes that are assigned to that
cluster and belong to the same true cluster. The average purity of the discovered
communities is reported as quality measure of the performance of DEEN.

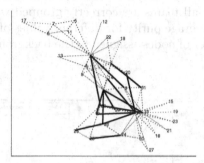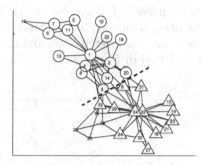

Fig. 1. (Application of DEEN to the Zachary social network (with $\gamma = 0.6$, minimum
and maximum size of clusters equal to 3 and 15, respectively). Left-hand side figure:
deleted edges are plotted using thick lines. Right-hand side figure: the two clusters
detected by DEEN with cluster identifiers denoted by a circle and a triangle symbol,
respectively. Nodes with no identifier are not assigned to any cluster and form the
background. The dash line separates the two true communities.

The Karate Club Network. The karate club network describes the friendship
relation between members of a karate club studied by Zachary [24]. During the
course of the study, the administrator and the club's instructor quarreled, and
the club split into two factions. We consider these fractions as a true clustering for
testing the performance of DEEN. The network contains 34 nodes and 156 edges.
Figure 1 (left-hand side) shows the network after the application of the edge
deletion step, while the plot on the right-hand side shows the clustering generated
by DEEN (obtained using $\gamma = 0.6$, $min\_size = 3$ and $max\_size = 15$). The
instructor and the administrator are represented by nodes 1 and 34, respectively.

The results show that DEEN correctly identifies the presence of two communities, each of them containing only elements belonging to the same true community. Therefore the average purity of DEEN applied to this network is equal to 1.
Five nodes are not assigned to clusters: these nodes are weakly connected to the
identified communities, and are considered by DEEN to be background.

When varying the value of γ a different number of nodes is not assigned to any cluster, while the average purity of the resulting clusters remains equal to 1 except for the case $\gamma = 1$ (no edge removal). In this case DEEN detects four clusters, node 3 is mapped to the wrong community, and 8 nodes are assigned to the background.

The US College Football Network. The US College football network [11] describes the schedule of Division 1 games for the 2000 season: the nodes are the teams and each edge represents a game between two teams. The network contains 115 nodes and 499 edges. The teams are divided into so-called conferences which provide a true clustering that we use for evaluating the results of DEEN.

Applying DEEN to this network, we find that it identifies the conference structure with a high degree of purity. Almost all teams are correctly grouped with the other teams in their conference. The average purity for different values of γ, the number of deleted edges and the number of nodes assigned to the background are plotted in Figure 2.

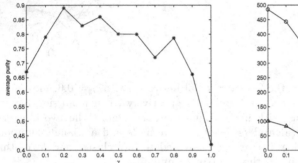 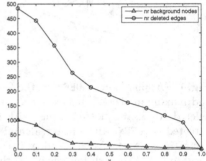

Fig. 2. Application of DEEN to the US College football network (with minimum and maximum size of clusters equal to 3 and 15, respectively. Left-hand side plot: average purity for different values of γ. Right-hand side plot: number of deleted edges and number of nodes assigned to the background for different values of γ.

4.2   Protein Complex Detection in the Budding Yeast PPI Network

With the exponential increase of data on protein interactions obtained from advanced technologies, data on thousands of interactions in human and most model species have become available [3,23]. PPI networks offer a powerful representation for better understanding modular organization of cells, for predicting biological functions and for providing insights into a variety of biochemical processes. In particular, PPI networks can be used for detecting protein functional modules and complexes and for assigning function to yet uncharacterized proteins.

Among the interactions produced by high-throughput methods there could be many false positives. In [16] the accuracy and the biases of 80 000 physical interactions among 5400 yeast proteins reported previously were assessed and a confidence value was assigned to each interaction.

In order to reduce the interference by false positives, the authors extracted interactions with high and medium confidence. This network was first used in [6] for detecting complexes. We retrieved a version of this network from `http://vlado.fmf.uni-lj.si/pub/networks/data/bio/Yeast/Yeast.htm`: it contains 6646 interactions among 2361 proteins.

Assignment of Annotation and p-values to Clusters. As an isolated cluster may involve different functional categories, here we p-values are used as criteria to assign each cluster a main function, as done previously e.g. in [6]. Specifically, hypergeometric distribution was applied to model the probability of observing at least k proteins from a cluster of size l by chance in a category containing C proteins from a network containing n proteins. The resulting p-value P is computed as

$$P = 1 - \sum_{i=1}^{k-1} \frac{\binom{C}{i}\binom{n-C}{l-i}}{\binom{n}{l}}.$$

The above test measures whether a cluster is enriched with proteins from a particular category more than would be expected by chance. If the p-value of a category is near 0, the proteins of the category in a cluster will have a low probability of being chosen by chance. Here, we assigned each cluster the main function with the lowest p-value in all categories.

For each cluster we calculated its p-value and annotated it based on the Munich Information Center (MIPS) hierarchical functional categories, using a set of functional categories provided in previous studies of this dataset [16] (see Table 1).

Table 1. MIPS functional categories from [16]

id	function
10	E Energy production
7	G Amino-acid metabolism
2	M Other metabolism
6	P Translation
1	T Transcription
12	B Transcriptional control
5	F Protein fate
9	O Cellular organization
13	A Transport and sensing
11	R Stress and defence
8	D Genome maintenance
4	C Cellular fate/organization
3	U Uncharacterized

We call *significant cluster* a cluster with p-value smaller than 0.05.

Moreover, in order to analyze the more pure clusters generated by the algorithm, we considered the subset of significant clusters satisfying the following two conditions: (a) their assigned functional category is different from "U" and (b) they contain only proteins of that category except possibly some uncharacterized proteins. We call these clusters *homogeneous*.

Results. In our analysis, we considered only clusters containing at least 3 elements (thus we set $min\_size = 3$), that is, clusters of a higher complexity than just a single interaction. We set the bound for the maximum size of a complex to be equal to 15, thus focussing on small functional complexes. Prior knowledge on the size of functional complexes could be used to select a more tight upper bound.

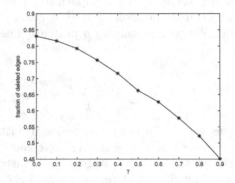

Fig. 3. Application of DEEN to the Budding Yeast PPI network. Fraction of edges deleted by DEEN for different values of γ.

Figure 3 plots the number of edges deleted by DEEN when varying the value of the parameter γ. The plot shows that a large number of the edges in the considered PPI network is removed, ranging from 45% to more than 80% of the total number of edges.

Figure 4 (the left plot) shows the fraction of significant clusters (that is, with p-value smaller than 0.05) and the number of homogeneous ones, respectively, for different values of γ. The right plot shows the behavior of DEEN when varying the value of γ with respect to the fraction of the proteins covered by significant clusters and by homogeneous ones, respectively. One can see that for any value of γ more than 70% of the clustered proteins are assigned to significant clusters. However, as shown on Table 2 (see values in the row with identifier tp) the number of proteins assigned to significant clusters tends to increase for higher values of γ, with a pick for $\gamma = 0.7$.

From the summary of the results contained in Table 2 we can draw the following observations. The best performance of DEEN is achieved for $\gamma = 0.7$, with the highest number of proteins assigned to significant and homogeneous clusters. When no edge deletion is performed (that is, for $\gamma = 1$) very few homogeneous

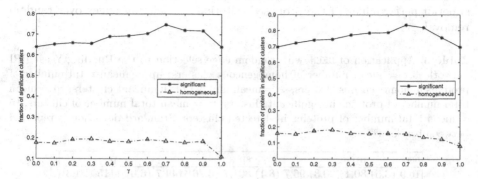

Fig. 4. Application of DEEN to the Budding Yeast PPI network. Left: the fraction of significant clusters and of homogeneous ones, respectively, for different values of γ. Right: the fraction of proteins covered by significant clusters and by homogeneous ones, respectively, for different values of γ.

Table 2. Application of DEEN to the Budding Yeast PPI network. Results for different values of γ. sc = number of significant clusters, hsc = number of homogeneous clusters, tc = total number of clusters, sp= total number of proteins in significant clusters, hp= total number of proteins in homogeneous clusters, tp = total number of proteins in detected clusters, de= number of deleted edges.

γ	0.0	0.1	0.2	0.3	0.4	0.5	0.6	0.7	0.8	0.9	1.0
sc	115	116	120	124	131	129	131	133	121	117	110
hsc	32	31	35	37	35	34	36	33	30	30	19
tc	180	178	182	189	190	186	186	178	168	163	172
sp	654	691	747	796	846	895	915	1009	974	846	879
hp	150	148	176	194	176	179	186	188	162	138	103
tp	938	957	1009	1068	1095	1139	1162	1207	1189	1121	1264
de	5520	5424	5267	5029	4756	4404	4169	3835	3466	2999	0

clusters are detected covering about 100 proteins, while using edge deletion with any other value of γ (in the considered set) results in the discovery of a larger number of homogeneous clusters covering more proteins. The number of significant clusters generated by DEEN with $\gamma = 1$ is less than that obtained using the other values of this parameter, while the number of proteins covered by these clusters is smaller than the one obtained using $\gamma \in \{0.6, 0.7, 0.8\}$ and similar or bigger than the one obtained using the remaining values of γ. These results indicate that deleting edges improves the quality of the "Expand Nodes" clustering procedure.

In order to test also the benefits of the type of edge deletion criterion used in DEEN, we replaced it with a random edge deletion procedure. Specifically, we run 10 experiments of DEEN with the randomized procedure for deleting 3835 edges, that is, using the number of edges deleted by the "Delete Edges" algorithm with $\gamma = 0.7$, since this value produced the best results of DEEN. The mean and standard deviation of the results are shown in Table 3. These results indicate superior performance of the proposed criterion for deleting edges over random removal.

Table 3. Application of DEEN with random edge selection to the Budding Yeast PPI network. hsc = mean number of homogeneous clusters, hp = mean total number of proteins in homogeneous clusters, sc = mean number of significant clusters, sp = mean total number of proteins in significant clusters, tc = mean total number of clusters, tp = mean total number of proteins in detected clusters. Standard deviation is reported between brackets.

hsc	hp	sc	sp	tc	tp
16.9 (3.5)	80.1 (20.3)	96.7 (8.1)	801.7 (6.26)	144.7 (6.0)	1115 (24.3)

Comparison with MCL. We compare the results of DEEN (using $\gamma = 0.6$) with those of a state-of-the-art clustering method, called Markov Clustering (MCL) [22,8].

We briefly describe MCL and refer the reader to [22] for a detailed presentation of this method, and to [8] for its first use for detecting protein families. MCL finds clusters in graphs by a mathematical bootstrapping procedure. The process deterministically computes (the probabilities of) random walks through the graph, and uses two operators transforming one set of probabilities into another. MCL simulates a flow on the graph by calculating successive powers of the associated adjacency matrix. At each iteration, an inflation step is applied to enhance the contrast between regions of strong or weak flow in the graph. The process converges towards a partition of the graph, with a set of high-flow regions (the clusters) separated by boundaries with no flow. The value of the inflation parameter is used to control the granularity of these clusters, hence it indirectly influences the number of clusters detected by the method. We set this parameter to the value 1.8 as reported in [5] and obtained by tuning for accuracy and separation. MCL with this inflation parameter value was shown to achieve best performance in a comparative experimental assessment of four state-of-the-art algorithms for detecting functional modules in PPI networks. Another recent comparative analysis of algorithms for protein complex detection [15] further substantiated the very good performance of MCL.

DEEN with $\gamma = 0.6$ detected 186 clusters, containing a total of 1162 proteins; 131 of these clusters have p-value less than 0.05, resulting in a percentage of 70.4 high quality clusters covering a total of 915 proteins.

MCL detected 272 clusters with at least 3 elements, containing a total of 2005 proteins; 168 of these clusters have p-value less than 0.05, resulting in a percentage of 61.76 high quality clusters.

The average p-values of MCL and DEEN were 0.0692 (standard deviation equal to 0.0862) and 0.0574 (standard deviation equal to 0.0851), respectively. Figure 5 shows the sorted p-values of the clusters found by DEEN and by MCL.

However, the above results should be considered with care due to the bias on the maximum size of clusters considered by DEEN, because larger clusters

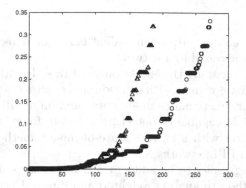

Fig. 5. Application of DEEN to the Budding Yeast PPI network. Sorted P-values of the clusters found by DEEN (triangle symbol) and by MCL (circle symbol).

discovered by MCL may tend to be less significant and homogeneous. Thus, to minimize the effect of this bias, we further focus only on significant and on homogeneous clusters.

MCL discovered 32 homogeneous clusters with 166 proteins in total while DEEN detected 36 homogeneous clusters containing a total of 186 proteins.

The average purity of the significant clusters generated by DEEN for varying values of γ and of those discovered by MCL are shown in Figure 6. The plot shows that the significant clusters detected by DEEN are more pure than those generated by MCL for all values of γ except when no edge deletion is performed ($\gamma = 1$).

These results show that DEEN is more conservative and more accurate than MCL for the following reasons: (1) it found less clusters and clustered less proteins than MCL, (2) it detected a higher number of homogeneous clusters (and covered proteins) as MCL, (3) it detected clusters having average p-value smaller than that of the clusters detected by MCL, and (4) it generated significant clusters with higher average purity than that of those generated using MCL.

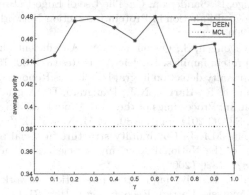

Fig. 6. Application of DEEN and MCL to the Budding Yeast PPI network. Average purity of MCL and of DEEN when varying γ.

5   Conclusion

We proposed a new efficient algorithm called DEEN for detecting high quality communities and background in a network.

We assessed experimentally the effectiveness of this algorithm on two benchmarks networks and we compared its performance with that of MCL, a state-of-the-art method for functional complex detection, on a PPI network. Results indicated that DEEN is capable of detecting accurate functional protein modules and is competitive with a current state-of-the-art methods for functional complex detection in PPI networks.

Possible interesting topics to be addressed in future work include extensions of the proposed method to analyze weighted and directed networks, as well as the development of methods for tuning the parameters of DEEN.

References

1. Alamgir, M., von Luxburg, U.: Multi-agent random walks for local clustering on graphs. In: Proceedings of the 2010 IEEE International Conference on Data Mining, ICDM 2010, pp. 18–27. IEEE Computer Society, Washington, DC (2010)
2. Altaf-Ul-Amin, M., Shinbo, Y., Mihara, K., Kurokawa, K., Kanaya, S.: Development and implementation of an algorithm for detection of protein complexes in large interaction networks. BMC Bioinformatics 7(1) (2006)
3. Bader, G.D., Donaldson, I., Wolting, C., Ouellette, B.F.F., Pawson, T., Hogue, C.W.V.: Bind–the biomolecular interaction network database. Nucleic Acids Res. 29(1), 242–245 (2001)
4. Becchetti, L., Boldi, P., Castillo, C., Gionis, A.: Efficient algorithms for large-scale local triangle counting. TKDD 4(3) (2010)
5. Brohee, S., van Helden, J.: Evaluation of clustering algorithms for protein-protein interaction networks. BMC Bioinformatics 7(1), 488+ (2006)
6. Bu, D., Zhao, Y., Cai, L., Xue, H., Zhu, X., Lu, H., Zhang, J., Sun, S., Ling, L., Zhang, N., Li, G., Chen, R.: Topological structure analysis of the protein-protein interaction network in budding yeast. Nucl. Acids Res. 31(9), 2443–2450 (2003)
7. Dunn, R., Dudbridge, F., Sanderson, C.: The Use of Edge-Betweenness Clustering to Investigate Biological Function in Protein Interaction Networks. BMC Bioinformatics 6(1), 39+ (2005)
8. Enright, A.J., Van Dongen, S., Ouzounis, C.A.: An efficient algorithm for large-scale detection of protein families. Nucleic Acids Research 30, 1575–1584 (2002)
9. Fortunato, S.: Community detection in graphs. Physics Reports 486, 75–174 (2010)
10. Fung, W.S., Hariharan, R., Harvey, N.J., Panigrahi, D.: A general framework for graph sparsification. In: Proceedings of the 43rd Annual ACM Symposium on Theory of Computing, STOC 2011, pp. 71–80. ACM, New York (2011)
11. Girvan, M., Newman, M.E.J.: Community structure in social and biological networks. Proceedings of the National Academy of Sciences of the United States of America 99(12), 7821–7826 (2002)
12. Jancura, P., Marchiori, E.: Dividing protein interaction networks for modular network comparative analysis. Pattern Recognition Letters 31(14), 2083–2096 (2010)
13. Jancura, P., Marchiori, E.: Detecting high quality complexes in a PPI network by edge deletion and node expansion. In: CIBB (2011)

14. Jiang, P., Singh, M.: SPICi: a fast clustering algorithm for large biological networks. Bioinformatics 26(8), 1105–1111 (2010)
15. Li, X., Wu, M., Kwoh, C.K., Ng, S.K.: Computational approaches for detecting protein complexes from protein interaction networks: a survey. BMC Genomics 11(suppl. 1), S3+ (2010)
16. von Mering, C., Krause, R., Snel, B., Cornell, M., Oliver, S.G., Fields, S., Bork, P.: Comparative assessment of large-scale data sets of protein-protein interactions. Nature 417, 399–403 (2002)
17. Mete, M., Tang, F., Xu, X., Yuruk, N.: A structural approach for finding functional modules from large biological networks. BMC Bioinformatics 9(S-9) (2008)
18. Molloy, M., Reed, B.A.: A critical point for random graphs with a given degree sequence. Random Struct. Algorithms 6(2/3), 161–180 (1995)
19. Radicchi, F., Castellano, C., Cecconi, F., Loreto, V., Parisi, D.: Defining and identifying communities in networks. Proceedings of the National Academy of Sciences of the United States of America 101(9), 2658–2663 (2004)
20. Satuluri, V., Parthasarathy, S., Ruan, Y.: Local graph sparsification for scalable clustering. In: Proceedings of the 2011 International Conference on Management of Data, SIGMOD 2011, pp. 721–732. ACM, New York (2011)
21. Ucar, D., Asur, S., Catalyurek, U., Parthasarathy, S.: Improving Functional Modularity in Protein-Protein Interactions Graphs Using Hub-Induced Subgraphs. In: Fürnkranz, J., Scheffer, T., Spiliopoulou, M. (eds.) PKDD 2006. LNCS (LNAI), vol. 4213, pp. 371–382. Springer, Heidelberg (2006)
22. Van Dongen, S.: Graph Clustering Via a Discrete Uncoupling Process. SIAM Journal on Matrix Analysis and Applications 30(1), 121–141 (2008)
23. Xenarios, I., Salwínski, L., Duan, X.J., Higney, P., Kim, S.M., Eisenberg, D.: Dip, the database of interacting proteins: a research tool for studying cellular networks of protein interactions. Nucleic Acids Research 30(1), 303–305 (2002)
24. Zachary, W.W.: An information flow model for conflict and fission in small groups. Journal of Anthropological Research 33, 452–473 (1977)
25. Zhao, Y., Levina, E., Zhu, J.: Community extraction for social networks. Proceedings of the National Academy of Sciences 108(18), 7321–7326 (2011)

Self-similarity in Physiological Time Series: New Perspectives from the Temporal Spectrum of Scale Exponents

Paolo Castiglioni

Fondazione Don C. Gnocchi, via Capecelatro 66, Milan, Italy
pcastiglioni@dongnocchi.it

Abstract. Most physiological time series have self-similar properties which reflect the functioning of physiological control mechanisms. Self-similarity is usually assessed by detrended fluctuation analysis (DFA) assuming that mono- or bi-fractal models generate the self-similar dynamics. Our group recently proposed a new DFA approach describing self-similarity as a continuous temporal spectrum of coefficients, thus not assuming that "lumped-parameter" fractal models generate the data. This paper reviews the rationale for calculating a spectrum of DFA coefficients and applies this method on datasets of signals whose self-similarity has been extensively studied in the past. The first dataset consists of six electroencephalographic (EEG) derivations collected in a healthy volunteer. The second dataset consists of cardiac intervals and diastolic blood pressures recorded in 60 volunteers at different levels of cardiac sympatho/vagal balance. Results reveal the limits of the traditional "lumped-parameter" approach, and provide information on the role of autonomic outflows in determining cardiovascular self-similarity.

Keywords: Fractals, Detrended Fluctuation Analysis, EEG, Heart Rate Variability.

1   Introduction

Most physiological systems are characterized by an intrinsic variability, even in steady-state conditions. This variability may reflect the response of control mechanisms to a multitude of external perturbations in the attempt to maintain homeostasis. It may also result from interactions with other physiological systems or from temporal changes in internal set-points, as determined, for instance, by postural changes, by physical or mental activity, or by fatigue. Stochastic models are usually assumed to describe these fluctuations given the large number of involved factors.

A typical feature of most stochastic processes in physiology is the so-called "self-similarity". A time series is considered self-similar if segments of its data have the same appearance, independently of the time scale at which they are observed, provided that the amplitude is properly rescaled. This property makes time series analogous to fractal objects. A geometric fractal can be split into smaller parts and still each

E. Biganzoli et al. (Eds.): CIBB 2011, LNBI 7548, pp. 164–175, 2012.

fragment looks like the original when enlarged. In the same way, a self-similar (or fractal) time series can be split into smaller segments and each segment may show fluctuations statistically similar to the original, if plot at higher time resolution properly rescaling the amplitude [1]. More formally, $x(t)$ is self-similar if it has the same statistical properties of $a^{-H}x(at)$ for any $a>0$. The coefficient H (called Hurst exponent) defines the vertical "stretching" factor, $1/a^H$, which preserves the statistical properties of $x(t)$ if the time axis is rescaled by a. The value of H depends on the degree of temporal correlation among data.

The first who described a natural phenomenon with self-similar dynamics and long-range dependence was H.E. Hurst. He was a geologist studying how high a dam should be designed to store the annual floods of the river Nile [2]. Analysing annual records of the flows, Hurst found that over a period of n years, the maximum level reached by the water in the reservoir, normalized by the standard deviation of the flow, $A(n)$, would be increased as a power of n: $A(n) \propto n^H$. This indicated the scale invariance (i.e., self-similarity) of the phenomenon because the ratio between A values at two time scales, n_1 and n_2, depends only on the ratio of the scales, n_1/n_2, and not on their absolute values:

$$A_1/A_2 = (n_1/n_2)^H \quad (1)$$

Interestingly, H was greater than 0.5, the expected value for independent observations [3]. This implies a long-range dependence, indicating that wet and dry periods are clustered over many years for the river Nile.

The work of Hurst led Mandelbrot and Wallis to discover that self-similar phenomena with long-range dependence are ubiquitous in nature [4]. They proposed two families of fractal processes with H between 0 and 1: the fractional Gaussian noises and their integral, the fractional Brownian motions. H defines the degree of dependence between samples of fractional Brownian motion. When $H=0.5$, each increment does not depend on past increments. Thus the series of increments is a white noise process, and the integrated series is a "random walk", or Brownian motion. When $0<H<0.5$, increments are anti-correlated (positive increments are more likely followed by negative increments and vice-versa) while when $0.5<H<1$ increments are correlated (any increment is more likely followed by an increment of the same sign).

Fractional Gaussian noises and fractional Brownian motions represent a simple dichotomous model [5] largely adopted in physiology. Assuming this model, self-similarity is assessed in two steps. The first step consists in evaluating whether the generating process is a stationary Gaussain noise or a nonstationary Brownian motion. The second step consists in estimating the corresponding H. Among the many methods for estimating H (see [6] for a review) Detrended Fluctuation Analysis (DFA) is very popular. In fact, DFA can be applied without knowing in advance whether the series should be modeled as Gaussian noise or Brownian motion, because it estimates a coefficient α equal to H for fractional Gaussian noise and to $H+1$ for fractional Brownian motion. This is useful because the self-similarity of physiological signals may range between the extremes of white noise ($\alpha=0.5$) and Brownian motion ($\alpha=1.5$) even in the same subject.

In the last years a large number of studies applied this dichotomous model to describe the fractal properties of physiological processes. In several cases it has been shown that a single H exponent cannot properly describe the full fractal dynamics of the series. In these cases, the "mono-fractal" model has been extended by calculating two (bi-fractal model) or more exponents separately, each of them defined over a specific range of time scales.

Recently our group further extended the DFA method in order to estimate a full temporal spectrum of scale exponents [7]. This approach leaves the traditional model which assumes that the series is generated by one or more fractional Gaussian noises or Brownian motions, each acting separately over a specific range of time scales. Therefore our DFA approach appears particularly useful for describing physiologically more realistic stochastic processes in which the characteristics of long-term dependence appear to change continuously with the time scale. Moreover, it avoids arbitrarily defining the order of the fractal model and "a priori" selecting the scale ranges over which one estimates the H exponents.

Aim of this paper is to illustrate how a temporal spectrum of DFA scale coefficients provides a richer description of the scaling structure of physiological time series, without requiring the strict assumptions usually assumed for the fractal models generating the data. The method will be illustrated with applications on electroencephalographic and cardiovascular time series collected in healthy volunteers. These examples will show how the assessment of a whole spectrum of DFA scale coefficients may help selecting the proper fractal model which better describes the data. They will also show how the temporal spectrum of scale coefficients may provide useful information for better understanding aspects of the control mechanisms producing fractal dynamics in physiology.

2   DFA and the Temporal Spectrum of Scale Exponents

DFA was originally introduced to describe long-range correlations in DNA sequences with noncoding regions [8]. Since then, it has been employed in a large number of studies to analyse heart rate [9], blood pressure [10], respiration [11], the electroencephalogram (EEG) [12], the electromyogram [13] and gait dynamics [14].

The method is based on the calculation of a variability index, $F(n)$, function of the time scale n. Briefly, given the series $x(t_k)$ of length N samples, first the mean value is calculated:

$$\bar{x} = \frac{1}{N} \sum_{k=1}^{N} x(t_k) \tag{2}$$

and the integrated series $y(t_k)$ is obtained after subtraction of the mean:

$$y(t_k) = \sum_{i=1}^{k} \left(x(t_i) - \bar{x} \right) \quad k=1,\dots,N. \tag{3}$$

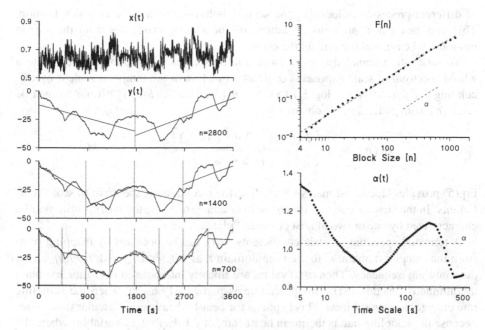

Fig. 1. DFA-based estimation of a temporal spectrum of scale exponents, $\alpha(t)$, for a beat-by-beat series of cardiac intervals $x(t)$, reciprocal of heart rate, of 1-hour duration (upper-left panel). The integral of $x(t)$ after mean subtraction, $y(t)$, is split into consecutive non-overlapping blocks of n beats. Lower left panels show blocks of 2800, 1400 and 700 beats, and the linear trend in each block. $F(n)$, root mean square of the deviations from the trend, is estimated for n between 4 and 2000 beats (upper-right panel). The log-log scale highlights an underlying power-law relation because $F(n) \propto n^{\alpha}$ and α can be estimated as slope of a linear regression (dashed line). Deviations from α are taken into account by $\alpha(t)$ (lower-right panel), derivative of log $F(n)$ vs. log n mapped from the beat domain to the time domain.

The integrated series is divided into nonoverlapping boxes of n samples. The local trend in each box, $y_n(t_k)$, is obtained by least square fit and subtracted. The root-mean square of the detrended series, $F(n)$, is calculated over all the blocks of size n:

$$F(n) = \sqrt{\frac{1}{N}\sum_{k=1}^{N}\left(y(t_k) - y_n(t_k)\right)^2} \qquad (4)$$

The calculation of $F(n)$ is repeated at different box-sizes n. For monofractal processes, $F(n)$ increases proportionally to n^{α} and α is estimated as slope of the regression line between log $F(n)$ and log n.

This procedure, however, cannot take into account possible deviations of real physiological data from a simple monofractal scaling behaviour. If correlations are of different types at short and at long scales, the scaling behaviour would be better described by a bi-fractal model with two coefficients, α_1 and α_2. In this case, the coefficients can be estimated by fitting regression lines separately over ranges of small and large n. But it is even possible that the fractal dynamics results from the superposition of different processes influencing the scaling behaviour in a more complex fashion. This may result in continuous deviations of the scaling exponents from the simple monofractal case, making critical the estimation of α.

To take into account also these more complex cases, we proposed to estimate a whole spectrum of scale exponents $\alpha'(n)$ as a function of the temporal scale n by calculating the derivative of $\log F(n)$ vs. $\log n$ [7]. Thus, if $F(n)$ is estimated over M scales n_p, with $p=1,\ldots,M$, we obtain:

$$\alpha'\left(n_p\right) = \frac{\log\left[F(n_{p+1})\right] - \log\left[F(n_{p-1})\right]}{\log\left[n_{p+1}\right] - \log\left[n_{p-1}\right]} \qquad 1<p<M. \qquad (5)$$

Eq.(5) provides "local" estimates which describe a continuous spectrum of scale coefficients. In the simpler cases of mono- or bi-fractal processes, the $\alpha'(n)$ profile will be characterized by one or two almost constant "plateaus".

A temporal spectrum of scale coefficients, $\alpha(t)$, can be obtained by mapping $\alpha'(n)$ from the samples domain, n, to the time-domain t, as $\alpha(t_p)=\alpha'(n_p)$ with $t_p = n_p/f_S$ and f_S the sampling frequency. Then $\alpha(t_p)$ values are linearly interpolated over time to obtain a continuous function $\alpha(t)$. This procedure is particularly useful when the sampling rate changes among subjects. This happens for beat-by-beat cardiovascular time series because the sampling rate is the mean heart rate, or for respiratory variables where the sampling rate is the mean breathing rate. Figure 1 illustrates the whole procedure.

3   DFA Temporal Spectrum of Physiological Time Series

Cardiovascular beat-by-beat series and the electroencephalogram (EEG) are the physiological signals studied more in details in terms of DFA. In this paragraph, the limits of the traditional DFA approach are illustrated by calculating the temporal spectrum of DFA scale coefficients in signals collected in healthy volunteers.

3.1   Temporal Spectrum of EEG

The EEG has been modelled as a self-similar process by DFA in different studies, but results in literature are somehow discrepant. When DFA was applied on short data segments (length of 10 s), it has been assumed that the EEG can be modelled by a "bifractal" process on the base of the shape of log-log plots of $F(n)$ vs. n; thus, a short-term coefficient, α_1, was defined between 11 and 49 ms, and a long-term coefficient, α_2, between 132 and 1250 ms [15]. A successive study confirmed the EEG bifractal nature but indicated a different range for α_2 (between 80 and 430 ms) [16]. When longer EEG series were considered (30 s), a more complex structure was described, with three coefficients (α_1, from 6.1 to 24.4 ms; α_2 from 40 to 157.8 ms; and α_4, from 1579 to 6000 ms) [17].

The estimation of a temporal spectrum of scale coefficients may clarify this issue by providing a more complete picture of the scaling structure of EEG. For this aim, we recorded EEG channels in one volunteer at rest for 2 minutes. The recording, free from muscular and ocular artefacts, was digitized at 512 Hz and 16 bits without filters (see details in [18]) and then split into 4 non-overlapping data blocks of 30 s. A DFA spectrum, $\alpha^k(t)$, was estimated for each block k, with $1 \leq k \leq 4$. The final estimate $\alpha(t)$ was obtained by calculating mean and confidence intervals over the 4 non-overlapping blocks. Two EEG channels on the frontal lobe (Fp1 on the left and Fp2 on the right hemisphere), two on the temporal lobe (T7 to the left, T8 to the right) and two on the occipital lobe (O1 to the left and O2 to the right) were considered.

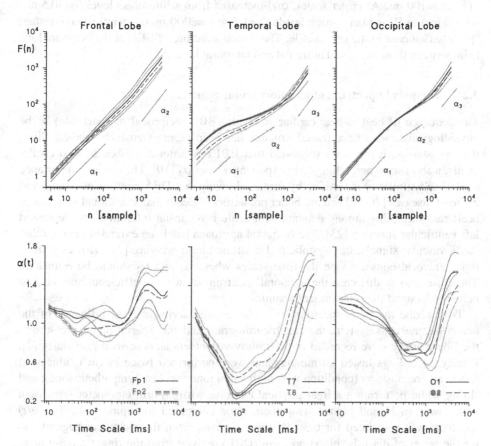

Fig. 2. F(n) functions and $\alpha(t)$ spectra with 95% confidence intervals of the estimates from DFA for EEG channels on frontal, temporal and occipital lobes in one volunteer. Upper panels also show the α_i parameters of lumped fractal models as traditionally derived from visual inspection of *log-log* plots.

Results are shown in figure 2. Upper panels display log-log plots of $F(n)$ vs. n. These plots suggest a bi-fractal structure for EEG on the frontal lobe, the slopes appearing steeper at scales greater than 512 samples (1000 ms). $F(n)$ plots of temporal and occipital lobes suggest a fractal structure with 3 coefficients: the slopes seem to decrease at scales n between 50 and 1000 samples, and to increase again at scales n greater than 1000 samples.

However, the $\alpha(t)$ spectra (figure 2, lower panels) provide a more detailed and complex picture of the EEG fractal structure. Actually EEG derivations on the frontal lobe might be modelled by a bi-fractal process, because $\alpha(t)$ appears approximately constant around the 1.1 level for time scales between 10 and 1000 ms, and tends to be higher at larger scales. By contrast, the $\alpha(t)$ profiles exclude that EEG derivations at the temporal lobe could be properly represented by a fractal model with 3 coefficients. In fact, $\alpha(t)$ decreases monotonically from 1.1 at t=10 ms to 0.3 (T7) or 0.5 (T8) at t=100 ms. At larger scales, $\alpha(t)$ increases from white noise levels (α=0.5 at t =1000 ms) to Brownian motion levels (α=1.5 at t =8000 ms). Therefore no constant "plateaus" appear in the $\alpha(t)$ profile. The fractal structure of EEG at the occipital lobe is in between those observed at frontal and temporal lobes.

3.2   Temporal Spectrum of Cardiovascular Signals

The sequence of beat-to-beat cardiac intervals (BBI, reciprocal of heart rate) is the physiological series whose fractal structure has been more extensively studied. Since the first studies, it has been suggested that BBI are better described by two coefficients, a short-term and a long-term exponent α_1 and α_2 [19]. The clinical importance of BBI self-similarity is testified by studies showing that DFA coefficients are altered by heart diseases [20-22] and are better predictors of death than traditional methods of heart rate variability among patients with acute myocardial infarction and depressed left ventricular function [23]. The bi-fractal approach has been extended also to other cardiovascular signals, like systolic and diastolic blood pressure [24]. However, there is no univocal consensus on the time scales where α_1 and α_2 should be estimated. Therefore also in this case the temporal spectrum of scale coefficients may help to better understand the self-similar dynamics.

To describe the DFA spectrum of cardiovascular series and the influence of the autonomic nervous system, the electrocardiogram and the arterial blood pressure at the finger artery were recorded in 60 healthy volunteers as described previously [7]. Briefly, recordings lasted 10 minutes and were performed twice in each subject: at rest in supine position (condition with high vagal tone and low sympathetic tone); and sitting while performing a light physical exercise with an arm ergometer (condition with lower vagal and higher sympathetic tone compared to supine rest). The $\alpha(t)$ spectrum was calculated for the BBI series derived from the electrocardiogram and for the series of diastolic blood pressure (DBP) derived from the finger arterial pressure recordings. The BBI dynamics is modulated by cardiac sympathetic and cardiac vagal outflows on the sinus node and therefore it is expected to reflect the cardiac sympatho/vagal balance. The DBP dynamics is strongly modulated by changes in vascular resistances and therefore it is expected to reflect changes in vascular sympathetic tone. Temporal scales between 5 and 100 s were considered.

Results are shown in figure 3. During supine rest, $\alpha(t)$ spectra of BBI and DBP differ markedly. The temporal spectrum of DBP decreases monotonically from values higher than 1.2 at t=5 s to values lower than 0.8 at t=60 s. This trend excludes that the DBP dynamics could be appropriately described by monofractal or bi-fractal models, as assumed in literature. By contrast, $\alpha(t)$ of BBI is always lower than 1. It decreases from 0.9 at t=5 s up to a minimum close to 0.7 at t around 14 s. At larger temporal scales it increases forming a "plateau" at time scales greater than 45 s, where a long-term scale coefficient α_2 could be therefore defined. The autonomic activation following the change of posture from supine to sitting and the increased level of physical activity produces important changes on $\alpha(t)$ of both BBI and DBP. The two temporal spectra look remarkably similar in this condition. They both decrease steeply from 1.2 at t=5 s up to 0.7 at t=18 s; at larger scales they both slowly rise up to 0.8.

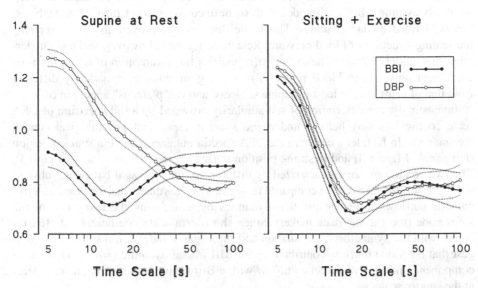

Fig. 3. Temporal spectra of scale coefficients for BBI and DBP in 60 volunteers supine (*left*) and sitting while performing a light physical exercise (*right*): mean and 95% confidence intervals over the group

4   Discussion and Conclusions

The examples of DFA spectra of self-similarity reveal the inadequacy of fractal models based on few "lumped parameters" to fully describe the dynamics of physiological signals. Even if at first sight the relation between $F(n)$ and n seems to strictly follow a power-law relation, as in the example of figure 1, the more detailed description provided by $\alpha(t)$ reveals substantial deviations from this trend. These deviations cannot be attributed simply to the variance of a noisy estimation. Therefore, they should be taken into account when selecting the model which better represents the data. Moreover, these deviations may reflect important features of physiological control mechanisms responsible for the observed fractal dynamics.

For instance, the temporal spectrum of DFA scale coefficients confirms that the fractal nature of EEG cannot be regarded as a simple monofractal process. However, it also suggests that its self-similar structure is more complex than usually considered.

In particular, the example of figure 2 suggests that the EEG self-similarity should be described by a continuous spectrum of scale exponents, rather than by a finite number of coefficients. In fact, a clear "plateau" in $\alpha(t)$ appears only in one of the considered couples of EEG derivations. The peculiar $\alpha(t)$ profile of EEG may also explain discrepancies previously reported in literature, when fractal models with "lumped-parameters" were assumed.

Applications on BBI and DBP evidenced the inadequacy of mono- or bi-fractal models to also describe cardiovascular data. Most of the studies on heart-rate self-similarity assume a bifractal model, with α_1 defined for n lower than 12 or 16 beats, and α_2 defined for larger scales. This model has been employed also for describing the scaling structure of blood pressure. Results of figure 3, however, seriously undermine this model. As to the heart rate, $\alpha(t)$ justifies the assumption of a long-term α_2 coefficient only. As to blood pressure, its scaling structure is remarkably different from that of heart rate, at least in supine subjects, and no "plateaus" appear in $\alpha(t)$.

Interestingly, the description of self-similarity provided by a full spectrum of DFA scale coefficients may help to understand specific aspects of physiological control mechanisms. In fact, let's compare the DFA spectra obtained at rest in supine position (left panel of figure 3) and in sitting position during exercise (right panel of figure 3). The two conditions are characterized by different sympatho/vagal balances, substantially greater during exercise compared to supine rest. Cardiac vagal and cardiac sympathetic outflows influence the BBI dynamics by modulating the firing rate of the sinus node (the cardiac pace maker). Since short term scale coefficients of BBI increase with the sympathetic stimulation and the vagal withdrawal, results would suggest that the vagal outflow contribute to the BBI fractal dynamics with a white noise component, and the sympathetic outflow with a Brownian motion component, at least at the shorter scale.

This hypothesis is supported by the recent observations that selective autonomic blocking agents have very different influences on the fractal structure of heart rate [25]. In particular, it has been shown that heart-rate scale coefficients reach values close to those characterizing 'white-noise' dynamics (i.e., $\alpha=0.5$) when the cardiac sympathetic outflow is blocked by propranolol while, when the vagal outflow is blocked by atropine, they reach much larger values, even close to those of Brownian motion ($\alpha=1.5$) at the shorter temporal scales. Our hypothesis is also in line with the transfer function between vagal outflow and BBI and between sympathetic outflow and BBI previously described in dogs [26].While the transfer function between vagal outflow and BBI is reported to be almost flat, indicating that a 'white' vagal outflow contributes to the BBI dynamics with a 'white-noise' component, the transfer function between sympathetic outflow and BBI is described as a one-pole low-pass filter (see figure 4). The cut-off frequency of the filter is determined by the much slower dynamics of noradrenaline removal compared to the dissipation rate of acetylcholine released by the vagal terminals [27]. This one-pole filter would act as an integrator for those components faster than the cut-off frequency. Therefore, a white noise sympathetic outflow would contribute with a Brownian motion component at the shorter scales, as observed in figure 3.

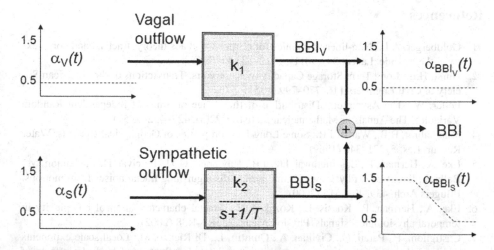

Fig. 4. An interpretative model for the changes in $\alpha(t)$ of BBI following changes in autonomic tone as observed in [7,25]. The blocks represent the transfer functions of the atrial sinus node, in terms of Laplace transforms, between cardiac vagal outflow and BBI and between cardiac sympathetic outflow and BBI. This latter block has been described as a single-pole filter with time constant T around 60 s [26]. Therefore, this block can be approximated by the k_2 constant for components of the sympathetic outflow with dynamics much slower than 60 s, and by the integration block k_2/s for much faster components. If sympathetic and vagal outflows are represented by white noise inputs ($\alpha_V(t)=\alpha_S(t)=0.5$), then the BBI component modulated by the vagal outflow (BBI_V) would also present a white noise dynamics and a constant DFA spectrum equal to 0.5. By contrast, the BBI component modulated by the sympathetic outflow (BBI_S) would be characterised by white noise dynamics only at temporal scales much greater than T, and by Brownian motion dynamics at temporal scales much shorter than T.

This physiological model may also explain why the DFA spectra of BBI and DBP differ markedly in supine rest, and are similar during exercise. Unlike BBI, DBP is not importantly influenced by the vagal outflow, while it is modulated by the vascular sympathetic outflow. Therefore it is reasonable to expect large differences between BBI and DBP fractal dynamics during supine rest, where the vagal outflow is highest, and similar dynamics during exercise, where the sympathetic tone modulating both BBI (through cardiac outflows) and DBP (through vascular outflows) is highest.

In the last years the DFA algorithm has proved capable to provide precious physiological and clinical information on the fractal structure of biosignals. Until now, however, this algorithm has been applied under the assumption that the self-similarity structure of real physiological signals can be modelled by relatively simple "lumped-parameter" fractal models. DFA methods able to take into account more complex fractal structures, like the proposed temporal spectrum of scale coefficients, may make self-similarity analysis in health and disease even more effective.

References

1. Goldberger, A.L.: Non-linear dynamics for clinicians: chaos theory, fractals, and complexity at the bedside. Lancet 347(9011), 1312–1314 (1996)
2. Hurst, H.E.: Long Term Storage Capacity of Reservoirs. Transactions of the American Society of Civil Engineers 116, 770–799 (1951)
3. Feller, W.: The Asymptotic Distribution of the Range of Sums of Independent Random Variables. The Annals of Mathematical Statistics 22(3), 427–432 (1951)
4. Mandelbrot, B.B., Wallis, J.R.: Some Long-Run Properties of Geophysical Records. Water Resour. Res. 5, 321–340 (1969)
5. Eke, A., Herman, P., Bassingthwaighte, J.B., Raymond, G.M., Percival, D.B., Cannon, M., Balla, I., Ikrenyi, C.: Physiological time series: distinguishing fractal noises from motions. Pflugers Arch. 439, 403–415 (2000)
6. Eke, A., Herman, P., Kocsis, L., Kozak, L.R.: Fractal characterization of complexity in temporal physiological signals. Physiol. Meas. 23, R1–R38 (2002)
7. Castiglioni, P., Parati, G., Civijian, A., Quintin, L., Di Rienzo, M.: Local scale exponents of blood pressure and heart rate variability by detrended fluctuation analysis: effects of posture, exercise, and aging. IEEE Trans. Biomed. Eng. 56, 675–684 (2009)
8. Peng, C.K., Buldyrev, S.V., Havlin, S., Simons, M., Stanley, H.E., Goldberger, A.L.: Mosaic organization of DNA nucleotides. Phys. Rev. E. Stat. Phys. Plasmas. Fluids Relat. Interdiscip. Topics 49, 1685–1689 (1994)
9. Tulppo, M.P., Kiviniemi, A.M., Hautala, A.J., Kallio, M., Seppanen, T., Makikallio, T.H., Huikuri, H.V.: Physiological background of the loss of fractal heart rate dynamics. Circulation 112, 314–319 (2005)
10. Schulz, S., Koschke, M., Bar, K.J., Voss, A.: The altered complexity of cardiovascular regulation in depressed patients. Physiol. Meas. 31, 303–321 (2010)
11. Busha, B.F.: Exercise modulation of cardiorespiratory variability in humans. Respir. Physiol. Neurobiol. 172, 72–80 (2010)
12. Abasolo, D., Hornero, R., Escudero, J., Espino, P.: A study on the possible usefulness of detrended fluctuation analysis of the electroencephalogram background activity in Alzheimer's disease. IEEE Trans. Biomed. Eng. 55, 2171–2179 (2008)
13. Chang, S., Hsyu, M.C., Cheng, H.Y., Hsieh, S.H., Lin, C.: Synergic co-activation in forearm pronation. Ann. Biomed. Eng. 36, 2002–2018 (2008)
14. Hausdorff, J.M.: Gait dynamics, fractals and falls: finding meaning in the stride-to-stride fluctuations of human walking. Hum. Mov. Sci. 26, 555–589 (2007)
15. Ferree, T.C., Hwa, R.C.: Power-law scaling in human EEG: relation to Fourier power spectrum. Neurocomputing 52-54, 755–761 (2003)
16. Abasolo, D., Hornero, R., Escudero, J., Espino, P.: A study on the possible usefulness of detrended fluctuation analysis of the electroencephalogram background activity in Alzheimer's disease. IEEE Trans. Biomed. Eng. 55, 2171–2179 (2008)
17. Jospin, M., Caminal, P., Jensen, E.W., Litvan, H., Vallverdu, M., Struys, M.M., Vereecke, H.E., Kaplan, D.T.: Detrended fluctuation analysis of EEG as a measure of depth of anesthesia. IEEE Trans. Biomed. Eng. 54, 840–846 (2007)
18. Castiglioni, P., Pugnetti, L., Garegnani, M., Mailland, E., Carabalona, R.: On the self-affinity of the electroencephalogram: evaluation of a whole spectrum of scale coefficients by detrended fluctuations analysis. In: Dössel, O., Schlegel, W.C. (eds.) WC 2009, 4th edn. IFMBE Proceedings, vol. 25, pp. 651–654 (2009)

19. Peng, C.K., Havlin, S., Hausdorff, J.M., Mietus, J.E., Stanley, H.E., Goldberger, A.L.: Fractal mechanisms and heart rate dynamics. Long-range correlations and their breakdown with disease. J. Electrocardiol. 28, 59–65 (1995)
20. Absil, P., Sepulchre, R., Bilge, A., Gérard, P.: Nonlinear analysis of cardiac rhythm fluctuations using DFA method. Physica A: Statistical Mechanics and its Applications 272, 235–244 (1999)
21. Lombardi, F., Sandrone, G., Mortara, A., Torzillo, D., La Rovere, M.T., Signorini, M.G., Cerutti, S., Malliani, A.: Linear and nonlinear dynamics of heart rate variability after acute myocardial infarction with normal and reduced left ventricular ejection fraction. Am. J. Cardiol. 77, 1283–1288 (1996)
22. Makikallio, T.H., Hoiber, S., Kober, L., Torp-Pedersen, C., Peng, C.K., Goldberger, A.L., Huikuri, H.V.: Fractal analysis of heart rate dynamics as a predictor of mortality in patients with depressed left ventricular function after acute myocardial infarction. TRACE Investigators. TRAndolapril Cardiac Evaluation. Am. J. Cardiol. 83, 836–839 (1999)
23. Huikuri, H.V., Makikallio, T.H., Peng, C.K., Goldberger, A.L., Hintze, U., Moller, M.: Fractal correlation properties of R-R interval dynamics and mortality in patients with depressed left ventricular function after an acute myocardial infarction. Circulation 101, 47–53 (2000)
24. Schulz, S., Koschke, M., Bar, K.J., Voss, A.: The altered complexity of cardiovascular regulation in depressed patients. Physiol. Meas. 31, 303–321 (2010)
25. Castiglioni, P., Parati, G., Di Rienzo, M., Carabalona, R., Cividjian, A., Quintin, L.: Scale exponents of blood pressure and heart rate during autonomic blockade as assessed by detrended fluctuation analysis. J. Physiol. 589, 355–369 (2011)
26. Berger, R.D., Saul, J.P., Cohen, R.J.: Transfer function analysis of autonomic regulation. Am. J Physiol. 256, H142–H152 (1989)
27. Levy, M.N., Yang, T., Wallick, D.W.: Assessment of beat-by-beat control of heart rate by the autonomic nervous system: molecular biology technique are necessary, but not sufficient. J. Cardiovasc. Electrophysiol. 4, 183–193 (1993)

Support Vector Machines
for Survival Regression

Antonio Eleuteri and Azzam F.G. Taktak

Department of Medical Physics and Clinical Engineering
Royal Liverpool and Broadgreen University Hospitals NHS Trust
Duncan Building 1st Floor, L7 8XP, Liverpool, United Kingdom
antonio.eleuteri@gmail.com,
afgt@liverpool.ac.uk

Abstract. In this paper we show how the survival analysis problem can be formulated in terms of support vector regression, starting from a quantile regression perspective. We define an appropriate weighted loss function which takes into account possibly censored observations, and we prove bounds on the estimation error and on the quantile property. We deduce that censoring is a limiting factor in the accuracy of solutions, though the overall rate of convergence is $O(n^{-1/2})$. Finally we show some applications of the model to synthetic data, and to the German Breast Cancer Study Group 2 data.

Keywords: Survival analysis, censored data, support vector machines, statistical learning theory, quadratic optimisation.

1 Introduction

Survival time prediction usually involves the estimation of survival functions, either by nonparametric (e.g. the Kaplan-Meier estimator) or semi-parametric (e.g. the Cox model) approaches [1]. These methods usually either do not allow the inclusion of clinical, patient-specific information; or, in the case of parametric models, make quite strong assumptions about the form of hazards, and their interaction with patient information.

Recent nonlinear parametric formulations of the survival analysis problem have been derived by means of neural networks [2][3][4][5]. Whereas these models exhibit great flexibility, they also have some drawbacks, among which their inherent non-identifiability, which may require many repetitions of the training process until a "good" solution is found. Non-identifiability also induces algebraic singularities in the parameter space, which makes Bayesian learning techniques the only reliable ones [6]. For recent parametric approaches to censored quantile regression see [7][8].

In this work we present a novel nonparametric approach to survival analysis, which efficiently uses the support vector machine (SVM) formalism, providing a unique solution to the problem. For detailed background on SVMs and statistical learning theory, see [9][10].

E. Biganzoli et al. (Eds.): CIBB 2011, LNBI 7548, pp. 176–189, 2012.

Previous attempts at using SVMs for survival analysis are reported in [11][12]. The former is based on minimisation of an approximate c-index [13] on suitable subsets of data points; the latter deals with censoring by using a target-interval formulation (the authors report this approach gives biased results, as we have verified in our simulations.) Recent survival analysis approaches based on alternative formulations of the SVM paradigm are reported here [14][15]. The former is described in terms of least-squares minimisation, and an additive kernel structure [9]. The latter is described in terms of empirical bayesian principles [2] and a degenerate kernel structure (which may result in potentially inconsistent estimates of the variance of the output [16]).

This paper is an extension of previously published work [17][18].

2   Survival Analysis as Quantile Regression

Definition 1. *Denote by $y \in \mathbb{R}$ an absolutely continuous random variable and let $\tau \in (0,1)$. Then, the conditional quantile $\eta_\tau(x)$ for a pair of random variables $(x,y) \in \mathcal{X} \times \mathbb{R}$ with joint measure $P(x,y)$ and cumulative distribution function F, is the function $\eta_\tau : \mathcal{X} \to \mathbb{R}$ such that pointwise $\eta_\tau(x) = \inf\{y : F(y|x) \geq \tau\}$*

Since a survival probability $S(y)$ is defined as $1 - F(y)$, it follows that the $(1-\tau)$-survival quantile is equivalent to the τ-quantile, so the problem of survival quantile regression can be formally handled as the problem of quantile regression [19][20]. We have also assumed without loss of generality that $y \in \mathbb{R}$; since quantile estimation is invariant with respect to monotonic transformations, in cases where we deal with positive data (e.g. survival times) we will implicitly assume a logarithmic transformation of the data; this assumption translates into an accelerated failure time model formulation [13].

In many practical applications y is right-censored, i.e. we do not directly observe the random variable y, rather the pair (z,d), where $z = \min(y,c)$, $d = 1\{y \leq c\}$ and c has (usually unknown) distribution function $1 - G$; $1\{\cdot\}$ is the set indicator function. The presence of censoring does not allow direct use of the formalism of quantile regression, so we will have to modify it to solve the survival analysis problem.

2.1   Loss Function

The basic idea behind quantile estimation derives from observing that minimisation of the ℓ_1 loss for location estimates results in the median [19]. This idea has been further generalised to obtain regression estimates for any quantile by an appropriate "tilting" of the ℓ_1 loss, which takes the form:

$$\mathcal{L}_\tau(\eta) = \begin{cases} \tau & \text{if } \eta \geq 0 \\ \tau - 1 & \text{if } \eta < 0 \end{cases}. \tag{1}$$

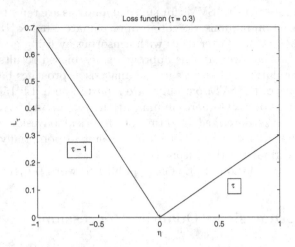

Fig. 1. Example of tilted loss function

Based on the above loss we can define the expected quantile risk (note the expectation is with respect to the measure $P(x, y)$):

$$R[f] = \mathsf{E}[\mathcal{L}_\tau(y - f(x))] \ . \tag{2}$$

If the data is not censored, then we may directly use the above risk (actually, its empirical variant). We will show next how to modify (2) to deal with censoring.

2.2 Censored Loss Function

We can get an expression for the expected censored quantile risk by using the properties of conditional expectations [21] (from now on we will omit the measure $P(x, y)$ from the expectations to avoid cluttering the notation):

$$
\begin{aligned}
R[f] &= \mathsf{E}[\mathcal{L}_\tau(y - f(x))] = \mathsf{E}\left[\frac{\mathcal{L}_\tau(y - f(x))}{G(y)}\mathsf{E}[1\{y \le c\}|(x, y)]\right] \\
&= \mathsf{E}\left[\frac{\mathcal{L}_\tau(y - f(x))}{G(y)}1\{y \le c\}\right] \\
&= \mathsf{E}\left[\frac{\mathcal{L}_\tau(z - f(x))}{G(z)}d\right] \ .
\end{aligned}
\tag{3}
$$

The above derivation assumes that c is statistically independent from both x and y. While this assumption is difficult to check in practice, it can be usually assessed by prior knowledge of the data. Also, the estimate assumes either random or (trivially) no censoring since it must be $G(y) > 0$ with probability one (this excludes fixed and constant censoring.) As usual, since the measure $P(x, y)$ is unknown and only data is available, we resort to the empirical censored quantile risk:

$$\hat{R}_n[f] = \frac{1}{n} \sum_i \frac{d_i}{G(z_i)} \mathcal{L}_\tau(z_i - f(x_i)) \ . \tag{4}$$

However, in most cases this form would not be usable in practice, since G is typically unknown. Therefore, we define the following *modified empirical censored quantile risk* functional which replaces the survival function G with its empirical estimate G_n (the Kaplan-Meier estimator [1]):

$$R_n[f] = \frac{1}{n} \sum_i \frac{d_i}{G_n(z_i)} \mathcal{L}_\tau(z_i - f(x_i)) \ . \tag{5}$$

While it has been proved elsewhere that the estimation error of the empirical quantile risk is bounded [20], it is not intuitive that the same property holds for the modified functional (5). In the next section we will prove this fact.

3 Theoretical Analysis

To assess the performance of the quantile estimator f_n, the minimiser of (5), we will use two criteria, namely:

- the estimate must satisfy the quantile property (bounds on the quantile property):

$$\mathsf{P}\left\{|F(f_n(x)) - \tau| \ge \epsilon\right\} \le \delta \ ; \tag{6}$$

- the estimate must be "close" (in some sense) to the true conditional quantile (bounds on the quantile risk):

$$\mathsf{P}\left\{|R[f_n] - R[f^*]| \ge \epsilon\right\} \le \delta \ . \tag{7}$$

In the above f^* denotes the optimum (generally unachievable) solution, and ϵ, δ are some small positive quantities.

As we will show in the next sections, the performance criteria can be expressed in terms of bounds and complexity classes of functions.

3.1 Bounds on the Quantile Risk

We will use the following definition:

Definition 2 (Rademacher Complexity). *Let $X = \{x_1, x_2, \ldots, x_n\}$ be drawn i.i.d. from $P(x)$ and let $\mathcal{F}$ be a class of functions from X to $\mathbb{R}$. Let σ_i be independent, uniform, $\{\pm 1\}$-valued random variables. Then the Rademacher Complexity $\mathcal{R}_n$ is defined as:*

$$\mathcal{R}_n(\mathcal{F}) \equiv \mathsf{E}_X\left[\mathsf{E}_\sigma\left[\sup_{f \in \mathcal{F}} \left|\frac{2}{n} \sum_i \sigma_i f(x_i)\right| \Big| X\right]\right] \ .$$

The following theorem provides the main tool to assess bounds based on Rademacher complexity.

Theorem 1 (Concentration for Lipschitz continuos functions). *For any Lipschitz continuous function ϕ with Lipschitz constant L and a function class $\mathcal{F}$ of real-valued functions on X and probability measure $P(x)$, then with probability $1 - \delta$ for all draws of x from $P(x)$ we have:*

$$\sup_{f \in \mathcal{F}} \left| \mathsf{E}[\phi(f(x))] - \frac{1}{n} \sum_i \phi(f(x_i)) \right| \le 2L\mathcal{R}_n(\mathcal{F}) + 2\sqrt{8\ln(2/\delta)/n}$$

Proof. For a proof of this result, see [22]. □

The next result shows that we can in practice use the empirical censored quantile risk (5) in place of (4). In fact, we can prove the following:

Lemma 1. *The empirical risk functional $R_n[f]$ almost surely converges to the empirical risk functional $\hat{R}_n[f]$:*

$$\sup_f \left| R_n[f] - \hat{R}_n[f] \right| \to 0 \quad a.s. \quad (n \to \infty)$$

Proof. We first note that the function $\mathcal{L}_\tau$ is a contraction on a compact (Lipschitz continuous with constant $L = \max\{\tau, 1 - \tau\}$), so its uniform norm is finite. Since G_n, G are nonincreasing positive functions, let $Y_F = \sup\{y : F(y) > 0\}$, we can write:

$$\sup_f \left| R_n[f] - \hat{R}_n[f] \right| = \sup_f \left| \frac{1}{n} \sum_i d_i \mathcal{L}_\tau(z_i - f(x_i)) \left(\frac{1}{G_n(z_i)} - \frac{1}{G(z_i)} \right) \right|$$

$$\le \frac{\|\mathcal{L}_\tau\|_\infty}{G_n(Y_F)G(Y_F)} \sup_{t \le Y_F} |G_n(t) - G(t)| \to 0 \quad a.s. \quad (n \to \infty)$$

where the last step follows by invoking a Glivenko-Cantelli result for G_n [23]. □

The following proposition proves Rademacher concentration bounds of the risk in terms of the modified empirical risk (5).

Lemma 2 (Concentration bounds for censored quantile risk)

Proof. By invoking the previous lemma and the Rademacher concentration bounds we have:

$$\sup_f |R[f] - R_n[f]| = \sup_f \left| R[f] + \hat{R}_n[f] - \hat{R}_n[f] - R_n[f] \right|$$

$$\le \sup_f \left| R_n[f] - \hat{R}_n[f] \right| + \sup_f \left| \hat{R}_n[f] - R[f] \right|$$

$$\le 2M\mathcal{R}_n(\mathcal{F}) + \sqrt{\frac{8\ln 2/\delta}{n}},$$

□

where M is the Lipschitz constant of the weighted loss $\mathcal{L}_\tau d/G$. Note that the constant is finite since by definition G is a strictly positive function.

We can now prove the following fundamental result.

Theorem 2. *The estimation error of the censored quantile risk is bounded.*

Proof. We denote by f^* the minimiser of $R[f]$ with respect to the chosen function class and by f_n the minimiser of the risk $R_n[f]$. We have then:

$$R_n[f_n] \leq R_n[f^*] \ .$$

Let us consider the uniform deviation:

$$R[f^*] \leq R_n[f^*] + \sup_f \left(R[f] - R_n[f] \right) \ ,$$

then we can write:

$$
\begin{aligned}
R[f_n] =& R_n[f_n] - R_n[f_n] + R[f_n] - R[f^*] + R[f^*] \\
\leq& R[f^*] + (R_n[f^*] - R[f^*]) + (R[f_n] - R_n[f_n]) \\
\leq& R[f^*] + 2\sup_f |R[f] - R_n[f]| \\
\leq& R[f^*] + 4M\mathcal{R}_n(\mathcal{F}) + 2\sqrt{8\ln(2/\delta)/n} \ ,
\end{aligned}
$$

where the last step follows from the Rademacher concentration results.   □

As an example, let us assume that the function space is a Reproducing Kernel Hilbert Space (RKHS), with a radial basis function kernel k normalised to unit variance. Let us also assume that all the functions in the space satisfy $\|f\| \leq C$. In this case, it can be shown [22] that $\mathcal{R}_n(\mathcal{F}) \leq 2C/\sqrt{n}$. This implies that the bounds in Theorem 2 translate into a rate of convergence $O(n^{-\frac{1}{2}})$. For nonlocalised estimates this result cannot be improved, and except for pathological cases, even the use of localised Rademacher estimates is unlikely to provide returns [24]. However it is quite possible that the hidden constants in the bounds could be improved, though we have not explored this matter further.

3.2   Bounds on the Quantile Property

In this section we establish bounds to assess to which degree the quantile estimate f_n satisfies the quantile property. In our derivation we will follow the argument of [20], though with the necessary corrections to take into account censoring.

We first observe that we can write the deviation in (6), and by taking into account the properties of conditional expectations in (3), as:

$$\mathsf{E}\left[\frac{\delta}{G(z)} 1_{(-\infty,0]}(z - f_n(x)) \right] - \tau \ . \tag{8}$$

Also note that (6) is not scale dependent, i.e. it's strongly affected by small changes in $f_n(x)$ around $y = f_n(x)$. One possible solution is to introduce two functions which provide a lower and upper bound to (6), and which depend on an artificial margin parameter ϵ:

$$r_u(\eta) \equiv \min(1, \max(0, 1 - \eta/\epsilon))$$
$$r_l(\eta) \equiv \min(1, \max(0, -\eta/\epsilon)) \ . \tag{9}$$

We can thus formulate the following:

Theorem 3. *Under the assumptions of Theorem 2 the expected censored quantile risk satisfies with probability $1 - \delta$ the following inequalities:*

$$\frac{1}{n} \sum_i \frac{d_i}{G_n(z_i)} r_l(z_i - f(x_i)) - \Delta \leq \mathsf{E}\left[\frac{\delta}{G(z)} 1_{(-\infty, 0]}(z - f_n(x))\right]$$
$$\leq \frac{1}{n} \sum_i \frac{d_i}{G_n(z_i)} r_u(z_i - f(x_i)) + \Delta \ , \tag{10}$$

where the confidence term Δ is:

$$\Delta \equiv 2K\mathcal{R}_n(\mathcal{F}) + \sqrt{\frac{-8\ln\delta}{n}} \ , \tag{11}$$

and $K \propto 1/\epsilon$ is the Lipschitz constant of the functions $\frac{d}{G(z)} r_{\{l,u\}}(z - f(x))$.

Proof. The result follows directly from Theorem 1 and the Lipschitz continuity of the ramp functions $r_l d/G$ and $r_u d/G$. Using the Rademacher bound on the class of censored losses induced by $r_l d/G$ and $r_u d/G$, and applying a union bound on the upper and lower deviations completes the proof.   □

It's interesting to note that, depending on the value of the ϵ parameter, we can get more or less loose bounds on the Rademacher averages of the induced function class. This implies that a small ϵ gives tight bounds on the quantile property, but a large confidence term; whereas a large ϵ reduces the confidence but induces a tight approximation of the empirical quantile.

4   Optimisation of the Risk Functional

In a practical application, we are actually going to minimise the empirical risk plus a regularisation term:

$$Q_n[f] \equiv R_n[f] + \lambda \|g\|_{\mathcal{F}}^2, \quad f = g + b, \ g \in \mathcal{F}, \ b \in \mathbb{R} \tag{12}$$

where the function class $\mathcal{F}$ is a RKHS [9]. It should be noted that the offset is not regularised, to ensure that the minimiser satisfies the quantile property [20]. It should be noted that it's necessary for the consistency of the risk estimate that the kernel of the RKHS be bounded [25]; this excludes in practice the class of polynomial kernels.

4.1   Dual Optimisation

Efficient numerical implementations rely on the formulation of the above problem in terms of a dual problem [9]. By using the properties of RKHSs, we can write $f(x) = \langle w, \phi(x) \rangle + b$, where $\langle \cdot, \cdot \rangle$ is a scalar product and $\phi(x)$ is a basis function, so that the optimisation problem can be written as:

$$\min_{w,b,\zeta_i,\zeta_i^*} \frac{1}{n\lambda} \sum_i \frac{d_i}{G_n(z_i)} \left[\tau \zeta_i + (1-\tau)\zeta_i^* \right] + \frac{1}{2} \|w\|^2$$

subject to:

$$z_i - \langle w, \phi(x_i) \rangle - b \leq \zeta_i,$$
$$- z_i + \langle w, \phi(x_i) \rangle + b \leq \zeta_i^*,$$
$$\zeta_i, \zeta_i^* \geq 0 .$$

(13)

The dual to this problem can be written by using Lagrange multipliers. We obtain the following quadratic optimisation problem:

$$\min_\alpha \frac{1}{2} \alpha^\top \mathbf{K} \alpha - \alpha^\top z$$

subject to:

$$\frac{d_i}{\lambda n G_n(z_i)} (\tau - 1) \leq \alpha_i \leq \frac{d_i}{\lambda n G_n(z_i)} \tau$$
$$\sum_i \alpha_i = 0 .$$

(14)

The Gram matrix $\mathbf{K}$ is obtained by evaluating the kernel function $k(\cdot, x)$ at the data points x_i. It should be noted that the constant b in the primal formulation is simply the dual variable to the constraint $\sum a_i = 0$. We recover the quantile estimator as the support vector expansion $f_n(x) = \sum \alpha_i k(x_i, x) + b$.

An important feature of the dual problem is that censored observations (for which $d = 0$) do not appear in the support vector expansion of the solution; for these observations the constraints above translate into $\alpha = 0$. Also note that the expansion maps all censored training patterns to the same value b.

A very efficient algorithm to solve the above problem is based on an interior point method with convex constraints set.

4.2   Monotonicity Constraints

It should be noted that estimates for different values of τ are not guaranteed to not cross, which would violate the definition of a survival curve [19][20]. Although it is known [19] that crossings don't happen around the expected values of the covariates, a formal solution of the problem for a set of τ's would require optimising w.r.t. a large set of variables (n times the number of τ's.)

We did not follow this route, but instead used a monotonization technique [26], which can be applied as a post-processing step. The end result is a fast and reliable estimate of survival quantiles.

5   Experiments

In this section we describe applications of the model to synthetic and real-world data. In all cases the available data was split into training and test set, with respective proportions 2/3 and 1/3. The regularisation parameter was set by 10-fold cross-validation [9] on the training set; the c-index was used to assess the validation and test set performances.

The software for the analyses was written and run on MATLAB® R2011a with the Optimisation Toolbox 6™ and R v2.12.2.

5.1   Simulated Data

We show here an example of the application of the above algorithm on a synthetic data set. To simplify the presentation, we consider the case $\tau = 0.5$ (which corresponds to predicting the conditional median of the data). We simulated an exponential survival process, with mean $\exp(x)$, $x \sim U(0, 1)$. We also simulated an exponential censoring process with mean 2, which amounts to about 30% censored observations. In the following graph we show the data and the theoretical conditional median, which is an exponential function.

The Gaussian kernel was used. The data set consists of three hundred observations. Fig. 2 shows the predictions on the test sample. The c-index on the test data is 0.72.

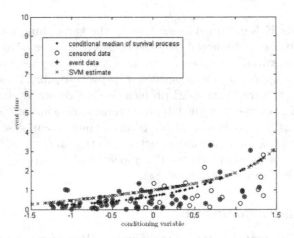

Fig. 2. Conditional median survival estimate of a censored exponential survival process

5.2   German Breast Cancer Study Group 2

In this example we use the German Breast Cancer Study Group 2 data [27], which contains 686 observations with 8 covariates: hormonal treatment, age,

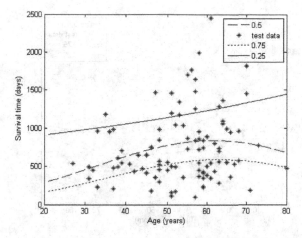

Fig. 3. Effect of age on survival

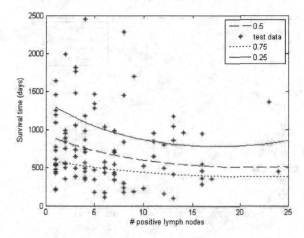

Fig. 4. Effect of number of nodes on survival

menopausal status, tumour size, tumour grade, number of positive lymph nodes, progesterone receptor, oestrogen receptor. 56.4% of the observations are censored. An additive Gaussian kernel was used, i.e. for each covariate we compute a Gaussian kernel, and the resulting kernels are added together. This choice restricts the space of functions to the sum of non-linear functions, each one depending on one covariate.

In Fig. 3 to 7 we show the survival probability contours (0.25, 0.5, 0.75) as functions of the continuous covariates (assuming the others are fixed at their median values.) The c-index on the test data for each of the quartiles are: 0.71 for $\tau = 0.5$; 0.69 for $\tau = 0.25$; 0.70 for $\tau = 0.75$.

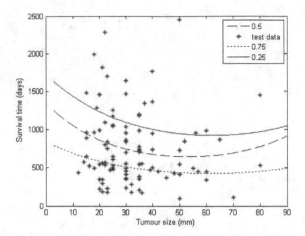

Fig. 5. Effect of tumour size on survival

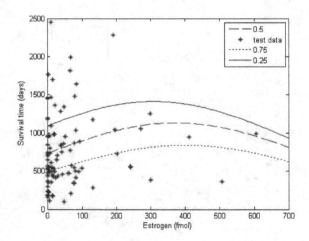

Fig. 6. Effect of oestrogen on survival

In Fig. 8 we report the Kaplan-Meier estimates (and related 95% confidence intervals) of the two test set prognostic groups identified by the model based on its median output. The log-rank test value is 41.3. Note that the prognostic groups don't have any predictive value per se; they are shown to graphically assess the overall discriminative ability of the model.

We compare these results with those obtained by a non-linear Cox model, for which 4th order restricted cubic splines were used to model the impact of high-cardinality variables (age, tumour size, number of positive lymph nodes, progesterone and oestrogen receptors.) The model was trained by maximum penalised likelihood. The c-index on the test data is 0.69, whereas the log-rank test value is 27.3. Note that whereas the log-rank results can be compared between

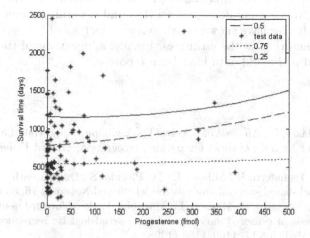

Fig. 7. Effect of progesterone on survival

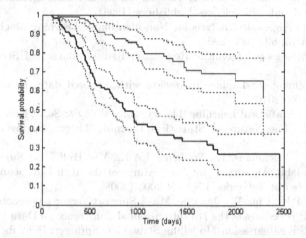

Fig. 8. Risk groups based on median model output

the two models, the c-index has a different interpretation. In the case of the SVM, we are measuring the concordance of each quartile (over all the times) vs. the ranks estimated from the data. In the case of the Cox model we get an overall measure (for all the times and probabilities;) obviously this is possible because the shape of the hazard rate does not change, only its scale.

6 Conclusions

In this paper we have described a new approach to survival analysis by SVMs. We have defined an empirical quantile risk estimator, which allows evaluation of survival quantiles even under right censoring. A major issue yet to be solved is the estimation of confidence intervals on predictions, which is a difficult problem even in classical linear quantile regression [19], and it's still an open problem in general for SVMs. We have shown convergence properties of the estimator, and the impact of censoring on the estimates. Finally, applications of the algorithm to synthetic and real-world data have been reported.

References

1. Cox, D.R., Oakes, D.: Analysis of Survival Data. Chapman and Hall, London (1984)
2. Bishop, C.M.: Neural networks for pattern recognition. Oxford University Press, Oxford (1995)
3. Eleuteri, A., Tagliaferri, R., Milano, L., De Placido, S., De Laurentiis, M.: A novel neural network-based survival analysis model. Neural Networks 16, 855–864 (2003)
4. Biganzoli, E., Boracchi, P., Mariani, L., Marubini, E.: Feed forward neural networks for the analysis of censored survival data: a partial logistic regression approach. Statistics in Medicine 17, 1169–1186 (1998)
5. Ripley, B.D., Ripley, R.M.: Neural Networks as Statistical Methods in Survival Analysis. In: Dybowsky, R., Gant, V. (eds.) Artificial Neural Networks: Prospects for Medicine. Landes Biosciences Publishers (1998)
6. Watanabe, S.: Algebraic Analysis for Non-identifiable Learning Machines. Neural Computation 13, 899–933 (2001)
7. Koenker, R.: Censored Quantile Regression Redux. Journal of Statistical Software 27 (2008)
8. Bottai, M., Zhang, J.: Laplace regression with censored data. Biometrical Journal 52, 487–503 (2010)
9. Vapnik, V.N.: Statistical Learning Theory. John Wiley & Sons, New York (1998)
10. Vapnik, V.N.: The Nature of Statistical Learning Theory. Springer, Heidelberg (1995)
11. Van Belle, V., Pelckmans, K., Suykens, J.A.K., Van Huffel, S.: Survival SVM: a Practical Scalable Algorithm. In: Proceedings of the 16th European Symposium on Artifical Neural Networks, ESANN 2008 (2008)
12. Shivaswamy, P.K., Chu, W., Jansche, M.: A Support Vector Approach to Censored Targets. In: Proceedings of the 7th International Conference on Data Mining (2007)
13. Harrell Jr., F.E.: Regression Modelling Strategies. Springer, Heidelberg (2005)
14. Van Belle, V., Pelckmans, K., Suykens, J.A.K., Van Huffel, S.: Additive survival least-squares support vector machines. Statistics in Medicine 29, 296–308 (2010)
15. Lama, N., Boracchi, P., Biganzoli, E.: Partial logistic relevance vector machines in survival analysis. Journal of Applied Statistics 38(11) (2011)
16. Williams, C.K.I., Rasmussen, C.E.: Gaussian Processes for Machine Learning. The MIT Press (2006)
17. Eleuteri, A., Taktak, A.F.G.: Survival time prediction by support vector regression. Proceedings of Royal Liverpool University Hospital Research Open Day (2007)
18. Eleuteri, A.: Support vector survival regression. In: 4th IET Conference on Advances in Medical, Signal and Information Processing (2008)
19. Koenker, R.: Quantile Regression. Cambridge University Press (2005)
20. Takeuchi, I., Le, Q.V., Sears, T.D., Smola, A.J.: Nonparametric Quantile Estimation. Journal of Machine Learning Research 7, 1231–1264 (2006)
21. Carbonez, A., Györfi, G., van der Meulin, E.C.: Partition-estimate of a regression function under random censoring. Statist. Decis. 13, 21–27 (1995)

22. Bartlett, P.L., Mendelson, S.: Rademacher and Gaussian complexities: Risk bounds and structural results. Journal of Machine Learning Research 3, 463–482 (2002)
23. Wang, J.L., Stute, W.: The strong law under random censorship. Annals of Statistics 21, 14–44 (1993)
24. Bartlett, P.L., Bousquet, O., Mendelson, S.: Localized Rademacher Complexities. In: Kivinen, J., Sloan, R.H. (eds.) COLT 2002. LNCS (LNAI), vol. 2375, pp. 44–58. Springer, Heidelberg (2002)
25. Christmann, A., Steinwart, I.: Consistency of kernel-based quantile regression. Journal of Applied Stochastic Models in Business and Industry 24, 171–183 (2008)
26. Chernozukov, V., Fernandez-Val, I., Galichon, A.: Improving point and interval estimators of monotone functions by rearrangement. Biometrika 96, 559–575 (2009)
27. Schumacher, M., Basert, G., Bojar, H., Huebner, K., Olschewski, M., Sauerbrei, W., Schmoor, C., Beyerle, C., Neumann, R.L.A., Rauschecker, H.F.: For the German Breast Cancer Study Group: Randomized 2x2 trial evaluating hormonal treatment and the duration of chemotherapy in node-positive breast cancer patients. Journal of Clinical Oncology 12, 2086–2093 (1994)

Boosted C5 Trees i-Biomarkers Panel for Invasive Bladder Cancer Progression Prediction

Alexandru George Floares[1], Irina Luludachi[2], Colin Dinney[3], and Liana Adam[3]

[1] SAIA & OncoPredict & IOCN
Department of Artificial Intelligence, Str. Vlahuta Bloc Lama C/45, 400310, Romania
alexandru.floares@ieee.org
[2] SAIA & OncoPredict
Department of Artificial Intelligence, Str. Vlahuta Bloc Lama C/45, 400310, Romania
irina.luludachi@saia.ro
[3] Department of Urology, UT-MD Anderson Cancer Center, Houston, Tx, USA
{cdinney,ladam}@mdanderson.org

Abstract. Bladder cancer is the fourth most common malignancy in men in the western countries. The aim of this study was to develop intelligent systems for invasive bladder cancer progression prediction. The proposed methodology combines knowledge discovery in data using artificial intelligence and knowledge mining. These are used both in feature selection and classifier development. The approach is designed to avoid overfitting and overoptimistic results. To our knowledge, these are the first intelligent systems for prediction of bladder cancer progression, based on boosted C5 decision trees, and their accuracy of 100% is the best published by now.

Keywords: C5 algorithm, boosting, invasive bladder cancer, progression, i-Biomarker.

1 Introduction

Bladder cancer (BCa) was estimated to reach a number of 70530 new cases in 2010 in the United States, representing the fourth most common diagnosis in men, while the estimated number of deaths was set at 14680 [1]. Bladder cancer is traditionally classified as superficial (Ta or T1) or invasive (T2, T3, and T4), the two subtypes being quite different in their overall characteristics. Long-recurrence free episodes are present in most cases of the superficial disease, while for the invasive cases a multimodal therapy is usually necessary, combining surgery and chemotherapy.

Important goals are the detection of cancer at an early stage, determining prognosis and monitoring disease progression and therapeutic response, in a personalized way. These can be achieved by analyzing alterations in gene sequences, mRNA and microRNA expression levels, protein structure or function. These alterations form cancer biomarkers that can be used to guide treatment (see [2]) and the success of personalized medicine depends on their availability. Despite decades of intense effort, few biomarkers are in clinical use.

E. Biganzoli et al. (Eds.): CIBB 2011, LNBI 7548, pp. 190–200, 2012.

Research in bladder cancer and mRNA expression has increased over the last several years, with high-throughput experiments investigating thousands of molecules in parallel. The final result of most of these studies are lists of selected and ranked molecules capable to discriminate between one or more clinical outcomes. Bioinformatics tools are used and the most common ranking criterion is the p-value of the statistical tests performed.

Although these lists are interesting, a challenging bioinformatics problem arises: developing accurate methods to include these lists as support in clinical decisions for cancer treatment. For example, a classifier for the prediction of bladder cancer progression has been developed with an accuracy on validation of just 66% (see [3]). A solution we proposed is the development of systems based on artificial intelligence (AI): Intelligent Clinical Decision Support Systems (i-CDSS), a concept first introduced by us in [4], and i-Biomarkers (see [5] for a general methodology), a subset of i-CDSSs. We have developed intelligent systems for bladder cancer diagnosis [6] and progression [7] based on plasma microRNA measurements, with an accuracy reaching as high as 100%.

This study is focused on invasive bladder cancer of urothelial origin, also known as transitional cell carcinoma. The goal was to develop i-Biomarkers for the prediction of bladder cancer progression based on mRNA measurements. Genes selection was performed by either knowledge discovery in data (KDD) alone, or by combining KDD and Knowledge Mining (KM). The C5 decision tree algorithm, with and without ensemble methods (boosting), was used to build i-Biomarkers. The i-Biomarkers based on KDD alone achieved 100% accuracy, only with boosted C5 trees. The i-Biomarkers based on combined KDD and KM achieved 100% accuracy, even without boosting. To our knowledge, these are the first intelligent clinical decision support systems based on C5 and boosting, for invasive bladder cancer progression, and the most accurate.

2   Methods

2.1   Data Preprocessing

The microarray data was obtained by material hybridization on a Illumina Human-6 expression beadchip version 2. We therefore quantile normalized and log2 transformed the raw data, by using the *lumi* package in Bioconductor, specific for Illumina microarray analysis [8].

Two methods of genes (feature) selection were used, resulting in two sets of genes, for i-Biomarker development. Both methods are designed such as to avoid overfitting or overoptimistic results. The first set was selected by KDD alone. It contains genes with a standard deviation higher than a chosen threshold. No information about the classes — progression and no progression — of the samples was used. The second set consisted of genes selected based on KM and KDD, and again, no information about the output was used. The KM method will be published elsewhere. A second feature selection was performed for both genes sets, by the build in feature selection capability of the decision trees used (see Section 2.2).

2.2   i-Biomarker Development Using C5 Decision Trees

In this study, we developed i-Biomarkers for BCa prognosis prediction: Progression vs. No Progression using C5 decision trees. The i-Biomarkers are classifiers that can accurately make the distinction between the two classes: Progression (Yes) versus No Progression (No), based on mRNA measurements. A team of such classifiers forms a panel of i-Biomarkers. Performing external validation is the best method to verify the accuracy of the i-Biomarkers in classifying new samples. However, due to the relative small number of samples usually available in microarray experiments, in comparison to the number of mRNAs, this process becomes a challenging task.

The alternative solution is to estimate the i-Biomarker's predictive accuracy on samples included in the dataset. In this case, an important rule must be followed: the samples used for the i-Biomarker validation must not intervene before or during the i-Biomarker's development. Two types of procedures can be applied to accomplish this goal (see [9]):

1. Randomly splitting the data in a training and a testing dataset: the training dataset is further used to develop the i-Biomarker, while the testing dataset intervenes only when evaluating the i-Biomarker's accuracy. This method performs well when a sufficient number of samples is available.
2. Performing cross-validation: this iterative process implies creating temporary training and testing datasets at each iteration (or fold). Although, in the end, all the samples intervene in both training and testing, at each fold the i-Biomarker is developed on samples selected for training and validated on different samples in the test set, so the rule is not violated. This procedure is preferred when the number of samples is not sufficient for the split-sample procedure described above.

To develop the i-Biomarkers, we tested different decision tree algorithms such as: CART [10], CHAID and the C4.5 [11]. Although all the decision trees performed well (results not shown), the C5 algorithm (which is the latest version of the C4.5 decision tree) gave the best results and was further used in this study.

A general method to building decision trees is described below:

1. The process starts with an empty tree and the whole training set.
2. The following steps are iteratively repeated until a stopping criterion is reached (for example, all the samples were correctly classified or the minimum number of samples can be found in each terminal node (leaf node)).
3. At the current node: if all training samples belong to the same category (Progression or No Progression) then the node becomes terminal.
4. Otherwise, the variable (or attribute, mRNA) which best splits correctly the training samples into the two categories is determined and becomes a decision node.
5. From the decision node, a branch is created and the samples are partitioned accordingly.

The splitting procedure is performed so as to maximize the purity of the classification at a given level, and it is different for each decision tree. The measure of purity (or equivalently saying, the method of selection of the best attribute) used by the C5 algorithm is based on the maximum information gain at each level.

The development of a decision tree is usually performed in two stages. In the first stage, the tree grows recursively by following the general algorithm described above. At each iteration, the attribute (mRNA) which best discriminates between the two possible outcomes (Progression vs. No Progression) is selected. The training samples are split into the two categories by comparing their values for the selected attribute with the determined threshold value for that attribute. The splitting procedure stops when all the samples were correctly assigned to a terminal node. However, requesting an 100% accuracy can sometimes lead to an overfitted model. A stopping criterion that helps to avoid this is based on setting a minimum number of samples per child branch. In this case, splitting continues only if the resulting new branches contain at least the minimum number of samples.

The second stage of decision tree development consists of a pruning procedure. Global pruning may be performed and this implies a first process of local pruning. To an extent provided by the pruning severity, local pruning examines subtrees and collapses branches to improve the tree's accuracy and simplifies it at the same time. By increasing the pruning severity, smaller trees are obtained, while decreasing this value leads to a higher accuracy of the model. Global pruning analyzes the tree as a whole and this can lead to further elimination of branches.

The goal of obtaining the highest accuracy possible can be achieved by using ensemble modeling, considered one of the greatest advances in statistical research over the past decade (see [12] and [13]). This approach implies combining multiple models having specified standards of accuracy and diversity to outperform a single model.

For our study we preferred the boosting ensemble method proposed by Freund and Schapire [14]. Boosting works by repeatedly developing classifiers on various distributions over the training data, and then combining these classifiers into a single composite model. Variety is created by assigning different weights to the cases studied, according to whether they were easier or harder to classify correctly (see [12] and [13] for details). The following steps describe a general algorithm for boosting applied to our study:

1. Assign equal weights to the samples.
2. Repeat the following steps for a given number T of trials (for $j = 1, T$):
   (a) Develop an i-Biomarker$_j$ (C5 decision tree) using the computed weights.
   (b) Give higher weights to the samples more difficult to classify correctly.
   (c) Give lower weights to the samples easier to classify accurately.
3. Combine i-Biomarkers from i-Biomarker$_1$ to i-Biomarker$_T$ to obtain the panel of i-Biomarkers (boosted C5 decision trees); perform this by assigning higher weights to the earliest i-Biomarkers, and lower weights to the last i-Biomarkers.

There are many advantages in developing i-Biomarkers using C5 and boosted C5 decision trees, regarding the following:

1. The input variables: from the multitude of mRNA inputs, only relevant mR-NAs are selected for the i-Biomarker's development. At every decision node all the inputs are evaluated, but only the attribute offering the best split is chosen for further use. This underlines the variable selection capability of the i-Biomarkers based on C5 decision trees.
2. The samples' data: decision trees can handle outliers and their accuracy is not diminished significantly by missing values.
3. Computational details:
   (a) The algorithm implies a limited number of tunable parameters, which makes it easy to use once the parameters are understood.
   (b) The building and running of the trees are fast in comparison to other iterative methods.
4. Model analysis: the resulting model given as a binary tree graphic is easy to interpret, at least to a few levels.

Certain disadvantages appear however. For example, the samples used to train the i-Biomarker are reduced after every split, thus, when reaching high dimensions this can lead to overfitting. Also, the greedy search strategy (local optima) implies that small changes in the data (e.g., sampling fluctuations) can result in big changes of the fully developed tree.

3   Results and Discussions

3.1   Samples Data

We used a dataset of primary BCa samples [15], accessible at NCBI GEO database [16] (accession GSE13507), consisting of 62 patients with invasive BCa (stages T2, T3 and T4), 42 samples with no progression and 20 samples with progression.

3.2   i-Biomarkers Development

We developed i-Biomarkers that can accurately predict bladder cancer progression using two different sets of genes. The data were preprocessed as described in Section 2.1. The first set, denoted as the Knowledge Discovery in Data or simply the KDD set consisted in 815 genes having a standard deviation higher than or equal to 1.5. The second, denoted as the Knowledge Mining or KM set, contained 416 genes determined as important through KM and KDD, i.e. they are differentially expressed genes in a surrogate mesenchymal to epithelial transition phenotype created by expressing a poor prognostic marker (miR-200c) in mesenchymal BCa cells. The two sets overlap having 24 genes in common.

The i-Biomarkers had a categorical binary output: Yes for progression and No for no progression. We applied the C5 decision tree algorithm for both sets of input genes.

To develop an i-Biomarker, we used a V-fold cross validation (CV) procedure and tested different values for V. This approach was chosen as the number of patients was relatively small ($n = 62$ samples), not allowing the splitting of the dataset into training and testing. The process is illustrated in Fig. 1, adapted from [9].

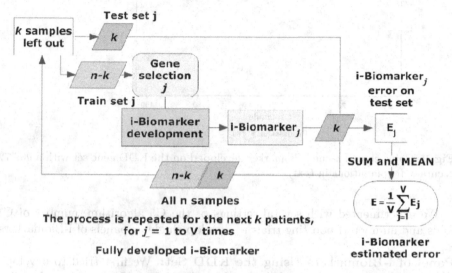

Fig. 1. Development of an i-Biomarker with a V-fold CV procedure. The i-Biomarker is for a binary outcome: Progression (Yes) vs. No Progression (No). From the initial dataset with n samples, k samples are withdrawn creating a temporary testing set and a training set with n - k samples. A different mRNA selection j is performed on the training set and a different i-Biomarker$_j$ is developed at each iteration of the CV. The i-Biomarker$_j$ developed is used to classify the left-out samples in the testing set as Yes or No progression. Final result: the fully developed i-Biomarker and the estimated error computed as the mean of each i-Biomarker$_j$'s error on the test set.

Each fold contains the same (or nearly the same) k number of patients obtained by splitting the total number of patients ($n = 62$) to the number of folds V. At each fold, the C5 algorithm made a selection of genes and an i-Biomarker$_j$ was developed using the temporary training dataset consisting of n - k patients. The temporary testing dataset containing the remaining k patients was used to test the accuracy of the i-Biomarker. The genes used to build an i-Biomarker$_j$ were different at each step of the cross validation procedure.

A fully developed i-Biomarker was obtained after performing all folds. An estimate of its error was computed as the mean of classification errors of each i-Biomarker$_j$ on the temporary test set j. The classification error of an i-Biomarker$_j$ was computed as the ratio between the number of patients it misclassified and the total number of patients.

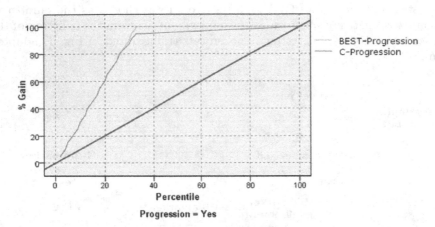

Fig. 2. Gains chart for the i-Biomarker developed on the KDD gene set with a 96.77% accuracy (explanations in text)

We experimented with several settings of the C5 algorithm, number of CV folds and number of boosting trials to develop single or panels of i-Biomarkers.

Panel of i-Biomarkers Using the KDD Set: We first tried to develop a single i-Biomarker using the C5 algorithm, the V-fold CV procedure described above and providing as input the genes from the KDD set. The settings for C5 were: perform global pruning, a pruning severity for local pruning of 75% and a minimum number of records (samples) per child branch of 2. We tested different CV folds, from $V = 3$ to $V = 62$, the last corresponding to the leave-one-out CV procedure.

The accuracy of the i-Biomarker was of 96.77% and constant with respect to the number of CV folds. Two samples were misclassified: one sample with progression classified as no progression (false negative) and one sample without progression labeled as having progression (false positive).

The accuracy of the i-Biomarker may also be observed by analyzing its cumulative gains chart. Gains are defined as the proportion of total hits that occurs in each quantile. Gains are computed as (number of hits in quantile / total number of hits) 100%. Besides the gains chart, we also presented the best line and the baseline. The best line indicates perfect confidence, where hits equal 100% of cases (samples), while the baseline indicates a perfectly random distribution of hits where confidence becomes irrelevant. In Fig. 2 the gains chart (C-Progression line) is closer to the best line (BEST-Progression line), but it does not level off at 100%. This suggests a good accuracy of the i-Biomarker, but not the highest of 100%.

An 100% accuracy using the KDD set was only obtained by developing a panel of i-Biomarkers. This was accomplished by using the C5 decision tree with boosting. We first set the same settings as above for C5 and experimented with different numbers of CV folds — $V = 3$, $V = 10$, $V = 62$ — and boosting trials — 3, 10 and 25. An 100% accuracy was obtained regardless of the number of boosting trials and CV folds. We then set the number of CV-folds to $V = 3$ and the number of boosting trials to 3 and tested different pruning severities — 75%, 80% and 85%— and different minimum number of records per child branch — 3, 4 and 5. The accuracy decreased only when setting 5 minimum records per child branch, reaching 98.39% and was not influenced by the pruning severity.

From the multitude of panels of i-Biomarkers developed with the above settings and having a 100% accuracy, we chose a panel of 10 i-Biomarkers: an i-Biomarker from the panel was obtained with a 10-fold CV procedure; the C5 settings were: perform global pruning, a pruning severity of 75% and 2 minimum number of records per child branch; boosting was performed with 10 trials.

The corresponding gains chart is presented in Fig. 3. The gains chart (C-Diagnosis line) levels off at 100%, thus implying that the maximum accuracy was reached.

The C5 algorithm selected and ranked as important 30 genes for this particular panel of i-Biomarkers (result not shown as it is patent pending). It is our belief that such a panel of 10 i-Biomarkers will provide better results on validation on a new dataset than panels with fewer i-Biomarkers, even though on this dataset they reached the same high accuracy.

Single i-Biomarker Using the KM Set: Due to the initial gene selection process in the KM set, classification with a 100% accuracy was obtained by developing a single i-Biomarker. The C5 decision tree had the following settings: perform global pruning, a pruning severity of 75% and 2 minimum number of records per child branch and the 10 fold CV procedure presented above was used. We experimented with different CV folds from $V = 3$ to $V = 62$ that had no influence on the accuracy. We also increased the minimum number of records per child branch to 3 and observed a decrease in accuracy, reaching 93.55% and thus decided to choose the i-Biomarker initially developed with 2 minimum number of records per child branch.

The i-Biomarker contains 7 genes selected and ranked by the C5 algorithm using its intrinsic capability of attribute selection. The importance of the genes is shown in Fig. 4. The Illumina Id of the genes was replaced with a generic notation (mRNA01,..., mRNA07), as this result is patent pending.

The decision tree of the i-Biomarker is presented in Fig. 5. The accuracy of 100% is confirmed by analyzing the terminal nodes of the tree: the samples in each terminal node belong to a single category: progression (Yes, red rectangles) or no progression (No, blue rectangles).

The decision tree is easy to interpret. For a new sample, we observe the values of the 7 genes included in the i-Biomarker and compare them with the threshold values identified at each node. For example, if the value of mRNA01 for the new sample is higher than the threshold value 8.73, then the sample is classified with progression (Yes); otherwise, we compare the value of mRNA02 for the sample with the threshold value 9.2: if it is higher, the sample is included in the

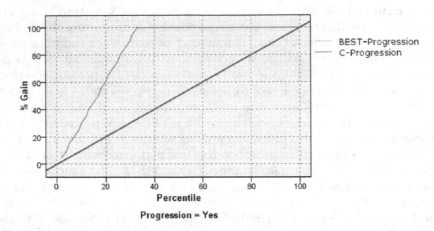

Fig. 3. Gains chart for the panel of i-Biomarkers developed on the KDD gene set with a 100% accuracy (explanations in text)

Variable Importance

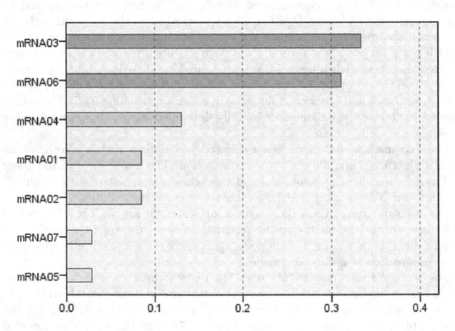

Fig. 4. Variable importance for the i-Biomarker developed on the KM gene set with a 100% accuracy (explanations in text)

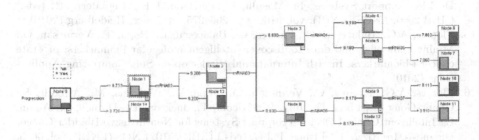

Fig. 5. Decision tree for the i-Biomarker developed on the KM gene set with a 100% accuracy (explanations in text)

progression cases; else, mRNA03 is investigated, and the process of evaluation continues until the sample is included in a terminal node, thus in a category.

Although one could argue that obtaining a single i-Biomarker with the highest accuracy would be the best solution, it is our belief that a panel of i-Biomarkers developed using ensemble methods will provide better accuracy on new, unseen cases. Passing a new case through multiple filters should reduce the probability of misclassification. Results have shown (see [17]) that ensemble methods do not perform overfitting in practical applications, leading to a contradiction with Ocam's Razor that "the simpler of competing alternatives should be preferred".

4 Conclusion

Using the white-box artificial intelligence algorithm boosted C5 decision trees, in a knowledge discovery in data approach, either alone or combined with knowledge mining, we developed intelligent clinical decision support systems, in the form of a panel of i-Biomarkers, for invasive bladder cancer progression prediction. The proposed methodology is specially designed to avoid overfitting and overoptimistic results and the accuracy is 100%, for the analyzed data.

References

1. Jemal, A., Siegel, R., Xu, J., Ward, E.: Cancer Statistics. CA Cancer J. Clin. (2010), doi:caac.20073
2. Tuma, R.S.: Biomarker Developers Face Big Hurdles. J. Natl. Cancer Inst. 100, 456–461 (2008)
3. Dyrskjot, L., Zieger, K., Real, F.X., Malats, N., Carrato, A., Hurst, C., Kotwal, S., Knowles, M., Malmstrom, P., de la Torre, M., Wester, K., Allory, Y., Vordos, D., Caillault, A., Radvanyi, F., Hein, A.K., Jensen, J.L., Jensen, K.M.E., Marcussen, N., Orntoft, T.F.: Gene Expression Signatures Predict Outcome in Non Muscle-Invasive Bladder Carcinoma: A Multicenter Validation Study. Clinical Cancer Research 13, 3545–3551 (2007)

4. Floares, A.G.: Using Computational Intelligence to Develop Intelligent Clinical Decision Support Systems. In: Masulli, F., Peterson, L.E., Tagliaferri, R. (eds.) CIBB 2009. LNCS (LNBI), vol. 6160, pp. 266–275. Springer, Heidelberg (2010)
5. Floares, A.G., Balacescu, O., Floares, C., Balacescu, L., Popa, T., Vermesan, O.: Mining knowledge and data to discover intelligent molecular biomarkers: prostate cancer i-biomarkers. In: 4th International Workshop on Soft Computing Applications (2010)
6. Floares, A.G., Floares, C., Vermesan, O., Popa, T., Williams, M., Ajibode, S., Chang-Gong, L., Lixia, D., Jing, W., Nicola, T., Jackson, D., Dinney, C., Adam, L.: Intelligent Clinical Decision Support Systems for Non-invasive Bladder Cancer Diagnosis. In: Rizzo, R., Lisboa, P.J.G. (eds.) CIBB 2010. LNCS (LNBI), vol. 6685, pp. 253–262. Springer, Heidelberg (2011)
7. Williams, M., Floares, A., Choi, W., Siefker-Radtke, A., McConkey, D., Dinney, C., Adam, L.: Prognostic significance of miR-200 family in bladder cancer progression. In: EMT and Cancer Progression and Treatment (2010)
8. Du, P., Kibbe, W.A., Lin, S.M.: lumi: a pipeline for processing Illumina microarray. Bioinformatics 24, 1547–1548 (2008)
9. Dupuy, A., Simon, R.M.: Critical Review of Published Microarray Studies for Cancer Outcome and Guidelines on Statistical Analysis and Reporting. Journal of the National Cancer Institute 99, 147–157 (2007)
10. Breiman, L., Friedman, J.H., Olshen, R.A., Stone, C.J.: Classification and Regression Trees. Chapman & Hall, New York (1984)
11. Quinlan, J.R.: C4.5: programs for machine learning. Morgan Kaufmann Publishers Inc., San Francisco (1993)
12. Nisbet, R., Elder, J., Miner, G.: Handbook of Statistical Analysis and Data Mining Applications. Academic Press, Canada (2009)
13. Seni, G., Elder, J.F.: Ensemble Methods in Data Mining: Improving Accuracy Through Combining Predictions. In: Han, J., Getoor, L., Wang, W., Hill, C., Gehrke, J., Grossman, J. (eds.) Synthesis Lectures on Data Mining and Knowledge Discovery. Morgan & Claypool, California (2010)
14. Freund, Y., Schapire, R.E.: Experiments with a New Boosting Algorithm. In: 13th International Conference on Machine Learning (ICML), pp. 148–156 (1996)
15. Kim, W.J., Kim, E.J., Kim, S.K., Kim, Y.J., Ha, Y.S., Jeong, P., Kim, M.J., Yun, S.J., Lee, K., Moon, S.K., Lee, S.C., Cha, E.J., Bae, S.C.: Predictive value of progression-related gene classifier in primary non-muscle invasive bladder cancer. Molecular Cancer 9, 3 (2010)
16. Barrett, T., Troup, D.B., Wilhite, S.E., Ledoux, P., Evangelista, C., Kim, I.F., Tomashevsky, M., Marshall, K.A., Phillippy, K.H., Sherman, P.M., Muertter, R.N., Holko, M., Ayanbule, O., Yefanov, A., Soboleva, A.: NCBI GEO: archive for functional genomics data sets – 10 years on. Nucleic Acids Research 39, D1005–D1010 (2011)
17. Domingos, P.: The Role of Occam's Razor in Knowledge Discovery. Data Mining and Knowledge Discovery 3, 409–425 (1999)

A Faster Algorithm for Motif Finding in Sequences from ChIP-Seq Data

Federico Zambelli and Giulio Pavesi

Dept. of Biomolecular Science and Biotechnology
University of Milan
via Celoria 26
Milan, Italy
{giulio.pavesi,federico.zambelli}@unimi.it

Abstract. Motif finding in nucleotide sequences for the discovery of over–represented transcription factor binding sites is a very challenging problem, both from the computational and the experimental points of view. Transcription factors in fact recognize very weakly conserved sequence elements, that in typical applications are very hard to discriminate against random sequence similarities. Recent advances in technology like ChIP-Seq can generate better datasets to be investigated, in which the degree of conservation of binding sites is higher: on the other hand, the size itself of the datasets has posed new challenges for the design of efficient algorithms able to produce results in reasonable time. In this work we present an updated version of our algorithm Weeder, in which time and space requirements are significantly reduced and, moreover, also the accuracy of the results is notably improved.

1   Introduction

Motif finding can be defined as the problem of finding short similar sequence elements shared by a set of nucleotide or protein sequences with a common biological function, in order to highlight which parts of the sequences could be more likely to be essential for the function itself. The identification of regulatory elements in nucleotide sequences, modulating the expression of genes, has been one of the most widely studied flavors of the problem, both for its biological significance and for its sheer difficulty.

The first step of gene expression, the transcription of a DNA region into a complementary RNA sequence, is finely regulated by the activity of *transcription factors* (TFs), which usually bind DNA in the neighborhood of the transcription start site of genes, in the *promoter* region. The transcription of a given gene can be said to be initiated when the "right" combination of TFs is bound to the DNA at the "right" time in its neighborhood [1].

The actual DNA region bound by a TF (called *transcription factor binding site*, or TFBS) usually ranges in size from 8-10 to 16-20 nucleotides (small sequence elements of this size are also called *oligonucleotides*, or *oligos*). TFs bind the DNA in a sequence-specific fashion, that is, they recognize sequences that are

E. Biganzoli et al. (Eds.): CIBB 2011, LNBI 7548, pp. 201–212, 2012.

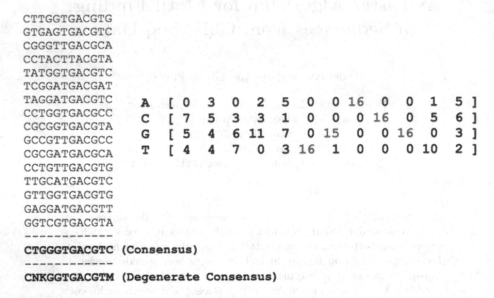

```
CTTGGTGACGTG
GTGAGTGACGTC
CGGGTTGACGCA
CCTACTTACGTA
TATGGTGACGTC
TCGGATGACGAT
TAGGATGACGTC   A  [ 0  3  0  2  5  0  0 16  0  0  1  5 ]
CCTGGTGACGCC   C  [ 7  5  3  3  1  0  0  0 16  0  5  6 ]
CGCGGTGACGTA   G  [ 5  4  6 11  7  0 15  0  0 16  0  3 ]
GCCGTTGACGCC   T  [ 4  4  7  0  3 16  1  0  0  0 10  2 ]
CGCGATGACGCA
CCTGTTGACGTG
TTGCATGACGTC
GTTGGTGACGTG
GAGGATGACGTT
GGTCGTGACGTA
-----------
CTGGGTGACGTC (Consensus)
-----------
CNKGGTGACGTM (Degenerate Consensus)
```

Fig. 1. Representing a collection of sites bound by the same TF (left column) with a consensus or a regular expression (left, bottom) or with a profile giving the frequency of each nucleotide at each position of the sites (right). Notice how all the sites contain five nucleotides almost perfectly conserved.

similar but not identical, tolerating a certain degree of approximation. The binding sequence preference of a given TF can be summarized and modeled starting from an experimentally validated collection of its sites [2], as shown in Figure 1. In the simplest form, we can take, position by position, the most frequent nucleotide, and build a *consensus* of the sites. All oligos that differ from the consensus up to a maximum number of nucleotide substitutions can be considered valid instances of binding sites for the same TF. Alternatively, we can build the alignment profile (or *position specific weight matrix*) of the sites, in order to estimate the frequency with which each nucleotide appears in each position of the sites. Notice in Figure 1 also how differences between the different oligos do not seem to be the effect of random mutations: rather, it can be easily seen how some adjacent positions are more conserved and tolerate less variation than others. This phenomenon is typical of TFBSs, that often exhibit a conserved core flanked by less conserved nucleotides.

2   The Problem

If we have measurements of the level of transcript of genes through technologies like microarrays, the rationale for the discovery of TFBSs is straightforward: TFs regulate the transcription of genes; genes with similar transcription patterns should be regulated by the same TFs; by investigating genomic regions taken from these co-expressed genes (for example, their promoters) one should be able to detect the presence of short "over-represented" sequence elements, corresponding to binding sites for the common regulators. As for representation, also the de novo discovery of over-represented candidate TFBSs has followed two main approaches, namely those *consensus-based*, which enumerate all the possible consensuses of feasible length matching them on the sequences, and those *profile-based*, which try to find the combination of sequence oligos building the best profile, that is the highest scoring one according to some measure of conservation like information content[3]. In the latter case, however, the problem of finding the most conserved profile is NP-hard under every feasible measure of significance: hence the introduction of heuristics for the exploration of the solution space with combinatorial approaches.

In the last few years the introduction of technologies like *Chromatin Immunoprecipitation* (ChIP [4]), coupled with *next-generation sequencing* (ChIP-Seq [5]), has permitted the direct genome-wide identification of regions bound *in vivo* by a given TF. Usually the number of genomic regions bound by a TF ranges from a few thousands to several thousands. Since the regions extracted are anyway usually much larger than the actual TFBS (200-300 bps), these experiments are a perfect case study for motif finding as well.

Regardless of the source experiment, the problem can be informally defined as follows: given a set of DNA sequences, typically a few hundred base pairs (bps) long, find a set of oligos (8-16 bps long) appearing in all or most of the sequences (thus allowing for experimental errors and the presence of false positives in the set) similar to one another enough to be likely to be instances of sites recognized by the same TF. Moreover, the same set of similar oligos should not appear with the same frequency and/or the same degree of similarity in a set of sequences selected at random (thus very unlikely to share any common regulator) or built with some model generating random but "biologically feasible" DNA sequences. The similar and over-represented oligos collectively build the *motif* recurring in the input sequences.

While the overall problem is virtually the same, there are some significant differences between the analysis of a set of promoters from co-expressed genes and of a set of sequences derived from a ChIP experiment[6]:

1. The size of the sequence sets: a genome-wide ChIP usually yields thousands of candidate regions, while a typical promoter analysis of co-expressed genes is performed on a few dozen sequences.
2. The length of the sequences: sequences extracted from experiments like ChIP-Seq are usually 200-300 bps long, as opposed to promoters which are usually defined as 500-1000 bps long.
3. The frequency with which binding sites for the same TF appear: in a ChIP they should appear in a very large percentage of the sequences examined, even more than once in a single sequence, while in a set of co-expressed genes there is no guarantee for this.

In other words, with ChIP we have a much larger but somewhat cleaner input sequence set and, more importantly, much more redundant, since in thousands of sequences we can expect to find several instances of binding sites very similar to one another. On the other hand, co–expression does not imply co–regulation. That is, the similar expression patterns shared by a set of genes could be, and often is, the effect of several different regulators, each acting on a subset of them. In traditional gene promoter analysis, thus, the input set is much less clean (there is no guarantee on how many sequences actually share the same motif), the sequence set is much smaller (and thus the similarities among different sites recognized by the same TF in the sequences can be very subtle) and the sequences are longer [8]. Thus, in ChIP we can expect to obtain a clearer separation of the signal (the motif) from the background "noise", and a better performance of motif finding methods.

From a computational point of view, the main drawback is the fact itself that genome-wide ChIP experiments yield much larger data sets than expression-based experiments, usually made of thousands of sequences. Profile-optimization becomes too time-consuming for the increase of the solution search space and of the number of candidate solutions to be optimized [7], and this fact has led to the development of consensus-based algorithms more specific for this type of data, which are usually based on consensus enumeration by matching on the input sequences all the possible oligos of a given length, and collecting the approximate occurrences of each one up to a given number of substitutions. To further speed up the exhaustive matching, the sequences can be organized with a suitable indexing structure like suffix trees [9, 10, 11], and mismatches can be confined to only some positions of the oligos by using regular expressions [11, 12].

3   The Algorithm

An algorithm we introduced for this problem a few years ago, called Weeder [10], is still one of the most widely used tools, even on ChIP-Seq data. It is a con-sensus based method that indexes sequences with a suffix tree without imposing restrictions on the positions of mismatches. Having being designed for finding subtle similarities in small sequence sets, however, it becomes significantly slow on "modern" data sets, and in its full implementation the suffix tree barely fits into the memory of a state of the art computer. We thus developed an updated version of the algorithm addressing these two points, that is, finding an index-ing strategy less space-consuming on one hand, and on the other introducing some heuristic able to trim the search space and hence the time required by the algorithm.

For the indexing of the input sequences, we replaced the suffix tree with a De Bruijn graph (DBG [13]). A DBG is a directed graph whose edges are labeled with substrings of the input sequences. The graph is built by splitting the sequences into overlapping substrings of a given length k (k-tuples), where two adjacent k-tuples overlap by $(k-1)$ characters. Each k-tuple corresponds to a directed edge of the graph, and each edge corresponds to identical k-tuples in the input sequences. Two edges are connected to a node if they represent two adjacent k-tuples of the input sequences. The node represents the k-tuple

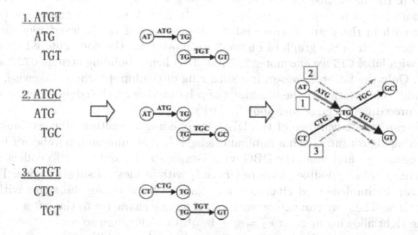

Fig. 2. De Bruijn Graph for strings ATGT, ATGC, and CTGT

overlap. An example is shown in Figure 2. For string $ATGT$ and $k = 3$, we have two k-*tuples* ATG and TGT that overlap, and the two corresponding edges are connected by a node. In this way, each of the input sequences corresponds to a unique path in the graph. If a k-*tuple* appears in different sequences, the corresponding sequence paths will intersect at the edge representing the k-*tuple*, and the number of sequence paths visiting the edge will correspond to the number of sequences containing the k-*tuple*. As in [13] we define the edge multiplicity as the number of sequence paths visiting the edge.

DBGs have proven themselves to be a very efficient indexing strategy for handling large number of sequences, like in sequence assembly [14], and have been recently applied to the multiple local alignment problem and to motif finding in amino acid sequences [13]. The key property of this structure is that in the graph edges corresponding to conserved motifs will tend to have higher multiplicity. To further exploit this property, during the construction of the graph we can further annotate each edge with a bit-string where the ith bit is set if the k-*tuple* appears in the ith input sequence. Now, let $p = p_1 \ldots p_k$ be an oligo of length k (the size of the k-*tuple*). The sequences p appears in can be retrieved from the bit-string in the corresponding edge of the graph. Likewise, the sequences p appears in with at most e substitutions are given by the bit-string resulting from the logical OR of the bit strings of the edges corresponding to strings within Hamming distance e from p.

Once the occurrences of p in the graph have been located on the corresponding edges, then the graph can be used as an indexing structure for pattern matching, since all the k-*tuples* overlapping p in the sequences will be connected to its edge by a node. Thus, we can move to the edge whose k-*tuple* ends with the character a we want to match. Notice that the bit string of the edge we end up on corresponds to the occurrences of $p_2 \ldots p_k a$, which are exactly those of $p_1 \ldots p_k$ only if a follows p in every sequence. Thus, by performing the logical

AND of the bit strings of the two edges we get an *upper bound* on the actual number of sequences $p_1 \ldots p_k a$ appears in. In fact, there is no guarantee that every path in the graph corresponds to a substring of the indexed sequences. For example, if in the graph of Figure 2 we move from the node entered by the edge with label CTG we encounter TGC and TGT, hence building strings CTGC and CTGT. Only the latter, however, is a substring of the input strings. Likewise, we can add a character a at the beginning of p by moving on the edges entering the node preceding the edge corresponding to p.

We can take advantage of the DBG by building a multiple-step exhaustive matching algorithm. Given a minimum length l_1 and minimum number of mismatches e_1, we first build the DBG with k-*tuple* size l_1, and use it to collect the occurrences of all possible motifs of length l_1 with at most e_1 substitutions. This step can be implemented efficiently for example by indexing the edges with a hash table. Then, we can extend each motif by one character to the left and one to the right allowing at most $e_2 = e_1 + 1$ substitutions, and so on.

Thus, the result is that we obtain, for each possible motif p, an upper bound on the number of sequences it appears in with at most e_2 substitutions, with the additional constraint of having at most e_1 mismatches in the middle l_1 characters, at most $e_1 + 1$ in the middle $l_1 + 2$, and so on. This step can be iterated any number of times, starting at each "expansion" step from the occurrences of a motif of length l with at most e_l substitutions, and adding one character to the left and one to the right allowing at most $e_l + 1$ substitutions. This procedure can be implemented recursively, like exhaustive pattern matching with a suffix tree, as outlined in Figure 3. Given a pattern p and pointers to its approximate occurrences in the graph, the procedure first adds a character a to the left of the pattern, locating it on the graph with the respective number of errors. Then, appends every possible character to the right of motif ap and locates each resulting motif in the graph as well.

Once a motif p has been located with the corresponding bit string, we can compute a significance score taking into account the number of strings p appears in, and its conservation in each of them. Given k input sequences $S_1, S_2, \ldots, S_k$:

$$W(p) = \sum_{i=1}^{k} I(p, S_i) \log_2 \frac{Obs(p, S_i, e_i)}{Exp(p, S_i, e_i)} \qquad (1)$$

Where $I(p, S_i)$ equals one if p appears in sequence S_i, zero otherwise; e_i is the minimum number of substitutions with which p appears in S_i, and $Obs(p, S_i, e_i)$ is the number of times p appears in sequence S_i with e_i substitutions; $Exp(p, S_i, e_i)$ is the expected value for the number of occurrences of p in sequence i with at most e_i substitutions, given by the frequency with which p appears in the promoters of the genome of the same organism of the input sequences multiplied by the length of sequence S_i. This is the score function we introduced in the original Weeder algorithm [10].

As we mentioned before, the occurrences collected in this way for each oligo p are an upper bound on the actual number. Our idea is to use the scores obtained anyway, as a pre-filtering step: we rank the motifs according to the scores just computed, and then fully match the h highest scoring ones on the sequences, collecting the actual occurrences and computing once again the score only for these.

Moreover, as an additional speed-up of the exhaustive search, we can limit the expansion step only to those motifs which were among the highest-ranking h at the previous step (those for which we computed the exact score). In this way, we end up expanding and matching on the sequences only motifs which have the "conserved-core" property we mentioned in the introduction.

All in all, the algorithm can be summarized as follows, starting from a minimum length l_{min}, and defining a priori the number of iterations (expansions) *itermax*:

1. Let $l = l_{min}$ and $e = e_{min}$
2. Build the DBG with $k - tuple$ size l.
3. Enumerate all possible oligos of length l, and locate their approximate occurrences on the corresponding edges in the graph with at most e substitutions. Score each motif and rank the motifs according to the score computed.
4. Let $i = i + 1$. Let $e = e + 1$.
5. Expand all the top t_{i-1} highest scoring motifs starting from the corresponding edges in the graph, allowing at most e substitutions in their occurrences.
6. Rank the new expanded motifs according to their score
7. Match in the sequences the top h_i motifs, re–computing their score according to the occurrences collected
8. Rank the motifs according to the new score
9. If $i < itermax$ goto 4

4   Experimental Evaluation

In our experiments we ran the algorithm with minimum motif size $l_{min} = 6$ and $e_{min} = 1$, followed by two expansion steps at length 8 and 10 with 2 and 3 mismatches, respectively. For length $l = 6$, all motifs are scored and ranked. Then, the top $h = 2000$ are passed to the expansion step of length 8 with two substitutions. Once the upper bound for the score has been computed by matching them on the graph, the top $h = 500$ motifs of length 8 are scored by collecting their occurrences in the sequences. Finally, the top 250 motifs of length 8 are passed to the last expansion step, with motifs of 10 bps with three substitutions.

As a benchmark, we applied our method to the "Metazoan compendium" presented in [12]. From this collection, we selected datasets of human or mouse gene promoters experimentally known to be bound by a given TF through genome-wide ChIP experiments. The sole exception are four datasets corresponding to genes expressed in the G1S and G2M phases of human cell cycle, and two of genes annotated with Gene Ontology term "Immune Response" in human and mouse, respectively. As in the original experiment, we considered sequences from -1000 to +200 base pairs with respect to the transcription start site. This dataset

```
Procedure expand(pattern p, Loc_p, n)
errmax = s_err + n;
for all x ∈ {A,C,G,T}
    p' = xp
    OccBits_p' = [0,0, ... 0];
    Loc_p' = ∅ ;
    for all (Pos, e) ∈ Loc_p
        for all edge ∈ Prev(Start(Pos))
            if First_Char(edge) = x
                OccBits_p' = OccBits_p' OR (OccBits_p AND OccBits_edge );
                Pos' = Insert_first_edge(Pos, edge);
                Loc_p' = Loc_p' ∪ (Pos', e);
            else if e + 1 ≤ errmax
                OccBits_p' = OccBits_p' OR (OccBits_p AND OccBits_edge );
                Pos' = Insert_first_edge(Pos, edge);
                Loc_p' = Loc_p' ∪ (Pos', e + 1);
            end if
        end for
    end for
    for all y ∈ {A,C,G,T}
    p'' = p'y;
    Loc_p'' = ∅ ;
    OccBits_p'' = [0,0, ... 0];
        for all (Pos', e') ∈ Loc_p'
            for all edge ∈ Next(End(Pos'))
                if Last_Char(edge) = y
                    OccBits_p'' = OccBits_p'' OR (OccBits_p' AND OccBits_edge );
                    Pos'' = Append_last_edge(Pos' , edge);
                    Loc_p'' = Loc_p'' ∪ (Pos'', e');
                else if e' + 1 ≤ errmax
                    OccBits_p'' = OccBits_p'' OR (OccBits_p' AND OccBits_edge );
                    Pos'' = Append_last_edge(Pos' , edge);
                    Loc_p'' = Loc_p'' ∪ (Pos'', e' + 1);
            end for
        end for
    end for
end for
```

Fig. 3. The pseudocode of the recursive expansion procedure using a De Bruijn Graph. Given a starting pattern p and its occurrences within the graph, the procedure locates all the occurrences of all patterns that can be derived from p by adding a character (nucleotide) at the beginning and appending another character at the end. n is the iteration number and s_{err} is the initial number of errors allowed. Pos is an ordered set of pointers to edges of the graph. For any oligo o the set contains pointers to all the edges $edge$ overlapped by o. The order of the edges of the set is given by the k-tuples composing o. Loc_p is a set of pairs (Pos, e) corresponding to the positions in the graph of all the approximate occurrences of pattern p with the respective number of errors e. $OccBits_{obj}$ is a bit string representing the occurrences of an object obj in the input strings. obj can be an edge, a set of edges or a pattern. $Start(Pos)$ returns a pointer to the first edge of Pos. $End(Pos)$ returns a pointer to the last edge of Pos. $Prev(edge)$ returns the set of edges connected to $edge$ by a node moving backwards in the graph. $Next(edge)$ returns the set of edges connected to $edge$ by a node moving forward in the graph. $First\_Char(edge)$ returns the first char of the k-tuple corresponding to $edge$. $Last\_Char(edge)$ returns the last char of the k-tuple corresponding to $edge$. $Insert\_first\_edge(Pos, edge)$ inserts $edge$ as first edge inside Pos. $Append\_last\_edge(Pos, edge)$ appends $edge$ as last edge inside Pos.

Table 1. Performance comparison of the new algorithm (Weeder2.0) on the Metazoan compendium [12]. See [12] for further details. Motifs for Weeder2.0 are considered as identified (YES) if one of the two highest scoring motifs of length 8 or 10 matches the known one as in [12] according to profile correlation.

Motif	Number of sequences	Trawler	Amadeus	Weeder	Weeder2.0
CREB	2354	NO	YES	YES	NO
E2F4_CAM	203	YES	YES	YES	YES
E2F4_REN	96	YES	YES	YES	YES
ERa	498	NO	NO	NO	NO
ETS1	1193	NO	YES	YES	YES
FOXP3	927	NO	NO	NO	NO
CellCycle_G1S	268	YES	YES	YES	YES
CellCycle_G2M	350	NO	YES	NO	YES
HNF1A	207	YES	YES	NO	YES
HNF4A	1485	NO	NO	NO	NO
HNF6	212	NO	YES	NO	YES
HSF1	333	NO	NO	NO	YES
Immune_HS	619	NO	YES	NO	YES
Immune_MM	335	NO	YES	NO	YES
MEF2	26	NO	NO	NO	YES
MYOD_BLAIS	105	YES	YES	YES	YES
MYOD_CAO	104	YES	YES	YES	YES
MYOG	78	YES	YES	YES	YES
MYOGENIN	110	YES	YES	YES	YES
NFkB	271	YES	YES	YES	YES
NRF1	679	YES	YES	YES	YES
OCT4	243	NO	YES	NO	YES
SRF	174	YES	YES	YES	YES
SOX2	580	NO	NO	NO	YES
YY1	721	YES	YES	YES	YES
Total		12	19	13	21

thus represents a compromise between the two different flavors of the problem we introduced, sequences coming mostly from ChIP datasets, but of full-promoter length. Differently from [12], however, we did not mask the sequences for repeats before processing.

The results are summarized in Table 1 and Figure 4, where data for the other methods are those reported in [12]. Programs were run on computational resources similar to the ones employed for our test. We can notice a dramatic improvement over the execution time, which is clearly comparable to, if not better than, other ChIP-specific tools, and especially much faster than the original Weeder implementation (see Figure 4) which in the test was run on motif lengths 8 and 10 as well. It should be noted also that both Trawler and Amadeus used masked sequences as input, and match motifs on the sequences using regular expressions, hence confining substitutions at fixed positions. The speed-up of

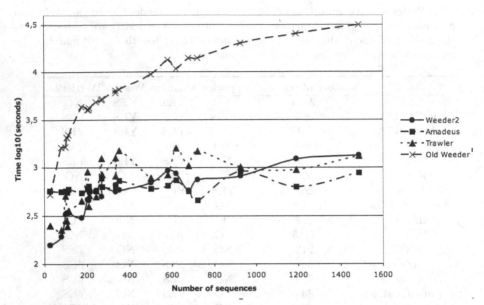

Fig. 4. Running time of different motif-finding tools according to the number of sequences analyzed (each 1200 bps long). The y-axis show the log_{10} of the time measured in seconds (taken from [12] for the other methods).

our method is due to the reduced number of motifs to be evaluated, and also to the usage of pre-computed frequency tables for approximate motif occurrences, which in the original Weeder implementation were computed on the fly. Further improvements on execution time were reached by employing masked sequences as in [12] (data not shown), but this led to a worse accuracy in the results.

Indeed, even more strikingly, in Table 1 we can notice a significant improvement on the accuracy of the results (motifs correctly identified) over the performance reported for our original Weeder algorithm, although no change on the significance measure adopted had been explicitly introduced. We consider this improvement due to three main factors. First of all, the results are significantly improved if input sequences are not masked. In other words, TFBS can be often located within several different repeated sequence regions. Second, and perhaps most important, there is no explicit threshold on the number of sequences that have to contain a motif. In our original Weeder algorithm this was set by default to half of the input sequences, so to reduce the number of motifs to evaluate, and this parameter was not changed by the authors employing Weeder the comparison of [12]. Third, requiring explicitly motifs to satisfy the "conserved core" property, and to be among the highest scoring ones also at shorter lengths has the effect of cleaning up the output from spurious or random sequence similarities. The sole exception seems to be the binding motif for CREB (see Table 1), that becomes a miss in our new test. Actually, the motif was present in the top 10 highest scoring motifs, but was no longer in the top two. Once again, we believe that the considerations we just outlined are valid also for the appearance of new motifs scoring better than CREB. On the other hand, the authors of the ChIP experiment of this TF remarked the fact that the canonical CREB binding motif was present only in a subset of the regions that had been identified, and that other motifs seemed to be required for the binding of CREB [15].

5   Conclusions

Preliminary results have clearly shown a dramatic improvement on the computational resources required by our original Weeder algorithm, with an unexpected side effect of a better performance also in the motif finding itself.

We are currently running more benchmark tests, in order to fully assess the performance of the algorithm, together with the implementation of additional ChIP-Seq specific features. For example, several experiments have shown that the actual binding sites for the TF investigated tend to be located near the summit of the peaks identified in the experiment. Introducing also positional bias with respect to the read enrichment in the ChIP-Seq could thus significantly improve the accuracy of the results. In other words, the scoring function should take into account also how the positioning of the motif in the sequences deviates from a random uniform model. Also, in most of the cases the binding site of the TF, as well as the corresponding motif, is already known, and motif discovery serves just as a validation of the accuracy of the ChIP experiment itself. But, in these cases what researchers are also interested in is which other TFs can interact or co-operate or compete with the one investigated. This, in turn, can be explained by finding "secondary motifs" in the sequences, not as conserved as the main one but nevertheless significantly over–represented [16]. Since secondary motifs can appear only in a limited number of sequences of the set, the effect is again a harder instance of the problem more similar to promoter analysis as discussed in the introduction, with the additional feature that there might be some positional conservation as well, with respect to the main motif, as for example in case of different TFs binding as heterodimers. Initial results obtained by our method have anyway been promising also from this point of view.

Acknowledgements. This work has been supported by the Italian FIRB project Laboratorio Internazionale di Bioinformatica (LIBI).

References

[1] Lemon, B., Tjian, R.: Orchestrated response: a symphony of transcription factors for gene control. Genes. Dev. 14, 2551–2569 (2000)

[2] Stormo, G.D.: DNA binding sites: representation and discovery. Bioinformatics 16, 16–23 (2000)

[3] Pavesi, G., Mauri, G., Pesole, G.: In silico representation and discovery of transcription factor binding sites. Brief Bioinform. 5, 217–236 (2004)

[4] Collas, P., Dahl, J.A.: Chop it, ChIP it, check it: the current status of chromatin immunoprecipitation. Front Biosci. 13, 929–943 (2008)

[5] Mardis, E.R.: ChIP-seq: welcome to the new frontier. Nat. Methods 4, 613–614 (2007)

[6] Pavesi, G.: Motif finding from Chips to ChIPs. In: Elnitski, L., Piontkivska, H., Welch, L.R. (eds.) Advances in Genomic Sequence Analysis and Pattern Discovery. World Scientific Publishing Co. (2011)

[7] Mercier, E., Droit, A., Li, L., Robertson, G., Zhang, X., Gottardo, R.: An integrated pipeline for the genome-wide analysis of transcription factor binding sites from ChIP-Seq. PLoS One 6, e16432 (2011)

[8] Tompa, M., Li, N., Bailey, T.L., Church, G.M., De Moor, B., Eskin, E., Favorov, A.V., Frith, M.C., Fu, Y., Kent, W.J., Makeev, V.J., Mironov, A.A., Noble, W.S., Pavesi, G., Pesole, G., Rgnier, M., Simonis, N., Sinha, S., Thijs, G., van Helden, J., Vandenbogaert, M., Weng, Z., Workman, C., Ye, C., Zhu, Z.: Assessing computational tools for the discovery of transcription factor binding sites. Nat. Biotechnol. 23, 137–144 (2005)

[9] Sagot, M.-F.: Spelling Approximate Repeated or Common Motifs Using a Suffix Tree. In: Lucchesi, C.L., Moura, A.V. (eds.) LATIN 1998. LNCS, vol. 1380, pp. 111–127. Springer, Heidelberg (1998)

[10] Pavesi, G., Mereghetti, P., Mauri, G., Pesole, G.: Weeder Web: discovery of transcription factor binding sites in a set of sequences from co-regulated genes. Nucleic Acids Res. 32, W199–W203 (2004)

[11] Ettwiller, L., Paten, B., Ramialison, M., Birney, E., Wittbrodt, J.: Trawler: de novo regulatory motif discovery pipeline for chromatin immunoprecipitation. Nat. Methods 4, 563–565 (2007)

[12] Linhart, C., Halperin, Y., Shamir, R.: Transcription factor and microRNA motif discovery: the Amadeus platform and a compendium of metazoan target sets. Genome Res. 18, 1180–1189 (2008)

[13] Zhang, Y., Waterman, M.S.: DNA sequence assembly and multiple sequence alignment by an Eulerian path approach. In: Cold Spring Harb. Symp. Quant. Biol., vol. 68, pp. 205–212 (2003)

[14] Zerbino, D.R., Birney, E.: Velvet: algorithms for de novo short read assembly using de Bruijn graphs. Genome Res. 18, 821–829 (2008)

[15] Martianov, I., Choukrallah, M.A., Krebs, A., Ye, T., Legras, S., Rijkers, E., Van Ijcken, W., Jost, B., Sassone-Corsi, P., Davidson, I.: Cell-specific occupancy of an extended repertoire of CREM and CREB binding loci in male germ cells. BMC Genomics 11, 530 (2010)

[16] Bailey, T.L.: DREME: motif discovery in transcription factor ChIP-seq data. Bioinformatics 27, 1653–1659 (2011)

Case/Control Prediction from Illumina Methylation Microarray's β and Two-Color Channels in the Presence of Batch Effects

Fabrice Colas and Jeanine J. Houwing-Duistermaat

MEDSTATS, Leiden University Medical Center, Leiden, The Netherlands

Abstract. Among the published studies that submitted Illumina Bead-Array 27k methylation datasets to the Gene Expression Omnibus (GEO), more than nine out of ten analyse β, thus making β a *de facto* standard. Further, as β combines the two color channels M and U into the ratio $M/(M+U)$, we also assume, maybe naively, that β conveys more biologically relevant information than a single color taken alone. As well, a fourth of the GEO studies do not report any analysis step to cancel for non-biological variation. Here, we farther assess the validity of β as a micro array methylation analysis measure by testing empirically whether β predicts more accurately the case/control status than the two color channels taken independently. In addition, we consider whether cancelling the non-biological effects due to the genotyping protocol influences the prediction accuracy. Our results show that M alone predicts better than β and U, interpreting that U's low prediction impacts negatively the one of β. We also confirm that without proper batch effect cancellation, non-biological variance hides the biological signal, making impractical the prediction of case status.

Keywords: DNA Methylation, Microarray, Batch Effect, Prediction.

1 Introduction

Even though monozygotic twins are genetically identical, significant phenotypic discordance exists between them [1]. To explain this differentiation, it is suggested that epigenetic, defined as the heritable changes in phenotype or gene expression caused by mechanisms *other* than changes in the underlying DNA sequence [2], plays a major role. Besides differentiation of twins, epigenetic is also involved in a number of other mechanisms like imprinting [3], a process by which parent-specific alleles are silenced, aging [1], trans-generational effects [4], tumorigenesis [5,6]. As the main epigenetic process, methylation attaches methyl-groups to the DNA. While the nucleotide sequence remains the same, the appearance and structure of the DNA changes, which may influence how genes are interpreted, e.g. when transcribing.

As a key genotyping solution provider, Illumina extended its Infinium II assay platform with its proprietary BeadChip micro array technology to the genome

E. Biganzoli et al. (Eds.): CIBB 2011, LNBI 7548, pp. 213–225, 2012.

wide analysis of methylation [7]. Covering 14495 genes, this technology measures methylation levels at 27578 sites [8]. As illustrated in Figure 1 (a), a single run may genotype up to 48 samples per plate through four BeadChips scanning at 12 different assay positions. To date[1], 41 published studies (half in the last eight months) submitted Illumina methylation 27k datasets to the Gene Expression Omnibus (GEO) [9,10]. Of those, more than nine out of ten (38) analyse methylation levels in terms of $\beta_i = M_i/(M_i + U_i)$, with M_i and U_i the number of methylated and unmethylated calls for each site i, $\beta = 0$ indicates absence of methylated molecules and $\beta = 1$ indicates that all identified molecules are methylated.

About a fourth of the studies (10) do not report any background correction, variance stabilization or batch effect cancellation. As instance of normalization strategy, we cite loess [11] and quantile normalization [12]. Widely used in gene expression micro array data analysis, these two techniques assume similar global expression levels between samples [13]. However, due to inter-individual, tissue or age differences, overall methylation levels may greatly vary between samples, resulting in normalizations that could remove some of the true biological signal. In practice, about one out of five (7) of the GEO-studies applied either a quantile or a loess normalization. And in our own research, we also found quantile normalization to reduce appropriately the distributional differences.

Here, we decided to compare the case/control prediction of M and U alone with respect to β. We hypothesized that if β combined M and U into a single ratio, it had to convey more *information* and therefore, it should predict with greater accuracy the case/control status. Moreover, although technical replicates of Illumina's methylation micro array exhibit high correlations $r > .99$ (5), a fourth of the GEO studies (10) do not report any batch effect cancellation procedure. But we can see from Figure 1 (b) that non-biological factors account for a large part of the variability in the raw data. Hence, we also monitored the influence on the prediction accuracies of cancelling the variance due to non-biological effects. We carried out this analysis protocol on two datasets from GEO with $N = 48$ and $N = 195$.

In the coming section, we present the methodological aspects of our study. Next, we present our main results. We follow with a discussion of our results in regard with current research. And last, we give concluding remarks.

2   Methods

In this section, we motivate the methodological design of our analysis protocol, starting with the data collections used and, following with the software elements, the data preparation, the selected batch effect cancellation procedure, the feature selection strategy, the adopted classification rule algorithm, the measurement of the classification accuracy and the validation strategy.

---

[1] 4th October 2011.

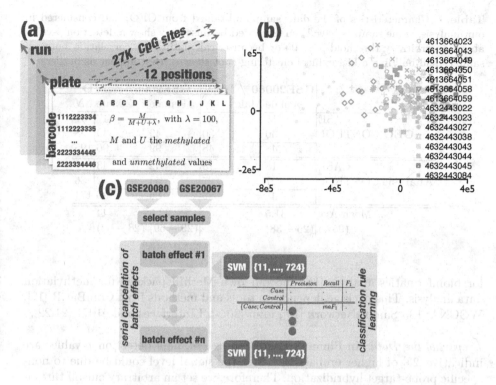

Fig. 1. (a) Outline of how DNA samples are disposed over plates on the Illumina Infinium platform. A plate is made of up to 4 BeadChips that can process 12 DNA samples at 12 positions ($N = 48$). To type more than 48 samples, several plates may be passed into a run. In meta-analyses, runs from different genotyping centers are combined. (b) Multi-Dimensional Scaling (MDS) plot characterizing the cluster of samples per barcode, which corresponds to each BeadChip's id. (c) Summary of our analysis.

Collecting Data. We analyse data from two genome wide DNA methylation case control studies obtained from the gene expression omnibus repository (GEO) under series numbers GSE20080 and GSE20067 [14].

In the first series, normal and pre-invasive cervical smear female samples infected with the human papilloma virus (HPV) are studied. Two types of controls (HPV+/-) and one type of cases (HPV+) were considered. In the present analysis, we merged the two control groups (HPV+/-) into one. In the second series, 192 male and female Irish patients with type 1 diabetes (T1D) mellitus are studied. Cases had T1D and nephropathy, while controls had T1D but no evidence of renal disease.

Table 1 summarizes the main characteristics of the two case control studies.

Software. The data analysis is carried out under the R (2.12.2) software environment for statistical computing [15], using its Bioconductor framework

Table 1. Characteristics of the data sample obtained from GEO, and considered in our analysis. Some samples have been discarded because they show a detection p-value above an arbitrary threshold $p > .05$ or because, calculating the correlation between samples and building a hierarchical clustering (not shown), they appear as outliers.

	GSE20080 / HPV			GSE20067 / T1D		
	Female	Male	N	Female	Male	N
GEO CASE	18	18		50	47	97
CONTROL	30	30		49	49	98
	48	48		99	96	195
Analysis CASE	18	18		42	43	85
CONTROL	27	27		44	42	86
	45	45		86	85	171
Mean Age	31.5			43.5	44	
(95%)	(26 − 38)			(29 − 69)	(28 − 62)	

for bioinformatics analysis [16] and our own MethIll package for methylation data analysis. This package depends on tools and methods from ComBat.R [17], WGCNA [18], SampleNetwork [19], lumi [20], MLInterfaces and e1071 [21,22].

Preparing the Data. In Illumina BeadChip assays, high detection p-values are indicative [23] of higher probabilities that the signal level could be due to non-specific probe-target hybridization. Therefore, we set an arbitrary cut-off threshold of $p < 0.05$ and we discard those samples showing a mean detection p-value above it.

However, as it is not yet clear how to normalize methylation assay data and as finding the most optimal normalization strategy for methylation data analysis is outside the scope of this present research, we limit our analysis to un-normalized data. Though, the next analysis step does center and scale down the data.

Cancelling Batch Effects. To remove non-biological experimental variation in the assay data, we use the empirical Bayes (EB) frameworks of [17]. This framework is referred to as ComBat, which stands for combating batch effects when combining batches of gene expression micro array data. In comparison to singular value decomposition and other location/scale methods, ComBat demonstrate the appealing property of handling very small sample sizes per batches while presenting robustness to outliers in those small samples.

ComBat relies on the assumption that phenomena resulting in batch effects often impact many genes in similar ways. Thus, [17] chose to estimate the location and scale parameters by pooling information across genes in batches to reduce parameter estimates towards the overall mean of the batch effect estimates across genes. Their approach proceeds in three steps: a standardization of the data, an EB-batch effect parameter estimates using parametric empirical prior and then, data adjustment.

More formally, supposing that the data Y contain m batches containing n_i samples each, with $i = 1, ..., m$, for gene $g = 1, ..., G$, and j samples, then the data model expresses as follows

$$Y_{ijg} = \alpha_g + X\beta_g + \gamma_{ig} + \theta_{ig}\epsilon_{ijg}. \tag{1}$$

The α_g correspond to the overall gene expression, the X to a design matrix for the batches, the β_g to the vector of regression coefficients, the $\epsilon_{ijg} \sim \mathcal{N}(0, \sigma_g^2)$ the error terms, the γ_{ig} and θ_{ig}, the additive and multiplicative batch effect for batch i and gene g.

In first, data is standardized in order to reduce the between gene differences which, if un-accounted for, could bias the empirical bias estimates of the prior distribution and therefore, make less effective the batch effect cancellation procedure. Standardization is calculated by

$$Z_{ijg} = \frac{Y_{ijg} - \hat{\alpha}_g - X\hat{\beta}_g}{\hat{\sigma}_g}. \tag{2}$$

Then, using parametric empirical prior, the EB batch effect parameters are estimated. The hyper-parameters of the parametric forms for prior distributions are estimated empirically from the standardized data. Last, the data is adjusted for the batch effects. The batch adjusted data is calculated as follows:

$$\gamma_{ijg}^* = \frac{\hat{\sigma}_g}{\hat{\theta}_{ig}^*}(Z_{ijg} - \gamma_{ig}^*) + \hat{\alpha}_g + X\hat{\beta}_g. \tag{3}$$

In the two series, we cancel out the systematic effects (illustrated in Figure 1 (a)) for: the barcode (BeadChips), the position, as well as the age taken as a factor. In series GSE20067, we also adjust for a gender effect since the study includes both males and females.

Selecting Features/Probes. For each combination of data (GSE20080, GSE20067) and assay (M, U and β), we simulate a series of binary classification problems, on which the accuracy of classification rules is evaluated when the size of the feature space is gradually increased; series $\mathcal{F}$ summaries the different number of predictors considered in the present simulation:

$$\mathcal{F} = \{11, 22, 45, 90, 181, 362, 724\}. \tag{4}$$

For instance, the 11 in the series means that 11 probes are **randomly** selected as predictors for the training of the classification rule. By fixing the random seed for all experiments, each larger subset of randomly selected probes includes the smallest, e.g. in the 22-subset, there are 11 new randomly selected probes in addition to the 11 previous ones. In turn, a classification rule learned from a larger subset of predictors relates to the previous ones and is therefore *comparable*. For practical reasons, the maximum number of predictors used to learn classification rules was 724 but it should not restrict the scope of our conclusions since the studied problems are sub-samples of the larger one due to the random sampling.

Classification Rule Learning. Since our aim is not to evaluate how various classification algorithms compare in the task of discriminating cases from controls in methylation data analysis but, to compare classification accuracies for the different assay data M, U and β, the choice of the classification algorithm is not of prime interest. Therefore, we orient our choice towards the Support Vector Machines (SVM) algorithms, based on Vapnik's statistical learning theory [24], and which are considered to work well with high dimension data. Further, as M, U and β are continuous, we opt for a radial kernel with default parameters. In our experiments, we used the libsvm implementation [25,26] that is available from within R in the package e1071.

Briefly, the SVM classification function of a test point $\boldsymbol{x}'$ is given by

$$\hat{\Phi}(\boldsymbol{x}') = sign(\langle \mathbf{w}.\boldsymbol{x}' \rangle + b) \tag{5}$$

with $\mathbf{w}$ and the scalar b, the coordinates of the separating hyperplane and the bias to the origin. The particularity of this hyperplane $\mathbf{w}$ is that it is the one separating the points of the two classes with the maximum distance when these are linearly separable. In the case of a radial basis kernel, $\mathbf{w}$ is defined as follows:

$$\mathbf{w} = k(\mathbf{x_i}, \mathbf{x_j}) = exp\left(\frac{||\mathbf{x_i} - \mathbf{x_j}||^2}{2\sigma^2}\right) \tag{6}$$

This concept of maximum separating distance is formalized by the *geometrical margin* which is defined as

$$\gamma = \frac{1}{2||\mathbf{w}||_2}. \tag{7}$$

Therefore, the SVM problem resides in searching the maximum of γ or, alternatively, the minimum of $||\mathbf{w}||_2$ given the constraints. To identify this $\mathbf{w}$, an optimization problem must be solved. Its primal form is expressed by

$$minimize_{\mathbf{w},b} \qquad \tfrac{1}{2}\langle \mathbf{w}.\mathbf{w} \rangle,$$
$$subject\ to \qquad y_i(\langle \mathbf{w}.\boldsymbol{x}_i \rangle + b) \geqslant 1, i = 1, ..., N, \tag{8}$$

where the $\boldsymbol{x}_i$ are the training instances in the database. Yet, as the number of training instances is typically several times smaller than the number of features, it is usually preferred to operate the SVM in the dual (that depends on the number of training instances). The dual form can be obtained by posing and deriving the Lagrangian according to $\mathbf{w}$ and b:

$$maximize_{\alpha} \sum_{i=1}^{N} \alpha_i - \tfrac{1}{2} \sum_{i=1}^{N} \sum_{j=1}^{N} y_i y_j \alpha_i \alpha_j k(\boldsymbol{x}_i.\boldsymbol{x}_j),$$
$$subject\ to \qquad \sum_{i=1}^{N} y_i \alpha_i = 0 \tag{9}$$
$$0 \leqslant \alpha_i \leqslant C, i = 1, ..., N.$$

In order to limit values of Lagrange coefficients α_i, an upper bound C is introduced so that each training instance has a maximum contribution when classes are not linearly separable. This type of SVM is referred to as soft-margin SVM.

Measuring Classification Accuracy. To evaluate the classification accuracy of learned rules, we visualize the prediction of the rule through a confusion Table illustrated in 2.

For each class $j \in C = \{A, B\}$ (case and control), we calculate the precision ($Prec_j$), the recall (Rec_j), and the F_1-score (F_1^j). F_1 is referred as the weighted average, or the harmonic mean between the precision and the recall. Besides F_1, we also calculate an average measure maF_1, which takes the mean of the individual F_1^j scores for twe two classes j.

In the following, we define each measure.

Table 2. Confusion matrix representing the joint distribution of a classification rule, where columns indicate the predicted class and rows, the true class

		Predicted	
		A	B
Given	A	TP	FN
	B	FP	TN

The *precision* represents the fraction of instances that, among all instances predicted as positive ($TP + FP$), are actually relevant (TP); for class $j \in C$ it expresses as

$$Prec_j = \frac{TP_j}{TP_j + FP_j}. \tag{10}$$

The *recall* represents the fraction of instances that, among all positive ($TP + FN$), are actually relevant (TP); it expresses as

$$Rec_j = \frac{TP_j}{TP_j + FN_j}. \tag{11}$$

The F_1 measure combines the $Prec$ and Rec; a value of one is best and of zero is worst. For class j, it defines as

$$F_1^j = 2 \times \frac{Prec_j \times Rec_j}{Prec_j + Rec_j}. \tag{12}$$

In particular, provided $TP, FP, FN, TN \geq 0$, we have

$$\lim_{FP,TP \to 0} Prec_j = \lim_{FN,TP \to 0} Rec_j = 0, \tag{13}$$

and
$$\lim_{Prec_j \to 0, Rec_j \to 0} F_1^j = 0. \tag{14}$$

Finally, the macro-F_1 score (maF_1) is an average measure of the F_1 scores from the different classes where each class is given equal weight. There exists also the micro-F_1 which, to the opposite of maF_1, weighs *a priori* the contribution of each F_1^j. The measure maF_1 defines as follows:

$$maF_1 = \frac{1}{2} \sum_{j \in C} F_1^j \tag{15}$$

Validation by Leave One Out (LOO). Cross validation techniques aim to assess how statistical analyses generalize to independent datasets. Cross validation is often referred to as a rotation technique because of the way the dataset is partitioned in complementary sub-samples and the way the statistical analysis is validated iteratively on the sub-sample that is left out.

Because of the *a priori* probability class-imbalance, we select the leave one out cross validation strategy, which is the particular case of cross validation when the number of samples left out for testing is one. Therefore, LOO proceeds iteratively on all instances but one, taken as the validation sub-sample.

3 Results

Non-biological Variation. In Figure 2 **(a,c)**, we report the variance in the first principal component, which is explained in the assay β by covariates like the barcode (BeadChips), the position, the case control status, the age and the gender. We remark that most of the variability in β is due to the barcode, a remark especially true for series GSE20067 with $p < 1e^{-50}$. Then, as the effect of the different batches are cancelled out, the signal of the control status is progressively recovered in GSE20067 with $p < .05$, and in GSE20080 with $p \sim .1$; see Figure 2 **(b,d)**. Although rounds of batch effect cancellation are performed for both the barcode and the age, we notice some residual variance for both covariates; Figure 2 **(b,d)**. A simple explanation for the effect of age is that we analyse it as a factor and not as a continuous variable. As a factor, the covariate looses the quantitative information of the effect. Concerning the barcode, some of the residual variance may associate with the case control status, e.g. there may be collinearity due to a sub-optimal randomization of the samples across the main systematic batch effects, which may render barcode adjustment incomplete.

Case/Control Prediction. We summarize the results in Figure 3 by means of 2×9 sub-figures, i.e. nine sub-figures for each series GSE20080 and GSE20067. Classification rule accuracy is compared on the *un-methylated* (U), the *methylated* (M) assays and the ratio measurements β (lowest, middle and highest row of each series), for the two classes (control in the first column, case in the second), each taken as target class when calculating the precision and the recall, and for the two-class problem when averaging with maF_1 the scores from the two classes (right column). In general, as batches are cancelled out one by one (from bottom up of each sub-plot), and when the number of predictors is increased (from left to right of each sub-plot), we observe F_1 scores getting higher.

First, as long as the data has not been adjusted for the main systematic effects of the barcode and the position, an obvious absence of learning of the classification rules happen. This is most clearly seen in the smallest study (GSE20080) but also in the other one (red in GSE20067). In fact, on unadjusted data, classification rules predict all samples into the majority class. Indeed, we read classification accuracies for GSE20080 of $F_1^{CONTROL} = 74\%$ and $F_1^{CASE} = 0\%$, which corresponds to the prior probability of the controls samples. We explain absence of learning by

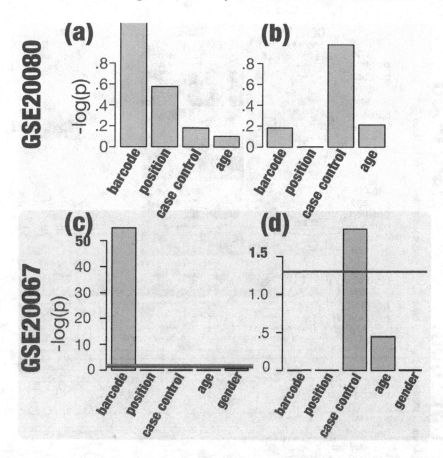

Fig. 2. Variance explained by systematic batch effects like the barcode (BeadChips) or the position in the first principal component of the assay data β. The p-value indicates the strength of the effect, e.g. in (c) the barcode accounts for most of the variance before it is cancelled out (in **d**), with $p < 1e^{-50}$. Sub-figures (**a**) and (**c**) characterize the variance structure in GSE20080 and GSE20067 before batch effect cancellation, while sub-figures (**b**) and (**d**) characterize the variance structure after.

the overwhelming variance from the barcode and the position, which makes it impossible to learn any other rule than the majority class. Further, we account the difference between the two series, in attained classification accuracies -and colors-, by the class imbalance that is sharper in the smallest series.

Second, we remark from Figure 3 that the highest F_1 and maF_1 scores are obtained on both case control studies for assay M (middle row of sub-plots for each series), irrespective of the number of predictors from $\mathcal{F}$ used to learn the classification rule. In contrast, U consistently exhibits the lowest F_1 and maF_1 scores, while ratio measurements β also appear systematically lower than accuracies attained with M alone. Therefore, we suggest that by combining both M and U into a single summary score, β is more affected by the lack of prediction information in U, than by its additional predictive information content.

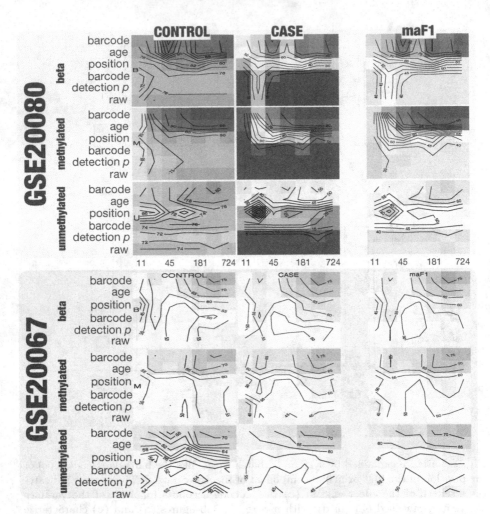

Fig. 3. Comparative view of the classification rule accuracy (F_1 for control and cases and maF_1, from left to right) as the number of probes randomly selected as predictors is increased (x-axis of each sub-plot), and as systematic effects are canceled out one by one (y-axis of each sub-plot). In y, the lowest row refers to the unadjusted data and the top to the fully adjusted. We reproduce our experimental protocol on series GSE20080 above and GSE20067 below. And for each, we repeat classification rule learning on the un-methylated (U), the methylated (M) and the β assay data (from bottom up for each series). In each sub-plot, the contour lines give the relative classification accuracy, from 0 to 100%.

4   Discussion

The standard in current genome wide DNA methylation research is to analyse β-values. In this empirical study, we reported prediction accuracies consistently lower for β than for the color channel M taken alone. To explain this unexpected results, we showed that M leads to higher prediction accuracies than the other color channel U and we interpreted that the lack of prediction information in U impacts negatively β that combines both measures into a single ratio. Our results suggest that an alternative to β should be searched for.

In fact, as an approximate percent methylation value, β varies continuously between zero and one and its variance appears larger for middle-range values than for the ones near the boundaries (see Figure 3 of [27]). This phenomena referred as heteroscedasticity may invalidate, if unaccounted for, testing for significance of differentially methylated regions (DMRs). Similarly, selecting probes based on their larger variance, a practice that was common in gene expression micro array analysis, may result in biased findings.

To overcome these limitations, some suggested $logit(\beta)$ as analysis measure of methylation micro array data [13,27]. But in practice, only three GEO-studies used the $logit(\beta)$ [27,28,29]. Besides β as a *de facto* standard, wide acceptance for a proper statistical analysis strategy has not been reached too. In fact, a fourth of the GEO studies do not report any adjustment for the presence of non-biological variance introduced in the genotyping phase.

Yet, the first Figure reported in this study illustrates raw methylation data confounded by non-biological variation. And to evaluate whether this non-biological variation would have any influence in the learning of case/control prediction, we cancelled the non-biological effects one by one and observed the variation in prediction accuracy. The dramatic improvement in classification accuracy, from random prediction to 90% prediction accuracies, is suggestive of the influence of that variance. While testing for hypotheses, we expect statistical power to improve in a similar way.

Nonetheless, some agreement appears among published studies that submitted their data to GEO. For instance, in terms of quality control, detection p-values are commonly set to .01 (3) or .05 (11), technical replicates exhibit high correlations $r \geq .99$ (5) and probes on the X/Y chromosomes are usually discarded (7). In terms of statistical analysis, some evaluate the difference in the number of hypo- and hyper-methylated probes according to $(lower, upper)$ thresholds like (.2, .8), (.3, .7) or (.344, .696), while others consider absolute differences in $\Delta(\beta) \geq .25$ or .45.

5   Conclusion

As we remarked from previously published studies and from the GEO repository, β happen to be a *de facto* standard in methylation data analysis. Yet, we found that the M assay provides higher classification accuracies than β and U. Combining M and U into a single ratio, β is negatively impacted by the lack of predictive information in U. We have also shown how adjustment for non-biological effects influences the learning of classification rules. If not accounted for, the learned classification rules predict everything into the majority class. Still, after batch effect cancellation, the true biological signal could be recovered and good case/control prediction accuracies could be achieved.

References

1. Fraga, M.F., Ballestar, E., Paz, M.F., Ropero, S., Setien, F., Ballestar, M.L., Heine-Suñer, D., Cigudosa, J.C., Urioste, M., Benitez, J., Boix-Chornet, M., Sanchez-Aguilera, A., Ling, C., Carlsson, E., Poulsen, P., Vaag, A., Stephan, Z., Spector, T.D., Wu, Y.-Z., Plass, C., Esteller, M.: Epigenetic differences arise during the lifetime of monozygotic twins. Proceedings of the National Academy of Sciences of the United States of America 102, 10604–10609 (2005)
2. Wikipedia. Epigenetics (2011) (online accessed April 14, 2011)
3. Wood, A.J., Oakey, R.J.: Genomic imprinting in mammals: emerging themes and established theories. PLoS Genetics 2, e147 (2006)
4. Jones, P.A., Laird, P.W.: Cancer epigenetics comes of age. Nature Genetics 21, 163–167 (1999)
5. Feinberg, A.P., Tycko, B.: The history of cancer epigenetics. Nature Reviews. Cancer 4, 143–153 (2004)
6. Pembrey, M.E., Bygren, L.O., Kaati, G., Edvinsson, S., Northstone, K., Sjöström, M., Golding, J.: Sex-specific, male-line transgenerational responses in humans. European Journal of Human Genetics: EJHG 14, 159–166 (2006)
7. Bibikova, M., Lin, Z., Zhou, L., Chudin, E., Garcia, E.W., Wu, B., Doucet, D., Thomas, N.J., Wang, Y., Vollmer, E., Goldmann, T., Seifart, C., Jiang, W., Barker, D.L., Chee, M.S., Floros, J., Fan, J.-B.: High-throughput dna methylation profiling using universal bead arrays. Genome Research 16, 383–393 (2006)
8. Weisenberger, D., Van Den Berg, D., Pan, F., Berman, B., Laird, P.W.: Comprehensive dna methylation analysis on the illumina infinium assay platform (2008)
9. Edgar, R., Domrachev, M., Lash, A.E.: Gene expression omnibus: Ncbi gene expression and hybridization array data repository. Nucleic Acids Research 30, 207–210 (2002)
10. Barrett, T., Troup, D.B., Wilhite, S.E., Ledoux, P., Evangelista, C., Kim, I.F., Tomashevsky, M., Marshall, K.A., Phillippy, K.H., Sherman, P.M., Muertter, R.N., Holko, M., Ayanbule, O., Yefanov, A., Soboleva, A.: Ncbi geo: archive for functional genomics data sets–10 years on. Nucleic Acids Research 39, D1005–D1010 (2011)
11. Cleveland, W.S.: LOWESS: A Program for Smoothing Scatterplots by Robust Locally Weighted Regression. The American Statistician 35(1) (1981)
12. Bolstad, B.M., Irizarry, R.A., Astrand, M., Speed, T.P.: A comparison of normalization methods for high density oligonucleotide array data based on variance and bias. Bioinformatics 19, 185–193 (2003)
13. Laird, P.W.: Principles and challenges of genome-wide dna methylation analysis. Nature Reviews. Genetics 11, 191–203 (2010)
14. Teschendorff, A.E., Menon, U., Gentry-Maharaj, A., Ramus, S.J., Weisenberger, D.J., Shen, H., Campan, M., Noushmehr, H., Bell, C.G., Maxwell, P., Savage, D.A., Mueller-Holzner, E., Marth, C., Kocjan, G., Gayther, S.A., Jones, A., Beck, S., Wagner, W., Laird, P.W., Jacobs, I.J., Widschwendter, M.: Age-dependent dna methylation of genes that are suppressed in stem cells is a hallmark of cancer. Genome Research 20, 440–446 (2010)
15. R Development Core Team. R: A Language and Environment for Statistical Computing. R Foundation for Statistical Computing, Vienna, Austria (2010) ISBN 3-900051-07-0
16. Gentleman, R., Carey, V., Bates, D., Bolstad, B., Dettling, M., Dudoit, S., Ellis, B., Gautier, L., Ge, Y., Gentry, J., et al.: Bioconductor: open software development for computational biology and bioinformatics. Genome Biology 5(10), R80 (2004)

17. Evan Johnson, W., Li, C., Rabinovic, A.: Adjusting batch effects in microarray expression data using empirical bayes methods. Biostatistics 8, 118–127 (2007)
18. Langfelder, P., Horvath, S.: Wgcna: an r package for weighted correlation network analysis. BMC Bioinformatics 9, 559 (2008)
19. Oldham, M., Langfelder, P., Horvath, S.: Network methods for describing sample relationships in genomic datasets: application to Huntington's disease. BMC Systems Biology 6(1), 63 (2012), http://www.biomedcentral.com/1752-0509/6/63, doi:10.1186/1752-0509-6-63
20. Du, P., Kibbe, W.A., Lin, S.M.: Lumi: a pipeline for processing illumina microarray. Bioinformatics 24, 1547–1548 (2008)
21. Carey, V., Gentleman, R., Mar, J., contributions from Vertrees, J.: MLInterfaces: Uniform interfaces to R machine learning procedures for data in Bioconductor containers. R package version 1.30.0
22. Dimitriadou, E., Hornik, K., Leisch, F., Meyer, D., Weingessel, A.: e1071: Misc Functions of the Department of Statistics (e1071), TU Wien, R package version 1.5-24 (2010)
23. Illumina. Normalization and Differential Analysis (2008)
24. Vapnik, V.N.: The Nature of Statistical Theory. In: Information Science and Statistics. Springer (1995)
25. Chang, C.-C., Lin, C.-J.: LIBSVM: a library for support vector machines (2001)
26. Fan, R.-E., Chen, P.-H., Lin, C.-J.: Working set selection using second order information for training support vector machines. J. Mach. Learn. Res. 6, 1889–1918 (2005)
27. Du, P., Zhang, X., Huang, C.-C., Jafari, N., Kibbe, W.A., Hou, L., Lin, S.M.: Comparison of beta-value and m-value methods for quantifying methylation levels by microarray analysis. BMC Bioinformatics 11, 587 (2010)
28. Liu, J., Zhang, Z., Bando, M., Itoh, T., Deardorff, M.A., Li, J.R., Clark, D., Kaur, M., Tatsuro, K., Kline, A.D., Chang, C., Vega, H., Jackson, L.G., Spinner, N.B., Shirahige, K., Krantz, I.D.: Genome-wide dna methylation analysis in cohesin mutant human cell lines. Nucleic Acids Research 38, 5657–5671 (2010)
29. Fang, F., Turcan, S., Rimner, A., Kaufman, A., Giri, D., Morris, L.T., Shen, R., Seshan, V., Mo, Q., Heguy, A., Baylin, S.B., Ahuja, N., Viale, A., Massague, J., Norton, L., Vahdat, L.T., Moynahan, M.E., Chan, T.A.: Breast cancer methylomes establish an epigenomic foundation for metastasis. Science Translational Medicine 3, 75ra25 (2011)
30. Boks, M.P., Derks, E.M., Weisenberger, D.J., Strengman, E., Janson, E., Sommer, I.E., Kahn, R.S., Ophoff, R.A.: The relationship of dna methylation with age, gender and genotype in twins and healthy controls. PLoS One 4(8), 6767 (2009)

Supporting the Design, Communication and Management of Bioinformatic Protocols through the Leaf Tool

Francesco Napolitano and Roberto Tagliaferri

Dpt. of Computer Science, University of Salerno, Fisciano, Salerno, Italy
fnapolitano@unisa.it,
www.neuronelab.dmi.unisa.it

Abstract. In Bioinformatic studies, a prototypical approach is common practice when dealing with data analysis. While the source code of such tools provides by itself a precious tool to replicate the analysis, this is in practice often hard to realize. In this paper we try to formalize the concept of protocol in bioinformatic data analysis and introduce the Leaf System, including a graph design language to define the main steps of the data analysis and a Python engine to automatically and efficiently apply it with support for the management of data resources. The tool is undergoing testing and documentation process and is available upon request from the authors.

Keywords: bioinformatics, protocols, leaf, python, computational biology.

1 Introduction

Experiments in natural sciences are designed and formalized before their realization with rigorous rules and standardizations in order to ensure safety, efficacy, precision and correctness of measurements and replicability. Such collection of rules and procedures is called "protocol". Today's research in many areas of natural science has been greately aided by technology and particulary by the advent of computers.

Bioinformatics is the application of Computer Science to Biological problems and is one of the most important example of pervasiveness of technology in research. Technologies like Microarrays or Deep Sequencing can provide punctual information about the whole genome of an organism. Huge amounts of data produced through the use of such or other high-throuput devices are necessarily transferred to matematicians, statisticians or computer scientsts for them to mine knowledge out of such complexity, otherwise not directly tractable by researchers.

Bioinformatic analyses are therefore necessarily divided across multiple research groups, starting from data producers, passing through data miners and finally arriving to application domain experts. Typically data producers use dedicated technology on biological specimen to extract data; data miners analyze

E. Biganzoli et al. (Eds.): CIBB 2011, LNBI 7548, pp. 226–237, 2012.

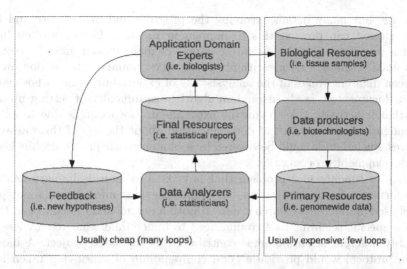

Fig. 1. Bioinformatic research collaboration scheme. This is a representation of a typical process in a bioinformatic study where different research units are involved. The left part of the scheme represents a cheap flow (no consumables or expensive technologies involved) and is expected to be iterated over many loops to refine the analysis basing on partial results.

data and try to put relevant informative aspects in evidence; application domain exports examine the filtered data to validate their hypothesis or to make new ones and typically verify them with more targeted biological experiments. Protocols are widely understood and used by researchers working in the first and last stage of this pipeline, probably due to the inherent difficulty, and thus urgency, of producing formal procedures in a physical environment. Mathematicians and Computer Scientists, on the other hand, use to deal only with formal systems and tend not to be concerned with the concept of protocol. Unfortunately, the assumptions relying upon the implicit formality of mathematical formulas and computer programs are often not met.

Data miners receive raw data to analyze with a computer and statistical tools. Bioinformatic laboratories may develop quite standard pipelines for the analysis and use already available or third party software. On the other hand, many experiments will often require a custom process. Programmers typically write scripts using high-level languages (Python, Ruby, R, Matlab) to quickly test ideas and new methodologies and present results to the other groups as soon as possible. In software engineering similar development models are called Agile Development, Extreme Programming or Prototypical development [4]. Data analysis software priority is about results: features like code maintainability, documentation, portability are often considered secondary, especially when the process is meant to be run just once.

Consider now the fundamental problem of experiment replicability. Results provided by a computer program are usually considered obviously easy to replicate, but many details involving the program and its software and hardware context can prevent this to happen in practice. Consider often hidden (that is, not documented in scientific papers or manuals and difficult to extract from code) variables as: algorithmic parameters; manual intervention on data between different stages of the analysis; use of external programs whose version is not documented; seeds in random algorithms; difficulty of setting up a system that is actually able to run the experiments (for example due to external dependencies); generic lack of documentation about the use of throwaway procedures. Such details could be covered by a bioinformatic protocol while keeping the development process agile.

Another fundamental problem that is typical of interdisciplinary fields like Bioinformatics is communication. The ability to share information about procedures used in different research groups is both a crucial and difficult task. People from a specific scientific background need to understand what researchers from possibly different scientific areas contributed to the same project. A bioinformatic protocol would provide a good compendium of every step taken in the analysis. We will show how this can be also produced in a visual form that is easy to understand and share.

Lastly, an often very time-consuming task is reconsidering past bioinformatic analyses. As mentioned, the data analysis phase of a bioinformatic study is usually controlled by a series of scripts written in high level languages, having a very specific aim and being not expected to be used again. However, the same analysis can be reconsidered in case of newly available data, ideas about improving parts of the analysis, need of partial results to submit to another type of analysis and so on. In this case the availability of a protocol would provide an easy tool to quickly get the system up and running again, while maintaining the details of all the steps in the analysis.

In this paper we try to formalize the concepts expressed in this introduction and provide tools to support their practical implementation. We will show how the basics of a bioinformatic protocol can be summarized by a graph visualization and introduce the Leaf System, which bases on such representation to induce the production of bioinformatic protocols in a way that is as transparent and automatic as possible. The system also provide automatic and optimized management of the resources produced during the analysis.

2   Formalizing Bioinformatic Protocols

The concept of protocol is not new in Bioinformatics [1,2,3]. Repositories of protocols exist that collect protocols for their application to future analyses and improve replicability. We stress that our concept of bioinformatic protocol deals also with the problems of simple communication of the procedures, optimization of the computational resources and maintainability of the developed tools. For these reasons we think that any analysis should be accompanied by a protocol, even for internal use only. For this to be practical, tools are needed to make the process of protocol development as automatic and transparent as possible.

In this section we try to formally describe the essential actors playing a part in the data analysis phase of a bioinformatic analysis. The concepts illustrated are easily extensible to any data analysis process.

The formal context of collaboration for a bioinformatic study that we assume is the one illustrated in Figure 1. Concepts analyzed in this paper regard the data analysis research unit.

2.1   Resources and Processors

There are basically two kinds of actors in a data analysis process: resources and processors. Resources are any kind of data, including raw data, processed data, images, files etc. Processors are basically computer programs that can create a new resource or modify an existing one.

We distinguish between two main kinds of resources:

- *Primary Resources.* Primary resources are the input to the data analysis system. They are usually raw data coming from high-throughput devices like Microarrays, eventually coming from a laboratory that is not the same that will perform the data analysis process. Under this exemplar assumptions, researchers from the data analysis group trust the incoming data and assume no responsibility on its correctness: they consider them their ground truth. Primary resources represent the starting point of the analysis and every protocols should record all actions taken from them, maintaining the possibility to revert any subsequent step back to these resources. Any unsafe modification to them could imply the necessity to request another copy of the original version the data producers.
- *Derived Resources.* If a primary resource is modified by a processor, a derived resource is born. The same happens when a processor creates a new resource. Derived resources can be always recreated relying only on processors and primary resources, as opposed to primary resources that can only be recreated by data producers. In general this means that loosing a derived resource (for example not storing it in order to save disk space) is usually not an issue: the resource can be rebuilt as needed. However some derived resource can be computationally expensive to obtain again: in such cases they can be as precious as primary resources or even more. Derived Resources can be in turn divided into two kinds:
  - *Derived Raw Resources.* Raw Resources are derived resources that are nor primary neither final. They represent internal steps in the analysis and may be useful to store partial results both for debugging purposes and to save computational time when resources derived from them are needed.
  - *Derived Final Resources.* Final resources are derived resources that represent results to be presented to the application domain experts. They have the special requirement of human readability and should be stored in a format that is easy to share among groups involved in the project. We call final resources "leaves": the meaning of the term becomes clear when considering the graph representation of the protocols (see next sections).

If R_d is a resource that is derived from R_p in one or more steps, we say that R_p is an ancestors of R_d. It is called a parent if the derivation is exactly in one step.

2.2   Protocols as Annnotated Directed Graphs

Primary resources go through a series of transformations made by processors in order to obtain final resources. Consider processors as nodes in a graph and resources as edges (this is in conformity with the Pipes and Filters design paradigm [4]). Given a primary resource R_p, a derived resource R_d and a processor P, the graph (N, V), with $N = \{P, S, E\}$ being the set of nodes and $V = \{R_p = (P, S), R_d = (S, E)\}$ being the set of edges, shows that resource R_d is obtained from a starting node S whose aim is to load R_p, and then applying P to it. The resource is then passed to the ending node, E whose aim is to export R_d for presentation.

A graph representation can show all the steps in the data analysis process, hide the unnecessary details and easily provide information about how derived resources are built. If a path exists from a resource R_1 to a resource R_2, then R_1 is needed to build R_2. If some modifications are made in the process that influence R_1 than R_2 must be recomputed, otherwise it is not necessary. These information are treated automatically in the Leaf System (see next sections) to optimize computations.

A graph does not include all possible information about the analysis. Particularly it does not contain explanations about what processors do. We call an annotated graph a graph accompanied by such documentation, and consider this an implementation of a bioinformatic protocol.

A software system aiming at supporting bioinformatic protocols should provide two subsystems: one for designing the protocol (the protocol design tool) and one for applying it (the protocol application engine).

Resources Management. Derived resources are produced during the analysis. High-throughput devices may produce Gigabytes or Terabytes of primary resources and the size of derived resources is often proportional. On the other hand, derived resources can be built on the fly applying the procedures described in the bioinformatic protocol. When a resource is requested, there are three possible way of *providing* it:

1. If the resource is already available in primary memory it is just *returned* as is.
2. If the resource is not available in primary memory but stored on disk it is *loaded* in primary memory and then returned.
3. If the resource is not available neither in primary memory nor on a permanent storage, it must be *factored*. In this case the protocol is applied in order to find the minimum cost path going from an available or stored resource to the requested resource. The path is than followed applying all the processors in it.

There is a trade-off to balance when deciding whether to store or not derived resources. Large resources can be an issue if one chooses to store all of them, but if their computational cost is high, it may be worthy. Small resources could be stored always, but some of them could just be faster to be computed on the fly than loaded from disk and would uselessly pollute the storage device.

The Leaf System automatically decides what to store and what to compute on the fly depending on resource size and computational time logged in previous runs of the analysis. Moreover, it can provide a requested resource with the minimal combination of ancestor resource loads and factoring.

Coherence and Consistency. The concept of Coherence and Consistency are well known in environments like database and multiprocessor systems with shared memory. When different actors are able to read and write any kind of resource the system must carefully manage accesses to avoid the production of inconsistent states.

In general, coherency deals with the correctness of a resource state, while consistency concerns the time when it becomes available.

In a bioinformatic protocol processors may read and modify resources. If one processor accesses a resource while it is being computed it will find it in an incoherent state. If a resource is updated but a processor works on a previous version of it, the state of the system is said to be inconsistent.

The case of inconsistency is very common. A bioinformatic data analysis is an ongoing process that is constantly subject to new ideas coming from partial results. This means that a branch of the analysis (for example a processor) can be modified in an unpredicted way. In such cases all the resources that are not dependent from such branch are still consistent with the new version of the processor, while all the others become inconsistent and must be refactored.

The Leaf System automatically takes care of consistency issues updating all the resources that fall in an inconsistent state. Coherence is not a problem at the moment because processors are not allowed to run in parallel.

3   The "Leaf" System

The Leaf system is composed of two subsystems: the Leaf Graph Language (LGL) and the Leaf Protocol Engine (LPE).

3.1   The Leaf Graph Language

There are many available visual tools to design graphs [8]. Also, the whole concept of bioinformatic protocol could be implemented under the framework of visual languages as a special case with peculiar features. We avoid both visual languages and visual graph design tools for the following reasons:

- Visual languages use to impose a thick Abstraction Layer between the visual interface and the final code. This model does not fit well with the urgency of quick patches and fixes that is common in a tight-loop prototypical development model, where requests from biologists must be implemented as soon as possible and results may in turn generate new requests. The Leaf model includes an extremely thin Abastraction Layer, such that, if needed, the programmer can completely avoid it, editing and running the code directly, but still having the possibility to restore it back again. There is no export/import process: it is only a matter of how the programmer decides to use his code, either trough an abstractio layer (AL) or directly. Having the graph design direclty embedded inside the source code helps making a completely white-box abstraction layer.

- Our ideal target of bioinformatic protocol tools is programmers. Programmers deal with code and the graph design phase would be just a very tiny percentage of their work. If they can do that directly from their code, in an easy way, they can gain in productivity avoiding context switch.
- Text instructions are often much more powerful than visual tools, mainly thanks to the power of parametric iterations. As an example, consider the task of mass-renaming files: it can usually be readily done through a general purpose command line interface, while it requires a dedicated tool in a visual environment.

LGL is a programming language, with the peculiarity of having a graphical appearance even though it is written in standard text. An LGL graph definition can be directly embedded in the code of any programming language. The resulting graph will be readily available and still very easy to read.

While a detailed description of the language is beyond the scope of this paper, we just show some examples to understand its basic philosophy (see Figure 3). LGL includes a compiler generated using the Flex and Bison tools [6,7]. The LGL compiler is able to output a graph in DOT format, which can be easily converted in a PDF visualization through the graphviz tools [5].

3.2   The Leaf Protocol Engine

The LGL is used in the Leaf System to design a graph representing the computational protocol of a bioinformatic analysis. The graph produced can be exploited by a computer program to apply all the steps described automatically. This is the main aim of the Leaf Protocol Engine. LPE is an engine coded in the Pyhon language that is able to embed an LGL graph, send it to the LGL compiler, get its output and apply the correspondig protocol to data.

LPE considers each node in the protocol as a Python function whose name is given by the node name. Without ever leaving the Python environment, a programmer can define the general design of the analysis through the computational protocol and fill in the details as Python functions, even in the same source file. This induces an important encapsulation level: the programmer will include in the general design of the analysis only steps that are important enough to be identified as processors in the protocol. Each processor is coded as a Python function and contains all the algorithmic details that are hidden in the graph.

The computational protocol is the main tool for communication of the analysis process to other research groups, so it must be as essential and clear as possible.

LPE includes resource and processors management. If the source code of any of the Python functions described in the protocol or any resource is changed, LPE will be aware of that and call all (and only) the processor that are necessary to update the whole analysis, even across different sessions.

LPE automatically stores all resources that are produced during the analysis in order to have them readily available upon request from the user. Through the Python console the user can interact with LPE in order to request or clear resources, as identified by the name of the processors producing them. LPE will search a requested resource in RAM first, then on disk from a previous computation and if the search fail it will automatically start its factoring basing on the protocol.

Finally, LPE can generate an annotated graph exploiting inline python comments. This means that Python self-documentation feature is used to strip docstrings out of the code and including it in the graph visualization of the protocol.

4   A Real Application Example

In this section we show the application of the concepts described in the paper as implemented in the Leaf System through a real use case.

The research collaboration of this study includes three research units:

1. University G. D'Annunzio, Chieti: biological research unit directing the aim of the project towards the formulation of biological hypothesis and validation through wet lab experiments. Also provides biological tissues to analyze.
2. Mario Negri Sud: provides high-throughput facilities through an Illumina Infinum SNP Array. Specialized staff operates the array and extract raw data.
3. University of Salerno: applies statistical and machine learning tools to extract relevant information from raw data and present it in the form of a synthetic and clear summary of results.

The three research units represent respectively: application domain experts, data producers and data miners. As research unit 3, we are concerned with: safely keeping primary resources provided by research unit 2 as our ground-truth; easily identifying, storing and retrieving primary and derived resources in order to quickly response to ongoing requests from research unit 1; providing a clear report of all the steps of our analysis; ensure that our analysis is documented with all necessary details that make it easy to replicate.

Detailed description of the analysis is going to be covered by a dedicated paper. What is important here are the practical issues concerning the development process of the analysis pipeline and how the idea of protocol and the Leaf System helped us in facing them efficiently.

```
LogR_BAF_FileName[F] -> prepareInput[F];

                /getSampleNames -> CNVboolVects, exportDistMats, intersMat_genes,
                |                   exportIntersMat_genes, exportCNVDiffMat, clustergram,
                |                   distMatGfx, CNVDiffMat, countCNVlenghts,
                |                   exportToCircos, intersectRegs, intersectTBRegs
 sampleSheet[F] <
                \                /genoTypeCheck
                 @prepareInput <
                              \
                              PennCNV[F] -> analyzeCNV;
analyzeCNV:
                 /makeBed
joinPennCNVout[F] <
                \                   /getGeneNames
                |                   |  -> @intersMat_genes,
                |                   |     @clustergram,
                |                   |     @exportIntersMat_genes,
                |                   |     @CNVDiffMat,
                |                   |     @exportCNVDiffMat
                |  addGeneInfo[F]   |
                     -> readFile    |
                      -> manualClean<
                                   \   /@intersectRegs
                                   | |    -> exportToCircos,
                                   | |       exportMergedRegs
                                   .<
                                    \   /@intersectTBRegs
                                    | |    -> exportMergedRegsTB
                                    .<
                                     \              /CompareRegionAndGenes
                                     |              |  -> exportComRegGen
                                    reformat <
                                              \   /exportPerRegion,
                                              | |  @countCNVlenghts,
                                              | |  @exportToCircos
                                             .<
                                              \geneCentricAnalysis;
geneCentricAnalysis:
        /@intersMat_genes  -> @exportIntersMat_genes
addStats <
        \                    /@exportCNVDiffMat,
        |                    |  @clustergram
        |   @CNVDiffMat <
        | /             \ computeFisher
        | |               -> @clustergram,
        | |                  @exportCNVDiffMat
       .<
        \  /@exportCNVDiffMat
         .<
          \
          |                   /@intersMat_genes -> @exportIntersMat_genes
          @CNVboolVects <
                         \ samplesDistMats -> @exportDistMats, @distMatGfx ;
```

Fig. 2. A computational protocol in LGL. Compare with Figure 4. Refer to figure 3 for syntax, considering that "|" and newline characters are ignored by the compiler. The graph is split into two unnamed subgraphs and two named subgraphs (wich is supported by LGL) to fit the page.

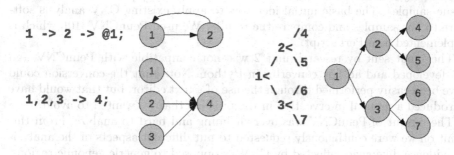

Fig. 3. Some example of graphs defined with the Leaf Graph Language. LGL sample code is accompanied by a visualization of the corresponding graph. The LGL compiler is able to parse LGL syntax and translate it into DOT source.

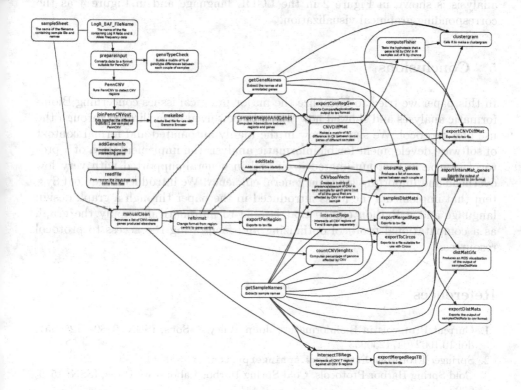

Fig. 4. Graphical representation of the LGL code of Figure 2. This figure is obatained automatically using the Graphviz tools on the DOT file that is output by the LGL compiler.

The project involved a copy number variation (CNV) [9] analysis of numerous tissue samples. The basic initial idea was to apply existing CNV analysis software to our samples and compare the results. We used PennCNV [10], which is implemented as a Perl script.

The input sent by research unit 2 was not compatible with PennCNV and we developed and ad hoc converter in Python. Note that the conversion could have been easily performed through the use of a text editor, but that would have introduced a manual intervention in the pipeline that we wanted to avoid.

The output of PennCNV was overwhelming and hard to analyze. From this point on we were continuously requested to put different aspects of the analysis in evidence, like genes affected by CNV as opposed to generic genomic regions, graphical representations of CNVs per chromosome as opposed to per sample, statistical synthesis through p-values for the most concordantly hit genes as opposed to analytic reports of all the CNVs for all the genes in each sample.

Such requests were heavily driven by partial results. This means that as new results arrived new analyses were decided that could start from the end of the last one or from any stage before it. The final computational protocol for the analysis is shown in Figure 2 in the LGDL language and in Figure 4 as the corresponding graphical visualization.

5   Conclusions

In this paper we tried to formalize the major practical issues concerning Bioinformatic analyses and showed how they can be solved or facilitated through the use of a protocol. We showed how in the highly automated and formal context of software development for bioinformatic analysis the implementation of a protocol can be in part automated itself and in general supported with very low overhead and important gains on general efficiency. We introduced the Leaf System that implements the ideas introduced in the paper through a graph design language and a Python engine that is able to automatically apply the graph as a computational protocol optimizing and facilitating the access to protocol resources.

References

1. Current Protocols in Bioinformatics. John Wiley & Sons, ISBN: 9780471250951, doi:10.1002/0471250953
2. Springer Protocols, http://www.springerprotocols.com/
3. Cold Spring Harbor Protocols. Cold Spring Harbor Laboratory Press, ISSN: 1559-6095
4. Bruegge, B., Dutoit, A.H.: Object-Oriented Software Engineering, 2nd edn. Prentice Hall (2003) ISBN-10: 0130471100
5. Graphviz - Graph Visualization Software, http://www.graphviz.org/
6. flex: The Fast Lexical Analyzer, http://www.gnu.org/software/flex/

7. Bison - GNU parser generator, http://www.gnu.org/software/bison/
8. Johnston, W.M., Hanna, J.R.P., Millar, R.J.: Advances in dataflow programming languages. ACM Computing Surveys 36(1), 1–34 (2004) (retrieved February 16, 2011), doi:10.1145/1013208.1013209
9. Hastings, P.J., Lupski, J.R., Rosenberg, S.M., Ira, G.: Mechanisms of change in gene copy number. Nature Reviews Genetics 10(8), 551–564 (2009), doi:10.1038/nrg2593; PMC 2864001. PMID 19597530
10. Wang, K., Li, M., Hadley, D., Liu, R., Glessner, J., Grant, S., Hakonarson, H., Bucan, M.: PennCNV: an integrated hidden Markov model designed for high-resolution copy number variation detection in whole-genome SNP genotyping data. Genome Research 17, 1665–1674 (2007)

Genomic Annotation Prediction Based on Integrated Information

Davide Chicco, Marco Tagliasacchi, and Marco Masseroli

Dipartimento di Elettronica e Informazione,
Politecnico di Milano Piazza Leonardo Da Vinci 32, 20133 Milan, Italy
{davide.chicco,masseroli@elet.polimi.it},
marco.tagliasacchi@polimi.it

Abstract. In the recent years, an increasingly large amount of biomedical and biomolecular information and data has become available to researchers, allowing the scientific community to infer new knowledge and reach new objectives. As these information increase, so does the difficulty in managing it efficiently. In this paper, we present a short overview of our proposal to solve this problem, a prototypal multi-organism Genomic and Proteomic Data Warehouse called GPDW, based at Politecnico di Milano. We also present the computational methods we implemented to exploit it. Experimental studies on datasets demonstrated the effectiveness of our resource and methods.

Keywords: Biomolecular databases, Bioinformatics data integration, Biomolecular annotation prediction, Information integration, Data warehouse, Software infrastructures.

Introduction. The amount of biomedical and biomolecular information and data has grown in recent years, presenting new challenges and goals in the bioinformatics scientific community. Such large amounts of information makes computerized integration and analysis of these data unavoidable [1] [2], in particular controlled annotations of biomolecular entities (mainly genes and their protein products) are of great value to support scientists and researchers.

These data can effectively support the biomedical interpretation of biomolecular test results and the extraction of knowledge; which can then be used to formulate and validate hypotheses, and possibly discover new biomedical knowledge. Several computational tools, such as those for enrichment analysis [3] [4] [5] [6] [7], are available to analyze such annotations.

The information is often present in multiple resources, in different locations and formats, and within different technologies and electronic infrastructures; so, the integration of these data, in order to infer new knowledge, can be very difficult [8] [9].

Different databank integration approaches exist. In order to build an integrated repository of distributed valuable biomolecular information and use it to support innovative knowledge discovery methods, for several reasons we decided to follow the *data warehousing* approach. The main motivation for this is that

E. Biganzoli et al. (Eds.): CIBB 2011, LNBI 7548, pp. 238–252, 2012.

having all the data together allows a quicker, more efficient and effective access to the data. The "on demand" approaches, instead, are slower and may only be effective for specific or singular queries.

Our approach comprises two different parts: the first is *integration* of data from different sources; and, secondly, *analysis* of the integrated data, with computational methods, to infer new knowledge.

Given integration architecture able to manage and integrate a large amount of information, the computational methods and tools needed to analyze the information are manifold, especially concerning controlled annotations (e.g. Gene Ontology (GO) annotations [10]). In this scenario, we propose a method for predicting new annotations of gene and gene products based solely on previously available annotations. Our first contribution extends and enhance the method in [11], hereafter denoted the SVD *(Singular Value Decomposition)* method, by incorporating a gene (or gene product) clustering algorithm based on the functional similarity between gene (or gene product) pairs. The proposed method, denoted the SIM *(Semantic IMprovement)* method, computes a separate set of eigen-terms for each identified cluster, while the original SVD method computes a global set of eigen-terms.

This paper is organized as follow: in Section 1, we will explain our data warehousing approach and information integration methods; in Section 2, we will briefly describe the computational methods we use to elaborate the integrated data; in Section 3, we will discuss our software implementation choices and performances. Finally conclusions and possible future developments are drawn in Section 4.

1   Data Warehousing and Information Integration

In this section we will explain about our prototypal multi-organism Genomic and Proteomic Data Warehouse, called GPDW, based at Politecnico di Milano (Subsection 1.1), and we will describe its information and data integration approach (Subsection 1.2).

1.1   Genomic and Proteomic Data Warehouse

Given the large amount of biomolecular information and data available nowadays in different web sources, information integration has become a very important task for the bioinformatics community. There are different data integration approaches available:

- *federated databases* (e.g. BioKleisli [12], K2 [13]);
- *link-driven federations* (e.g. SRS [14]);
- *link-driven integration of data sources* (e.g. Entrez [15], GeneCards [16], SOURCE [17]);

- *mediator-based architecture* (e.g. BioDataServer [18], DiscoveryLink [19]);
- *data warehousing* (e.g. EnsMart [20], BioWarehouse [21]).

In order to integrate heterogeneous bioinformatics data available in a variety of formats from many different sources, we decided to follow this last approach, *data warehousing*. This is because, generally, accessing to data warehouse systems is quicker, and more efficient and effective than accessing the "on demand" systems. When used for singular and specific queries, "on demand" approaches could be preferable. In our case, we decided to divide our system into two parts: an *integration* part, where all the data sources are put together; and an *analysis* part, where all the data are used to infer new knowledge.

Our objective was to generate, maintain updated and extend a multi-species Genomic and Proteomic Data Warehouse (GPDW) that provided transparent provenance tracking, quality checking of all integrated data, comprehensive annotation based analysis support, identification of unexpected information patterns and which fostered biomedical discoveries. This data warehouse constitutes the back-end of a system that we will exploit through suitable web services, and will allow discovery of new knowledge by analyzing our large amount of information and data available.

1.2 Information and Data Integration Approach

The integration of data from different sources in our data warehouse is managed in three phases: *importing*, *aggregation*, and *integration*. In the former (*importing*), data from the different sources are imported into one repository. In the second (*aggregation*), they are gathered and normalized into a single representation in the instance-aggregation tier of our global data model. In the third (*integration*), data are organized into informative clusters in the concept-integration tier of the global model.

During the initial importing and aggregation phases, tables of the features described by the imported data are created and populated. Then, similarity and historical ID (*IDentification*) data are created by translating the IDs provided by the data sources to our internal OIDs (*Own IDentification*).

In doing so, relationship data are coupled with their related feature entries. According to the imported data sources and their mutual synchronization, relationship data may refer to feature entries or features that have not been imported into the data warehouse. In this case, missing integrated feature entries are synthesized and labeled as such (i.e., inferred through synthesis from relationship data). However, if a missing entry has an obsolete ID and through unfolded translated historical data it is possible to get a more current ID for it, the relationship is first moved to the latest ID and is marked as *inferred* through historical data. In this way, all the relationships expressed by the imported relationship data are preserved and allows their subsequent use to infer new biomedical knowledge discoveries (e.g., by transitive closure inference, also involving the synthesized entries).

The final integration phase uses similarity analysis to test whether single feature instances from different sources represent the same feature concepts. In this case, they are associated with a new single concept OID. To keep track of the inference method used to derive an entry, an *inferrence* field is used in all tables that have been integrated. Furthermore, a summary quality rate for each concept instance is computed based on the source–specific instances contributing to the concept instance and its *inferred* attribute value.

At the end of the integration process, the defined indexes, unique, primary and foreign key integrity constraints of all the integrated tables are enforced in order to detect and resolve possible data inconsistencies and duplications, thus improving the speed of access to the integrated data, as well as their general quality.

2 Computational Methods

In this section we describe how to exploit the integrated data integrated in the data warehouse in order to generate good predictions of new biomolecular annotations.

2.1 Prediction of Biomolecular Annotations

Genome sequencing has completely revolutionized the approach of studying biological functionalities. To better understand the functions of genes and proteins, the concept of *annotation* (association of nucleotide or amino acid sequences with useful information) was developed. This information is expressed through controlled vocabularies, sometimes structured as ontologies, where every controlled term of the vocabulary is associated with a unique alphanumeric code. Such a code associated with a gene or protein ID constitutes an annotation.

The annotation curator's task is paramount for the correct use of the annotations. Curators discover and/or validate new annotations; and publish them in online web databanks, thereby making them available to scientists and researchers. However, available annotations are incomplete, and, for recently studied genomes, they are mostly computationally derived. So only a few of them represent highly reliable human–curated information. To support and quicken the time–consuming curation process, prioritized lists of computationally predicted annotations are extremely useful. In our work, we assessed, improved and extended a prediction method already available in literature, based on SVD (*Singular Value Decomposition*) [11] of the annotation matrix, by proposing a new method, SIM (*Semantic IMprovement*). A flow chart describing SVD and SIM methods is provided in Figure 1.

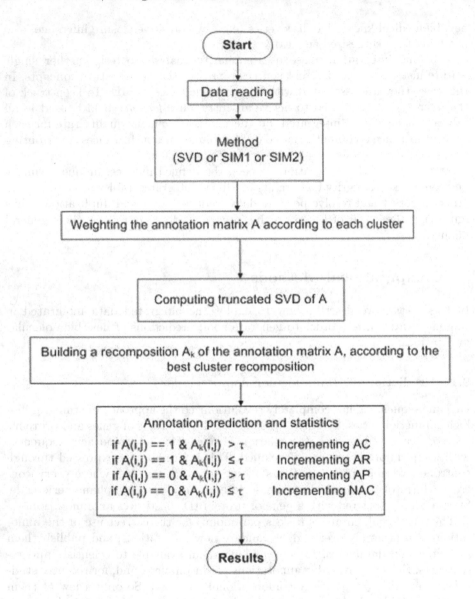

Fig. 1. The flow chart describing SVD and SIM methods

2.2   SVD - Singular Value Decomposition

Let the matrix $A \in \{-1, 0, 1\}^{m \times n}$, with m rows corresponding to genes and n columns corresponding to annotation terms, represent all the considered annotations of controlled vocabularies for a certain organism. The entry $A(i, j)$ assumes a value of 1 if gene i is annotated to term j or to any descendant of j in the considered ontology structure. It assumes a value of -1 if it is known that gene i must not be annotated to term j, or a valure of 0 otherwise. Then, we considered the SVD of the annotation matrix A, i.e. $A = U \Sigma V^T$, where U is a $m \times p$ unitary matrix (i.e. $U^T U = I$), Σ is a non-negative diagonal matrix of size $p \times p$, and V is a $n \times p$ unitary matrix, where $p = min(m,n)$. An annotation prediction, based on this SVD, is performed by computing a reduced rank approximation A_k of matrix A by means of singular value decomposition (where $0 < k < r$, with r the number of non zero singular values). A_k contains real valued entries related to the likelihood that gene i shall be annotated to term j. For a defined threshold τ, if $A_k(i,j) > \tau$, gene i is predicted to be annotated to term j. The threshold τ can be chosen in order to obtain the B best predicted annotations (with $B \in \mathbb{N}$). Values of k and τ can be heuristically chosen according to preliminary tests on the specific data considered.

2.3   SIM - Semantic IMprovement

The SVD method implicitly adopts a global term-to-term correlation matrix $T = A^T A$, estimated from the whole set of available annotations. In contrast, we propose an adaptive approach, called the SIM method, which clusters genes (the rows of matrix A) based on their original annotation profile and values a set of distinct correlation matrices, T_c, one for each cluster. For each matrix, T_c, a predicted annotation profile for gene i is computed. The selected predicted annotation profile for gene i is the one that minimizes variation, measured by the ell-2 norm, with respect to the original annotation profile of the gene.

We heuristically fix a number C of clusters, and completely discard the columns of matrix U where $j = C+1, ..., n$. Each column, u_c, of SVD matrix U represents a cluster, and the value $U(i,c)$ indicates the membership of gene i to the cth cluster [22]. We use this membership degree to cluster the genes (the rows of matrix A). As such, each gene might belong to more than one cluster with different degrees of membership. We notice that the columns of U are a set of eigenvectors for the matrix $G = AA^T$, i.e. the similarity between gene pairs is measured by the inner product of their annotation profiles. To estimate the correlation matrices, T_c, we cluster genes based on their functional similarity, expressed through their annotations, by exploiting SVD of matrix A. To calculate T_c, for each cluster, first we generate a modified gene-to-term matrix $A_c = W_c A$ (where $W_c \in \mathbb{R}^{m \times m}$ is a diagonal matrix with the entries of u_c along the main diagonal), in which the ith row of A is weighted by the membership score of the corresponding gene to the cth cluster. Then, we compute $T_c = A_c^T A_c$.

Furthermore, to effect more accurate clustering, we compute the eigenvectors of the matrix $\tilde{G} = ASA^T$ where $S \in \mathbb{R}^{n \times n}$ is the term similarity matrix. Starting from a pair of ontology terms, j_1 and j_2, the term functional similarity $S(j_1,j_2)$ can be calculated using different methods; here we use the Lin's similarity metrics [23].

An overview of the SIM algorithm is described in Fig. 2.

An important and interesting difference between our method and that of Draghici et al. [11] is the choice of the predicted annotations. While Draghici et al.

1. Given a number $C \in \mathbb{N}$ of clusters
2. Consider only the columns U_j of matrix U, where $j \in \{1, ..., C\}$ and $A = U\Sigma V^T$
3. Use the membership degree U(i,c) of gene i to cluster c, to group the genes
4. For each cluster c, generate $\boldsymbol{A_c} = \boldsymbol{W_c A}$, where $W_c = diag(u_c)$ and $W_c \in \mathbb{R}^{m \times m}$
5. For each cluster c, compute the correlation matrix, $\boldsymbol{T_c} = \boldsymbol{A_c^T A_c}$
6. Compute the term functional similarity matrix $\boldsymbol{S}$, using the Lin's similarity metrics
7. Compute the gene-similarity matrix $\tilde{\boldsymbol{G}} = \boldsymbol{ASA^T}$
8. Compute the set of k eigenvectors $\boldsymbol{V_{k,c}}$ of $\tilde{\boldsymbol{G}}$, where k is the number of the largest eigenvectors of $\boldsymbol{T_c}$, fixed heurisiticaly
9. Compute every row $a_{k,i}$ of output matrix $\boldsymbol{A_k}$:
   $a_{k,i} = a_i * \boldsymbol{V_{k,c,i}} * \boldsymbol{V_{k,c,i}^T}$
10. Compare $\boldsymbol{A}$ with $\boldsymbol{A_k}$ elements:
    - if $\mathbf{A(i,j)} \leq 0$ & $\mathbf{A_k(i,j)} > \tau$:
      suggestion of new annotation
    - if $\mathbf{A(i,j)} \leq 0$ & $\mathbf{A_k(i,j)} \leq \tau$:
      annotation absence confirmed
    - if $\mathbf{A(i,j)} = 1$ & $\mathbf{A_k(i,j)} > \tau$:
      original annotation presence confirmed
    - if $\mathbf{A(i,j)} = 1$ & $\mathbf{A_k(i,j)} \leq \tau$:
      original annotation suggested to be reviewed

Fig. 2. Overview of the SIM algorithm

[11] took all the predicted annotations above a certain threshold τ as equally correct, our method provides the predicted annotations in order of accuracy. Thus, the user can select the B most correct annotations by choosing the value of τ threshold.

To assess the performance of the SVD and SIM methods, we considered the Gene Ontology annotations of different organisms, including *Saccharomyces cerevisiae* and *Drosophila melanogaster*, excluding annotations with evidence code IEA (*Inferred Electronic Annotations*), since they have not been checked by a manual curator. After this, the *Saccharomyces cerevisiae* dataset included 3,676 genes related to 1,256 ontology terms, for a total of 23,384 annotations. For the sake of brevity in this paper, we present only the result for the *Saccharomyces cerevisiae* dataset, but similar results where obtained also for the *Drosophila melanogaster* dataset.

2.4   Results

We assessed the performance of the SVD and SIM methods by performing K-fold cross-validation as in [24] and [25], and discarding terms used to annotate less than M genes, in order to avoid considering very low reference annotation terms which could bias the evaluation. As for the SIM method, we evaluated two variants. In SIM1, we set $\boldsymbol{S} = \boldsymbol{I}$, i.e. the clustering step does not rely on the functional similarity between terms. In SIM2, matrix S is computed by means of the Lin's metrics [23]. In both cases we heuristically set a fixed number of clusters $C = 5$ for all ontology, based on our own tests ($C \ll p$). With a threshold value τ, if $\mathbf{A(i,j)} \leq 0$ and $\mathbf{A}_k(\mathbf{i,j}) > \tau$, a new annotation is suggested; this case is denoted as a *predicted annotation* (AP). Conversely, if $\mathbf{A(i,j)} = 1$ and $\mathbf{A}_k(\mathbf{i,j}) \leq \tau$, an existing annotation is suggested to be semantic inconsistent with the available data; this case is denoted as an *annotation to be reviewed* (AR). The *confirmed annotations* (AC) rate and *no annotations confirmed* (NAC) rate are similarly defined.

The curve in Figure 3 depicts the trade-off between the annotations to be reviewed rate (AR / (AC + AR)) and predicted annotations rate (AP / (AP + NAC)) of annotations of *Saccharomyces cerevisiae* (SGD) genes, when the prediction is performed using heuristically the first k = 40 eigenvectors of the available annotation matrix, $\mathbf{A}_k$.

To improve reliability of validation, we performed several validations with different $\mathbf{A}_k$ values by retaining Gene Ontology terms used to annotate at least M = 3 or M = 10 genes of the considered organism and excluding annotations with evidence code IEA (inferred electronic annotations), since they have not been checked by a manual curator. As an aggregated indicator of the prediction performance, we computed the area above the AR rate versus AP rate curve (AAC) in the [0;0:01] range, for *Saccharomyces cerevisiae* (SGD). Indeed, we are typically interested in the low range of AP rate, since it corresponds to top-ranked predictions of newly inferred annotations (AP) with the highest score.

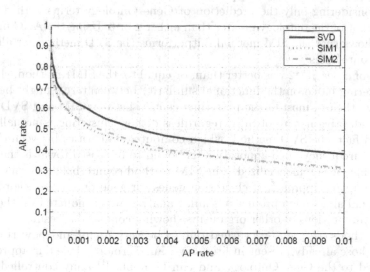

Fig. 3. Annotations to be reviewed (AR) rate versus predicted annotations (AP) rate for the prediction of the Gene Ontology Biological Process annotations of *Saccharomyces cerevisiae* (SGD) genes

Table 1. Area above the curve of annotations to be reviewed (AR) rate versus predicted annotations (AP) rate of the Gene Ontology annotations of *Saccharomyces cerevisiae* (SGD), at Gene Ontology level greater than 2 (L > 2) and 6 (L > 6) predicted with different methods when only terms annotating at least M genes are considered for prediction. BP: biological processes, MF: molecular functions, CC: cellular components GO ontologies; k: number of eigenvectors of the considered annotation matrix retained for prediction. Testing values 20 and 40 for k were heuristically chosen as sample values based on preliminary tests made.

M	method	k	BP L > 2	BP L > 6	MF L > 2	MF L > 6	CC L > 2	CC L > 6
3	SVD	20	0.58	0.35	0.47	0.51	0.39	0.50
		40	0.65	0.57	0.57	0.60	0.32	0.51
	SIM1	20	0.64	0.53	0.56	0.64	**0.41**	**0.60**
		40	0.70	0.61	0.52	0.61	0.37	0.56
	SIM2	20	0.64	0.50	**0.59**	**0.70**	0.37	0.56
		40	**0.71**	**0.62**	0.55	0.62	0.36	**0.60**
10	SVD	20	0.53	0.34	0.43	0.49	0.35	0.43
		40	0.60	0.53	0.53	0.59	0.31	0.47
	SIM1	20	0.62	0.52	0.50	0.56	**0.43**	**0.56**
		40	0.65	**0.60**	0.46	0.39	0.39	**0.56**
	SIM2	20	0.63	0.52	**0.54**	**0.65**	0.37	0.53
		40	**0.67**	0.58	0.49	0.47	0.35	**0.56**

The normalized AAC metrics are limited to the [0;1] interval, where a value closer to 1 implies more accurate predictions. In all cases, we computed the AAC metrics considering only the prediction of Gene Ontology terms with depth L from the root of the ontology greater than either 2 or 6. Using the AAC metrics, Table 1 shows that the SIM method outperforms the SVD method for all Gene Ontology ontologies.

In 66% of cases SIM2 was better than, or equal to, the SIM1 method, showing that clustering based on the functional similarity between terms might be beneficial. Nevertheless, most of the performance gain between SIM and SVD stems from the adaptive nature of SIM, regardless of how clustering is actually performed. In fact, the SVD method, which computes similarities between clusters in terms of frequency of co-annotation, is bound to be biased towards the larger clusters, since it is unnormalized. The SIM method counterbalances such a bias with its adaptive approach of clustering genes (or gene products) according to their original annotation profile. A similar analysis was conducted on the Gene Ontology annotations of other organisms showing comparable results.

The methods we proposed turned out to be very useful and powerful compared to those already present in literature. Furthermore, since our approach is not limited to the Gene Ontology and can be applied to any controlled annotation, increasingly available multiple annotations of genes and gene products from different controlled vocabularies and ontologies could be jointly considered to further improve prediction reliability.

3   Software Infrastructure and Performances

Since the amount of data was very large and the objectives and computation quite demanding, we had to pay particular attention to software performance and memory usage. To satisfy the facility of the software to be modified and extended, we first chose the Java programming language for implementation. Java results to be very independent from platform and from operating system, that is a very important value for the software objectives. However, Java shows some limitations, too: it provides a high response time, and uses a lot of memory. The response delay clearly results you comparing matrix operation rapidity in Java and C++ environments with native solutions that use very highly optimized mathematical kernels. The high memory usage problem is especially relevant for the virtual machine.

Given these issues, we decided to implement the mathematical core of our software in C++ programming language, using a multiplatform, multithreading, optimized mathematical kernel, such as AMD Core Math Library (ACML) [26]. This library provides a high level of optimization on generic processors, and is simple to use, given that it does not need to be compiled. In addition, ACML is freely available for both Linux/Unix, Microsoft Windows and Solaris systems. Another effective library we used for the mathematical core was SVDLIBC [27]. The multithreading native part was developed by using OpenMP (Open Multi-Processing, OPM) [28] compiler directives which exploited by the mathematical kernels, independently from the operating system. The interaction between the native C++ code and Java code was though Java Native Interface (JNI) [29].

Library choices are described in the following Subsection 3.1, while in the later Subsection 3.2 we will discuss performance times and memory peaks.

3.1   ACML and SVDLIBC

We needed a way to implement a complex data processing efficiently, and we chose ACML and SVDLIBC libraries to manage this issue. The AMD Core Math Library (ACML) implements a set of multithread functions optimized for *high performance computing*. It is formed by the following main components, relevant to our implementation:

- Complete implementation of the Basic Linear Algebra Subprograms (BLAS) [30].

  BLAS is a *standard* application programming interface, supported by most of the mathematical libraries to execute vector and matrix operations. Implemented in different libraries, developed both by open source communities (GotoBLAS, ATLAS, etc) and processor inventors (ACML, Intel's MKL, IBM's ESSL, etc), BLAS provides different operators, mainly for: operations between vectors, between vectors and matrices, and between matrices.

- Complete implementation of the Linear Algebra PACKage (LAPACK) [32]. LAPACK is a set of functions, written in Fortran to make high level scientific calculations. It is mainly used to solve: linear simultaneous equations, systems with linear least squares solutions, factoring problems, and for eigenvalue and eigenvector investigations.

Moreover, the ACML could be compiled for 32-bit and 64-bit systems, on Linux/Unix, Microsoft Windows or Solaris systems. ACML takes great advantage of OpenMP [28] resources; this allows implementation with simple threading models and a simplified debug. OpenMP also permits multithreading usage on any system.

SVDLIBC is a C library based on the SVDPACKC library [31], used mostly for SVD and truncated SVD operations. Its intent is to provide an easy to use interface and a set of functionalities to manage, and convert matrices. The SVDPACKC algorithm used in the software is *las2*, which proved to be very powerful for the SVD calculation despite of having some inaccuracies in the minor eigenvalues calculation.

3.2   Performances

As previously stated, the use of Java Native Interface code and extremely optimized mathematical libraries allowed much faster execution times. Our software flow can be divided into five different performance steps.

The first step is the reading of initial annotations. As described in the previous sections, data are retrieved from the Java code software and then submitted to the native code. During this phase, the software retrieves all the annotations related to a certain organism, possibly deleting any duplicated annotations, that may be present because of different *evidence codes*.

The second step relates to annotation unfolding. This part is executed by an iterative algorithm on the ontology controlled vocabularies native memory structure. We decided that the software would be used to manage already-unfolded data, because this would have drastically increased the database working load.

The third step is the computation of truncated SVD, that is implemented using the Lanczos algorithm in the SVDLIBC library. This reduces occupied memory for the initial annotation matrix A, and allows direct computation of the already-truncated resulting matrices.

The fourth step saves data into files. For this operation, we implemented a buffered writing method, in order to minimize the disc access number.

Finally, the fifth step rebuilds the original matrix, by extracting the K best annotations from it. This extraction is optimized by the implementation of a data structure (a memory buffer containing the best annotations, over a certain threshold).

Tests were executed on a personal computer with an Intel Centrino T8100 2.10Ghz processor and a 5600RPM Hitachi disk with 8Mb cache. Comparative test results are shown in Table 2.

Table 2. Performances of the previoulsy-described steps for SVD, SIM1 and SIM2 methods, for prediction of annotations having; Homo Sapiens taxonomy (9606); ontologies *biological function feature, cellular component, biological process*; not having evidence code IEA (*Inferred Electronic Annotations*). SIM1 and SIM2 are considered for C=3 clusters.

Method	Annotation and ontology reading	Unfolding	Truncated SVD execution	Saving of the matrices into files	Prediction of 1000 new annotations	Total	Memory peak
SVD	4 153 ms	10 661 ms	6 488 ms	595 ms	15 177 ms	37 sec	152 Mb
SIM1	4 153 ms	10 661 ms	17 196 ms	595 ms	91 619 ms	124 sec	155 Mb
SIM2	4 153 ms	10 661 ms	17 196 ms	595 ms	101 070 ms	133 sec	163 Mb

As you cas see in Table 2, the most onerous step is prediction, because it has to rebuild the initial matrix and order all the obtained values to complete the ranking operation. SIM methods show similar performance times and memory peaks, with a little increment corcerning SIM2, because of the computation of functional similarity between terms in S matrix. Concerning *Truncated SVD execution*, the performance time is proportional to the number of clusters used in SIM methods (in this case, 3 clusters).

Annotation and ontology reading, Unfolding, and *Saving of the matrices into files* phases need similar time for all the methods, while the *Prediction of 1000 new annotations* phase times are slighty different, because of the different operations made in the three procedures.

4 Conclusions

Easy and integrated access to the high amount of biomolecular information and knowledge now available in many heterogeneous and distributed data sources is required to answer biological questions. Data warehousing and computational systems can provide support for comprehensive use and analysis of sparsely available genomic and proteomic structural, functional and phenotypic information and knowledge. We designed a method for integrating biomolecular knowledge (mainly expressed through controlled terminologies or ontologies), into a data warehouse, and exploiting such integrated data to predict new biomolecular annotations.

We proposed a novel contribution in the context of prediction of genomic ontological annotations, SIM. Our Semantic IMproved (SIM) version of the Single Value Decomposition (SVD) method produced better predictions than the SVD method alone. In the future, our software implementation could be improved in many ways. For example, an algorithm for the automatic computation of k, τ and C parameters based on Receiver operating characteristic (ROC) curves [34] could be added. Furthermore, since our approach is not limited to a specific type of annotations, can be applied to any controlled annotation. Increasingly available multiple annotations of genes and gene products from different ontologies and controlled vocabularies could be jointly considered to further improve prediction reliability.

Finally, our aim is to provide web service access to our implemented method and integrate such web service with other available services within the Search Computing framework [35] [36] in order to provide support for answering complex life science questions [37].

Acknowledgments. This research is part of the Search Computing project (2008-2013) funded by the European Research Council (ERC), IDEAS Advanced Grant.

References

1. Galperin, M.Y., Cochrane, G.R.: Nucleic Acids Research Annual Database Issue and the NAR Online Molecular Biology Database Collection in 2009. Nucleic Acids Res. 37(Database issue), D1–D4 (2009)
2. EMBL Nucleotide Sequence Database Statistics,
   `http://www3.ebi.ac.uk/Services/DBStats/`
3. Huang, D.W., Sherman, B.T., Lempicki, R.A.: Bioinformatics Enrichment Tools: Paths toward the Comprehensive Functional Analysis of Large Gene Lists. Nucleic Acids Res. 37, 1–13 (2009)
4. Al-Shahrour, F., Minguez, P., Tárraga, J., Medina, I., Alloza, E., Montaner, D., Dopazo, J.: FatiGO+: A Functional Profiling Tool for Genomic Data. Integration of Functional Annotation, Regulatory Motifs and Interaction Data with Microarray Experiments. Nucleic Acids Res. 35(Web Server issue), W91–W96 (2007)
5. Huang, D.W., Sherman, B.T., Tan, Q., Kir, J., Liu, D., Bryant, D., Guo, Y., et al.: DAVID Bioinformatics Resources: Expanded Annotation Database and Novel Algorithms to Better Extract Biology from Large Gene Lists. Nucleic Acids Res. 35(Web Server issue), W169–W175 (2007)
6. Masseroli, M., Martucci, D., Pinciroli, F.: GFINDer: Genome Function INtegrated Discoverer through Dynamic Annotation, Statistical Analysis, and Mining. Nucleic Acids Res. 32, W293–W300 (2004)
7. Masseroli, M.: Management and Analysis of Genomic Functional and Phenotypic Controlled Annotations to Support Biomedical Investigation and Practice. IEEE Trans. Inf. Technol. Biomed. 11, 376–385 (2007)
8. Sujansky, W.: Heterogeneous Database Integration in Biomedicine. J. Biomed. Inform. 34, 285–298 (2001)
9. Hernandez, T., Kambhampati, S.: Integration of Biological Sources: Current Systems and Challenges ahead. SIGMOD Record 33, 51–60 (2004)
10. The Gene Ontology Consortium: Creating the Gene Ontology Resource: Design and Implementation. Genome Res. 11, 1425–1433 (2001)
11. Khatri, P., Done, B., Rao, A., Done, A., Draghici, S.: A Semantic Analysis of the Annotations of the Human Genome. Bioinformatics 21, 3416–3421 (2005)
12. Davidson, S.B., Overton, C., Tanen, V., Wong, L.: BioKleisli: A Digital Library for Biomedical Researchers. Int. J. Digit. Libr. 1, 36–53 (1997)
13. Davidson, S.B., Crabtree, J., Brunk, B., Schug, J., Tannen, V., Overton, C., Stoeckert, C.: K2/Kleisli and GUS: Experiments in Integrated Access to Genomic Data Sources. IBM System Journal 40, 512–531 (2001)

14. Etzold, T., Ulyanov, A., Argos, P.: SRS: Information Retrieval System for Molecular Biology Data Banks. Methods Enzymol. 266, 114–128 (1996)
15. Tatusova, T.A., Karsch-Mizrachi, I., Ostell, J.A.: Complete Genomes in WWW Entrez: Data Representation and Analysis. Bioinformatics 15, 536–543 (1999)
16. Safran, M., Solomon, I., Shmueli, O., Lapidot, M., Shen-Orr, S., Adato, A., et al.: GeneCards 2002: Towards a Complete, Object-Oriented, Human Gene Compendium. Bioinformatics 18, 1542–1543 (2002)
17. Diehn, M., Sherlock, G., Binkley, G., Jin, H., Matese, J.C., Hernandez-Boussard, T., et al.: SOURCE: A Unified Genomic Resource of Functional Annotations, Ontologies, and Gene Expression Data. Nucleic Acids Res. 31, 219–223 (2003)
18. Freier, A., Hofestädt, R., Lange, M., Scholz, U., Stephanik, A.: BioDataServer: A SQL-Based Service for the Online Integration of Life Science Data. Silico Biol. 2, 37–57 (2002)
19. Haas, L.M., Schwarz, P.M., Kodali, P., Kotlar, E., Rice, J.E., Swops, W.C.: DiscoveryLink: A System for Integrated Access to Life Sciences Data Sources. IBM Systems Journal 40, 489–511 (2001)
20. Kasprzyk, A., Keefe, D., Smedley, D., London, D., Spooner, W., Melsopp, C., et al.: EnsMart: A Generic System for Fast and Flexible Access to Biological Data. Genome Res. 14, 160–169 (2004)
21. Lee, T.J., Pouliot, Y., Wagner, V., Gupta, P., Stringer-Calvert, D.W., Tenenbaum, J.D., Karp, P.D.: BioWarehouse: A Bioinformatics Database Warehouse Toolkit. BMC Bioinformatics 7, 1–14 (2006)
22. Drineas, P.: Clustering large graphs via the singular value decomposition: Theoretical advances in data clustering. Machine Learning 56, 9–33 (2004)
23. Lin, D.: An Information-Theoretic Definition of Similarity. In: Shavlik, J.W. (ed.) Proceedings of the 15th International Conference on Machine Learning (ICML 1998), pp. 296–304. Morgan Kaufmann Publishers Inc., San Francisco (1998)
24. King, O.D., Foulger, R.E., Dwight, S.S., White, J.V., Roth, F.P.: Predicting Gene Function From Patterns of Annotation. Genome Res. 13, 896–904 (2003)
25. Tao, Y., Sam, L., Li, J., Friedman, C., Lussier, Y.A.: Information theory applied to the sparse gene ontology annotation network to predict novel gene function. Bioinformatics 23, 529–538 (2007)
26. AMD Core Math Library (ACML), http://developer.amd.com/cpu/libraries/acml/
27. Rohde, D.: SVDLIBC, http://tedlab.mit.edu/~dr/SVDLIBC
28. Dagum, L., Menon, R.: OpenMP: an industry standard API for shared-memory programming. IEEE Computational Science & Engineering 5, 46–55 (1998)
29. Gordon, R.: Essential JNI: Java Native Interface. Prentice-Hall, Inc., NJ (1998)
30. Lawson, C.L., Hanson, R.J., Kincaid, D.R., Krogh, F.T.: Basic Linear Algebra Subprograms for Fortran Usage. ACM Transactions on Mathematical Software (TOMS) 5 (1979)
31. Berry, M., Do, T., O'Brien, G., Krishna, V., Varadhan, S.: SVDPACKC (Version 1.0) User's Guide. Citeseer (1993)
32. Angerson, B., Dongarra, G., McKenney, D.C., et al.: LAPACK: A portable linear algebra library for high-performance computers. In: Proceedings of the 1990 ACM/IEEE Conference on Supercomputing, pp. 2–11. IEEE Computer Society Press, Los Alamitos (1990)
33. Hofmann, T.: Probabilistic Latent Semantic Indexing. In: Proceedings of the 22nd Annual International SIGIR Conference on Research and Development in Information Retrieval (SIGIR 1999). ACM, New York (1999)

34. Egan, J.P.: Signal Detection Theory and ROC Analysis. Academic Press, New York (1975)
35. Search-Computing.org, http://www.search-computing.org
36. Ceri, S., Brambilla, M. (eds.): Search Computing. LNCS, vol. 5950. Springer, Heidelberg (2010)
37. Masseroli, M., Ghisalberti, G.: Bio-SeCo: Integration and Global Ranking of Biomedical Search Results. In: Ceri, S., Brambilla, M. (eds.) Search Computing II. LNCS, vol. 6585, pp. 203–214. Springer, Heidelberg (2011)

Solving Biclustering with a GRASP-Like Metaheuristic: Two Case-Studies on Gene Expression Analysis

Angelo Facchiano[1], Paola Festa[2], Anna Marabotti[3],
Luciano Milanesi[3], and Francesco Musacchia[2]

[1] Istituto di Scienze dell'Alimentazione - CNR, Italy
angelo.facchiano@isa.cnr.it
[2] University of Napoli "Federico II", Italy
{paola.festa,francesco.musacchia}@unina.it
[3] Istituto di Tecnologie Biomediche - CNR, Italy
{anna.marabotti,luciano.milanesi}@itb.cnr.it

Abstract. The explosion of "omics" data over the past few decades has generated an increasing need of efficiently analyzing high-dimensional gene expression data in several different and heterogenous contexts, such as for example in information retrieval, knowledge discovery, and data mining. For this reason, biclustering, or simultaneous clustering of both genes and conditions has generated considerable interest over the past few decades. Unfortunately, the problem of locating the most significant bicluster has been shown to be NP-complete. We have designed and implemented a GRASP-like heuristic algorithm to efficiently find good solutions in reasonable running times, and to overcome the inner intractability of the problem from a computational point of view.

Experimental results on two datasets of expression data are promising indicating that this algorithm is able to find significant biclusters, especially from a biological point of view.

Keywords: Biclustering, gene expression analysis, GRASP, combinatorial optimization, approximate solutions.

1 Introduction

Traditional clustering tasks take as input a data set and a similarity (or distance) function over the domain, with the aim of finding a partition of the data into groups of mutually similar elements. Biclustering (term coined by Hartigan [1]) is a variant of this task that is needed when the input data comes from two domain sets and some relation over the Cartesian product of these two sets is given. In this case, one could be interested in partitioning each of the sets, such that the subsets from one domain exhibit similar behavior across the subsets of the other domain. Roughly speaking, bi-clustering can be viewed as simultaneous data clustering and feature selection, i.e., detection of significant clusters and the features that are uniquely associated with them, given that not all features are relevant to certain clusters.

E. Biganzoli et al. (Eds.): CIBB 2011, LNBI 7548, pp. 253–267, 2012.

In the pioneering work by Cheng and Church [2] biclustering was first introduced for the purpose of gene expression analysis. In the scientific literature devoted to biclustering [3], several classes of biclusters have been identified, depending on the chosen definition of homogeneity.

The state-of-the-art methods proposed for approaching the problem can be divided into five main classes: 1) exhaustive enumeration algorithms, that exhaustively search in the input matrix the best biclusters with very high computational running times [4, 5]; 2) iterative row and column clustering combination algorithms, that first apply separately clustering algorithms to the rows and columns of the data matrix and then combine the results using some sort of iterative procedure [6, 7]; 3) divide and conquer algorithms, that divide the problem in subproblems and are potentially very fast but usually split good biclusters before they can be identified [1, 8]; 4) greedy iterative search algorithms, that, based on the steepest descent idea, create biclusters by adding and/or removing rows and columns optimizing a local gain criterion [9–11], and 5) distribution parameter identification algorithms, that try to identify the distribution parameters used to generate the data [12–14]. Very recently, Aradhya et al. [15] proposed an approach based on Modular Singular Value Decomposition (Mod-SVD), that first partitions the input data matrix into a set of equally sized submatrices and applies a SVD to each of the submatrices to be then concatenated. It is only in the past few years that the biclustering task has been approached via metaheuristic algorithms, especially in the presence of large scale problem instances. They include a Simulated Annealing [16], a Genetic Algorithm [17], and a Reactive GRASP [18]. The reader can refer to [3] and [19] for recent surveys.

We have implemented Dharan and Nair's proposal and in our experience we observed that, even if robust and elegant, the local search applied at each iteration is time consuming and very rarely improves the constructed solution. In this paper, we propose a novel Reactive GRASP-like that overcomes the drawback of the Reactive GRASP proposed by Dharan and Nair in [18].

The paper is organized as follows. In Section 2 biclustering tasks are formally stated. Section 3 introduces the main issues in designing a GRASP method and Section 4 describes our Reactive GRASP-like proposal. In Section 5 we synthesize the whole analysis process and report and discuss the experimental results obtained on two case studies of gene expression experiments. We also report some consideration on future work in this challenging research area.

2   Problem Formulation

The goal of biclustering techniques is to identify subgroups of genes and subgroups of conditions, by performing simultaneous clustering of both n rows and m columns of a given gene expression matrix $\mathcal{A} \in \mathbb{R}^{n \times m}$, where each element a_{ij} represents the expression level of gene i under condition j. As in [3], in order to coherently represent all possible scenarios of biclustering real–world applications we will consider the general case of a data matrix $\mathcal{A} = (X, Y)$, where $X = \{x_1, \ldots, x_n\}$ is its set of rows, Y is its set of columns $Y = \{y_1, \ldots, y_m\}$, and the element a_{ij}, $(i \in X, j \in Y)$, corresponds to a value representing the relation between row i and column j.

Let $I \subseteq X$ and $J \subseteq Y$ be subsets of the rows and columns, respectively. Then, $\mathcal{A}_{IJ}$ denotes the submatrix of $\mathcal{A}$ that contains all the elements a_{ij} of $\mathcal{A}$ such that $i \in I$ and $j \in J$ and a *bicluster* $\mathcal{B} = \mathcal{A}_{IJ}$ is a $k \times s$ submatrix of $\mathcal{A}$, where $I = \{x_{i_1}, \ldots, x_{i_k}\} \subseteq X$ and $J = \{y_{j_1}, \ldots, y_{j_s}\} \subseteq Y$, i.e. it is a subset of $k \leq n$ rows defined over a subset of $s \leq m$ columns or, equivalently, a subset of $s \leq m$ columns defined over a subset of $k \leq n$ rows.

A natural representation of data matrices in clustering/biclustering problems is by means of a *complete weighted bipartite graph* $G = (V, E)^1$, where $V = X \cup Y$ (clearly, $X \cap Y = \emptyset$) and $E = \{[x_i, y_j] \mid x_i \in X, \ y_j \in Y\}$. Moreover, a *weight function* $w : E \mapsto \mathbb{R}$ is defined that to each edge $[x_i, y_j] \in E$ assigns a weight $w_{ij} = a_{ij} \in \mathbb{R}$.

This graph theoretical representation helped in understanding the inner intractability of the problem of finding a maximum size bicluster in a data matrix $\mathcal{A}$. In fact, even in its simplest form where $\mathcal{A} \in \{0, 1\}^{n \times m}$ the problem is **NP**-complete, since it reduces to finding the maximum edge biclique in the corresponding bipartite graph G [20]. Generally speaking, given a data matrix $\mathcal{A}$, biclustering aims at identifying a set of biclusters $\{\mathcal{B}_1 = (I_1, J_1), \ldots, \mathcal{B}_k = (I_k, J_k)\}$ such that each bicluster $\mathcal{B}_q$, $q = 1, \ldots, k$, satisfies some specific characteristics of "homogeneity", whose definition varies from approach to approach and plays an important role to evaluate a biclustering algorithm and the quality of the type of biclusters that it is able to find. In this paper, we want to identify "biclusters with coherent values". Therefore, we want to analyze directly the numeric values in the data matrix $\mathcal{A}$ and try to find subsets of rows and subsets of columns with similar behaviors. For this class, biclusters cannot be found simply by considering that the values within the bicluster are given by additive or multiplicative models that consider an adjustment for either the rows or the columns. More sophisticated statistical approaches are needed to evaluate the quality of the resulting bicluster or set of biclusters. According to Cheng and Church [2], we have used as a measure of the coherence of the rows and columns in the bicluster the *mean squared residue score* to be minimized and defined as the sum of the squared residues, where the residue of an element a_{ij} in $\mathcal{B}$ is the difference between its actual value and its expected value predicted from the corresponding row mean, column mean, and bicluster mean.

3   GRASP

GRASP (Greedy Randomized Adaptive Search Procedures) [21, 22] is a multi-start metaheuristic for producing good-quality solutions of hard combinatorial optimization problems and it has been efficiently applied to many problems. Each GRASP iteration is usually made up of a construction phase, where a

---

[1] A graph $G = (V, E)$ is said a *bipartite graph* if $V = V_1 \cup V_2$, $V_1 \cap V_2 = \emptyset$, and for each $[i, j] \in E$, $i \in V_1$ and $j \in V_2$. Moreover, G is *complete*, if for each $v_1 \in V_1$ and for each $v_2 \in V_2$, $[v_1, v_2] \in E$.

feasible solution is constructed in a *greedy, randomized,* and *adaptive* manner, and a local search phase which starts at the constructed solution and applies iterative improvement until a locally optimal solution is found. The reader can refer to [23–25] for a study of a generic GRASP metaheuristic framework and its applications.

Stopping criteria could be maximum number of iterations, maximum number of iterations without improvement of the incumbent solution, maximum running time, or solution quality at least as good as a given target value. A complete solution is iteratively constructed in the construction phase, one element at a time. At each construction iteration, the choice of the next element to be added is determined by ordering all candidate elements (i.e. those that can be added to the solution) in a candidate list C with respect to a greedy function $g : C \to R$. This function measures the (myopic) benefit of selecting each element. The heuristic is adaptive because the benefits associated with every element are updated at each iteration of the construction phase to reflect the changes brought on by the selection of the previous element. The probabilistic component of a GRASP is characterized by randomly choosing one of the best candidates in the list, but not necessarily the top candidate. The list of best candidates is called the *restricted candidate list* (RCL).

As is the case for many deterministic methods, it is almost always beneficial to apply a local search to attempt to improve each constructed solution. A local search algorithm replaces the current solution by a better solution in the neighborhood of the current solution, until a *locally optimal* solution is found.

In the next section, we describe the details of the Reactive GRASP-like algorithm that we have designed and implemented for the biclustering task.

4   A Reactive GRASP-Like Algorithm for Biclustering

GRASP is a multi-start high-level procedure that coordinates simple heuristics and rules (i.e., construction and local search) to find good (often optimal) approximate solutions of computationally hard combinatorial optimization problems.

In our GRASP-like proposal for biclustering, we adopted the stopping criterion that counts a maximum number of iterations without improvement of the incumbent solution (MaxNoImpr) and we implemented the reactive version of the metaheuristic framework. The pseudo-code is reported in Figure 1.

Our novel Reactive GRASP-like overcomes the drawback of the Reactive GRASP proposed by Dharan and Nair in [18]. We have implemented Dharan and Nair's proposal and in our experience we observed that, even if robust and elegant, the local search applied at each iteration is time consuming and very rarely improves the constructed solution, since it decides if to add or not a new element in the current solution on the only merit function basis. To overcome this drawback, we have designed a completely different local search strategy that uses two local improvement procedures that successively replace a bicluster in the current solution by a better bicluster in its neighborhood made of all biclusters that differ either because they have one more element (row or column)

```
algorithm GRASP-like-bicluster(A,MaxNoImpr,MaxDist,δ)
1   Δ := {α₁,...,αₗ};          /* αᵢ ∈ [0,1], i = 1,...,ℓ */
2   for i = 1 to ℓ do
3       p_{αᵢ} := 1/ℓ;
4   endfor
5   B = {B₁,...,Bₖ} :=filtered-Kmeans(A);  /* H(B_q) ≤ δ, q = 1,...,k */
6   for q = 1 to k do
7       B̂_q :=grasp(B_q,Δ,,A,MaxNoImpr,MaxDist);
8   endfor
9   return (B̂ = {B̂₁,...,B̂ₖ});
end
```

Fig. 1. Pseudo-code of our GRASP-like algorithm for biclustering

```
procedure grasp(B_q,Δ,,A,MaxNoImpr,MaxDist)
1   count := 0;
2   repeat
3       (c,B̄_q):=build-columns(B_q,Δ,A);
3       (bool,B'_q):=local-improvement-columns(c,Δ,B̄_q,,A,MaxDist);
4       if (bool) then count := 0;
5       else count := count + 1;
6       endif
7   until (count =MaxNoImpr)
8   count := 0;
9   repeat
10      (c,B̄_q):=build-rows(B'_q,Δ,A);
11      (bool,B'_q):=local-improvement-rows(c,Δ,B̄_q,,A,MaxDist);
12      if (bool) then count := 0;
13      else count := count + 1;
14      endif
15  until (count =MaxNoImpr)
16  return (B');
end
```

Fig. 2. Pseudo-code of grasp procedure invoked in our GRASP-like algorithm

and/or one less element. The specific element to be removed and/or added is chosen on the basis either of the diversity or of the improvement in terms of objective function value given by the mean squared residue.

In more detail, our algorithm starts from a partial solution made of a set $B = \{B_1,\ldots,B_k\}$ of k biclusters found by applying a k-means procedure and retaining only biclusters with small mean squared residue, i.e. those biclusters $B_q = (I_q, J_q)$ such that $H(B_q) \leq \delta$, where δ is a given input parameter.

As shown in Figure 2, the method proceeds in the attempt of finding a larger and locally better solution iteratively considering first the columns in Y (lines 1–7) and then the rows in X (lines 8–15), until MaxNoImpr iterations are performed

```
procedure build-columns(B_q,Δ,A)
1   C := ∅; g_min := large; g_max := 0;        /* B_q = (I_q, J_q), A = (X,Y) */
2   for each y ∈ Y \ J_q do
3       C := C ∪ {y};
4       g(y) := H(I_q, J_q ∪ {y});             /* mean squared residue */
5       if (g_min > g(y)) then g_min := g(y);
6       if (g_max < g(y)) then g_max := g(y);
7   endfor
8   α := select(Δ);
9   μ := g_min + α(g_max − g_min);
10  RCL := {c ∈ C | g(c) ≤ μ};
11  c := select(RCL); J_q := J_q ∪ {c};
12  return (c, B_q = (I_q, J_q));
end
```

Fig. 3. Pseudo-code of `build-columns` procedure invoked in our GRASP-like algorithm

```
procedure build-rows(B_q,Δ,A)
1   C := ∅; g_min := large; g_max := 0;        /* B_q = (I_q, J_q), A = (X,Y) */
2   for each x ∈ X \ I_q do
3       C := C ∪ {x};
4       g(x) := H(I_q ∪ {x}, J_q);             /* mean squared residue */
5       if (g_min > g(x)) then g_min := g(x);
6       if (g_max < g(x)) then g_max := g(x);
7   endfor
8   α := select(Δ);
9   μ := g_min + α(g_max − g_min);
10  RCL := {c ∈ C | g(c) ≤ μ};
11  c := select(RCL); I_q := I_q ∪ {c};
12  return (c, B_q = (I_q, J_q));
end
```

Fig. 4. Pseudo-code of `build-rows` procedure invoked in our GRASP-like algorithm

without improving the current better bicluster. The best incumbent bicluster is returned in line 16. Both procedures `build-columns` (Figure 3) and `build-rows` (Figure 4) take as input a partial bicluster $\mathcal{B}_q$ and try to enlarge it. The choice of the next element to be added to the partial solution is determined by ordering all candidate elements in a candidate list C with respect to their incremental costs given by evaluating a greedy function $g : C \to R$ that is the mean squared residue. The RCL then is the list of best candidates. The heuristic is adaptive because the incremental costs associated with every element are updated at each iteration to reflect the changes brought on by the selection of previous elements. The probabilistic component of our GRASP-like algorithm is characterized by randomly choosing one element from the RCL, but not necessarily the top candidate. In more detail, let $g(i)$ be the incremental cost associated with

```
procedure local-improvement-rows(c,Δ,B̄_q,A,MaxDist)
1   score := H(Ī_q, J̄_q);           /* B̄_q = (Ī_q, J̄_q), A = (X,Y) */
2   D := Ī_q; new :=select(X); dist :=distance(new,c);
3   if (new ∈ D) then
4       if (dist >MaxDist) then D := D \ {new};
5   else
6       if (dist ≤MaxDist) then D := D ∪ {new};
7   endif
8   new := argmin H(D \ {d}, J̄_q);      /* mean squared residue */
            d∈D
9   D := D \ {d}; new :=select(D);
10  dist :=distance(new,c);
11  if (dist >MaxDist and H(D \ {new}, J̄_q) < H(D, J̄_q)) then D := D \ {new};
12  if (score > H(D, J_q)) then
13      reevaluate-probabilities(Δ);
14      Ī_q := D; bool := true;
15  else
16      bool := false;
17  endif
18  return (bool,B̄_q = (Ī_q, J̄_q));
end
```

Fig. 5. Pseudo-code of `local-improvement-rows` procedure invoked in our GRASP-like algorithm

the incorporation of element i in the solution under construction and let g_{min} and g_{max} be the smallest and the largest incremental costs, respectively, i.e.

$$g_{min} = \min_{c \in C} g(c), \qquad g_{max} = \max_{c \in C} g(c). \qquad (1)$$

The restricted candidate list RCL is made up of elements $c \in C$ with the best (i.e., the smallest) incremental costs $g(c)$. There are two main mechanisms to build this list: a *cardinality-based* (CB) and a *value-based* (VB) mechanism. In the CB case, the RCL is made up of the z elements with the best incremental costs, where z is a parameter. In the VB case, the mechanism that we adopted, the RCL is associated with a parameter $\alpha \in [0,1]$ and a threshold value $\mu = g_{min} + \alpha(g_{max} - g_{min})$. In fact, all candidate elements c whose incremental cost $g(c)$ is no greater than the threshold value are inserted into the RCL. Note that, the case $\alpha = 0$ corresponds to a pure greedy algorithm, while $\alpha = 1$ is equivalent to a random construction.

As already underlined, we have implemented the *reactive* version of the GRASP metaheuristic framework. Reactive GRASP is the first enhancement that incorporates a learning mechanism in the memoryless construction phase of the basic GRASP. In Reactive GRASP, the value of the RCL parameter α is selected in each iteration from a discrete set of possible values with a probability that depends on the solution values found along the previous iterations. One way to accomplish this is to use the rule proposed in [26]. Let $\Delta = \{\alpha_1, \alpha_2, \ldots, \alpha_\ell\}$ (Figure 1 line 1)

```
procedure local-improvement-columns(c,Δ,B̄_q,A,MaxDist)
1   score := H(Ī_q, J̄_q);        /* B̄_q = (Ī_q, J̄_q), A = (X,Y) */
2   D := J̄_q; new :=select(Y); dist :=distance(new,c);
3   if (new ∈ D) then
4       if (dist >MaxDist) then D := D \ {new};
5   else
6       if (dist ≤MaxDist) then D := D ∪ {new};
7   endif
8   new := argmin H(Ī_q, D \ {d});        /* mean squared residue */
           d∈D
9   D := D \ {d}; new :=select(D);
10  dist :=distance(new,c);
11  if (dist >MaxDist and H(Ī_q, D \ {new}) < H(Ī_q, D)) then D := D \ {new};
12  if (score > H(I_q, D)) then
13      reevaluate-probabilities(Δ);
14      J̄_q := D; bool := true;
15  else
16      bool := false;
17  endif
18  return (bool,B̄_q = (Ī_q, J̄_q));
end
```

Fig. 6. Pseudo-code of `local-improvement-columns` procedure invoked in our GRASP-like algorithm

be the set of possible values for α. At the first GRASP iteration, all ℓ values have the same probability to be selected (lines 2–4), i.e.

$$p_{\alpha_i} = \frac{1}{\ell}, \qquad i = 1, \ldots, \ell. \tag{2}$$

At any subsequent iteration, let $\hat{z}$ be the incumbent solution objective function value and let A_i be the average objective function value of all solutions found using $\alpha = \alpha_i$, $i = 1, \ldots, \ell$. The selection probabilities are periodically reevaluated (Figure 5 line 13 and Figure 6 line 13) as follows:

$$p_i = \frac{q_i}{\sum_{j=1}^{\ell} q_j}, \tag{3}$$

where $q_i = \hat{z}/A_i$, $i = 1, \ldots, \ell$. If values of $\alpha = \alpha_i$ ($i \in \{1, \ldots, \ell\}$) lead to the best solutions on average, then the value of q_i is increased and larger values of q_i correspond to more suitable values for α. The probabilities associated with these more appropriate values will then increase when they are reevaluated.

Due to greater diversification and less reliance on parameter tuning, Reactive GRASP has lead to improvements over the basic GRASP in terms of robustness and solution quality. In fact, it has been successfully applied in power system transmission network planning [27] and in a capacitated location problem [28].

We next focus on the local search strategy that we have designed. We have implemented two local search algorithms, whose pseudo-codes are reported in Figures 5 and 6, respectively. Both the procedures successively replace a bicluster $\bar{B}_q = (\bar{I}_q, \bar{J}_q)$ in the current solution by a better bicluster in the neighborhood of $\bar{B}_q$ made of all biclusters that differ from $\bar{B}_q$ either because they have one more element (row or column) and/or one less element. The element *new* to be removed and/or added is chosen on the basis either of the diversity (Figures 5 and 6 lines 3–7) or of the improvement in terms of objective function value given by the mean squared residue (Figures 5 and 6 lines 8–11). If a better mean squared residue neighbor bicluster is found (Figures 5 and 6 line 12), then the selection probabilities of the α's in Δ are accordingly reevaluated (Figures 5 and 6 line 13).

Example. Suppose that we have a matrix $\mathcal{A}$ of 10 genes (rows) and 5 conditions (columns). Fixed as input the number of sets of genes and conditions (in the following example, 3 and 2, respectively), k-means algorithm will provide as output the required sets. Those sets may contain common elements but there will never be identical.

Then, biclusters seeds $(\mathcal{B})$ are created: in our example, 3×2 combinations are made to find a match between each set of genes and each set of conditions $(\mathcal{B}_1, \ldots, \mathcal{B}_6)$. Among these combinations, only those whose mean squared residue (hScore) is less than or equal to a given threshold δ are saved. Suppose that only 3 out of the 6 candidates are selected $(\mathcal{B}_1, \mathcal{B}_2, \mathcal{B}_3)$.

Now, the 3 biclusters are given as input to an iterative refinement procedure that tries to add and/or remove items, considering first the columns and then the rows.

Let us suppose that $\mathcal{B}_1$ has 6 rows and 3 columns (1,3,5). The procedure evaluates the improvement that could be obtained from the insertion of one of the remaining columns (2 and 4), in terms of hScore. If hScore is below a given threshold μ, then the corresponding column is inserted within a list of elements (RCL). Suppose that both columns 2 and 4 are included. One element (suppose column 4) is selected at random from the RCL and added to $\mathcal{B}_1$.

Once modified the current solution, the local search tries to improve it, by performing the following three steps.

1. Extract a new random element from the columns not included in the current solution (in our example, column 2). If the distance of column 2 from the column previously extracted from RCL (column 4) is less than or equal to a threshold given in input (MaxDist), column 2 is added to $\mathcal{B}_1$. Let us suppose this is the case.
2. From $\mathcal{B}_1$ the column that makes the hScore value of the bicluster worst is then eliminated. Suppose that this column is 3. Therefore, the set of columns in the new bicluster $\mathcal{B}_1$ is 1,2,4,5.
3. A further column is selected at random from all the columns of $\mathcal{B}_1$. It will be removed only if an improvement in terms of hScore is obtained. Supposing that this happens for column 5, the final bicluster consists of columns 1,2,4.

This procedure stops after a certain number of iterations without improvement (MaxNoImpr) and performs the above described operations on the set of rows of the bicluster under the same stopping condition.

The whole iterative procedure is applied on each selected bicluster ($\mathcal{B}_1$, $\mathcal{B}_2$, and $\mathcal{B}_3$).

5   Experimental Results and Biological Significance

Our Reactive GRASP-like algorithm has been implemented in C language, compiled with the Apple Xcode 3.1, and run on a MacBookPro 2GHz Intel Core Duo running MAC OSX 10.6. We have performed several iterations adopting the stopping criterion that counts a maximum number of iterations without improvement of the incumbent solution and inspected the results obtained.

A series of experiments has been conducted on the Yeast (Saccharomyces cerevisiae) cell cycle expression dataset [29] and on the dataset coming from the Lymphoma/Leukemia Molecular Profiling Project [30] to evaluate the quality of the proposed algorithm.

The first dataset includes 2884 genes and 17 conditions, with the expression level reported as an integer value in the range 0 to 600. Missing values in Yeast dataset are represented by -1. The second dataset is formed by 4026 genes and 96 conditions, with the expression level reported as an integer value in the range -300 to 300.

Table 1. Statistics on results of biclustering on the Yeast cell cycle expression dataset and on the Lymphoma/Leukemia molecular profiling project. The table lists the mean values of number of genes, number of conditions, volume, squared residue H, and running time over 10 trials using 10 different random number generator seeds. The last row reports the mean squared residual Hr obtained on a set of 33 (for yeast dataset) and 11 (for Lymphoma dataset) biclusters with the same cardinality of the bicluster obtained by our Reactive GRASP-like algorithm but with randomly selected membership.

Statistics	Yeast Dataset	Lymphoma Dataset
mean number of genes	97,33	59,63
mean number of conditions	10,52	8,18
mean volume	1000,06	478,93
mean H value	195,73	0,03
mean running time (in secs)	4044,43	5012,03
mean H_r value	1821,76	0,56

Table 1 shows results for a set of 33 biclusters generated for Yeast, and 11 biclusters generated for Lymphoma, in terms of number of genes, number of conditions, mean volume, mean squared residue H and mean running time over 10 trials using 10 different random number generator seeds. The differences in the values of H scores and volumes for the two datasets depend on the numerical values of the data included in each bicluster. In the last row, Table 1 reports the mean squared residual H_r obtained on a set of 33 and 11 biclusters with the same cardinality of the biclusters obtained by our Reactive GRASP-like algorithm but with randomly selected membership. Comparing this mean squared residual with the mean squared residual obtained with our approach, it is evident that our proposal is outperforming a simple random approach, since the H_r value is in both cases about one order of magnitude larger than the H.

Looking at the bicluster plots in Figure 7 and 8, one can notice that the genes in sample biclusters present a similar behavior under a set of conditions. This proves that our method is able to identify coherent biclusters from gene expression data.

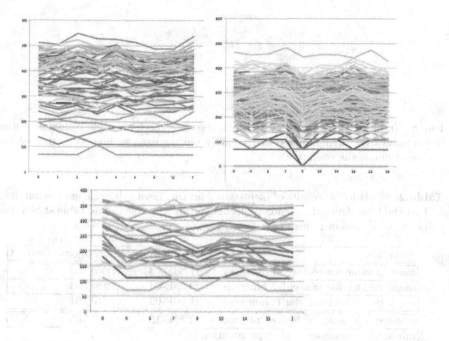

Fig. 7. Graphical representation of the expression levels for sample biclusters obtained in our analysis on Yeast dataset ([29]). On the rows we have the gene behaviour and on columns the conditions.

In order to verify the biological significance of biclusters obtained, we used GO annotation database and tools online. In GO annotation, terms describing biological processes, cellular components, and molecular functions are assigned to genes, so that a list of genes can be analyzed, looking for terms associated. The statistical significance to which the genes matches with the different GO terms or categories can be indicated by p-value. We used the Yeast Genome Gene Ontology Term Finder [31] to evaluate the biological significance of the 33 biclusters obtained in our analysis of the Yeast dataset, and the PANTHER (Protein ANalysis THrough Evolutionary Relationships) Classification System [32] for the analysis on Lymphoma results.

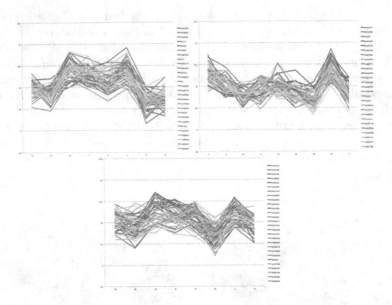

Fig. 8. Graphical representation of the expression levels for sample biclusters obtained in our analysis on Lymphoma dataset ([30]). On the rows we have the gene behaviour and on columns the conditions.

Table 2. Statistics on results of biclustering on the Yeast cell cycle expression dataset and on the Lymphoma/Leukemia molecular profiling project. The table shows a summary of the results in terms of p-values.

Statistics	Yeast Dataset	Lymphoma Dataset
mean p-value for biological process	1,83E-03	1,15E-03
mean p-value for molecular function	9,28E-04	5,88E-03
mean p-value for cellular component	1,60E-03	1,38E-01
minimum p-value for biological process	3,89E-15	5,25E-05
minimum p-value for molecular function	5,08E-17	3,27E-08
minimum p-value for cellular component	6,62E-22	1,05E-03

We reported in Table 2 a summary of the results, in terms of the mean p-value and the best p-value obtained for each of the three main categories, i.e. biological process, cellular component, molecular function. The analysis has been performed by submitting each gene list to the tool, and when a significant result was obtained, the p-value was selected. When two or more GO terms were significantly associated to the gene list, only the lowest p-value was selected. Figure 9 shows an example of the graphical result of the analysis for one of the biclusters analyzed. The analysis has found at least one GO term significantly associated to the gene list for 29 out of 33 biclusters in Yeast database, and for 11 out of 11 biclusters in Lymphoma dataset. This means that biclusters are made of

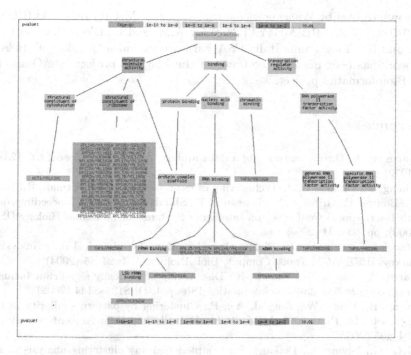

Fig. 9. The graphical output of the Yeast Genome Gene Ontology Term Finder tool for a sample bicluster obtained in our analysis

genes not only associated in terms of similar expression levels in the experimental data, but also with biological relationships, with a statistical confirm of the significance of this relationship. In the example of Figure 9, the GO term "structural costituent of ribosome" and its parent "structural molecule activity", have p-value ¡=1e-10, and are those most significantly associated to the list of genes included in the specific bicluster analyzed. This example shows that our analysis identified in this case a bicluster enriched by genes whose function, at level of protein expressed, is focalized on structural functions of ribosome. Therefore, the GO analysis confirms from a biological point of view the coherence of the bicluster analysis, being most of the gene clusters characterized by a common function, or cellular localization, or by the involvement in a biological process.

In conclusion, our Reactive GRASP-like algorithm is able to overcome several drawbacks of previous approaches for biclustering of biological data. We plan to perform further validation with other datasets from literature, as well as to design further variants of the algorithm to incorporate an intensification procedure by means of path-relinking [33, 34] and/or designing variable neighborhood structures [35, 36].

Acknowledgments. We acknowledge the support by MIUR FIRB ITALBIONET (RBPR05ZK2Z and RBIN064YAT_003) for A.M. and L.M. contribution to the work, and by "Programma Italia-USA Farmacogenomica Oncologica" to A.F.. This work has been made in the frame of the Flagship project InterOmics and CNR-Bioinformatics project.

References

1. Hartigan, J.: Direct clustering of a data matrix. J. Am. Stat. Assoc. 67, 123–127 (1972)
2. Cheng, Y., Church, G.M.: Biclustering of expression data. In: Altman, R., Bailey, T., Bourne, P., Gribskov, M., Lengauer, T., Shindyalov, I. (eds.) Proceedings of the 8th International Conference on Intelligent Systems for Molecular Biology (ISMB 2000), pp. 93–103 (2000)
3. Madeira, S., Oliveira, A.: Biclustering algorithms for biological data analysis: A survey. IEEE/ACM Trans. Comput. Biol. Bioinform. 1, 24–45 (2004)
4. Tanay, A., Sharan, R., Shamir, R.: Discovering statistically significant biclusters in gene expression data. Bioinformatics 18(suppl. 1), S136–S144 (2002)
5. Wang, H., Wang, W., Yang, J., Yu, P.: Clustering by pattern similarity in large data sets. In: Proc. 2002 ACM SIGMOD Int'l Conf. Management of Data, pp. 394–405 (2002)
6. Getz, G., Levine, E., Domany, E.: Coupled two-way clustering analysis of gene microarray data. Proc. Natl. Acad. Sci. USA 97 22, 12079–12084 (2000)
7. Tang, C., Zhang, L., Zhang, I., Ramanathan, M.: Interrelated two-way clustering: An unsupervised approach for gene expression data analysis. In: Proc. Second IEEE Int'l Symp. Bioinformatics and Bioeng., pp. 41–48 (2001)
8. Duffy, D., Quiroz, A.: A permutation based algorithm for block clustering. J. Classif. 8, 65–91 (1991)
9. Cho, H., Dhillon, I., Guan, Y., Sra, S.: Minimum Sum-Squared Residue Co-clustering of Gene Expression Data. In: Berry, M., Dayal, U. (eds.) Proceedings of the 4th SIAM Int'l Conf. Data Mining (2004)
10. Yang, J., Wang, W., Wang, H., Yu, P.: δ-clusters: Capturing subspace correlation in a large data set. In: Proc. 18th IEEE Int'l Conf. Data Eng., pp. 517–528 (2002)
11. Yang, J., Wang, W., Wang, H., Yu, P.: Enhanced biclustering on expression data. In: Proc. Third IEEE Conf. Bioinformatics and Bioeng., pp. 321–327 (2003)
12. Klugar, Y., Basri, R., Chang, J., Gerstein, M.: Spectral biclustering of microarray data: Coclustering genes and conditions. Genome Res. 13, 703–716 (2003)
13. Segal, E., Taskar, B., Gasch, A., Friedman, N., Koller, D.: Rich probabilistic models for gene expression. Bioinformatics 17(suppl. 1), S243–S252 (2001)
14. Sheng, Q., Moreau, Y., Moor, B.D.: Biclustering microarray data by gibbs sampling. Bioinformatics 19(suppl. 2), ii196–ii205 (2003)
15. Manjunath Aradhya, V.N., Masulli, F., Rovetta, S.: A Novel Approach for Biclustering Gene Expression Data Using Modular Singular Value Decomposition. In: Masulli, F., Peterson, L.E., Tagliaferri, R. (eds.) CIBB 2009. LNCS, vol. 6160, pp. 254–265. Springer, Heidelberg (2010)
16. Bryan, K., Cunningham, P., Bolshakova, N.: Application of simulated annealing to the biclustering of gene expression data. IEEE Trans. Inf. Technol. Biomed. 10(3), 519–525 (2006)

17. Mitra, S., Banka, H.: Multi-objective evolutionary biclustering of gene expression data. Pattern Recogn. 39, 2464–2477 (2006)
18. Dharan, S., Nair, A.: Biclustering of gene expression data using reactive greedy randomized adaptive search procedure. BMC Bioinformatics 10(suppl. 1), S27 (2009)
19. Tanay, A., Sharan, R., Shamir, R.: Biclustering Algorithms: A Survey. In: Aluru, S. (ed.) Handbook of Computational Molecular Biology. Computer and Information Science Series. S. Chapman & Hall/CRC (2005)
20. Peeters, R.: The maximum edge biclique problem is NP-Complete. Discrete Appl. Math. 131(3), 651–654 (2003)
21. Feo, T., Resende, M.: A probabilistic heuristic for a computationally difficult set covering problem. Oper. Res. Lett. 8, 67–71 (1989)
22. Feo, T., Resende, M.: Greedy randomized adaptive search procedures. J. Global Optim. 6, 109–133 (1995)
23. Festa, P., Resende, M.: GRASP: An annotated bibliography. In: Ribeiro, C., Hansen, P. (eds.) Essays and Surveys on Metaheuristics, pp. 325–367. Kluwer Academic Publishers (2002)
24. Festa, P., Resende, M.: An annotated bibliography of GRASP – Part I: Algorithms. International Transactions in Operational Research 16(1), 1–24 (2009)
25. Festa, P., Resende, M.: An annotated bibliography of GRASP – Part II: Applications. International Transactions in Operational Research 16(2), 131–172 (2009)
26. Prais, M., Ribeiro, C.: Reactive GRASP: An application to a matrix decomposition problem in TDMA traffic assignment. INFORMS J. Comput. 12, 164–176 (2000)
27. Binato, S., Oliveira, G.: A Reactive GRASP for transmission network expansion planning. In: Ribeiro, C., Hansen, P. (eds.) Essays and Surveys on Metaheuristics, pp. 81–100. Kluwer Academic Publishers (2002)
28. Delmaire, H., Díaz, J., Fernández, E., Ortega, M.: Reactive GRASP and tabu search based heuristics for the single source capacitated plant location problem. INFOR 37, 194–225 (1999)
29. Tavazoie, S., Hughes, J., Campbell, M.J., Cho, R.J., Church, G.M.: Systematic determination of genetic network architecture. Nat. Genet. 22, 281–285 (1999)
30. Alizadeh, A., Eisen, M., Davis, R., Ma, C., Lossos, I., Rosenwald, A., Boldrick, J., Sabet, H., Tran, T., Yu, X., Powell, J., Yang, L., Marti, G., Moore, T., Hudson, J., Lu, L., Lewis, D., Tibshirani, R., Sherlock, G., Chan, W., Greiner, T., Weisenburger, D., Armitage, J., Warnke, R., Levy, R., Wilson, W., Grever, M., Byrd, J., Botstein, D., Brown, P., Staudt, L.: Distinct types of diffuse large b-cell lymphoma identified by gene expression profiling. Nature 403, 503–511 (2000)
31. http://www.yeastgenome.org/cgi-bin/GO/goTermFinder
32. Mi, H., Dong, Q., Muruganujan, A., Gaudet, P., Lewis, S., Thomas, P.: PANTHER version 7: improved phylogenetic trees, orthologs and collaboration with the gene ontology consortium. Nucleic Acids Res. 38, D204–D210 (2010)
33. Frinhani, R.M.D., Silva, R.M.A., Mateus, G.R., Festa, P., Resende, M.G.C.: GRASP with Path-Relinking for Data Clustering: A Case Study for Biological Data. In: Pardalos, P.M., Rebennack, S. (eds.) SEA 2011. LNCS, vol. 6630, pp. 410–420. Springer, Heidelberg (2011)
34. Laguna, M., Martí, R.: GRASP and path relinking for 2-layer straight line crossing minimization. INFORMS J. Comput. 11, 44–52 (1999)
35. Festa, P., Pardalos, P., Resende, M., Ribeiro, C.: Randomized heuristics for the MAX-CUT problem. Optim. Methods Softw. 7, 1033–1058 (2002)
36. Mladenović, N., Hansen, P.: Variable neighborhood search. Comput. Oper. Res. 24, 1097–1100 (1997)

Author Index